615

TRUTH AGAINST THE WORLD

Frank Lloyd Wright, circa 1938.
Photograph from the collections of the Library of Congress.

TRUTH AGAINST THE WORLD

FRANK LLOYD WRIGHT SPEAKS FOR AN ORGANIC ARCHITECTURE

Patrick J. Meehan, AIA, Editor

The Preservation Press
National Trust for Historic Preservation

The Preservation Press
National Trust for Historic Preservation
1785 Massachusetts Avenue, N.W.
Washington, D.C. 20036

The National Trust for Historic Preservation is the only private, nonprofit organization chartered by Congress to encourage public participation in the preservation of sites, buildings, and objects significant in American history and culture. Support is provided by membership dues, endowment funds, contributions, and grants from federal agencies, including the U.S. Department of the Interior, under provisions of the National Historic Preservation Act of 1966. The opinions expressed here do not necessarily reflect the views or policies of the Interior Department. For information about membership in the National Trust, write to the Membership Office at the above address.

Printed in the United States of America
96 95 94 93 92 5 4 3 2 1

Library of Congress Cataloging in Publication Data
Wright, Frank Lloyd, 1867–1959
Truth against the world : Frank Lloyd Wright speaks for an organic architecture / edited with introductions by Patrick J. Meehan.
p. cm.
Originally published: New York: Wiley, © 1987.
Includes bibliographical references and index.
ISBN 0-89133-174-3
1. Wright, Frank Lloyd, 1867–1959—Contributions in organic architecture.
2. Organic architecture—United States. I. Meehan, Patrick Joseph. II. Title.
(NA737.W7A35 1992b)
720'.92—dc20 92-14034

Cover design by White Space Design Inferno, Minneapolis, Minnesota

Printed by Arcata Graphics, Kingsport, Tennessee, on 60-pound Finch Opaque Smooth

∞ The paper used in this publication meets the minimum requirements of the American National Standard for Permanence of Paper for Printed Library Materials Z39.48-1984.

Front cover: Frank Lloyd Wright, c. 1936, and the countryside surrounding Taliesin, Green Spring, Wisconsin. (Bill Hedrich, Hedrich-Blessing)
Back cover: Wright and his Taliesin Fellowship apprentices, fall 1937. (Hedrich-Blessing)

To Karen, Ryan, Sean, and the young architects of the future—

There is no past we should long to resurrect,
There is eternal newness only, reconstituting itself
Out of the extended elements of the past
and true yearning should always be towards productive ends
Making some new, some better thing.

JOHANN WOLFGANG VON GOETHE

The truth shall make you free.

JOHN, 8:32

Preface

Frank Lloyd Wright once said that he did

> *not believe much in these events where a man stands up and makes a talk. There is a lot of that going on, and really it does not amount to very much. You can talk a lot about a great many things, but never get anywhere. . . . People talk more because they found out that they could do more of it than anything else. Now that they found out they could talk, they take it out in talking. They talk everything to death, talk the arm off of everybody. If I had to translate. . .(my) buildings into talk and persuade you to take them, I would have a hard time because other people talk too.*

I believe, however, that the readers of this collection of Wright's speeches will find this to be untrue in his case. In his prolific architectural career of more than seventy years he became the most famous architect of the twentieth century, if not of all time, by the creation of more than 900 architectural designs that follow his philosophy of organic architecture.

Truth Against the World: Frank Lloyd Wright Speaks for an Organic Architecture presents a major, extensively illustrated treatise on Wright's philosophy of architectural design through the presentation of thirty-two of his most significant speeches. *Truth Against the World* is my third book on Frank Lloyd Wright and the second volume in my predominantly oral trilogy concerning him. My first book, *Frank Lloyd Wright: A Research Guide to Archival Sources* (New York: Garland Publishing, Inc., 1983), served as my introduction to the many well-known as well as obscure published and unpublished Wright letters, manuscripts, speeches, and other related items that are available to the scholarly researcher. My second book, *The Master Architect: Conversations with Frank Lloyd Wright* (New York: John Wiley and Sons, 1984), the first volume of the oral trilogy, allowed me to preserve in one volume the illustrated texts of rare audio- and audiovisual-related conversations, which were destroyed, had deteriorated beyond further use, or just were no longer available to the public from any source. *Frank Lloyd Wright Remembered* (Washington, D.C.: The Preservation Press, 1991), the third volume of the oral trilogy, presents him from the perspective of those who knew him best: fellow architects, clients, apprentices, acquaintances and friends, and members of his immediate family.

A Druid symbol of inverted rays of the sun was cut into a stone set in 1886 by an elderly Welsh mason into the wall of the Lloyd-Jones sisters' Home School near Spring Green, Wisconsin. Signifying the struggle of "Truth Against the World," the symbol was placed there by Wright's maternal relations—the Lloyd-Jones family—and became the family crest, brought from Wales by his grandfather, Richard Lloyd Jones. In part, the Druid symbol was the manifestation or embodiment of the liberal spirit of the Lloyd-Jones family and, most certainly, of Frank Lloyd Wright. Later this ancient Druid symbol was incised in the stone gate posts of Unity Chapel, the family chapel, also near Spring Green, Wisconsin. Still later, in 1902, the symbol appeared on the sandstone walls of another school run by Wright's aunts—the Hillside Home School, a building designed by him that in 1932 became a part of the Taliesin Fellowship Complex. Wright's own search for the truth in life represents a quest even more profound than his efforts to improve the human environment. Wright's speeches provide a clear-cut record of this relentless pursuit. In chapter one, Wright humorously quips: "Do you think he (grandfather) was thinking of me when he chose that motto?"

Truth Against the World represents a goal not too dissimilar from that of the first and third books of the oral trilogy. The purpose of *Truth Against the World* is to provide the interested reader, for the first time, with a comprehensive collection of Mr. Wright's most important speeches on architecture and contemporary society in one generously illustrated volume. *Truth Against the World* adds considerably to the current body of literature about Frank Lloyd Wright, because it produces new insights into his thought processes and personality as well as his great architecture.

Truth Against the World complements *The Master Architect*, which deals primarily with Wright's talks when he was in a more relaxed informal conversational setting, and *Frank Lloyd Wright Remembered*, which primarily presents the memories of others who knew him. *Truth Against the World*, on the other hand, presents Wright as a dynamic, seasoned, and polished orator, who, always in command of his subject, as well as his philosophy of organic architecture, spoke to and with large audiences in a public forum—audiences who sometimes rejected him and his revolutionary ideas.

During many of his speeches he was outspoken, but on rare occasions there were also glimpses of a profound humility. Wright's 1949 acceptance speech for the Gold Medal of the American Institute of Architects (AIA) is one example of this (see chapter 16). For over a half century, the AIA and Wright openly did not get along. Finally, in 1949, the AIA awarded him its highest honor—the Gold Medal. During his acceptance of the medal, Wright eloquently commented:

> *. . .no man climbs so high or sinks so low that he isn't eager to receive the good will and admiration of his fellowman. He may seem reprehensible in many ways; he may seem to care nothing about it; he may hitch his wagon to his star and, however he may be circumstanced or whatever his ideals or his actions, he never loses the desire for the appreciation of his kind.*
>
> *So I feel humble and grateful. I don't think humility is (a) very becoming state for me. . .but I really feel by this token of esteem from the home boys. . .*
>
> *. . .I don't know what change it's going to effect upon my course in the future. It's bound to have an effect! I am not going to be the same man when I walk out of here that I was when I came in. Because, by this little token in my pocket, it seems to me that a battle has been won. . .*

Mr. Wright was not only a master of architecture but also of public speaking. He spoke passionately. This quality is revealed in most of the speeches presented in this collection. This was particularly true when in 1957 he addressed his clients for the Marin County Civic Center (chapter 29):

> *The carelessness with which our people get their buildings built, who they will let plan them, is almost as though anybody that could poke a fire could plan a building. It should take the greatest experience that can be had to so plan. The best is none too good! And when people choose an architect, they ought to go at it prayerfully and if necessary go on their hands and knees as far as they could go to get the best there is because in the realm of such planning none is good enough.*

Wright's passion for architecture came from his soul.

The overwhelming majority of the thirty-two speeches in *Truth Against the World* are carefully selected from rare, obscure, and sometimes foreign publications, many of which have been out of print for half a century or longer. Several of them include Wright's personal and informal dialogue with his audiences after his formal speech presentation—a format he often used. Only on rare occasions would he read a prepared speech (such as his 1947 address to Princeton University presented in chapter 21). In addition, three of the talks contained in this volume (see chapters 1, 29, and 30) have never been published as written documents, although they have appeared in other audio or audiovisual form. This comprehensive collection of speeches spans almost six of Wright's seven decades in architecture by covering the period from 1900 to 1958 (several months before his death). These speeches, organized into nine parts based on their themes and subject matter, fully reveal Frank Lloyd Wright, the master architect, and Frank Lloyd Wright, the man, in his relentless pursuit of truth in architecture and mankind. The general topical areas presented in the nine parts of the book include his ideas on organic architecture, the machine, improving the human condition, honor, education, democracy, city planning and, in particular, his Broadacre City and government. The reader should note the consistency of his philosophies expressed in his words.

As in my past research in the study of Wright, a book like this would have been impossible to coordinate into an integrated organic whole without the kind assistance from many persons to whom I am especially indebted. I want to thank the following for their help in providing me with necessary materials and permissions to complete this work: Patricia Akre, photograph curator, San Francisco Public Library; Richard Alwood of American Commercial Photo, Detroit; Barbara Chapman, Billboard Publications; Dr. S. E. T. Cusdin, architect, of London, England; Elizabeth Dixon, librarian, and E. A. Underwood, Architectural Association of London; L. H. Falgie, managing editor, *Journal of the Franklin Institute*; Van Gillespie, clerk of the board, Board of Supervisors of Marin County, San Rafael, California; Helen Dwight Reid Educational Foundation; Randolph C. Henning, architect, Winston-Salem, North Carolina; Ada Ishii of *The New Yorker*; Mrs. Robert Furneaux Jordan; Wendy A. Jordan, executive editor, *Builder*; Edward L. Kamarck, former editor, *Arts in Society*; Dr. Joseph K. Kugler, Hastings, Minnesota; Marta Ladd, director of public relations, and Brad Beck, photographer, Florida Southern College, Lakeland, Florida; Cynthia Lowry; Kristine MacCallum and Daniel J. May; Edwin M. Mathias and Emily Sieger, reference librarians, Motion Picture, Broadcasting and Recorded Sound Division, Library of Congress; Robert S. McGonigal; Robert Meloon, former executive publisher, and Leigh A. Milner, former librarian, *The Capital Times*, Madison, Wisconsin; Michigan Society of Architects Board of Directors and Rae Dumke, executive director; Margaret M. Mills, executive director, American Academy and Institute of Arts and Letters; Lynn Nesmith, director of research, *Architecture* (formerly the *AIA Journal*); June P. Payne, assistant director of University Publications, Arizona State University, Tempe, Arizona; Marilyn Pustay, librarian, *The Sun/The Daily* Herald, Biloxi, Mississippi; Kate Rafine, Illinois Department of Conservation; Frances Stafford, executive administrative assistant, WLOX-AM Radio, Biloxi, Mississippi; George Talbot and Myrna Williamson of the State Historical Society of Wisconsin; William N. Thurston, historic preservation supervisor, Division of Archives, History and Records Management of the Florida Department of State; Gavin Townwend, Architectural Drawing Collection, University of California, Santa Barbara, California; the staff of the Interlibrary Loan Office, Golda Meir Library, University of Wisconsin-Milwaukee; Kathryn Vaughn, reference librarian, Art Institute of Chicago; Sam Venturella, president, Henry George School of Social Science, Chicago; Coreen Wallace of WNET/Thirteen Television of New York; Wilsons Solicitors of Salisbury, England; and Tony P. Wrenn, archivist, American Institute of Architects Archives.

I would also like to thank Buckley C. Jeppson, Janet Walker, and Margaret Gore of The Preservation Press for their valuable assistance in publishing this softcover edition of *Truth Against the World.*

Journalist Clifford L. Helbert once said that

> *three things distinguish the legacy of each man: his search for truth, chimerical and elusive as it is; his search for artistic integrity and the beauty and utility he achieves in things he makes; his search and response in love for his fellow man. To excel in one is amazing; to excel in two is astounding; to excel in all is the mark of genius. . .to strive in all is to live life to the fullest.*

Frank Lloyd Wright was such a genius.

PATRICK J. MEEHAN, AIA

Contents

PART ONE
Introduction

1 The Beginnings of Truth

A Talk with Mary Margaret McBride

One should select one's grandparents with even greater care than one's parents.

Introduction

On Friday, December 2, 1949, Frank Lloyd Wright appeared on *The Mary Margaret McBride Show,* a radio program broadcast over WEAF the New York station of the National Broadcasting Company (NBC), located at Radio City. In March of the same year Mr. Wright was the recipient of the Gold Medal of the American Institute of Architects (see Chapter 16). During the thirty-five-minute talk show Mr. Wright appeared to relax in the company of Ms. McBride, whose ability to make her guest feel at home by listening attentively and interjecting only an occasional question or comment encouraged him to expound at some length on his Welsh ancestors who brought with them to America their family motto—the Druid symbol that represented their strong belief in "Truth Against the World." It seems fitting that Frank Lloyd Wright's talk with Mary Margaret McBride should serve as the introduction to this book.

The text of this heretofore unpublished conversation was transcribed by the editor from *The Mary Margaret McBride Show,* a radio program broadcast on December 2, 1949, from Radio City in New York and rebroadcast on March 14, 1950. The original recordings of these two programs are housed in the Motion Picture and Recorded Sound Division of the Library of Congress in Washington, D.C. Recordings and transcriptions are used by permission of the estate of the late Mary Margaret McBride, Cynthia Lowry legatee.

Frank Lloyd Wright at his desk in Taliesin near Spring Green, Wisconsin, circa 1924. Photograph courtesy of the State Historical Society of Wisconsin.

The Talk

MARY MARGARET McBRIDE: I wonder how people feel about age today, compared with fifty years ago? I think quite differently.

VINCENT CONNOLLY (*Ms. McBride's cohost*): I would say so. You often hear people say: "When I was a child my grandmother, at fifty, was an old lady," or something of that sort.

McBRIDE: Of course, as we get older, Vincent, fifty doesn't seem so old.

CONNOLLY: Well, you have something there!

McBRIDE: Yes. When you're a child, I suppose, it always would. What I was thinking was that there are so many older people doing such wonderful jobs and today on this program we have one of them. We have a man who is considered, perhaps, the world's greatest architect alive today—Frank Lloyd Wright.

Well, Frank Lloyd Wright, you and I are both one-hundred percent American aren't we? You were born in Wisconsin.

WRIGHT: I think that you are a hundred and one percent! (laughter)

McBRIDE: (laughter) What are you? Seventy-five [percent]?

WRIGHT: I'm probably ninety-seven and a half or something like that!

McBRIDE: Ninety-seven and a half? Well, that voice is the voice of Frank Lloyd Wright, considered by many the most famous—the best—architect in the world. He is a congenital heretic. He says so himself in something I read that he wrote. He has been under fire a good many times from people who didn't agree with him. How is it now Frank Lloyd Wright?

WRIGHT: Well, you know any good thing too-long continued becomes a heresy.

McBRIDE: Why did they call you a heretic and why did you call yourself one?

WRIGHT: Well, I'm just learning that they did call me a heretic! I didn't know they did!

McBRIDE: Well, you called yourself one!

WRIGHT: Have I called myself a heretic?

McBRIDE: Yes, congenital and congenial. You were talking about your meeting with Mr. Sullivan [Louis H. Sullivan].

WRIGHT: Oh!

McBRIDE: You said he was a heretic and you were also a heretic. That's what you said!

WRIGHT: Did I say that? Well, I had forgotten.

McBRIDE: (laughter)

WRIGHT: But, anyway, heretic or no heretic here we are!

McBRIDE: Here we are!

WRIGHT: Isn't that what the clown says in the circus when he comes on over—"Well, here we are again!"?

McBRIDE: Here we are again—year after year.

WRIGHT: But this is not again. This is the first time and I'm glad to see you taking up architecture. I wish the country would take it up. Can't you persuade the country to take up architecture and learn something about it? It's a fascinating study!

McBRIDE: Well, isn't it rather difficult for a layman? How would I start taking it up?

WRIGHT: Well, it's the most subjective of the arts, of course, and the one probably most difficult to learn about. But [it] seems to me it's the one most worthwhile, because if our environment is not important to us what is important? I don't think we can talk about a culture or pretend to have one until we are familiar with what makes environment admirable and what makes [it] educable or what makes a good building or a bad building. Wouldn't you say so?

McBRIDE: I'd say so. I can't help wondering, what sort of building were you born in and did you live in when you were a little boy?

WRIGHT: It was in Richland Center, Wisconsin, and I went to see it some years ago and it had disappeared—thank God!

McBRIDE and WRIGHT: (laughter)

WRIGHT: I'm sure it was a hideous little box such as they build out there in the Middlewest . . . .

McBRIDE: Do you remember it at all?

WRIGHT: . . . these little imitations of the Cape Cod Colonial you know—siding, corner boards, . . .

McBRIDE: What should they build out in the Middlewest?

WRIGHT: What should it be?

McBRIDE: Yes.

WRIGHT: Well, it should be Middlewest, shouldn't it?

McBRIDE: I know! But what is Middlewest? I don't know!

WRIGHT: Middlewest now, I suppose, is anywhere west of where you're sitting!

McBRIDE: Yes. I came from Missouri which I'm sure would be Middlewest.

WRIGHT: Oh, that's Middlewest! That's still Middlewest.

McBRIDE: What would the Middlewest be, expressed in architecture?

WRIGHT: Well, we refer to it as the cradle of democracy. We refer to it as the heart of the nation. We refer to it as anything that's in the middle of things because that's where we are!

McBRIDE: But I still don't know how you would express it architecturally!

WRIGHT: Architecturally? Oh, it's something quiet

This house, which stood at 774 South Park Street, in Richland Center, Wisconsin, is believed to have been the birthplace of Frank Lloyd Wright (circa mid-1800s; demolished early 1970s). Photograph by Joe W. Koelsch.

and broad and sensible and belonging where it stood—belonging to the ground, you know? All those other little incidental things that buildings mostly miss.

McBRIDE: That's what you believe about *all* houses people live in.

WRIGHT: That's right. I think that when you're in the Middlewest you should particularly observe all those things. When you come East, of course, well that's different.

McBRIDE: But a Middlewesterner in the East should conform to the East then, architecturally?

WRIGHT: Yes. A Midwesterner in the East should still be true to the principles that made the Middlewest the heart of democracy.

McBRIDE: Do you believe it really is?

WRIGHT: I believe it is.

McBRIDE: I know a lot . . .

WRIGHT: If democracy has a heart, of course, that's the thing that particularly distinguishes it, isn't it, from other -isms?

McBRIDE: Don't you think so?

WRIGHT: The fact that it has a heart. The fact that it insists upon the individual as such and defends him. [It] has to live on genius—democracy. Democracy can't take the handrail down the stair. A democrat has to have courage—keep his hand off the handrail and take the steps down the middle. That's a democrat!

McBRIDE: You're a democrat?

WRIGHT: Well, I'd like to call myself one—look myself in the face. It's a very high faith!

McBRIDE: Will democracy last in this world?

WRIGHT: This world won't last unless democracy does!

McBRIDE: I think you're right on that!

STUDIO PERSONNEL: (loud applause)

McBRIDE: I'd like, Frank Lloyd Wright, for you to go back to Wisconsin because you once wrote a charming little book about yourself as a little boy. Do you remember how you started the book? Do you remember telling about a walk you took with an uncle and the snow had just fallen . . .

WRIGHT: Oh yes . . . I do remember and I remember that I wrote that book that my little family might continue to eat. It was a purely defensive affair. I had never written a book and didn't want to write a book but I thought that, perhaps, it was the only way I could get some money.

McBRIDE: Did you?

WRIGHT: So I wrote the first *An Autobiography* under very trying circumstances and it's more or less, of course, oh . . . what shall we say? You finish it!

McBRIDE: I gather that you didn't care for it. I liked it.

WRIGHT: Well, I've read it recently again—portions of it—and I like a number of things in it. I thought my "To Her" was rather good. People familiar with the situation at that time would naturally think that "To Her" meant some charming young person. As a matter of fact, it was a cow!

McBRIDE AND STUDIO PERSONNEL: (loud laughter)

WRIGHT: "To Her" referred to the cow. And I do think that the cow has been neglected by the many singers down the ages and it was time that somebody sang the glory of the cow! The calf-bearing, cud-chewing, all-forbearing cow.

McBRIDE: Who's always in the right position for pictures, you've also said.

WRIGHT: That's right! That's *true!* You've read it I see! (laughter)

McBRIDE: Oh dear me! (laughter)

WRIGHT: Well, that's more than I could have expected!

Forty members of Frank Lloyd Wright's maternal Lloyd-Jones family clan, circa 1883–1885. Frank Lloyd Wright is seated right of the empty chair with his sister, Maginel Wright [Barney], on his lap. Mr. Wright's mother Anna [Hannah] Lloyd-Jones Wright stands in the back row (third from right)*; his father William Carey Wright also appears in the back row* (seventh from left)*. The elderly gentleman seated on a chair in the front row is Frank Lloyd Wright's maternal grandfather Richard Lloyd-Jones, Sr. The empty chair in the front row symbolizes the presence of the deceased Mary [Mallie] Thomas Lloyd-Jones, his maternal grandmother and wife of Richard Lloyd-Jones, Sr. Photograph courtesy of the State Historical Society of Wisconsin.*

McBRIDE: It is? What do you expect now?

WRIGHT: I received a letter from the north of Scotland—way up—from a woman who had three children and she had read *An Autobiography* and wanted to thank me for what it had done for her and her little children. It amazed me because I didn't know there was anything like that in it.

McBRIDE: Maybe it gave her courage!

WRIGHT: I don't know what it gave her, but she gave me quite a thrill when she wrote that little note to me.

McBRIDE: Yes. You have a wonderful picture in there of your Welsh grandfather that I love.

WRIGHT: Well, he was a wonderful man to picture!

McBRIDE: He was a hat maker and he made a hat that looked a little like a witch's hat.

WRIGHT: Well, you've seen them riding on broomsticks—these witches with these pointed cone hats.

McBRIDE: Yes.

WRIGHT: They're Welsh hats.

McBRIDE: But men wore them!

WRIGHT: You can stand on them [and] throw them on the floor—he used to—and [he'd] say "stand [on] it "and if it would hold them up they'd buy the hat, I suppose.

McBRIDE: (laughter) Was he the one that had the motto on his crest or was that the other grandfather?

WRIGHT: The family, yes. Richard Lloyd Jones was a preacher and a hatter. He was a Unitarian in Wales and they were not very popular in those days, so he thought he'd come over here where men were free and thought was free. After he had been here for a few months they wanted to try him—he went to Ixonia [Wisconsin]. [He] had a church there and they wanted to try him for heresy. So that's what he got when he first got here.

McBRIDE: But he preached anyhow?

WRIGHT: But he preached anyhow and he survived. He came over here with that Druid—What shall we call it? The Japanese call it a "mawn "[sic]. We call it a motto. It's the Druid symbol—the inverted rays of the sun—and it signifies *Truth Against the World.* If that isn't enough trouble for one family!

McBRIDE: I thought that it was very appropriate that your grandfather should have that because it seems to me, Frank Lloyd Wright, that you fought for that your entire eighty years.

The Druid symbol of the Lloyd-Jones family, represented by inverted rays of the sun, signifies "Truth Against the World." This symbol was the manifestation or embodiment of their liberal spirit and that of Frank Lloyd Wright as well. Sketch by the editor.

WRIGHT: Do you think that he was thinking of me when he chose that motto?

McBRIDE: (laughter) No. I guess he didn't have you in [mind]. . . . Maybe he did!

WRIGHT: Maybe I was thinking of him!

McBRIDE: Yes, you never know about these things. No, he may have been thinking about his descendants.

WRIGHT: One should select one's grandparents with even greater care than one's parents.

McBRIDE: Your grandmother I thought you did select with great care. She was the one—the one that I'm talking about—the one that mended the tree.

WRIGHT: Oh yes! Sewed a bandage around its trunk and there it stands today eighty-five feet tall. A beautiful pine. A beautiful white pine.

McBRIDE: A pine tree and [she] took a little sewing box and put a bandage on it as if it were a human being.

WRIGHT: A patch. A patch around the trunk and then wound a bandage around it to save the little tree and there it is.

McBRIDE: And when this gentle woman died the prayer that grandfather sent up to heaven was the most beautiful and strongest anybody had ever heard him pray.

WRIGHT: I've heard my uncles and my aunts and my mother say that and might I say it could be, from what I know of him. I was taught in my early days as a youngster to answer to: "well, whose farmer are you now?" And I was taught to say to him: "bora dake tadke [sic] good morning grandfather." And he would say "kiske salyong" [sic], which would mean: "Have you slept sound?" So that's about all I remember about grandfather except that his wife taught him to smoke for the asthma and he got rid

Frank Lloyd Wright's maternal aunts and uncles and his mother Anna [Hannah] Lloyd-Jones Wright (seated, center), *circa 1883—1885. The children of Richard Lloyd-Jones Sr. (Mr. Wright's maternal grandfather) are* (back row, left to right) *Enos, Jennie, Jenkin, Mary, John; and* (front row, left to right) *James, Nell, Anna, Margaret, and Thomas. Photograph courtesy of the State Historical Society of Wisconsin.*

of the asthma but he never got rid of the pipe after that. It was a great mortification to the family!

McBRIDE: And he was the one who used to give tobacco to the Indians who came and brought venison.

WRIGHT: That's right. Yes he did. He was one of the pioneers out there and he had his ten children—lost one coming over—there were nine survivors and there were four of those strong, tall fellows who began to civilize that neck of the woods.

McBRIDE: And there was your mother.

WRIGHT: My mother was one of them.

McBRIDE: This mother who hung up. . . . Tell why you were an architect because your mother planned it.

WRIGHT: Certainly I never had to choose a profession. I never could understand how one would conduct oneself in the direction of the choice of a profession. I was to be an architect when I was born—never had any other thought. [I] put up with an engineering course in Wisconsin [University of Wisconsin-Madison] because they didn't have a course in architecture and then left three months before they would have given me a degree in engineering because I couldn't wait any longer to become an architect.

McBRIDE: Tell about your mother hanging these woodcuts of the cathedrals.

WRIGHT: My father was a preacher, of course, a musician, and he subscribed to a little magazine—not so little, it was a large one—called *Old England* and with each number came a wood engraving of one of the English cathedrals, so my mother hung them up around the room in which I was born and I came into that room where they were hung and that was her preparation for her architect.

McBRIDE: (laughter) You recognized it early?

WRIGHT: Well, I don't know what you mean about recognizing it? I accepted it as a foregone conclusion.

Frank Lloyd Wright's "Lieber Meister" Louis H. Sullivan, circa late 1800s. Photograph courtesy of The Art Institute of Chicago, © The Art Institute of Chicago, All Rights Reserved. Reproduced by permission of The Art Institute of Chicago.

McBRIDE: Now we have two gentlemen here [in the studio]—one is a physicist and one is a chemist—and they, I suppose, went through all the periods of "I'd like to be this or I'd like to be that" and I just wondered if you did, too?

WRIGHT: No, never.

McBRIDE: You just knew!

WRIGHT: I never questioned it. I accepted it without question and I thought it was the finest thing in the world and I didn't believe that anybody had such a nobility of opportunity or character or purpose as an architect. My mother taught me that and she got me born into it, in that sense, and I used to be very proud of being an architect and I would expect a reaction when I told people that I was an architect. I'd expect to see them wilt a little bit and be a little more respectful but it never made much impression.

McBRIDE AND OTHERS IN STUDIO: (laughter)

McBRIDE: Maybe they agreed with Mr. Sullivan [Louis H. Sullivan, architect] about draftsmen? Mr. Sullivan . . .

WRIGHT: Well, maybe they did! But I think most of them thought that an architect was just a case of a lot of mortar and some bricks and blueprints. I think they didn't think anything about him as anything else.

McBRIDE: They probably didn't know that you had to be a . . . . Wasn't Mr. Sullivan a draftsman before he drew ornamentation sketches?

WRIGHT: I don't think he ever regarded himself as such.

McBRIDE: No. He only regarded you as such.

WRIGHT: And I never regarded myself as such.

McBRIDE: Well, he did when he lost his temper at you, though.

WRIGHT: He could draw beautifully. So beautifully that he didn't have to regard himself as a draftsman.

McBRIDE: No. Why did he say he couldn't get by [as] a draftsman?

WRIGHT: Well, you see, a draftsman per se as such can never be an architect. He can never be anything but a draftsman. He becomes somehow habituated to the drawing board and the pencil and the triangle and eraser; that's his life. He does as he's told. He seldom emerges from draftsmanship. I hope that many of them aren't listening now!

McBRIDE: (slight laughter) Well, if they are they have a lot of company because there are many jobs one gets into and ruts where one does the same thing; maybe not drawing lines but . . .

WRIGHT: I wish we wouldn't use that word *jobs* so much in our country.

McBRIDE: You do?

WRIGHT: I don't like to think of them . . .

McBRIDE: What should we call them?

WRIGHT: . . . how the building that I am building is a job. I don't like to think of how the man that wants me to build one as a client, either! All these things get into categories with us and become standardized and somehow the life goes out of them. Don't you think so?

McBRIDE: Yes, I certainly do think so. I remember Mr. Sullivan telling you in [what] you're doing "put life in it, make it live" and, if everything could, that would be best.

WRIGHT: That's right. Make it come alive. Make it come alive! Well, he did—he could. There is more than one way of making things come alive. You could make them come alive in so many different styles and ways of being—don't you know?

McBRIDE: Yes, that's *true.* Anything you do can come alive don't you think?

WRIGHT: He made it come alive his way and I was determined that someday I'd make it come alive my way.

McBRIDE: What do you mean by USONIA? Is that the way you pronounce it?

WRIGHT: Well, we are a country without a name really. We speak of America . . . well, when I was in Brazil some years ago—I think it was in thirty-nine [1939]—I used to speak of America as the place I came from but they were the Americans, not we. So then I thought—and I had been thinking of it before—it was rather unfair for us to take the name Americans to ourselves. So I was reading Samuel Butler's *Erewhon*—you ever read it?

McBRIDE: Yes.

WRIGHT: [It is] a very interesting, fascinating book by Samuel Butler. He was the father of the great English realistic novel. Well, he pitied us because we had no name and so he gave us one and he gave us USONIA. And USONIA, of course, means simply—well, it has its roots in union, of union, for union—USONIA. So, in the early days people used to ask me what style my houses were and I couldn't tell them, you know, and that didn't please them, so I was held back a good deal by not working in a style. Now if I could have said Usonian that would have satisfied them.

Perspective rendering of the William H. Winslow residence (1893) at River Forest, Illinois. Drawing from Frank Lloyd Wright, Ausgeführte Bauten und Entwürfe von Frank Lloyd Wright *(Berlin: Ernst Wasmuth, 1910).*

The low hip roof projecting over the walls, with wide eaves that emphasized horizontality and a closeness to the ground, is a hallmark in American home design introduced by Frank Lloyd Wright in the William H. Winslow residence (1893) at River Forest, Illinois. Photograph by the editor.

McBRIDE: (laughter) They wouldn't have known what you meant!

WRIGHT: They wouldn't have known the difference (laughter).

McBRIDE: They would have been satisfied because that was a label.

WRIGHT: Well, now we do Usonian houses.

McBRIDE: But, Frank Lloyd Wright, you do have to have words to express ideas. Of course sometimes houses or churches express ideas but . . .

WRIGHT: You have to have bad words to express certain states of feeling . . .

McBRIDE: Yes.

WRIGHT: . . . and you have to have good words to express other states of feeling and words are important—I guess. Too important! Or could they be? I don't know.

McBRIDE: They are important but I am just trying to think about *job,* for instance, . . .

WRIGHT: The word *job* . . .

The playroom terrace on the west side of the Paul R. Hanna residence, Honeycomb (1936), at Stanford, California. The construction was based on a hexagonal modular unit system from which the name Honeycomb was derived. This is one of Frank Lloyd Wright's largest Usonian residential designs and the first with a pitched roof. Photograph by the editor.

McBRIDE: . . . is overworked.

WRIGHT: . . . has a vulgar sound, doesn't it? *Job.*

McBRIDE: It *is* an ugly word when you come right to it.

WRIGHT: For instance, a sailor is a gob, isn't he?

McBRIDE: He was in the war before the last [i.e., World War I].

WRIGHT: Well gob and job and hob . . . well I don't know—let it stand. Of course it's English and . . .

McBRIDE: But I thought perhaps you'd . . .

A Usonian design on a steep-sloped site. The George D. Sturges residence (1939) at Brentwood Heights, California. Photograph by the editor.

WRIGHT: . . . we can't change language!

McBRIDE: . . . help me and tell me what to do!

WRIGHT: Well, I don't know what to do concerning the language.

McBRIDE: It's been reported to me, Mr. Frank Lloyd Wright, that you said that in fifty-five years, at the very least, all these . . . this building we're sitting in right now would be condemned.

WRIGHT: Fifty-five years? Yes, I think that would be about the life of the building.

McBRIDE: Radio City?

WRIGHT: Of course, it was dated when it was built; that is a great misfortune. I noticed coming in here this morning piles of this, that, and the other thing, and I had to make my way through and I suppose nobody ever thought of a storage space for a studio. Did they?

McBRIDE: No (slight laughter).

STUDIO PERSONNEL: (laughter)

WRIGHT: Well, perhaps you better call the fifty-five years up now and build another one. Build another building suitable to your purpose!

McBRIDE and STUDIO PERSONNEL: (continued laughter)

McBRIDE: What will happen now when this is condemned; they'll just put up another one?

WRIGHT: Well, I suspect that Bob Moses will have to be called in to construct three bridges . . .

McBRIDE and STUDIO PERSONNEL: (laughter)

WRIGHT: . . . one below the Washington and two above the Washington to the other shore and the other shore will have to be annexed as New York [City] to the left. Or would it be to the right? It would depend on whether you were coming in or going out. But I think that would be a good move!

McBRIDE: Yes.

WRIGHT: Then I think above that the taxicabs in the street should be cut in two. The average fare on a taxicab would be one and a half passengers. Now why have a great place that you could really move into and keep house in just to tote that one and a half around the city?

The sign above the entrance to Radio City Music Hall in New York. Frank Lloyd Wright's conversation with Mary Margaret McBride took place in a studio at WEAF (radio), a National Broadcasting Company (NBC) affiliate, on December 2, 1949. Photograph courtesy of the New York Convention and Visitors Bureau.

McBRIDE: (laughter) Well, what would you do with cities?

WRIGHT: Oh! I, of course, am an advocate of Broadacre City [see Chapters 26 and 27], which is everywhere and no where. But I would have, of course, *nature* take her course, which she's doing—the city is disappearing. The city is going to the country whether we want it or not and, of

Wright: "Of course it was dated when it was built; that is a great misfortune." Radio City Music Hall, New York. Photograph courtesy of the New York Convention and Visitors Bureau.

course, you know that every city is a vampire. Don't you?

McBRIDE: Is a vampire?

WRIGHT: A vampire.

McBRIDE: I think so.

WRIGHT: It can't live on its own birthrate more than three years unless it's refreshed from the country—the villages—it's gone! And I was reading the other day that every city in the United States is insolvent—bankrupt.

McBRIDE: And they'll just vanish? Won't they?

WRIGHT: They will vanish all except places at the ports. Every port will be a city. Every center of distribution of natural materials—like great mines and great oil deposits—will have cities. But pretty soon we aren't going to know the city from the country. It's a terrible thing to think that we won't know the country from the city but the city won't be like the cities we see now.

McBRIDE: What will they be like?

WRIGHT: Well, something that we haven't yet recognized. Very beautiful and very, very much to be desired. It would be pretty hard to put it into words because I work with a pencil and a drawing board and triangles and so on.

McBRIDE: There'll be space?

WRIGHT: Well, it will recognize space as the reality of the building rather than walls and bricks and mortar and the shell of the thing. The spirit of the thing will come more and more into being and we'll come to love more and more the ground—realize that it is the basis of culture—and try to make up for lost time!

McBRIDE: We've wasted a good deal of time!

WRIGHT: We've wasted most of the time that we've been here on what we call merchandising, manufacturing, and money making and we've made nearly everything quite successfully except the thing that it would be worth making for—which would be a *true* culture of our own. That's something we've forgotten or never knew. Of course, we were originally colonials—weren't we? We came over here with customs and manners and pretty nearly everything set and we continued with it not realizing that now we had a chance to live in a greater and more satisfying way. So we continued to be English, I suppose. Of course, the English people are the most habituated people in the world—aren't they? Well, we've inherited that habituation, so we've been inhibited by that habituation.

McBRIDE: I don't quite see why you think we'll get out of it though.

WRIGHT: Because . . . things can't endure forever even abuses!

McBRIDE: (slight laughter)

WRIGHT: And we've had almost enough and by now a great many of our people are awakening to the loss that we've sustained. They're awakening to the fact that we do not have culture of our own; that we are as that witty Frenchman said—I never could remember his name, if I ever knew it; I've used his quotation often—that "we were the only great nation in the world to have proceeded directly from barbarism to degeneracy with no civilization of our own in between."

McBRIDE and STUDIO PERSONNEL: (loud laughter)

WRIGHT: Well, we laugh but it's *true!* We should weep and tear our hair and we should get busy and do something about it. Don't you think so?

McBRIDE: It's chiefly because we've just imitated, isn't it?

WRIGHT: Well, of course, that's the little book that I've just written—*Genius and the Mobocracy.* And the *mobocracy*—I meant by *mobocracy*—not what the critics that criticized the book seemed to think I meant. I meant the maintainers of mediocrity, not the workers, not the simple people, but those people who really are sitting in armchairs as professors and who function as critics and who sign the biggest checks—the people who really would not allow life to be lived, will not allow real building to occur. Like our insurance companies, [they] must always bank on yesterday; like our bankers looking ten years behind our times in order to be safe instead of ten years ahead in order to be safer. But we can't do anything about that except to do what we are doing—making life as uncomfortable for them as we can!!!

McBRIDE: (loud laughter) Thank you very much! Who published your *Genius and the Mobocracy?*

WRIGHT: *Genius and the Mobocracy* was published by Duell, Sloan, and Pearce.

McBRIDE: Duell, Sloan, and Pearce.

WRIGHT: I don't think it would be such a good book to read because it's hard to read. Most people who have read it say they've read it a second time in order to understand what is was all about the first time [they read it]!!

McBRIDE and STUDIO PERSONNEL: (laughter)

WRIGHT: There is a book that I think you should know about and everybody in America should know about because, don't you see, we're getting to be the most arrogant people on earth. The most arrogant nation and we've been up against something now that . . . or we are up against something now that's going to be pretty serious for us if we don't cease our arrogance and become a little more understanding, and that is of the life of the Orient, the philosophy of the Orient, the Oriental peoples—that profound and deeper philosophy of the East of which we've allowed ourselves to learn nothing. But there was a great man who died just lately in Paris [and] he's been referred to in a book . . . his name was Gurdjieff.

McBride: ". . . his family had had on the farm in Wisconsin a chapel of their own with rocking chairs in the front of the chapel for uncles and aunts." The Unity Chapel (1887), Helena, Wisconsin (near Spring Green). This building was designed by Joseph Lyman Silsbee, architect, under whom Frank Lloyd Wright worked at the time as a draftsman. The chapel is at the site of the Lloyd-Jones family cemetery, where Mr. Wright was buried from 1959 until 1985. Photograph by the editor.

Frank Lloyd Wright's motto inscribed in wood above the living room fireplace of his home (1889) in Oak Park, Illinois, states: Truth Is Life. Good Friend, Around These Hearth Stones Speak No Evil Word of Any Creature. *Photograph by the editor.*

We who knew him called him "Gurdovanich" [sic]. Well, Kipling said, you know, that "the East and the West, these twain shall never meet." But in this philosopher—in this great scientist, because he's a greater scientist I think than perhaps any who now live or who have lived—he pursued this ancient culture even into the fastnesses of Tibet and he came out with the most profound analysis of our *organic* relationship to the cosmos. And we will learn from him and by way of a mind like his, which was superb, to be a little more careful of how we misjudge the philosophy and ideals of other people than our own and we need that. So read this book and read this man. I think the book, which is published now, is called *In Search of the Miraculous,* published by Harper and Bruce and I think the other book to be published soon will be published by them which is Gurdovanich's own book—the tale of his travels—and I think that he calls it "Tales of . . . to His Grandson" or something like that.

McBRIDE: We'll look out for it.

WRIGHT: Well, thank you very much. Good-bye.

McBRIDE: Thank you Frank Lloyd Wright. It was a pleasure to have you here.

WRIGHT: You've been very nice and it's been very pleasurable.

McBRIDE: You didn't mind it?

WRIGHT: Boys, you carry on! [Mr. Wright exits the studio]

McBRIDE: (laughter) I didn't really spring on him two of the best little yarns I had about him. He had long golden curls until he was eleven years old when they were cut off [and] that's in his first *An Autobiography.* [He] used to get up at four o'clock in the morning to milk—he learned to milk very well and maybe that's why he had an ode "To the Cow"—and his family had on the farm in Wisconsin a chapel of their own with rocking chairs in the front of the chapel for uncles and aunts. Wasn't he an interesting man?

You notice that he talked about where we were broadcasting from—well, it's Radio City in case you've wondered yourself. We're right in Radio City.

Frank Lloyd Wright, circa 1920. Photograph courtesy of the R. M. Schindler Archive, the Architectural Drawing Collection, University of California, Santa Barbara.

2 This Is American Architecture

. . . God is the great mysterious motivator of what we call nature, and it has been said often by philosophers, that nature is the will of God. And, I prefer to say that nature is the only body of God that we shall ever see. If we wish to know the truth concerning anything, we'll find it in the nature of that thing.

Introduction

The text of the speech contained in this second introductory chapter was transcribed from a lecture Frank Lloyd Wright gave in 1957 to more than 1000 high school students at the former Fine Arts Building of the 1893 Columbian Exposition in Chicago. Mr. Wright discusses with a quiet and reserved audience the definition of the word *architect,* the Beaux Arts architecture that permeated the 1893 Columbian Exposition and its later influence on architecture during the early part of the twentieth century, the Declaration of Independence and the sovereignty of the individual, related to the emergence of a

---

Text of a speech, edited and reprinted with additional material, from Frank Lloyd Wright's "This Is American Architecture, "*Design,* Vol. LIX, January/February 1958, pp. 112–113, 124, 127–128, by permission of the Helen Dwight Reid Educational Foundation. The additional material is derived from a Pacifica Tape Library audio recording titled "Frank Lloyd Wright and His Impact" (Catalog #BB3612).

free American architecture, nature study and its importance to architecture, and the concept of architectural principle opposed to architectural precedent. Mr. Wright always enjoyed talking to and with the youth of America and had a certain mystical rapport with the young, made obvious in this speech by the attentiveness of the large student audience.

By the end of 1957, the year of this speech, Mr. Wright had already designed 864 projects, which represented about ninety percent of his lifework. In addition, 1957 was his most prolific year of architectural practice in terms of the number of projects created (forty-three). Before his death on April 9, 1959, one and one-half years after this speech, he was to design another ninety-two revolutionary projects in an astonishing lifetime achievement of 956, of which 448 were executed.

The year 1957 was a busy one not only with respect to his prolific architectural outpouring but also to the frequency of his public appearances. In late April of 1957 he addressed another interested group of students who attended the Department of Architecture at the University of California, Berkeley.[1] Mr. Wright was invited to give a number of lectures and seminars to that student group as a Bernard Maybeck Lecturer. On June 18 he spoke to the editors of *Arts in Society* regarding his philosophies of education and art (see Chapter 20), and on July 31 he stood before the Marin County [California] Board of Supervisors in regard to his commission to design the Marin County Civic Center (see Chapter 29). In September he was interviewed twice by Mike Wallace for the nationally televised *The Mike Wallace Interview.*[2] Mr. Wright was eighty-nine years old in 1957.

---

[1] For the complete text of these lectures and seminars see Patrick J. Meehan (Editor), *The Master Architect: Conversations with Frank Lloyd Wright* (New York: John Wiley and Sons), 1984, pp. 185–228.

[2] *Ibid*, pp. 291–310.

The Speech

WRIGHT: Well, I suppose you're here—most of you—to hear something about architecture, aren't you? And, [do] you know, first of all, what *architecture* means? What the word *architect* means? How many of you know? Let's hear it! Can somebody tell me what the meaning of the word *architect* is really? I've asked so many young people and always got *no* for an answer. Then I would turn to the bellwether—the leader—who'd be standing by the window and I'd say "well, he knows!" No, rather embarrassed—red in the face—he doesn't know! Well, now it's strange that you should wear the name *architect* all your life and never know what the word means! Isn't it? Now, is there anybody here who can give me the meaning of the word *architect?*

AUDIENCE: (no response)

WRIGHT: Why surely this is not possible! You're all students of architecture, aren't you? You youngsters down there, are you seniors? Juniors? Or what? Seniors! Well, now, the word *arch*—the archbishop—*arch* means the top; it means way up above everything; really master. There you have *arch!* Now *itect*—what does *tect* mean? You know that! Technician, technology—it means know-how—knowing the way and the means—*tect. Architect*—there you have the master of the know-how. Well, now, if I've never done anything else for you, [I] came down here to tell you what the name that you wear, or [are] going to wear, means—I ought to get a posy for that, shouldn't I?

AUDIENCE: (laughter)

WRIGHT: Isn't it strange, boys and girls, isn't it a little strange that things as fundamental, as elemental as all of that are escaped in your educational adventure? And you've escaped nearly everything else, I imagine, in much the same way!

What is *architecture,* anyway? What does *architecture* mean to you? Is it, like the meaning of the word, also something you take for granted? An architect builds buildings, doesn't he? He is supposed to know why he builds those buildings. He is supposed to do something in the design and construction of those buildings that makes them eloquent of their purpose, that makes them features of their site so that they grace it and do not disgrace it. In other words, it's a great mother art—*architecture.* And for 500 years, of course, as you know, architecture has been more or less a cliché, more or less an exterior, not *true* to conditions, not *true* to life. And what we have here and what we're in today is characteristic, I think, of how the world got its architecture.

Well now, it serves a purpose. I remember when this building was built the American people got their first impressive view of the *classic* at the Columbian Exposition, where this building was the [Fine] Arts Building. It was filled with paintings and sculpture and it came straight over from the Beaux Arts, where all of the architecture that we knew any-

The Fine Arts Building of the 1893 Columbian Exposition at Chicago, Illinois, Charles B. Atwood, architect, in which Frank Lloyd Wright delivered his speech "This Is American Architecture" to more than 1000 high school students in 1957. Photograph by Robert S. McGonigal.

thing about in America—where the architects themselves—had come from. I don't suppose we had a real important architect in those days who was not a Beaux Arts graduate. And therefore he was inoculated with the major axis and the temple forms and the columns and all that—he came over here furnished forth [sic] to give to America what all the other civilizations and all the other cultures of the world had had. But somehow that didn't square in my mind or in the mind of Louis [H.] Sullivan, in the minds of Dankmar Adler and a few other people at that time, with this Declaration of Independence. We had declared something new in the world and that was—what? The *sovereignty of the individual* and *that* was a very brave thing in government to do. Magna Charta in England was the nearest thing to it that had ever been proclaimed as government; we got something from that and France was toying with the idea. But we came out—our forefathers—with that declaration of the sovereignty of the individual per se as such.

When all this architecture that we had to draw upon—if we were going to go on building buildings in the old way—were monarchic; they were all the product of authority, none of them were the children or the expression of freedom, freedom of spirit, freedom of soul. So, we were up against, as I saw it, the necessity for a culture of our own, an expression of our own, worthy of the greatest gift of ground the world has ever seen anywhere—most beautiful, most extensive, and all the riches beyond imagination. No nation ever inherited such a material wealth as we inherited! So what to do with it?

We had no means of doing anything with it except as we tried to make over or in some way modify these old patterns, patterns of an old life and an old civilization not at all like ours. So something had to be born from within the man. Something had to be born in a *new spirit* and you had nothing to go by except *principle.*

Now *principle* never changes. The expressions of principle do. Like morals, you see. Morality and ethics have only this in common: that in morals you're endeavoring to apply the principles of ethics and they may be very far wrong, and morals are no surer than the classic architecture was surer, or principle. In fact, morals are oftentimes not on speaking terms with ethics. So here was this proposition—let's call it a proposition: how are we going to satisfy the conditions of this new life? Here's the machine, here's quality now available, here are certain things that a new tool the world hadn't seen before could do very well—could do better than it could be done by hand. But still we had for a pattern to do those things with was what had been done by hand. So, first of all, the machine began imitating in architecture those things which had been done by hand. Well, they soon looked pretty dead and pretty tough and not worthy of man's time or a second look. So someone had to devise ways and means of building whereby the machine could render even more beautifully than ever before the *nature* of the material, the *nature* of steel.

We didn't understand anything; we were taking everything on faith, by cliché, until we began to dig in and find out what the *nature* of these things really amounted to, architecturally—how to express wood as wood. Now, of course, wood is the tree—the greatest friend of man that he has—wood is very friendly to man, he feels it so! Stone is under his feet, the ribs of the earth he inhabits—stone. And here comes glass as an entirely new material to keep air out. And all these new things lying there [that] the Greeks never knew anything about. I'm sure that if the Greeks had known [or] had these materials that we've had we'd be copying the Greeks now! We wouldn't be building anything but Greek buildings. But they didn't have these things. So we've had to get forms that were new to express them. We've had to find integrity that was lacking in the Beaux Arts performance; it was lacking in this kind of building that we're in here now [i.e., the Fine Arts Building of the Columbian Exposition of 1893 in Chicago]. And we had to come out with something that had a fresh new expression of continence, at least, if not integrity of feature, and we went in that direction;

studied it; worked hard at it; came out with certain simple forms that belong to the prairie here.

That's a feature of architecture, too—the thing has to belong there where it stands, as much of it as possible. It has to be *true* to the materials of which it is built—which may be what?—steel and glass largely now. And also various other things.

Here comes the stature of the human being. Here comes the *nature* of the human being. For the first time we began to build according to a human scale. The old grandomania, as you know, took into effect only giving humanity an inferiority complex. That was the aim, of course, and the result of the old Gothic architecture. The old classic [style] was much the same—make a man feel small. And he was small in those days; the individual didn't amount to much.

But now all that changed. Here [in America] the individual did amount to a great deal. So, we took the scale of the human being as the new scale. Well, we didn't get too far with this idea of *principle* instead of *precedent* before the World's Fair corrupted the whole taste of the nation [i.e., the Columbian Exposition of 1893] and we went back about fifty years to the old, old practices inculcated by the Beaux Arts. So, what [we] finally got out of the World's Fair was buildings like this [i.e., the Fine Arts Building of the Columbian Exposition of 1893 at Chicago]; buildings of this character. And the *new* was suspended—oh, I guess not for fifty years, say forty—we'll compromise for thirty-five.

Then we began to have another influx [of], should we say, *intelligence?* Feeling a desire for something substantially our own; something that represented our civilization, our time, and our place, and our man. Well, that's what we've been working at now and, to the degree that we have succeeded, we are on the path of a great future and a great demonstration of what the human mind—if it's related to the human heart—can accomplish. But now we've arrived at a point where being lost out of this progress [or] progression is the *nature* of the human heart.

We're getting to the point now where we're satisfied with the old steel framing, where we build a building with a wall and put the inside against it this way [Editor's note: Mr. Wright motions with his hands]; where the old ideals of principle which make a building like this [Editor's note: Mr. Wright again motions with his hands] one by way of steel in tension—that was the Imperial Hotel [and] that's what kept it from destruction [because] you couldn't pull it apart. Steel in tension first went into actual experience against the earthquake in the Imperial Hotel.

Well it seems that, of course, the foundation was another feature but essentially it was tension—steel in tension—that saved the building and it's been saving it ever since. Just three weeks ago [there] was one of the greatest quakes they've [Tokyo] had; the Imperial [Hotel] does this thing—it goes this way and then it comes back again [Editor's note: Mr. Wright motions again with his hands] and everybody in it is perfectly safe.

Steel in tension. Well, now, all these new things, like glass, have properties. Steel has a property. Now, of course, when we first got steel there was nothing to do. We had been using lumber, we had beams and we had posts, and so we rolled the steel into lumber [shapes] and we used the steel as beams and we used it as posts and we used all that sort of thing, just as though we were using wood. But here's [John] Roebling coming along and some of these minds that are based on *principle*—elemental thinkers—and Roebling said "but steel is strongest as a strand." You've got the properties of steel, [a] property used in construction is the strand like the spider, spinning. And there lies the secret of what steel can do for modern times. It can give indefinite span—indefinite lightness of span.

And, here comes glass to use in large open surfaces filling these spans lightly and there you had an architecture that the Greeks knew nothing about—Gothic Goths knew nothing about. In fact, the Goths tried for this delicacy and width and span and everything by way of stone until the stone began to fall down—until the buildings began to

Wright: "Steel in tension first went into actual experience against the earthquake in the Imperial Hotel." View of the pool (foreground) *and main entrance of the lobby wing at the Imperial Hotel (1915), reconstructed at the Museum Meiji Mura near Nagoya, Japan (1976). The original building was constructed in Tokyo, Japan, and because of its unique structural design survived the great earthquake of 1923. Photograph by Juro Kikuchi.*

fall! They carried it as far as it could be carried.

Now we've started on a new course—new buildings and inasmuch as they had nothing in that time to use except steel lumber, they used the steel framing and they used steel the way lumber is to be used, you see? Now, of course, when you frame steel together like lumber and make a steel building like a lumber building the joints can never get the paint that is necessary to keep the building living. As long as you paint the steel, the steel will stand. But the paint doesn't get into the joints! So, [for] most of those nineteenth-century [buildings] . . . that was a cliché. That's what the nineteenth century produced by way of thinking for structure—the lumber-framed steel building! Well, now, the joints of course, were exposed and have been exposed and they're the only life the building had, and today, of course, our buildings are more or less dying of arthritis at the joints! I think that when they built the first skyscrapers in New York City they said they would stand for fifty-five years. Well, they'll stand a good deal longer than fifty-five years but they're only temporary. As compared with ancient buildings, we haven't built a building in America by way of steel construction that's going to last measurably long. So that was a wrong, wrong way to use steel if you wanted permanence! But, of course, the whole steel industry was set up on that basis and if you wanted to do something else it would be very troublesome and expensive. So, they made the best of the old steel framing and did pretty well with it. They reduced it to a facade and all you had to do with a facade after you got it was to devise some type of wallpaper pattern for the face of it and hang it there or plaster it on. So the architect became a facade mummer and a paper hanger, more or less, on a steel frame.

Well, now, that's all right for nineteenth-century architecture and it's good enough for the city, probably because the city isn't going to last very long now with the car. You've got to choose between the car and the city and the choice about fifteen years from now is going to be quite evident that it is not going to be the city! They're

View of the Brooklyn Bridge in New York, a suspension bridge that spans some 1595 feet over the East River between Brooklyn and Manhattan, was designed by John Augustus Roebling (1867) and completed by his son Washington Roebling (1883). Steel strands in tension make up the vertical and radiating suspenders of steel cable. Photograph courtesy of the New York Convention and Visitors Bureau.

doing everything possible to make it stand for the time being.

Now all these elemental things are inherent in the *nature* of architecture today, and only as you study *nature*. And *nature* doesn't mean out-of-doors, you know—*nature* doesn't mean horses and cows and streams and storms only—that's only one little element. *Nature* means the essential significant life of the thing, whatever the thing is. That thumb of mine, what's the *nature* of the thumb? Why is this nail on the thumb? It's the *why,* the questioning concerned with the very life and character of whatever is, that is the study of *nature*. Now there's no architect possible for future use or who is able in the least to reckon with these terrific impulses released by the facilities of machinery and modern science, who can interpret them in terms of beauty, until he has mastered and become a master in the realm of the study of *nature.* That's why I think we made a great mistake when we took the capital "N "off *nature* and put it only on God. [Putting it] on God is all right—leave it there because God is the great mysterious motivator of what we call *nature*—and it has been said often by philosophers that *nature* is the will of God. And I prefer to say that *nature* is the only body of God that we shall ever see. If we wish to know the *truth* concerning anything, we'll find it in the *nature* of that thing. Now we've had great philosophers who are masters of what we call human *nature;* we've had great poets, and this is a matter for the poet: I think the *nature* of *nature* lies, so far as our grasp on it or our intimacy with it is concerned, is a matter of our learning from our great poets.

Of course, when we made this great declaration in the face of the world of a new integrity that was going to come out of the freedom of the individual to be greatly himself, we had no religion to go with it, don't you see? The old religion was all gone and the only thing we had was the saying of Jesus himself, that the kingdom of God is within you! That we cling to *now.* That is what the great Declaration of Independence means: that the kingdom of God *is* within you and that's where you'll find it, and it's in the *nature* of what you *are* that this thing is going to come that we call *appropriate architecture,* that we call the *nature* of building beautifully man's life according to time, to place, and to man. And, of course, we have nothing that is it. We're working toward it by way of proper uses of materials. If we use steel as steel in strands, vary it so that it has a flesh of its own, so that it cannot degenerate, take the sheets, slit them, pull them open, make a net that can be buried in concrete.

And we've given concrete a great deal of attention, too, because now concrete is practically strengthening, as it goes from year to year. The older the concrete is, if it's good concrete, the stronger it is! So it's practically imperishable. The old Roman cement today is there—it was magnesite; we used it; I used it in building the Larkin Building in Buffalo [New York]. They extract the carbonic acid gas from the soda water—fountain from it—and the residue is magnesite—that's the old Roman cement. Well it went very far with that in building. The Larkin Building was magnesite. So today we are pretty well in advance of nearly everything in this way of the flesh. Concrete becomes the flesh of our modern world and steel becomes the fibrous integument in the flesh just as it is in you, as it is in the tree; and now we build as *nature* builds—from the inside out. We no longer think of building frames such as you see all over the city, such as you see in every city in the United States, and then trying to do something with the exterior to make them attractive facades. So they're all today not buildings exactly, they are steel frames on the old lumber pattern of framing and they're all perishable and none of them permanent; all complex, expensive, except for the standardization that comes from the lumberizing of steel. And there you have a situation in the middle of the nineteenth century. Think of it, children, we're seven years past the center of the twentieth century [1957], building nineteenth-century buildings! In the nineteenth century way!

Well, now, Adler and Sullivan built them that way. When I was a young architect that was all there was! And it's all there is now except for a voice in protest like mine here to you and others who feel as I feel.

So, these things begin in and come out of the study of *nature.* It is out of the study of the *nature* of steel that you arrive at these conclusions which I'm giving you. It's out of the study of the *nature* of glass that I'm giving you what I'm giving you now. And that's where all the things will come from. That's your university; that's where you ought to go to school.

Well, let's see now, we've had a demonstration of what I've been talking about in Mexico. You heard

Drawing of the Seneca Street elevation of the Larkin Company Administration Building (1903), Buffalo, New York (demolished 1949—1950). Drawing from Frank Lloyd Wright, Ausgeführte Bauten und Entwürfe von Frank Lloyd Wright (Berlin: Ernst Wasmuth, 1910).

very little about it in this country. I don't think it was very welcomed news to the architects of the country—what the earthquake did to the steel framing filled with glass in Mexico. One poor architect committed suicide, three others went to jail, the frames were contorted, twisted, [and] the glass flew all over Mexico City. Because when you build a steel frame and gusset plate the joints, or do what you can to stiffen them, the slightest deviation from square will crack the glass. And, if the pressure is even almost invisible as this pressure [was], that will crack the glass; but if it becomes visible, it will explode the glass and that glass flew all over Mexico City from those so-called "modern buildings." Well, now, the buildings may be modern buildings but they were not new, they were the old thing carried to a long conclusion. Now, that we do; we're quite good at it. We'll take a thing and run it into the ground in a few decades. Now that's what we've done with the old steel-framed building—we've run it beyond its limitation, we've made a cliché out of it. You boys all laugh it up in the school. I went into the Beaux Arts in Paris about three months ago [and there were] 3500 students in the great hall where they were showing their clichéd work and I walked down the aisles here and there [and] they gradually learned that I was there and became a big queue behind me and went along. [And they] saw nothing! Nothing but the facade—facade after facade after facade! Nothing below the curtain screen wall patterned in different ways—sometimes very elaborate now—some of them got quite gay! But it was all the same thing; there was no thought of structure. There was nothing there that gave you the evidence of understanding of how things were built! You see? Well, of course, you can't live on that in a country like ours.

We're a great growing people with a great growing sense of life, and we're not satisfied with all these shallow clichés. We want something that expresses our own heart, our love of life, our own feeling for it. And, gracious! If we get into *nature,* out of *nature* can come miracles of structural integrity with an expression of beauty the world has never even dreamed of!

It's gone wrong now; it's going cliché. It's going away from the standard that we started to raise here in Chicago. Chicago was the birthplace of what I'm talking about, and it went abroad and astonished Europe and came back and we've been importing it ever since, but it was originated here. This is where we began to think that way. And we found a poet—Walt Whitman. We read Emerson, Thoreau, and we found the thing that was *truly* in the spirit of our life here and of our nation and that we have still to go by. Every once a year I have the boys around me read Emerson's "American Scholar." Get it and read it if you haven't read it. I don't know whether you have or not. And he couldn't go back to Harvard for 23 years after he delivered that lecture there! So now you can read it and various other things down the line. We've had great Americans. We're going to have greater ones and they're going to come from the teenagers. I doubt if there [are] very many of them visible now above that area, above that grade. It's all with the young; it's all with the youngsters who have fresh minds, who can *see in* when they look at things, not just *see at;* who can learn by analysis, not only by comparison. You see, when you compare this with that and that with that, you're on the surface all around; you never get the real *truth* about anything and you never really know anything. It's only as you say, well, what is the *nature* and character of this man, *nature* and character of that man, and begin to know who's who, why is why, and what is what. Only then are you on the road to the future that this nation was established not merely to proclaim but to build! And architecture is the cornerstone of that culture of which we now have none or little, but we only have an amazing civilization.

The mother art is architecture. Without an architecture of our own we have no soul of our own civilization. Now, of course, architecture is a blind spot of our life in America today. How many millions of students go to the university to be educated? They come away conditioned, not enlightened, and they know nothing of architecture, although they have a department somewhere around—probably in the basement or maybe in some buildings outside there where they had soldiers at one time; but architecture has not received, and is not receiving now, its due, if we mean by way of the word *democracy* a genuine culture which can become the soul of our civilization.

3 The Architect

In the arts every problem carries within its own solution and the only way yet discovered to reach it is a very painstaking way—to sympathetically look within the thing itself, to proceed to analyze and sift it, to extract its own consistent and essential beauty, which means common sense truthfully idealized. That is the heart of the poetry that lives in architecture.

Introduction

Frank Lloyd Wright delivered "The Architect" on the morning of Friday, June 8, 1900, at the Second Annual Convention of the Architectural League of America at the Fullerton Memorial Hall of The Art Institute of Chicago. Mr. Wright's address followed a talk given at the convention by his *Lieber Meister,* Louis H. Sullivan, architect. Recounting Mr. Wright's delivery, one reviewer commented:

Text of a speech reprinted with minor editorial corrections from Frank Lloyd Wright's "The Architect," *The Brickbuilder,* Vol. 9, No. 6, June 1900, pp. 124–128.

Frank Lloyd Wright, circa 1910—1920. Photograph by DeLonge Studio, courtesy of the State Historical Society of Wisconsin.

. . . his long paper on "Architects" belabored every existing condition and every ordinary practitioner, right and left, up and down, front and back, without an exception either as to practice or design. It was at times quite bright and funny, but such an exaggeration and perversion of (undoubtedly occasionally existing) facts can give but little serious weight to his paper.[1]

Another reviewer of Mr. Wright's speech had a different opinion and stated that it was carefully prepared:

. . . he devoted himself to questions of professional practice mainly and did not spare the plan-factory magnate, the shyster, and the charlatan. He hit from the shoulder and hit hard. His paper was full of flashes of wit, which carried home to his hearers the points on which he dwelt. The man of "eminence" he showed up in his true colors, and he made a strong plea for the man of obscurity striving after an ideal other than money and a large practice. His paper was a fearless and outspoken utterance on a subject of moment to every person interested in architecture.[2]

Regarding the Convention in general, another reviewer commented further:

. . . delegates were a rather unusually sharp, bright and attractive looking set, and represented evidently very faithfully the general make-up of the clubs that they appeared for. The majority were unquestionably draughtsmen or young architects probably with comparatively limited practical experience but certainly with enormous and unbounded enthusiasm for their work and profession as they saw it. The impression (probably false) would be that many of them, or certainly of their constituents, were not the so-called school-trained men. Partially, probably, because of their enthusiasm, and partially because of their lack of such training, they frequently desired to break over the traces, and would receive with applause condemnation of all design, school, styles and general existing conditions; and yet when it came to a vote upon any particular and specific point, their good American common-sense generally brought them quite squarely to more conservative ideas of even design.[1]

It is interesting to note that Mr. Wright opened his speech with the quotation *"Liberal sects do their work not by growing strong, but by making all others more liberal."* The following is the complete text of this important speech.

---

[1] "Second Annual Convention of the Architectural League of America," *The American Architect and Building News*, Vol. 68, June 16, 1900, p. 87.

[2] "Second Annual Convention of the Architectural League of America, held at Chicago, June 7–9," *The Brickbuilder*, Vol. 9, No. 6, June 1900, pp. 112–115.

The Speech

WRIGHT: A vital difference between the professional man and a man of business is that money making to the professional man should, by virtue of his assumption, be incidental; to the business man it is primary. Money has its limitations; while it may buy *quantity,* there is something beyond it and that is *quality.*

When the practice of a profession touching the arts is assumed, certain obligations to the public concerning quality and beyond money making are also assumed, and without their faithful discharge the professional man degenerates to the weakest type of social menial in the entire system—an industrial parasite. An architect practices a fine art as a profession, with the commercial and the scientific of his time as his technique. Men are his tools.

In this age of *quantity* there is a growing tendency on the part of the public to disregard the architect in favor of the plan-factory magnate or architectural broker, and there is consequent confusion in the mind of the young architect of today and tomorrow as to the sound constitution of his ideal, if that ideal is to be consistent with the *success* every man of him hopes to achieve. This confusion exists, and naturally enough, because the topography of his field of action has changed. It has changed to such an extent that in the letter, at least, the antique professional standard he may not recognize if he would. But the spirit of practice in the old field is still sound to the core—the spirit that made of the professional man a champion of finer forces in the lives of his people.

The influence chiefly responsible for this change and most easily recognized is that of science and its commercialism. The tremendous forward march of scientific attainment, with attendant new forces and resources—cultivation of the head at the cost of the heart, of mind and matter at the expense of the emotions—has nevertheless given to him new and masterful tools that demand of him their proper use and have taken from him temporarily his power to so use them. Because he has failed to realize and grasp his situation in its new bearings, he is not quite like his brother the artist—a *thing afraid* of organization and its symbol the machine; but the architect, the master of creative effort whose province it was to make imperishable record of the noblest in the life of his race in his time, for the time being has been caught in the commercial rush and whirl and hypnotized into trying to be the commercial himself. He has dragged his ancient monuments to the market places, tortured them with ribs of steel, twisted and unstrung them, set them up on pins, and perforated them until he has left them—not a rag! He has degenerated to a fakir. A fakir who flatters thin business imbecility with "art architecture shop fronts," worn in the fashion of the old "dickie," or panders to silly women his little artistic sweets. His "art is upon the 'town' to be chucked beneath the chin by every passing gallant, coaxed within the drawing room of the period, and there betrayed as a proof of culture and refinement."

Do you wonder at the prestige of the plan factory when architecture has become a commodity—"a thing" to be applied like a poultice or a porous plaster? Do you wonder that architecture becomes of less and less consequence to the public and that the architect has small standing except as he measures his success by the volume of business he transacts?

Divorced from fine art, the architect is something yet to be classified, though he is tagged with a license in Illinois. So is the banana peddler and the chiropodist.

Do you wonder that his people demand that he be at least a good business man, a good salesman, as something that they can understand and appreciate—when as far as the commodity he is selling, it has been dead to them so long [so] as to be unrecognizable except by virtue of association with the dim past, and it is not quite respectable even yet to do without something of the sort. That commodity is as dead to the salesman as to the buyer, and to the fact that the thing is more easily handled dead than alive the salesman, captain of industry though he be, owes his existence.

In business it is in the stock pattern that fortunes are made. So in architecture it is in the ready-made article that the money lies, altered to fit by any popular "sartorial artist"—the less the alteration, the greater the profit—and the architect.

The present generation of the successful architect has been submerged, overwhelmed by the commercialism of his time. He has yielded to the confusion and feverish demand of the moment and has become a high-grade salesman of a high-priced imported article. His duty to the public as professional man [has been] laid aside, if it was ever realized, and merely because the public was ignorant of its claim and willing to buy even if the paint came off and the features peeled.

What has been gained by his feverish haste to offer his art on the altar of commercial sacrifice has been quantity at expense to quality—a general depreciation of architectural values and a corruption of the birthright of the buyers. In consequence, architecture today has not even commercial integrity; and the architect as he practices his profession is humiliated and craven.

Robbed by his own cowardice and mediocrity of his former commanding position in the arts, he hesitates between stalking his victim outright or working wires—otherwise his friends—for the *job,* as his opportunity is now styled.

He joins the club and poses, or hanging to the coat-tails of his friends he teases for the *jobs* they may carry in their pockets, his mouth sticky and his hands dirty, pulling and working for *more.* Then he starves in the lower ranks of a doubtful aristocracy unless he comes by influence in other than architectural ways—by inheritance, by marriage, or by politics. Does a sale of property appear in a trade journal, immediately the owner is besieged by ten "first-class architects," suing for the privilege of submitting "samples free of charge," assuring the owner, meanwhile, that he would be granting a personal favor in permitting them to do so; and if the samples were not what he wanted they would love each other none the less. Or his friend drops in shortly after the owner decides to build and incidentally mentions so and so as a good fellow and a winning architect. His wife, perhaps, has had influence brought to bear before he gets home, and while against the principles of the architect to work for nothing, yet the combination is of such a friendly nature as to form a special case, and "sketches," in this instance, in place of "samples" are finally submitted to all intents and purposes as before, but a little higher in the social scale, inasmuch as the method is less rude and abrupt.

The latest development is the hiring of a professional promoter by the year to drum up "trade"—[to] mine and countermine the special system with pitfalls for the unwary to be ensured for the practice of his principal. And talk to the best of him concerning "professional" advertising, making capital of himself in subtle telling ways—poor devil, the naïveté of some of him would wring the tear of pity from commerce herself. How many architects would live—and they are just the number that *should* live—if they depended upon the work that came to them because of intelligent, critical appreciation of actual qualifications or work performed? There would be a good many, but probably about seven percent of the profession. There is usually the maneuver, the pull, sometimes methods more open, but no more weak and shameful.

Because this matter of architecture itself has become of little moment to the average client, architecture as a fine art is really out of it, and for the present architecture as a commodity is a case of friendly favor and interference or a matter of fashion. The fact that all this has become so generally accepted as good form is proof of the architect's danger and the damnable weakness of his position. Another feature of his present plight is that, not wholly respecting himself—how can he?—he is apt to be a hypersensitive individual, and like other unfortunates who depend upon preeminence of personality to get in the way of "the choosers" he is interested in pretty much everything as long as he counts one, and at that *No. 1;* none of his bloom or luster is to be rubbed off by contact. So, concerted effort in matters touching the welfare of his profession is rare among him.

Perhaps this is in the nature of the proposition. There are intelligent architects who argue that only the selfish few give value to art, the highlights only give value to the pattern of the fabric; but I believe it is because of warp and woof, undertone and motive, that he has any value as a "highlight," and that type of individualism is one of the superstitions he must shed before he comes to his own.

The *architect,* so-called today, is struggling in a general depression in the level of his art owing to the unknown character of the country patiently awaiting his exploration, prophesied by the past, but of which no map may yet be made and of which no chart has been provided by the schools. He is complacent inanity personified and counts not at all; or blinded by the baser elements of commerce, choked by greed, goaded by ambition for "success" of the current type, the feverish unrest, common to false ideals, racks of bones and waste his substance [sic] until he finally settles, dazed and empty, in his muddy tracks, which amounts, I suppose, to giving the people what they want.

For the generalization of the situation, then, the architect is rapidly accepted as a middleman, or broker, with the business instinct and ability, but who can have no business integrity because of the

The Frank Lloyd Wright residence (1889) at Oak Park, Illinois, a structure clad with wood shingles. Photograph by the editor.

The Frank Lloyd Wright studio (1895) at Oak Park, Illinois. Like the Frank Lloyd Wright residence (1889), the exterior of this adjoining structure is covered with wood shingles. Photograph by the editor.

nature of his self-imposed occupation. He sells the public ready-made imported architecture that he himself buys in a job lot of unfortunates in a home which he establishes to protect them from a condition which he himself has developed and fostered. This architecture is applied to his client's condition as a poultice or porous plaster would be applied to his aching back and is accepted with a clamor for more through lack of acquaintance with the real thing, lack of an ideal and of educational force in the profession itself. Meanwhile the younger aspirant for better things is either assimilated by the winners, plucked and shoved behind the scenes with the unfortunate, or settles down to give the people what they want, which simply means producing more of the type the plan factory fashions.

An example of a once-noble profession prostituted by the "commercial knight of untiring industry," abandoned to her fate by the "architect"—in quotation marks—who shrugs his shoulders, looks aghast, and contributes innocuous [sic] expectation of her ability "to pull out," and pull him out, too, to the general blight.

And why this network of cross purposes? Is it because the architect is now confronted with a condition which they say demands a combination of two of him and a corps of trained experts, where before one was absolute? Is it because he is now in a position that demands that an intricate commercial machine be perfected to carry into effect an idea? Or is it because architecture is a great thing in small hands, and ideals, noble theories, if you will, "the rails of the track on which the car of progress runs," have fallen to disrepute?

"Give me a great thought," cried the dying herder, "that I may refresh myself with it." He was the stuff from which an *architect* is made.

The regeneration of architecture does not lie in the hands of [the] classicist, or fashion-monger, of the East nor of the West. Their work is almost written at its length, and no spark of life and but a shroud of artistic respectability will cling to it half a century hence. It is but archaeological dry bones bleaching in the sun! America will regard it as crude; Chicago, even now, regards her County Courthouse as something weak and servile, an insult to the people who entrusted to chosen ones the fruit of honest toil and were betrayed to perpetuate the degenerate art of a degenerate people.

The American nation has a heart and backbone of its own and is rapidly forming a mind of its own. It has not yet been taught self-expression except in the matter of dollars and cents and recently of war [i.e., Spanish-American War]. Presently, light, grace, and ethics, *true* to as virile an individuality as history has known, will come as *naturally* to her as the breath of life that is already hers; and then, oh, ye Stuffed Prophets of Plethoric "Success," will she look with pride upon the time you bedizened her with borrowed finery; pierced her ears for borrowed ornaments; taught her to speak with a lisp and [put a] mince in her gait? No! Your very success was your undoing and her disgrace.

In her new code no one man will be entrusted with the amount of work that occasioned the *plan factory.* As no Rockefeller may rise to a legitimate point of vantage that would justify the control of such a vast share of the earth's resources, *how unspeakably vulgar and illegitimate will it be for one man to undertake in the fine arts more than he can characterize in noble fashion as a work of art!*

The plan factory is the product of a raw commercial state, perhaps a necessary evil to be passed through as we pass through the dark before the day. Perhaps the epidemic of Renaissance, French, Dutch, and English that encumbers the land was a contagious malady such as little children bring from school. Soonest over, soonest mended.

It is argued that we are witnessing the same development in architecture that we see is legitimate enough as a means to an end in trade, as the department store and the trust. But it is not in architecture a development, but a *reflection* or reflex action that is passing but causing painful confusion. It is making of art a network of cross purposes, but temporarily. Art will reign as long as life, and greater than ever her prestige when the harmony between commerce, science, and art is better understood.

It is this harmony, this commercialism, that the younger architect should strive to understand and appreciate, for it is the measure of his technique in his new field; but he should strive to understand it as a *master,* not as a *huckster;* to poetize and deify it as an instrument in his hands. He should help his lame, halt, and blind profession again to its place by respecting his art and respecting himself; by making the solution of problems that come fairly his way such as will compel the recognition that there is no commercial dignity without that kind of art; that will make the man of business see that a Greek temple made over to trade is an unhallowed joke, and that he is the butt when genuine dignity and beauty might be his for less money; that will make the householder realize that if he would live in a Louis XV environment he is but a step removed from the savage, with a ring in his nose; and make it felt that architecture is not a matter of the scene painting of periods nor [a] mere matter of scene painting in any sense whatever.

Give back the slogan "a good copy is better than a poor original" to those whose desire for *success* outmeasured their capacity to perform and who framed it in self-defense. "A poor thing but mine own" is better stuff for men when coupled with reverence and honesty and carries the fundamental principle of harmonious independence graven over the gate of the new country promised of old.

The architect should help the people to feel that

The James Charnley residence (1891), Chicago, Illinois. Frank Lloyd Wright designed this house while employed by the architectural firm of Adler and Sullivan. Photograph by the editor.

architecture is a destroyer of vulgarity, sham, and pretense, a benefactor of tired nerves and jaded souls, an educator in the higher ideals and better purposes of yesterday, today, and tomorrow.

Such an art only is characteristic of the better phase of commercialism itself and is *true* to American independence, America's hatred of cant, hypocrisy, and base imitation. When once Americans are taught in terms of building construction the principles so dear to them at their firesides, the architect will have arrived.

But his own education is a matter of the greatest concern. We all catch a glimpse of the magnificence awaiting him, but how to prepare him is a more difficult matter. It is for a higher law and more freedom in his architectural school that we plead, not anarchy—a deeper sense of the significance to his art of *nature,* manly independence, and vigorous imagination, a *truer* reverence for his precedent. He should learn a method of attack, have cultivated in him the quality that gets at an architectural proposition from the inside outward, for and by itself. He should be a thinking quantity when he leaves school, standing on his own legs—such as they are—with ears and eyes wide open, receptive, eager, and enthusiastic, his faculties sharpened by metaphysical drill, his heart wide open to beauty, whether of a specific brand or no, and a *worker* first, last, and all the time a *worker,* his mind alive to opportunity, knowing the direction in which it lies, gauging his own fitness in relation to it, far-sighted enough to decline the opportunity that he was unfitted to undertake if it should come to him—and many such do come to all architects—courageous enough to decline it and [to] wait for one "his size." And when it came he would make it count without making his client pay too large for a share of his education in the field.

He would gain experience and strength and build up solidly, if slowly; and the respect and confidence would in time be his that would make his personality a power for the architectural good of his country. His experience is to be gained only by solving problems for and by themselves. Advice never built a character worth the name, though advice is good.

So an architect may practice architecture extensively with book and precedent and die without experience, without a character. The man who has worked out the salvation of a summer cottage on his merits, held the conditions in rational solution, and expressed them in terms of wood and plaster, with beauty germane to the proposition, has more valuable experience than he who builds a city with the pomp and circumstance of established forms.

The education of an architect should commence when he is two days old—three days is too much—and continue until he passes beyond, leaving his experiments by the wayside to serve his profession as warning signs or guideposts. The kindergarten circle of sympathetic discernment should be drawn about him when he is born, and he should be brought into contact with *nature* by prophet and seer until abiding sympathy with her is his. He should be a *true* child of hers, in touch with her moods, discerning her principles and harmonics until his soul overflows with love of *nature* in the highest and his mind is stored with a technical knowledge of her forms and processes. Braced and stayed by that, he should move into the thick of civilization to study man and his methods in the things that are his and the ways thereof, taking his averages and unraveling seeming inconsistencies, shoulder to shoulder with his fellow men as one with them. Meanwhile, as his discipline, he should acquire the technical skill of the mill, forge, and try-pit of commerce in the light of science, study the beauty of the world as created by the hand of man as his birthright and his advantage, [and] finding his passion and delight in various initial steps of composition with the encouraging guidance of a catholic-minded, *naturewise,* and loving master. In short, a master that would make the distinction between *fine arts* and *fine artisanship* plain.

Now he is taught certain architectural phraseology of form and color, dubbed "grammar" by his professors, and much foreign technique.

If teaching him that minutes and modules of the architraves and cornices of one type in certain measure make Greek and of another type in combination make Roman and when they corrode each other the result is Renaissance—there he is taught grammar. I imagine it to be a more difficult matter to teach him the grammar of Goth and Moore. But architecture has no business primarily with this grammar, which, at its best, I suppose, might mean putting the architectural together correctly but as taught means putting the architectural together as predetermined by fashion of previous races and conditions.

So the young student is eternally damned by the dogmas of Vignola and Vitruvius, provided with a fine repertoire of stock phrases as architectural capital, and technique enough to make them go if he is let alone and conditions are favorable, which he never is and they never are. He comes to think [that] these fine phrases and this technique are architecture and sells both in judicious mixture to the "buyers" as such with the circumstance of the "scholar" and the "classical," and he would be shocked if told that he is a swindler. He is sent out a callow, complacent fledgling, sure of his precedent, afraid of little but failure to succeed, puffed up with architectural *excelsior* and wadded with *deafening,* to become soaked and sodden in the field, hopelessly out of shape.

The architect primarily should have something of his own to say or keep silence. There are more legitimate fields of action for him than the field of architecture. If he has that something to say in noble form, gracious line, and living color, each expression will have a grammar of its own, using the term in its best sense, and will speak the universal language of *beauty* in no circumscribed series of set architectural phrase as used by people in other times, although a language in harmony with elemental laws to be deduced from the beautiful of all peoples in all time. This elemental law and order of the beautiful is as much more profound than the

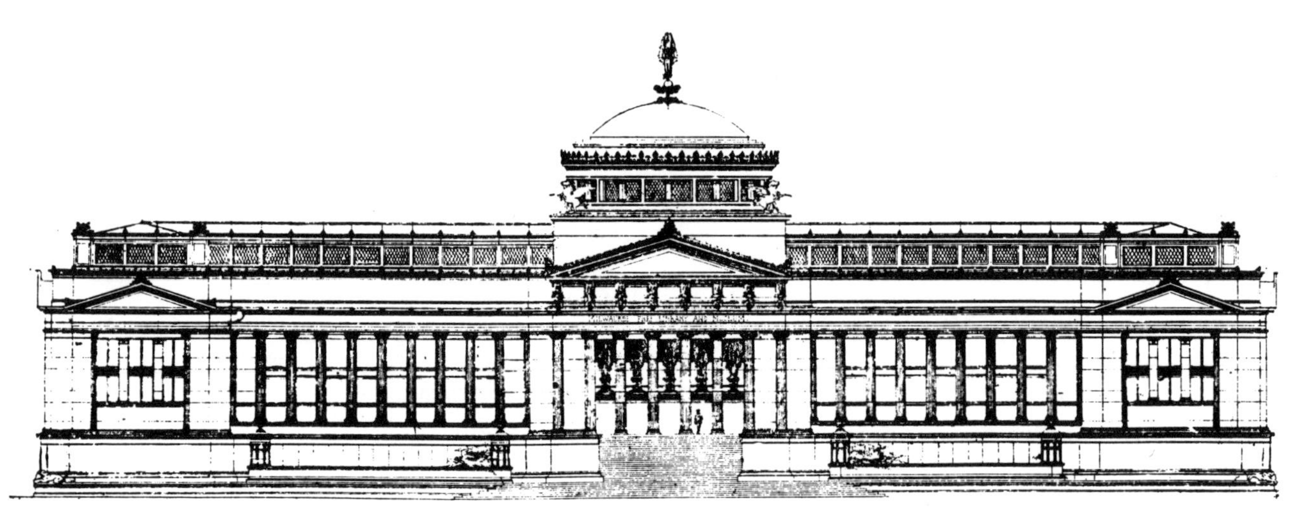

Drawing of the Grand Avenue (now Wisconsin Avenue) elevation of the Library and Museum for the City of Milwaukee Competition Project (1893), Milwaukee, Wisconsin. This project (later constructed by another architect with his own design) may represent Frank Lloyd Wright's only contribution to an architectural competition. Drawing reproduced from the Catalogue of the Seventh Annual Exhibition of the Chicago Architectural Sketch Club (Chicago: The Art Institute of Chicago, May 1894), courtesy of the Wisconsin Architectural Archive of the Milwaukee Public Library, Milwaukee, Wisconsin.

accepted grammatical of phrase in architecture as *nature* is deeper than *fashion.*

Let the young student add to his wisdom the strength and wisdom of past ages; that is his advantage. *But let him live his own life, nor mistake for the Spirit the Letter.* I would see him relieved of the unnatural, educational incubus that sowed the seed of the plan factory and nurtured the false ideals that enable it to exist. I would see him relieved of architectural lockjaw, not by prying the set of teeth of his art apart with a crowbar, nor by cracking its jaws with a sledge hammer, but by a realization that life was given the architect that architecture may grow and expand *naturally* as a noble fine art and as becomes a free-hearted, vigorous young people. It may be that the very cosmopolitan nature of our nation will prevent a narrow confirmation of any one type.

I hope that we are destined to greater variety in unity than has yet existed in the art of a great people. The very strength of individuality developed in a free nation, and the richness of our inheritance, will find expression in more diverse and splendid ways than could be expected of a more narrowly nurtured race. Yet it will find expression in an art that is indigenous and characteristic as an architecture measured by the laws of fine art, the hardy grace of the wild flower, perhaps, rather than the cultivated richness of the rose, but a further contribution to the art of the world—not a servile extraction!

The architect has a hard road to travel and far to go. He should know what he is to encounter in the field and be trained to meet it by men who have faced it in all its ugly significance with unconquerable soul and clear vision. He should understand that to go into the field penniless with a family to support means the ultimate addition of one more craven to the ranks, unless some chance saves him or his fortitude is of the stuff that will see his wife and children suffer for ideals that may seem ridiculous and are to the mind incomprehensible. If he goes single-handed, he must be content to walk behind, to work and wait. The work to be done by the *young* architect entering the lists would better be done by him whose board and lodging is assured

The Warren Hickox residence (1900), Kankakee, Illinois; abuts Frank Lloyd Wright's B. Harley Bradley residence "Glenlloyd" and stable (1900). Photograph by the editor.

for life and whose communication with his base of supplies is not apt to be cut off. He is going into a country almost abandoned to the enemy.

Yet the hardy pioneer who takes his architectural life in hand and fares boldly forth in quest of his ideal, not scorning hardtack for food nor a plank for a bed—

> *Withal a soul like the bird,*
> *Who pausing in her flight*
> *Awhile on boughs too slight,*
> *Feels them give way beneath her and yet sings,*
> *Knowing that she hath wings—*

is perhaps the stuff from which the missionary we need is to come—the spirit that conquered Western wilds and turned them to fallow fields transmuted to the realm of art, a boy with the heart of a king, the scent of the pine woods deep in his nostrils, sweetness and light in his soul, the erudition of the world at his fingers' ends. Will the flickering art spirit of this age produce him? If he is the stuff that architects are made of, he is not to be discouraged by limitations—the limitations within which an artist works do grind him and sometimes seem insurmountable; yet without these very limitations there is no art. They are at once his problems and his best friends—his salvation in disguise.

In the arts every problem carries within its own solution and the only way yet discovered to reach it is a very painstaking way—to sympathetically look within the thing itself, to proceed to analyze and sift it, to extract its own consistent and essential beauty, which means its *common sense truthfully idealized.* That is the heart of the poetry that lives in architecture. That is what they should teach the young architect in the schools, beginning early. But the schools will have to be taught before they will ever teach him. His scientific possibilities and demands have outrun his handmade art as planned for him in the school curriculum. He is without lettered precedent as he stands today on the threshold of great development in the industrial direction of the world.

The B. Harley Bradley residence "Glenlloyd" and stable (1900), Kankakee, Illinois; adjacent to the Warren Hickox residence (1900). Photograph by the editor.

A highly organized, complex condition confronts him. He will understand it, learn the secret of its correspondencies and their harmonics, and work with them, not against them. For art is of life itself; it will endure. Life is preparing the stuff to satisfy the coming demand; and the architect will know the capacities of modern methods, processes, and machines and become their master. He will sense the significance to his art of the new materials that are his, of which steel is but one. He will show in his work that he has been emancipated from the meager unit established by brick arch and stone lintel, and his imagination will transfigure to new beauty his primitive art. He will realize that the narrow limitations of structure outlined in his precedents are too mean and small to be longer useful

or binding and that he is comparatively a free man to clothe new structural conditions in the living flesh of virile imagination.

He will write large, in beautiful character, the song of steel and steam:

> *Lord, thou hast made this world below the shadow of a dream,*
> *And taught by time, I take it so, exceptin' always steam.*
> *Romance! Those first-class passengers, they like it very well,*
> *Printed and bound in little books, but why don't poets tell?*
> *I'm sick of all their quirks and turns, the loves and doves they dream.*
> *Lord! Send a man like Bobbie Burns to sing the song of steam,*
> *To match with Scotia's noblest speech, yon orchestra sublime,*
> *Whereto—uplifted like the Just—the tall rods mark the time,*
> *The crank-throws give the double bass, the feed-pump sobs and heaves;*
> *And now the main eccentric start their quarrel on the sheaves,*
> *Her time—her own appointed time—the rocking link-head bides.*
> *Till—hear that note—the rods return, whings glimmering through the guides.*
> *They're all away, true beat, full power, the clanging chorus goes*
> *Clear to the tunnel where they sit, my purring dynamos.*
> *Interdependence absolute, foreseen, ordained, decreed,*
> *To work ye'll note at any tilt, on any rate of speed,*
> *From skylight lift to furnace bars, backed, bolted, braced, and stayed.*
> *And singing like the morning stars for the joy that they are made;*
> *While, out o'touch of vanity, the sweating thrust-block says:*
> *Not unto us the praise, or man—not unto us the praise.*
> *Now all together, hear them lift their lessons, theirs and mine:*
> *Law, Order, Duty, and Restraint, Obedience, Discipline.*
> *Mill, forge, and try-pit taught them that when roaring they arose,*
> *And th' while I wonder if a soul was gied them wi' the blows.*
> *Oh for a man to weld it then in one trip-hammer strain,*
> *Till even first-class passengers could tell the meanin' plain.*

The architect will weld that strain and build that song in noble line and form. He will write that record for all time. He may not last to judge her line or take her curve, but he may say that he, too, has lived and worked; whether he has done well or ill, he will have worked as a man and given a shoulder to his fellows climbing after.

PART TWO
Organic Architecture and Some Elements

4 Organic Architecture

Nothing can live without entity. Now, organic architecture seeks entity, it seeks that completeness in idea in execution which is absolutely true to method, true to purpose, true to character, and is as much the man who lives in it as he is himself. . . .

Introduction

In this chapter Frank Lloyd Wright describes *organic architecture.* His speech on the subject was delivered before the 31st Annual Meeting of the Michigan Society of Architects in Detroit on Thursday, March 22, 1945. In later years Mr. Wright was to address the Society a number of times; once on May 27, 1954 (see Chapter 25) and again on October 21, 1957 (see Chapter 11), among other occasions.

In 1945 he was introduced to the Society by Michigan architect Alden B. Dow, an early participant in the Taliesin Fellowship for apprentice architects established by Wright in 1932. Dow was a member for only a short period, from

Text of a speech taken from Frank Lloyd Wright's "On Organic Architecture," *Michigan Society of Architects Weekly Bulletin,* Vol. 19, April 10, 1945, pp. 8–9. Reprinted by permission of the Michigan Society of Architects.

Frank Lloyd Wright, circa 1920—1930. Photograph from the Meuer Photoart Collection, courtesy of the State Historical Society of Wisconsin.

May of 1933 to the fall of that year, but Mr. Wright's profound influence on his later performance as an architect is evidenced by Dow's own *organic* architectural achievements.[1]

In 1982 Dow was the recipient of the first Frank Lloyd Wright Creativity Award from the Frank Lloyd Wright Foundation which recognizes persons whose creative achievements have changed the world and whose concerned efforts have helped others to realize their creative potential. Olgivanna Lloyd Wright (Mrs. Frank Lloyd Wright), in presenting the award to Dow, stated that he had been selected because of "the celebrated creativity of his architecture and the effect it has on his community" [i.e., Midland, Michigan] and because of the "creative brilliance apparent in his landscape design, especially evident in the Dow Gardens."[2] Shortly before his death in 1983, Michigan Senate Resolution No. 117 named Alden B. Dow as the first Architect Laureate of Michigan.[3]

---

[1] Two publications that explore in detail the relationship between Frank Lloyd Wright and Dow, his former apprentice, are Sidney K. Robinson's *Life Imitates Architecture: Taliesin and Alden Dow's Studio*, Ann Arbor, Michigan: Architectural Research Laboratory of the University of Michigan, 1980, and Sidney K. Robinson's *The Architecture of Alden B. Dow*, Detroit: Wayne State University Press, 1983.

[2] "First Frank Lloyd Wright Award Goes to Alden Dow of Michigan," *The AIA Journal*, Vol. 71, No. 12, October 1982, pp. 20, 22.

[3] "Michigan's Architect Laureate," *Progressive Architecture*, Vol. 64, No. 10,, October 1983, p. 45.

The Speech

WRIGHT: I shall have to stick pretty closely to this microphone tonight. People are downstairs listening.

Since this young man [Alden B. Dow], who is a highly gifted young man, has taken the liberty of talking to you about me, I think I shall talk to you a little about him. I was giving a Princeton lecture. I do not remember the date, it was so long ago. There was a young man sitting at the end of the front row, and through all six lectures he sat in the same place.

After the lectures were over and the exhibition was on, he came to me and said, "Mr. Wright, I want to come to work for you." I said, "My dear boy, I have no work. If I had, I would be glad to take you."

About a year later I thought of this plan which we call the Taliesin Fellowship for apprentices in architecture. We sent out a little circular to save ourselves from starvation and get a nickel to pay carfare. Then, up the steps comes Alden Dow, and Alden said, "You have got to take me now," so Alden was one of our first apprentices in [the] Taliesin Fellowship. He left too soon for him and for us, but we are proud of him.

If I listened very carefully to what he said tonight, I know I would be very proud of that, too, but I have learned not to take anything of the sort too seriously because it does not really matter.

And now it is remarkable, as I see all this tonight. It is very like a place in England where some lectures were given with equally young architects, I suppose, and that was a memorable English occasion [see Chapter 19]; everything we are, and everything we have, not alone architecturally, but in nearly every other way, we have inherited from the other side.

I admire this building which you have devoted to yourselves and to your purposes; and it is inevitable, *truly,* but the same mistake was made—no recognition, no preparation was made for the poor devil of a speaker. He had no way to get in, independently of the audience. He has no rest room of his own, and he is not anybody, and I guess that is right. Anyway, that is the way it is in our country, because I have been around a lot and met with the same neglect everywhere.

Now, I think that coming into the field a veteran—Alden said forty years, but he should have said fifty, because this architecture is about 125 years old, for I am sure I began to practice architecture long before I was born—now, here we are. You can best get from me something that I want to give you and you would want to have me give it to you by taking it out of me.

I do not believe much in these events where a man stands up and makes a talk. There is a lot of that going on, and really it does not amount to very much. You can talk a lot about a great many things, but never get anywhere.

If you knew how difficult it is to think about anything. We mistakenly call association of ideas and rationalization thinking. It is not. To think seven minutes a day, I do not think it would be possible. Some man has said that it could be done, but I doubt it. I think if you could take three minutes a day it would be wonderful for the human race, and I do not believe we can think except in flashes here and there, when we see and get something, and that is that.

Now, we in this nation are at a point in our national life, which is your life and my life, where we have got to do some thinking. And the thing that we should do to get a great springboard to start from is to take architecture into account as the thing we are calling *organic* architecture.

I wish you would stop speaking of architecture as *modern* architecture, because it does not mean a thing. Anything is modern that is built at the present time. I do not know how it ever got started, but I suppose because everything was antique, everything was from the antique shops. Even the things we wore came across in the same fashion, washed up on the shores of the nation, so we thought it was marvelous that we should have everything modern. Well, maybe it is.

But as to modern architecture, let us drop it and let us take modernistic out and shoot it at sunrise, because there is a great travesty on a great idea. So do please refer to *organic* architecture.

Organic can merely mean something biological, but if you are going to take the word *organic* into your consciousness as concerned with entities, something in which the part is to the whole as the whole is to the part, and which is all devoted to a purpose consistently, then you have something that can live, because that is vital.

Nothing can live without entity. Now, *organic* architecture seeks entity, it seeks that completeness in idea in execution which is absolutely *true* to method, *true* to purpose, *true* to character, and is as much the man who lives in it as he is himself, so that he loves it, lives it, and boasts of the fact that his house is the only house ever built. And he believes it. And it is, for him, if *organic* architecture has done its proper work.

So you see, here you have the centerline of something that goes back thousands of years. It was lost 500 years before Jesus, who enunciated the *principles* which we practice in building today, when he said that the reality of the building does not consist of four walls and a roof, but in the interior space.

The significance of that is not apparent just by the dropping of a hat. It is an entire change in the whole thought of the western world. Because western architecture, and what we call classic architecture, was merely a block of building material sculptured into some kind of style or fashion from the outside.

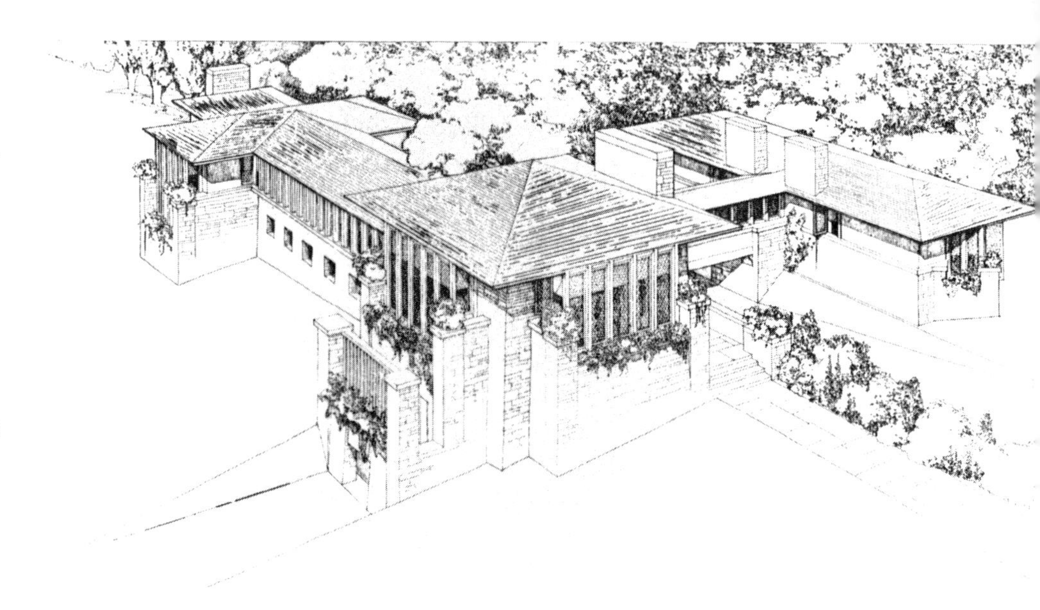

Aerial perspective rendering of the Nell and Jane Lloyd-Jones Hillside Home School II (1901), near Spring Green, Wisconsin. Nell and Jane Lloyd-Jones were Frank Lloyd Wright's aunts and teachers at the school. Later in the early 1930s this building of native stone and wood was to become an integral part of the Taliesin Fellowship Complex. Drawing from Frank Lloyd Wright, Ausgeführte Bauten und Entwürfe von Frank Lloyd Wright *(Berlin: Ernst Wasmuth, 1910).*

Well, here was something that rejected all that and got inside the thing, and when you get inside with that idea you are inside the man. You are seeking things of the spirit by way of the spirit, and you have a philosophy which can become the centerline of a culture of a great nation. It should become the culture of a democracy because it is the first statement of a democratic *principle.*

If it should ever become recognized by education, poor backward education such as we have had in this nation, we would grow, we would live, we could not be destroyed as all these other civilizations have that were monarchic, that were founded upon dictatorships or state socialism, because there you have the core of a democratic faith in man, faith in the man as a man, in him as an individual, which we have confounded always with personality. We have so little faith in the individual, I think because we have confounded *personality* with *individuality. Individuality* is that thing which makes me, me, and makes you, you. Regardless of your idiosyncrasies and your personal appearance, something inside that stands up within and will not sell out, something within that gives the man faith in the within of all men, and makes him all men and all men himself. For others he wishes what he wishes for himself, and he will stand staunch and straight to get it for himself so that all men may have it.

That is the essential phase of democracy, and it is what we had once upon a time set up as an ideal to follow. We had the men who had in the first days of the dawning of that conviction the courage to endeavor, in spite of perfidy, in spite of solicitations, in spite of self-interest, to make it the core of a great nation such as this one.

I am getting away from architecture, am I? Not at all. That is the basis of this ideal of an *organic* architecture. Would the basis not be a recognition of the essential character of the endeavor?

Now, we have never taken time out from making money and becoming Successful with a capital "S" to look ourselves in the face and demand of ourselves something better than anything we have got and something better than anything we have seen. Why, this nation is a neglected backyard from coast to coast and border to border.

I have motored across it fifty times if once, and the buildings from coast to coast and border to border are such as the little carpenters built and little carpenter work transplanted from the Middlewest

Drive and entrance gates to Taliesin I (1911), near Spring Green, Wisconsin. Taliesin I was partly destroyed by fire in 1914. Photograph courtesy of the State Historical Society of Wisconsin.

onto the great Western plains. Up north or down south, it does not make much difference. Out on the Kansas plains, what have you? The same thing, no thought, no feeling, nothing of the interior feeling of manhood we call democracy. Today democracy has built nothing, and I mean it, and I can prove it.

When democracy builds it will be when we recognize the *nature* and character of this idea that we call an *organic* architecture. It is from within, and those of you who used to go to Sunday School, and who read the Sermon on the Mount, and who used to believe in the words of Jesus should have been prepared for it, but you were not.

There was something missing in the Christian religion, something vitally missing, and it let the whole core of this ideal of a *truly* independent nation drift down the river as it has this faith in man which is essential to democracy. It is religion that has failed and failed just at the time when we need it most. But we are not going into that.

You want to know what constitutes physically this thing we call *organic* architecture. I have been asked time and again to show examples and lantern slides and show you what the root of the thing is, but I am not going to do it and I have never done so.

To show you something is very dangerous. I found it dangerous. Here I stand, having built, let us say the last opus, number 497. It went to the *Ladies' Home Journal,* because one went there forty-five years ago and they asked for another one now.

But it is dangerous to show somebody something you have done because they think that is it. You show somebody a house totally unsuited to his wants and it is nothing he would care about, but there is something there if he would look for the basis for it or examine the circumstances which caused it to come into being. But, no, they look at it and say, "Would I like to live in that? No!" Stupid. Perhaps that is a harsh word, but certainly ignorance.

And so it is with everything else. You show them a church and they want you to build a museum. Well, they do not think that would make a good museum. They want to see a good museum in that building, and so they go to some other architect.

Well, it is all extremely unfinished. There is no use calling names or using harsh words. You see, English is a great name-calling language. If you can get a name for anything in our language, you have got that thing practically if you will reiterate the name enough times.

We pay a terrific price for speaking English. We do. We do not know how much, because it is not a language in which to tell the *truth.* Is that a vicious statement? No, it is not. English is not a language in which to tell the *truth.* It is a beautiful language for politicians to use. They could not have found a language superior to ours for their purpose. It is the great language of propaganda.

But we speak it and we have got to sift it out. A young fellow, and I think he was Japanese, God help us all, in Chicago wrote a book on Semitics who made the idea profitable.

You must get the meaning of words into your mind so when we do talk about something we are talking about the same thing. That seldom happens in English. It is a very slippery, ambiguous language, but there is much beauty in it, too, if you read Shakespeare, or some of our master columnists.

Well, where were we? We were talking about architecture. And still, believe it or not, English is architecture. It should be and it is good architecture. If you get a proper definition of architecture in your mind, you will see how important this thing is to a nation that has no environment that is worthy of the nation or the people in it. You see, architecture rightly defined is the structure of whatever is.

Your structure, a building? Yes. But music, no less. It is music, the structure of music in Beethoven and Bach. It is the structure of things that should interest us now and never has.

We should have a system of economics that is structure, that is *organic* tools. We do not have it. We are all hanging by our eyebrows from skyhooks economically, just as we are architecturally. I think you can make it even more insulting than that, architecturally, although I do not know. For there we are.

Ornamental gates and entrance drive to Taliesin II (1914), near Spring Green, Wisconsin. Like Taliesin I earlier in 1914, Taliesin II was partly destroyed by a fire in 1925. Photograph courtesy of the State Historical Society of Wisconsin.

Aerial view of Taliesin III for Frank Lloyd Wright (1925 ff), circa 1953, near Spring Green, Wisconsin. Photograph by John Newhouse, courtesy of the State Historical Society of Wisconsin.

Now, why should not the professors do a little thinking? Why should not the schools go a little deeper into the basis for the thing which they talk about so glibly? They have a language of their own, and if you listen it sounds pretty well, sounds as though there was something in it, and there is nothing in it. You have to sift it.

I went to school for three years and some months, would have graduated and got a degree in three months more, but I walked out three months before graduation. That is the way I feel about the whole business today, only more so.

I think the time has come now when you youngsters, a lot of you here, and the young architects should begin to think for themselves. It is only by thinking and challenging the state of things at every step, at every point, that you can ever get anywhere, because you are imbedded today in the greatest conflicting mass of circumstantial evidence to the contrary that ever existed. It has been deplorably fostered and developed until you cannot trust anything you see or hear, unless you have had some contact and made some connection with this inner thing which is called the *law of nature.*

Now, when you can make a proper study of the *law of nature* for yourselves, you do not take it as something that you know, that is handed to you by way of information. You know a lot of things and realize nothing. You can know all the books have to tell you and not be able to do one single thing. You have to acquire this intimacy by way of contact with doing and only by doing will you learn. Where you come into the drafting room, at the end, there are some letters carved in the wall, "It is what a man does that he has." And do you know that he has nothing else? You will find it out. I found it out, and I think to find that out is what is essential at this step in our dangerous, drifting career.

Exterior view of the living room and long, cantilevered balcony at Taliesin III. Note the corn growing in the foreground. Photograph by the editor.

Detailed view of the long cantilevered living-room balcony at Taliesin III. Photograph by the editor.

View of the rolling Wisconsin countryside from the long cantilevered living-room balcony at Taliesin III. Photograph by the editor.

Detailed view of the living-room facade at Taliesin III, viewed from the living-room balcony. Photograph by the editor.

The hill-garden area at Taliesin III, looking toward the dining room and kitchen (hidden by the leaves of a large tree). Photograph by the editor.

Exterior view of the loggia (far left), *Frank Lloyd Wright's bedroom* (center and right), *and his outdoor bedroom terrace* (far right) *at Taliesin III. Photograph by the editor.*

View from the outdoor terrace adjoining Frank Lloyd Wright's bedroom (right) *and the dining room and kitchen* (left, background) *at Taliesin III. Photograph by the editor.*

The dining room (left) *and kitchen wing* (right) *at Taliesin III. Photograph by the editor.*

Now, you think all this, perhaps, is sidestepping the issue of architecture. It is right to the point. It is right where we have got to begin, at the beginning, before we [can] ever have architecture.

You know that architecture is the only proof of the quality of civilization that we have ever had, all we will ever have. There is nothing else. As a man builds, so he is. As a nation builds, so is that nation.

Were we to be destroyed tomorrow, what would be found by the people who come after us centuries hence? What would they find? There would be nothing except water closets, bathtubs, and washbowls. Anything else? Perhaps some pieces of terra-cotta harkening back to every civilization that ever was, and they could not find one except as it might be called inferior and therefore a replica.

We have nothing. Now, having nothing, why should we not be more humble? Why should we be so confoundedly arrogant? Was it not one of the great Greek philosophers who told us why nations perish? First success, then arrogance, then downfall, and such arrogance as ours cannot fail to be on the threshold of either an awakening or a downfall.

Why not wake up? I believe we should, and I believe it lies in the hands of architecture to be the prophetic cornerstone of that awakening because, until you get down to first principles and get back willingly to the beginning of the thing you are interested in, you are not going to really learn anything about it, are you?

I do not think so, and I have tried hard for a long time to learn. They have said of me that I was experimenting when I built something. It is *true.* I have never built a building that was not an honest experiment but an experiment in the interest of the man I built it for, which makes a difference.

I make this difference between an honest experiment and something merely experimental; a gen-

The interior of the living room at Taliesin III. Note the furniture designed by Frank Lloyd Wright. Photograph by Richard Vesey, courtesy of the State Historical Society of Wisconsin.

Exterior view of the drafting room of the Taliesin Fellowship Complex (1933 ff), near Spring Green, Wisconsin. Photograph by the editor.

Interior view of the drafting room of the Taliesin Fellowship Complex. Photograph courtesy of The Capital Times, Madison, Wisconsin.

The Taliesin Midway barns and dairy and machine sheds (1938—1947), circa 1985, near Spring Green, Wisconsin. Note that part of the building has collapsed. Note also the cornfield in the foreground. Photograph by the editor.

uine experiment is predicated upon something the man knows to be so by experience and believes that if it were just a little bit more so in that direction it would be better. And he tries it, but whenever he tries it he has got something that will save harmless himself and the people he is experimenting for.

Now, when you are developing the ideas of an *organic* architecture, that is inevitable and it is good. So I always explain that I am an "experimenting architect." And I am not ashamed of the fact because I know it is inevitable and should be.

Many a time I have notified a client that if he objected to paying for the education of a young architect—meaning myself—he had better not hire me! So I have been fair and square about it, too. That is one way to learn, an honest way to learn if you are honest about it.

But the building codes now, as they are framed, all stand in your way. They all stand in the way of growth. Building codes are framed in the same spirit exactly that your university education has been framed and developed, with the same trouble with it all. It is the experience of a few men making statements which may be merely a mirror of their limited experience and may be entirely wrong. They stand across the way of progress, but they are the law.

Well, in England I found they had done a wise thing where the code is concerned. They have set up a little court of independent thinkers, of really good men, to whom anybody with an idea rejected by the code may appeal. They are continually meeting with success in trying out new ideas.

Although we are a nation absolutely the son or the daughter or the child of this older nation, I do not think we should be going back to mama for everything, but still they have some good things over there we have not tried yet. I recommend that as one thing to try.

I say this most of all to the young architects. I do not think there is much use addressing the older ones. I do not mean that to be harsh because I am one of them.

Ornamental art-glass light fixture, wood, stone, and plaster are combined effectively with a relief sculpture in a bedroom at Taliesin III. Photograph by the editor.

5 Ornamentation

True ornament is not a matter of prettifying externals. It is organic with the structure it adorns, whether a person, a building, or a park. At its best it is an emphasis of structure, a realization in graceful terms of the nature of that which is ornamented.

Introduction

Frank Lloyd Wright spoke before the Nineteenth Century Club at Oak Park, Illinois, on the subject of ornamentation in January of 1909. It was reported in the local newspaper that

> *he pointed out that the work of ornamenting the person and habitations of the people take up two-thirds of the economic resources of the country, and condemned practically all of this vast effort. Ornamentation is a problem before every woman every day, and for this reason the lecturer received close attention. He not only indicated existing ornament and the culture it suggests, but gave the cure. Many an old idol and deified curlicue was knocked over and room made for Mr. Wright's ideas of ornament, which have made him one of the most famous architects in the world.*[1]

This chapter is a transcription of part of that speech.

Text of a speech reprinted from "On Ornamentation: Frank Lloyd Wright Pleads for New Culture Before Nineteenth Century Club—Other Events," *Oak Leaves* (Oak Park, Illinois), January 16, 1909, p. 20. This speech later appeared as "Ethics of Ornament," *The Prairie School Review*, Vol. 4, No. 1, First Quarter 1967, pp. 16–17.

[1] As reported in *Oak Leaves* (Oak Park, Illinois), January 16, 1909, p. 20.

The Speech

WRIGHT: The desire for works of ornament is coexistent with the earliest attempts of civilization of every people and today this desire is consuming at least two-thirds of our economic resources. Understanding is essential to a real sense of loveliness, but this we have lost; exaggeration serves us now instead of interpretation; imitation and prettifying externals combine in a masquerade of flimsy finery and affectation that outrages sensibility.

Modern ornamentation is a burlesque of the beautiful, as pitiful as it is costly. We never will be civilized to any extent until we know what ornament means and use it sparingly and significantly. Possession without understanding and appreciation means either waste or corruption. With us almost all these things which ought to be proofs of spiritual culture go by default and are, so far as our real life is concerned, an ill-fitting garment. The environment reflects unerringly the society.

If the environment is stupid and ugly or borrowed and false, one may assume that the substratum of its society is the same. The measure of man's cul-

Ornamental stained-glass windows permit the integration of the interior and exterior space at the Frederick G. Robie residence (1906) in Chicago, Illinois. Photograph by the editor.

Integral cast-in-place concrete and specially designed windows ornament the roofline of the A. D. German Warehouse (1915) at Richland Center, Wisconsin. Photograph by the editor.

Wood and glass integrated into an organic whole form a window ornamenting this wall. Special wood panels perforated with an ornamental pattern were made, and glass was inserted to allow for interior natural lighting in the Maynard P. Buehler residence (1948) at Orinda, California. Photograph by the editor.

In this example, as in the Buehler residence, concrete blocks and glass are integrated into an organic whole to form ornament that is an integral part of the structure and walls of the Robert Levin residence (1948) at the Frank Lloyd Wright-designed Parkwyn Village Development (1947) in Kalamazoo, Michigan. The glass permits natural light to form a pattern on an interior wall. Photograph by the editor.

Ornamental light fixtures (foreground) *and art glass* (background) *form an integral part of the interior space at Unity Church (1905) in Oak Park, Illinois. Photograph by the editor.*

ture is the measure of his appreciation. We are ourselves what we appreciate and no more.

The matter of ornament is primarily a spiritual matter, a proof of culture, an expression of the quality of the soul in us, easily read and enjoyed by the enlightened when it is a real expression of ourselves. The greater the riches, it seems, the less poetry and less healthful significance.

Many homes are the product of lust for possession and in no sense an expression of a sympathetic love for the beautiful. This is as *true* of the New York millionaire as of his more clumsy Chicago imitator.

He who meddles with the aesthetic owes a duty to others as well as to himself. This is *true* not only where the result is to stand conspicuous before the public eye but also in regard to the personal belongings of the individual. Back of all our manners, customs, dogmas, and morals there is something preserved for its aesthetic worth and that is the soul of the thing.

We are living today encrusted with dead things, forms from which the soul is gone, and we are

devoted to them, trying to get joy out of them, trying to believe them still potent. It behooves us, as partially civilized beings, to find out what ornament means, and the first wholesome effects of this attitude of inquiry is to make us do away with most of it, to make us feel safer and more comfortable with plain things. Simple things are not necessarily plain, but plain things are all that most of us are really entitled to, in any spiritual reckoning, at present.

True ornament is not a matter of prettifying externals. It is *organic* with the structure it adorns, whether a person, a building, or a park. At its best it is an emphasis of structure, a realization in graceful terms of the *nature* of that which is ornamented. Above all, it should possess fitness, proportion, harmony, the result of all of which is repose. So it is that structure should be decorated.

Decoration should never be purposely constructed. *True* beauty results from that repose which the mind feels when the eye, the intellect, the affections, are satisfied from the absence of any want—in other words, when we take joy in the thing.

Now to make application, I would impress upon you one law concerning which all great artists agreed and that has been universally observed in the best periods of the world's art and equally violated when art declined; it is fundamental, therefore inviolable. Flowers or other natural objects should not be used as ornaments but as conventional representations founded upon them, sufficiently suggestive to convey the intended image to the mind without destroying the unity of the object decorated. With birds and flowers on hats, fruit pieces on the walls, imitation or realism in any form, ornamentation in art goes to the ground.

This conventional representation must always be worked out in harmony with the *nature* of the ma-

Ornamental, hanging light fixture constructed of wood decorates the exterior of the Melvyn Maxwell Smith residence (1946) at Bloomfield Hills, Michigan. Photograph by the editor.

Triangle-shaped light is ornamentally compatible with the structural element it emphasizes in the interior of the Richard Davis residence (1950) at Marion, Indiana. Photograph by the editor.

terials used, to develop, if possible, some beauty peculiar to this material. Hence one must know materials and apprehend their *nature* before one can judge an ornament. Fitness to use and form adapted to function are part of the rule.

Construction should be decorated. Decoration never should be purposely constructed, which would finally dispose of almost every ornamental thing one possesses.

The principles discoverable in the works of the past belong to us. To take the results is taking the end for the means.

6 Hardware

. . . the architect must be a prophet . . . a prophet in the true sense of the term . . . if he can't see at least ten years ahead don't call him an architect.

Introduction

The speech presented in this chapter is Frank Lloyd Wright's address before the Fourth Annual Pacific Coast Regional Conference of the National Contract Hardware Association. It was delivered in the ballroom of the Wright-designed Arizona Biltmore Hotel in Phoenix, Arizona, in 1949. A short time earlier, on March 17, 1949, Mr. Wright made his famous speech before the American Institute of Architects (AIA) at Houston, Texas, on receipt of the AIA Gold Medal for 1948 [see Chapter 16]. In this speech to these producers of hardware he tells them that "the less that is in evidence [in the building] the better . . ." and "the more you get the hardware out of sight, and make less of it, the more you are going to be modern. . . ."

Text of a speech reprinted from Frank Lloyd Wright's "Frank Lloyd Wright Speaks On Hardware," *Weekly Bulletin, Michigan Society of Architects,* Vol. 23, No. 33, August 16, 1949, pp. 1–3, by permission of the Michigan Society of Architects. This speech appeared first as Frank Lloyd Wright's "I Don't Like Hardware," in *Hardware Consultant and Contractor,* Vol. 13, May 1949, pp. 22, 24, 26, and 28.

View of the front of the Arizona Biltmore Hotel (1927) at Phoenix, Arizona. The building utilizes an economic modular concrete block construction system. Mr. Wright delivered his 1949 speech before the Fourth Annual Pacific Coast Regional Conference of the National Contract Hardware Association in the ballroom of this building designed with Albert Chase McArthur. Photograph by the editor.

The Speech

WRIGHT: This is about the first time, or one of the few times, that I've been taken in on the ground floor where things are really done and happening. An architect usually is offstage. I am sometimes afraid that the men who do the selling and producing, and who are making the things of today, don't generally consider the architect very much.

I don't know who makes these designs for hardware or where you get them or how you come by them. Anyway, you don't keep up with the procession as I see it today. Hardware is still too ornamental—it isn't sufficiently simple.

I remember my old master, Louis [H.] Sullivan, making designs for hardware and all he had anything to do with were the escutcheon plates, which in those days were very ornamental. Do you remember? The Yale and Towne people here will surely remember. Those were the Adler and Sullivan doorplates. And then the knob came in for a little dickering too. So the whole thing became a little ornamental touch on a plain door. And I think all the architect had to do with it was just a little effect on the surface of things, as it were.

He really has never criticized hardware, properly speaking. My efforts ever since I've been practicing for myself is to get rid of it. The less hardware that is in evidence the better, or do you think so? Perhaps you feel the way the automobile manufacturers seem to feel about chromium. There must have been a great overstock of chromium in the country after the war. Anyway, they make all these cars look like jukeboxes and I've always felt I'd like to go up and drop in a nickel and see if they'd play. Well, hardware is a little like that, isn't it?

I recall the days when the hardware and the plumbing were goldplated when the capitalists had money. As a matter of fact, the field of plumbing and hardware aren't so far apart. I remember, when designing the Imperial Hotel [Tokyo, Japan], I tried to get some union in the simplicity of the plumbing and the hardware. Why shouldn't it be done? Why don't you go into that more? It is a field that hasn't been overworked.

A door with an ornamental hardware grill that conceals a pane of glass. Note the metal mailbox plate on the lower panel of the door. The James Charnley residence (1891), Chicago, Illinois. Photograph by the editor.

The more you get the hardware out of sight and make less of it, the more you are going to be modern and in line with modern architecture. Whatever of it is in sight should be adapted to the land and feel right and commodious. Nothing is more annoying than to have to use several fingers on a lever handle designed to hurt those fingers. Have you ever thought seriously of criticizing your product on the basis of that simple standard of the use of the thing you make?

Modern architecture is supposed to be based on form following function, but it isn't. It would be a good thing if that were the platform from which it could spring and until, we haven't got the thing we are really hoping for as modern architecture. When this is achieved, hardware is going to be very sensible, simple, and efficient. Does that cheer you up?

I think, in a meeting like this, you should be chiefly interested in trends. You want to see what's ahead, don't you? You should get together to talk things over, swap experiences, and try to weed out the mistakes of the past. Plan the direction of your future. I am prophesying the future for you now as I have helped make that future and I am not finished yet.

Detail of an ornamental and functional pull/push grip on a door at the Aline Barnsdall "Hollyhock" residence (1917), Los Angeles, California. Photograph by the editor.

A pair of doors with ornamental and functional push bars with grip and foot bolts at the Aline Barnsdall "Hollyhock" residence (1917), Los Angeles, California. Photograph by the editor.

Wright: ". . . when designing the Imperial Hotel, I tried to get some union in the simplicity of the plumbing and the hardware." View of the main entrance to the lobby wing of the Imperial Hotel (1915), reconstructed at the Museum Meiji Mura near Nagoya, Japan (1976). Photograph by Juro Kikuchi.

I came into architecture about fifty-six years ago when it was a pretty slim prophecy. Fifty-six years ago in selecting the hardware for a building the architect had a sense of frustration and usually a spell of prostration. Can you remember back to those days when hardware was not hardware but foolishness, aggravation, and extravagance? I can and I guess some of you can. What does it mean, then, to produce a good line of fine and effective hardware? Not what it used to mean—ornamental outside and then fix up the inside as best you can. Hardware should be something that really works and should be out of sight like a good floor hinge. Locks must be automatic and simple and mostly inside, and what does appear outside, easy to work with. That is an architect's point of view as to what the future of hardware should be like.

Now as to the marketing of it, its handling, and selection. I suppose most of you men have plans submitted to you, and then you go over them, make a list, and bid on what you think would be appropriate for the doors, windows, and the various necessities of the job. Isn't that the way you do it? Or does the architect come down to the merchant's store and pick out this and that and tell you what you use on each door and window? Besides being concerned with that, some of this group are representatives from the producers who are really designing and producing hardware. Well, then that's a fine get-together because it will really be effective. You can then really arrive at some conclusions regarding your products and improve them, which should be the outcome of a meeting like this. Incidentally, I am speaking in a ballroom that I designed in 1927. A very nice little place, isn't it?

Well, I came down here not to deliver a lecture to you but to talk the matter over and discuss hardware. This is not a formal occasion, mind you. What would you say, hardware man to architect, was your chief trouble today? What confuses you most? Perhaps it's a material affair—something regarding prices. Then my opinion wouldn't be worth anything. But, if you are really concerned with the char-

A decorative and functional metal horse hitch embedded in concrete at the Susan Lawrence Dana residence (1902), Springfield, Illinois. Photograph by the editor.

acter, usefulness, beauty, and appropriateness of your product, I am pretty valuable to you as I stand here. I think I have told you where you are heading.

The poor devil of an architect has many subinterests and hardware always is a subinterest which he is awfully glad to get rid of. Thus he welcomes any help that a hardware man offers him. I think that is quite right. The average architect is floored by hardware. He hasn't the time, and do you know of anything in this world requiring more detailed knowledge, more finicky adjustments, and realizations than this hardware business? Of course, when an architect gets entangled in devices, he must rise superior to them in some sensible adjustment that he makes with the man who produces them or he's going to have an awful drain on his good nature, his resources, and his time.

So I believe more and more that we're going to go into the hands of the hardware expert, and the hardware consultant will probably become a middleman between the hardware producer and the consumer. The consumer is always going to be mainly the architect. Perhaps the architects who devise and design the buildings that you men are going to hardware are going to be more and more the prey of your experts. I've hired and fired hundreds of experts myself because I know they can be pointed in any direction you want to point them. So I don't think highly of them and I don't employ many because to me an expert is a man who has stopped thinking. He thinks he knows everything. Now when a man gets to the point where he knows and is an authority he's finished, isn't he? There's no progress beyond that.

Well, a good architect wants to remain an amateur as far as he can remain one. He doesn't wish to become an authority. He doesn't wish to call a turn beyond his own vision, and he doesn't wish his own vision to be curtailed by being regarded as an authority. Is this subtle or is it sensible? My feeling is that the architect must be a prophet. I don't mean with an "it" on the word, either, because he'll never be that, but a prophet in the *true* sense of the term. He must keep open-minded and he must keep his eyes on the future. To him, all that can be seen of the future is now. It's today, immediately, it's here. Sometimes we say this man sees fifty years ahead, or he sees at least ten, but if he can't see at least ten years ahead, don't call him an architect.

There are three kinds of architects. I remember in my early days in Chicago hearing them referred to as ARCHitects. Then there were others who called them ARTitects, considered curious individuals. The ARCHITECT, pure and simple, was extremely rare. But he was somebody and he was a great guy, if you are old enough to remember that era. They were real characters and they were strong men.

This is not true of the profession as I see it practicing today because there have been too many paper degrees handed out to the men more ambitious to become architects in four years. So, today, I don't think it's so much to be an architect and I think more and more he's going to be the kind of individual that's going to depend upon you fellows, the plumbers, the electricians, the engineers, and in fact depend on everybody but [himself].

I remember Adler of Adler and Sullivan was a perfect terror to every contractor on the job, no matter who he was. Before the contractor came in to see the old man, he'd take two or three drinks to keep his courage well jacked up but I've seen the old gentleman literally take him and shake him as a mastiff might shake a rat. He'd go out all crumpled up. It doesn't happen that way today; it's usually the other way around. The poor young architect will be the fellow that goes out with his tail between his legs.

Have any of you ever stopped to think how much technique and how much knowledge have to enter into the life of a pretty good architect? It's a wonder he ever gets anything done at all in the way of design, which is the thing he's really supposed to contribute to society.

To me, today, in looking over the situation, what we lack most is an environment. When art is mentioned, we think of what? The art museum or the art exhibition, what is it? It certainly isn't a building. Painting is pictures and to the American people, art means pictures. Yes, be honest about it. Did you ever think of buildings when you heard the term art in this country? Well, to me that's exactly like one of our good wives interested chiefly in a hat and not being so much concerned about clothing for her body. She has to have a hat and it has to be a beautiful hat, so she goes shopping for a hat without regard for the clothing for her body. She might wear an insinuating smile and a beautiful hat and that would be as far as she'd get where art is concerned. It's just like that with our civilization and architecture today.

Art is not a matter of the actual clothing of our civilization, which must be buildings. It's more a question of environment which must be buildings,

The automobile gate and its associated hardware at the S. C. Johnson and Son Administration Building (1936), Racine, Wisconsin. Photograph by the editor.

the way we live in them, and the way we furnish them, and all that. That should be our great art. Now, if we get to the point in our teaching and our schooling and if going to the university is a matter of becoming more and more developed in this way of art, it might be worthwhile. But unfortunately it all seems to be set up contrariwise.

The very things that are important and should be connected with our everyday life are not matters of art. Then, what are they a matter of? I leave it to you to say. You meet each other, you visit each other's homes, and what's important there?

A metal fireplace wine kettle and its associated hardware form an integral organic part of the design of the Edgar J. Kaufmann, Sr. "Fallingwater" residence (1935) at Ohiopyle, Pennsylvania. Photograph by the editor.

To what can you point to prove that American civilization is really tops? That we really have a culture of our own; that we really know the difference between what is merely curious and what is *truly* beautiful. Where do we go to learn it? Who is teaching us? Are we asking for it or are we demanding it? My answer is, no. We are taking a lot of ugliness for granted. We only have left what we call eminent domain for a utility company that is going to give you electricity or water. It is something that can go anywhere it pleases and can destroy the beautiful landscapes and views that may exist. The utility companies and the politicians are our civilization and are as materialistic as anything that ever existed in the world.

Now, that materialistic side is up against an enemy and the enemy is Russia. Two ideologies are clashing and are going to clash more and more. It is the doctrine of the have-nots coming against the doctrine of the haves and the haves endeavoring to justify having and the have-nots trying to get hold of a little something. It's been the same since the world started to become civilized. It hasn't changed but the issue has become concentrated. It has got down to brass tacks.

All this is directly allied to the question of art in our environment and of the architect in his relation to society. Because if we really are what we profess and if we really are a honest democracy we wouldn't be afraid of Communism. We could make it look so bald, bare, and forbidding nobody would ever think of bringing it forward. But you see we are guilty of not being a democracy but being an industrial plutocracy. Now, an industrial plutocracy can't meet Communism and stand.

I went to Houston recently; I went down to be crowned titular head of the architectural profession [see Chapter 16]. I came back with a gold medal and a marvelously beautiful citation. While there, I went over to see the Shamrock [Hotel] open and view six carloads of movie stars in a monument to Frenchified American vulgarity. Or, if you wish, you can put it differently, but that is what essentially it was. And the city itself—to point the features of

The triangular shapes of interior lighting fixtures and air-duct grilles represent the hardware that is organically integral with the total design of the Price Company Tower built for Harold Price, Sr. (1952) in Bartlesville, Oklahoma. Photograph by the editor.

the thoughts I've just thrown at you—was a capitalistic city. Now what is a capitalistic city? Have any of you ever thought this out? A capitalistic city is a broad way paved with pretty much everything on it. At one end and usually at the center of it are downtown skyscrapers—tall buildings. On the other end, little or no paving and shanties. Well, that's Houston. Only Houston has done something very remarkable. Houston has extended the center avenue seven miles and built a skyscraper at the other end of it. On each side of it there are the shanties—and they are shanties—no pavements, and there is mud. That is your capitalistic city.

Where is democracy and show me something in this nation that democracy has really built. Do you know of anything? Is the skyscraper democratic? Is this type of city that Houston represents—and it's pretty fairly indicative of most American cities—is that democratic? What is democracy? Have you ever come to any conclusion concerning it? Have you ever thought it over among yourselves? What it represents, what it stands for, and what it could accomplish were it a success? Well, a hardware conference is a good place maybe to think it over because it's a hard question. Harder than hardware—a lot!

PART THREE

The Machine and Architectural Production

Frank Lloyd Wright (circa 1924), seated on a drafting table before a model of his Press Building Project of 1912 for the San Francisco Call (San Francisco, California) at Taliesin II, near Spring Green, Wisconsin. Photograph courtesy of the State Historical Society of Wisconsin.

7 The Art and Craft of the Machine

. . . in the Machine lies the only future of art and craft—as I believe, a glorious future. . . .

Introduction

"The Art and Craft of the Machine" is one of Frank Lloyd Wright's most famous speeches. His first presentation was made before the Chicago Arts and Crafts Society at Hull House on Friday March 1, 1901[1]; the second delivery occurred before the Western Society of Engineers on March 20 of that year.[2] Later, in 1902, Mr. Wright read a slightly revised text to the Chicago Chapter of the Daughters of the American Revolution at the University Lecture Hall of the Fine

Text of a speech reprinted precisely without editing from Frank Lloyd Wright's "The Art and Craft of the Machine," in the Chicago Architectural Club's *Catalogue of the Fourteenth Annual Exhibition of the Chicago Architectural Club,* Chicago: Architectural Club, The Art Institute of Chicago, 1901, unpaginated.

[1] The date of Mr. Wright's first presentation of this speech is often incorrectly given as March 6, 1901. However, based on the editorial that appeared in the March 4, 1901, issue of *The Chicago Daily Tribune,* which referenced this speech, the date of its first delivery now stands corrected to March 1, 1901.

[2] "The Art and Craft of the Machine" appeared in print for the first time in the *Catalogue of the Fourteenth Annual Exhibition of the Chicago Architectural Club* (Chicago: Architectural Club, The Art Institute of Chicago, 1901): excerpts were printed in *Brush and Pencil,* Vol. 8, May 1901, pp. 77–90 and a revised text appeared in the Daughters of the American Revolution (Illinois), *The New Industrialism* (Chicago: National League of Industrial Art, 1902, Part III, pp. 79–111), excerpts and revised text in Frank Lloyd Wright's *Frank Lloyd Wright On Architecture: Selected Writings (1894–1940)* (Chicago: Duell, Sloan, and Pearce, 1941, pp. 23–24, 26–28), in Edgar Kaufmann and Ben Raeburn (Editors), *Frank Lloyd Wright: Writings and Buildings* (New York: Horizon Press, 1960, pp. 52–73), and excerpts in William A. Coles and Henry Hope Reed, Jr., *Architecture in America: A Battle of Styles* (New York: Appleton-Century-Crofts, Inc., 1961, pp. 51–57).

Arts Building.[3] On Monday, March 4, 1901, the following editorial, which appeared in *The Chicago Daily Tribune*,[4] discussed the importance of Mr. Wright's first presentation of "The Art and Craft of the Machine":

There has lately been set to music a translation of some termes [sic] entitled "The Sweatshop," by the Yiddish poet—himself a sweatshop employe—Morris Rosenfeld of New York. The impression from the song is that of clattering wheels which "cannot sleep or for a moment stay" and of "toiling and toiling and toiling—endless toil. "It is the picture of one of the most marvelous and presumably socially useful of modern inventions, the sewing machine, as the ally and instrument of unwholesome and revolting conditions of industry.

A different view of "the machine" was presented in a paper read at the meeting of the Arts and Crafts society on Friday evening. It was heralded, not as the mere agent of modern commerce, but as potentially and prospectively the instrument of an entirely genuine and incomparably expanded art expression. The ugliness of the machine's products at present was attributed primarily to its prostitution to mere imitation of handiwork—as, for example, "pressed" chair back panels—and often imitation in one material of handiwork belonging to an entirely different material—as, for example, machine simulation in zinc of a carved stone cornice.

It was accordingly insisted that the legitimacy of the machine should be frankly recognized; that its distinctive capabilities should, instead of being forced or distorted, be honestly adhered to, and that under these circumstances machine products would, in their individuality, have as true artistic character as do tool products.

It is widely recognized that machine production—sometimes exhausting, often times monotonous, and nearly always highly subdivided in respect to labor—sometimes does sacrifice the workers so that they "sink into the night". The song of the Yiddish poet is realistic. Yet there is a conviction in the common mind that modern progress in mechanics should serve as a boon to society in general, and must somehow be made to do so. Indeed, the sweatshop is under the ban, and the law is demanding that the sewing machine be transferred to well-lighted rooms and be operated by power for reasonable hours only.

That machine production itself, however—conformed not to the characteristics of handicraft, but to its own creative possibilities—can and is destined to become as genuinely worthy and as pleasing to the finer sensibilities as is the more subtle, though now almost obsolete, production of the hand, is an idea not only new but one apparently indigenous, as far as its plain statement goes, to this city. In place of Mr. C.R. Ashbee's suggestion that the machine should for the modern world take the place of the slave for the Greek, this idea—which has found expression in the Arts and Crafts Society since its organization three years ago—says that there

---

[3] The text of this revised speech appeared in the Daughters of the American Revolution (Illinois), *The New Industrialism* (Chicago: National League of Industrial Art, 1902, Part III, pp. 79–111), and was a limited edition of 500 copies.

[4] The editorial is reproduced here in its entirety from "Art and the Machine," *The Chicago Daily Tribune*, Vol. LX, No. 63, March 4, 1901, p. 6.

should be neither slave nor slavish products. It asserts instead that machine production, at least in important subjects, can be and should be genuinely artistic.

Indeed, as a modest but real step in this direction, two artists of the society named have recently, after studying the processes of lithographing, designed a picture for the decoration of school walls with special reference to the possibilities of those processes, rather than with reference to the qualities of some oil or water color painting sought to be imitated.

It would seem that to the phrase and ideal, "Art and Labor," must now be added—and at the suggestion of Chicago—"Art and the Machine".

Years later, after this editorial appeared, Mr. Wright quipped that "Jane Addams herself must have written it, I suspect. She sympathized with me, . . ."[5]

"The Art and Craft of the Machine" is important because in this speech Mr. Wright was one of the first artists, if not the first, not only to feel but to express the thought that the "machine" could be seized by the creative artist and craftsman as a new, dynamic tool for creativity.[6] During this period the machine was more often feared by both as a potential threat to their *true* creativity. Mr. Wright later adapted this philosophy to his own architectural work and persisted in advancing the concept of the machine as a *true,* creative, artistic tool for almost sixty more years, as evidenced not only in his own architectural achievements but also in his speeches (Chapters 8, 9, 10, and 11).

[5] See Frank Lloyd Wright's *An Autobiography,* New York: Horizon Press, 1977, pp. 155–156. See also, Mr. Wright's speech presented in Chapter 10 of this volume for another similar reference to Jane Addams.

[6] A detailed discussion of Mr. Wright's "The Art and Craft of the Machine" can be found in David A. Hanks' "Frank Lloyd Wright's 'The Art and Craft of the Machine,'" *The Frank Lloyd Wright Newsletter,* Vol. 2, No. 3, Second Quarter 1979, pp. 6–9, and also in David A. Hanks' *The Decorative Designs of Frank Lloyd Wright,* New York: E.P. Dutton, 1979, pp. 64–66.

The Speech

WRIGHT: As we work along our various ways, there takes shape within us, in some sort, an ideal—something we are to become—some work to be done. This, I think, is denied to very few, and we begin really to live only when the thrill of this ideality moves us in what we will accomplish. In the years which have been devoted in my own life to working out in stubborn materials a feeling for the beautiful, in the vortex of distorted complex conditions, a hope has grown stronger with the experience of each year, amounting now to a gradually deepening conviction that in the Machine lies the only future of art and craft—as I believe, a glorious future; that the Machine is, in fact, the metamorphosis of ancient art and craft; that we are at last face to face with the machine—the modern Sphinx—whose riddle the artist must solve if he would that art live—for his nature holds the key. For one, I promise "whatever gods may be" to lend such energy and purpose as I may possess to help make that meaning plain; to return again and again to the task whenever and wherever need be; for this plain duty is thus relentlessly marked out for the artist in this, the Machine Age, although there is involved an adjustment to cherished gods, perplexing and painful in the extreme; the fire of many long-honored ideals shall go down to ashes, to reappear, phoenixlike, with new purposes.

The great ethics of the Machine are as yet, in the main, beyond the ken of the artist or student of sociology; but the artist's mind may now approach the nature of this thing from experience, which has become the commonplace of his field, to suggest, in time, I hope, to prove, that the machine is capable of carrying to fruition high ideals in art—higher than the world has yet seen!

Disciples of William Morris cling to an opposite view. Yet William Morris, himself, deeply sensed the danger to art of the transforming force whose sign and symbol is the machine, and though of the new art we eagerly seek he sometimes despaired he quickly renewed his hope.

He plainly foresaw that a blank in the fine arts would follow the inevitable abuse of new-found power and threw himself body and soul into the work of bridging it over by bringing into our lives afresh the beauty of art as she had been, that the new art to come might not have dropped too many stitches nor have unraveled what would still be useful to her.

That he had an abundant faith in the new art his every essay will testify.

That he miscalculated the machine does not matter. He did sublime work for it when he pleaded so well for the process of elimination its abuses had made necessary, when he fought the innate vulgarity of theocratic impulse in art as opposed to democratic, and when he preached the gospel of simplicity.

All artists love and honor William Morris.

He did the best in his time for art and will live in history as the great socialist, together with Ruskin, the great moralist: a significant fact worth thinking about, that the two great reformers of modern times professed the artist.

The machine these reformers protested because the sort of luxury which is born of greed had usurped it and made of it a terrible engine of enslavement, deluging the civilized world with a murderous ubiquity which plainly enough was the damnation of their art and craft.

It had not then advanced to the point which now so plainly indicates that it will surely and swiftly, by its own momentum, undo the mischief it has made and the usurping vulgarians as well.

Nor was it so grown as to become apparent to William Morris, the grand democrat, that the machine was the great forerunner of democracy.

The ground plan of this thing is now to the point where the artist must take it up no longer as a protest: genius must progressively dominate the work of the contrivance it has created, to lend a useful hand in building afresh the "Fairness of the Earth."

That the Machine has dealt Art in the grand old sense a deathblow none will deny.

The evidence is too substantial.

Art in the grand old sense—meaning Art in the sense of structural tradition, whose craft is fashioned upon the handicraft ideal, ancient and modern; an art wherein this form and that form as structural parts were laboriously joined in such a way as to beautifully emphasize the manner of the joining: the million and one ways of beautifully satisfying bare structural necessities, which have come down to us chiefly through the books as "Art."

For the purpose of suggesting hastily and therefore crudely wherein the machine has sapped the vitality of this art, let us assume Architecture in the old sense as a fitting representative of Traditional-art, and Printing as a fitting representation of the Machine.

What printing—the machine—has done for architecture—the fine art—will have been done in measure of time for all art immediately fashioned upon the early handicraft ideal.

With a masterful hand Victor Hugo, a noble lover and a great student of architecture, traces her fall in "Notre Dame."

The prophecy of Frollo, that "The book will kill the edifice," I remember was to me as a boy one of the grandest sad things of the world.

After seeking the origin and tracing the growth of architecture in superb fashion, showing how in the Middle Ages all the intellectual forces of the people converged to one point—architecture—he shows how, in the life of that time, whoever was born poet became an architect. All other arts simply obeyed and placed themselves under the discipline of architecture. They were the workmen of the great work. The architect, the poet, the master, summed up in his person the sculpture that carved his facades, painting which illuminated his walls and windows, music which set his bells to pealing and breathed into his organs—there was nothing which was not forced in order to make something of itself in that time, to come and frame itself in the edifice.

Thus down to the time of Gutenberg architecture is the principal writing—the universal writing of humanity.

In the great granite books begun by the Orient, continued by the Greek and Roman antiquity, the Middle Ages wrote the last page.

So to enunciate here only summarily a process it would require volumes to develop; down to the fifteenth century the chief register of humanity is architecture.

The Arthur Heurtley residence (1902) at Oak Park, Illinois. Drawing from Frank Lloyd Wright, Ausgeführte Bauten und Entwürfe von Frank Lloyd Wright *(Berlin: Ernst Wasmuth, 1911).*

In the fifteenth century everything changes.

Human thought discovers a mode of perpetuating itself, not only more resisting than architecture, but still more simple and easy.

Architecture is dethroned.

Gutenberg's letters of lead are about to supersede Orpheus' letters of stone.

The invention of printing was the greatest event in history.

It was the first great machine, after the great city.

It is human thought stripping off one form and donning another.

Printed, thought is more imperishable than ever—it is volatile, indestructible.

As architecture it was solid; it is now alive; it passes from duration in point of time to immortality.

Cut the primitive bed of a river abruptly, with a canal hollowed out beneath its level, and the river will desert its bed.

See how architecture now withers away, how little by little it becomes lifeless and bare. How one feels the water sinking, the sap departing, the thought of the times and people withdrawing from it. The chill is almost imperceptible in the fifteenth century, the press is yet weak, and at most draws from architecture a superabundance of life, but with the beginning of the sixteenth century the malady of architecture is visible. It becomes classic art in a miserable manner; from being indigenous, it becomes Greek and Roman; from being true and modern, it becomes pseudoclassic.

It is the decadence which we call the Renaissance.

It is the setting sun which we mistake for dawn.

It has no power to hold the other arts; so they emancipate themselves, break the yoke of the architect, and take themselves off, each in its own direction.

One would liken it to an empire dismembered at the death of its Alexander and whose provinces become kingdoms.

Sculpture becomes statuary, the image trade becomes painting, the canon becomes music. Hence Raphael, Angelo, and those splendors of the dazzling sixteenth century.

Nevertheless, when the sun of the Middle Ages is completely set, architecture grows dim, becomes more and more effaced. The printed book, the gnawing worm of the edifice, sucks and devours it. It is petty, it is poor, it is nothing.

Reduced to itself, abandoned by other arts because human thought is abandoning it, it summons bunglers in the place of artists. It is miserably perishing.

Meanwhile, what becomes of printing?

All the life, leaving architecture, comes to it. In proportion, as architecture ebbs and flows, printing swells and grows. The capital of forces which human thought had been expending in building is hereafter to be expended in books; and architecture, as it was, is dead, irretrievably slain by the printed book; slain because it endures for a shorter time; slain because human thought has found a more simple medium of expression, which costs less in human effort; because human thought has been rendered volatile and indestructible, reaching uniformly and irresistibly the four corners of the earth and for all.

Thenceforth, if architecture rises again, reconstructs, as Hugo prophesies she may begin to do in the latter days of the nineteenth century, she will no longer be mistress, she will be one of the arts, never again *the* art; and printing—the Machine—remains the second Tower of Babel of the human race.

So the organic process, of which the majestic decline of Architecture is only one case in point, has steadily gone down to the present time, and still goes on, weakening the hold of the artist upon the people, drawing off from his rank poets and scientists until architecture is but a little, poor knowledge of archeology, and the average of art is reduced to the gasping poverty of imitative realism; until the whole letter of Tradition, the vast fabric of precedent, in the flesh, which has increasingly confused the art ideal while the machine has been growing to power, is a beautiful corpse from which the spirit has flown. The spirit that has flown is the spirit of the new art but has failed the modern artist, for he has lost it for hundreds of years in his lust for the *letter,* the beautiful body of art made too available by the machine.

So the artist craft wanes.

Craft that will not see that human thought is stripping off one form and donning another, and artists are everywhere, whether catering to the leisure class of old England or ground beneath the heel of the commercial abuse here in the great West, the unwilling symptoms of the inevitable, organic nature of the machine, they combat, the hell-smoke of the factories they scorn to understand.

And, invincible, triumphant, the machine goes on, gathering force and knitting the material necessities of mankind ever closer into a universal automatic fabric; the engine, the motor, and the battleship, the works of art of the century!

The Machine is Intellect mastering the drudgery of earth that the plastic art may live; that the margin of leisure and strength by which man's life upon earth can be made beautiful, may immeasurably widen; its function ultimately to emancipate human expression!

It is a universal educator, surely raising the level of human intelligence, so carrying within itself the power to destroy, by its own momentum, the greed which in Morris' time and still in our own time turns it to a deadly engine of enslavement. The only comfort left the poor artist, sidetracked as he is, seemingly is a mean one; the thought that the very selfishness which man's early art idealized, now reduced to its lowest terms, is swiftly and surely destroying itself through the medium of the machine.

The artist's present plight is a sad one, but may he truthfully say that society is less well off because Architecture, or even Art, as it was, is dead and printing, or the Machine, lives?

Every age has done its work, produced its art with the best tools or contrivances it knew, the tools most successful in saving the most precious thing in the world—human effort. Greece used the chattel slave as the essential tool of its art and civilization. This tool we have discarded, and we would refuse the return of Greek art upon the terms of its restoration because we insist now upon a basis of Democracy.

Is it not more likely that the medium of artistic expression itself has broadened and changed until a new definition and new direction must be given the art activity of the future and that the Machine has finally made for the artist, whether he will yet own it or not, a splendid distinction between the Art of old and the Art to come? A distinction made by the tool which frees human labor, lengthens and broadens the life of the simplest man, thereby the basis of the democracy upon which we insist.

To shed some light upon this distinction, let us take an instance in the field naturally ripened first by the machine—the commercial field.

The tall modern office building is the machine, pure and simple.

We may here sense an advanced stage of a condition surely entering all art for all time; its already triumphant glare in the deadly struggle taking place here between the machine and the art of structural tradition reveals "art" torn and hung upon the steel frame of commerce, a forlorn head upon a pike, a solemn warning to architects and artists the world over.

We must walk blindfolded not to see that all that this magnificent resource of machine and material has brought us so far is a complete, broadcast degradation of every type and form sacred to the art of old; a pandemonium of tin masks, huddled deformities, and decayed methods; quarreling, lying, and cheating, with hands at each other's throats—or in each other's pockets; and none of the people who do these things, who pay for them or use them, knows what they mean, feeling only—when they feel at all—that what is most truly like

Perspective rendering of the Susan Lawrence Dana residence (1902) at Springfield, Illinois. This house represents Frank Lloyd Wright's early use of a two-story open living space. Drawing from Frank Lloyd Wright, Ausgeführte Bauten und Entwürfe von Frank Lloyd Wright *(Berlin: Ernst Wasmuth, 1910).*

the past is the safest and therefore the best; as typical Marshall Field, speaking of his new building, has frankly said: "A good copy is the best we can do."

A pitiful insult, art and craft!

With this mine of industrial wealth at our feet we have no power to use it except to the perversion of our natural resources? A confession of shame which is the merciful ignorance of the yet material frame of things, mistakers for glorious achievement.

We half believe in our artistic greatness ourselves when we toss up a pantheon to the god of money in a night or two or pile up a mammoth aggregation of Roman monuments, sarcophagi, and Greek temples for a postoffice [sic] in a year or two—the patient retinue of the machine pitching in with terrible effectiveness to consummate this unhallowed ambition—this insult to ancient gods. The delicate, impressionable facilities of terra cotta becoming imitative blocks and voussoirs of tool-marked stone, badgered into all manner of structural gymnastics or else ignored in vain endeavor to be honest; and granite blocks, cut in the fashion of the followers of Phidias, cunningly arranged about the steel beams and shafts, to look "real"—leaning heavily upon an inner skeleton of steel for support from floor to floor, which strains the "reality" and would fain, I think, lie down to die of shame.

The "masters"—ergo, the fashionable followers of

Exterior view of the east facade of the Susan Lawrence Dana residence (1902) at Springfield, Illinois. Photograph by the editor.

Phidias—have been trying to make this wily skeleton of steel seem seventeen sorts of "architecture" at once, when all the world knows—except the masters—that it is not one of them.

See now, how an element—the vanguard of the new art—has entered here, which the structural-art equation cannot satisfy without downright lying and ignoble cheating.

This element is the structural necessity reduced to a skeleton, complete in itself without the craftsman's touch. At once the million and one little ways of satisfying this necessity beautifully, coming to us chiefly through the books as the traditional art of building, vanish away—become history.

The artist is emancipated to work his will with a rational freedom unknown to the laborious art of structural tradition—no longer tied to the meagre unit of brick arch and stone lintel, nor hampered by the grammatical phrase of their making—but he cannot use his freedom.

His tradition cannot think.

He will not think.

His scientific brother has put it to him before he is ready.

The modern tall office building problem is one representative problem of the machine. The only rational solutions it has received in the world may be counted upon the fingers of one hand. The fact

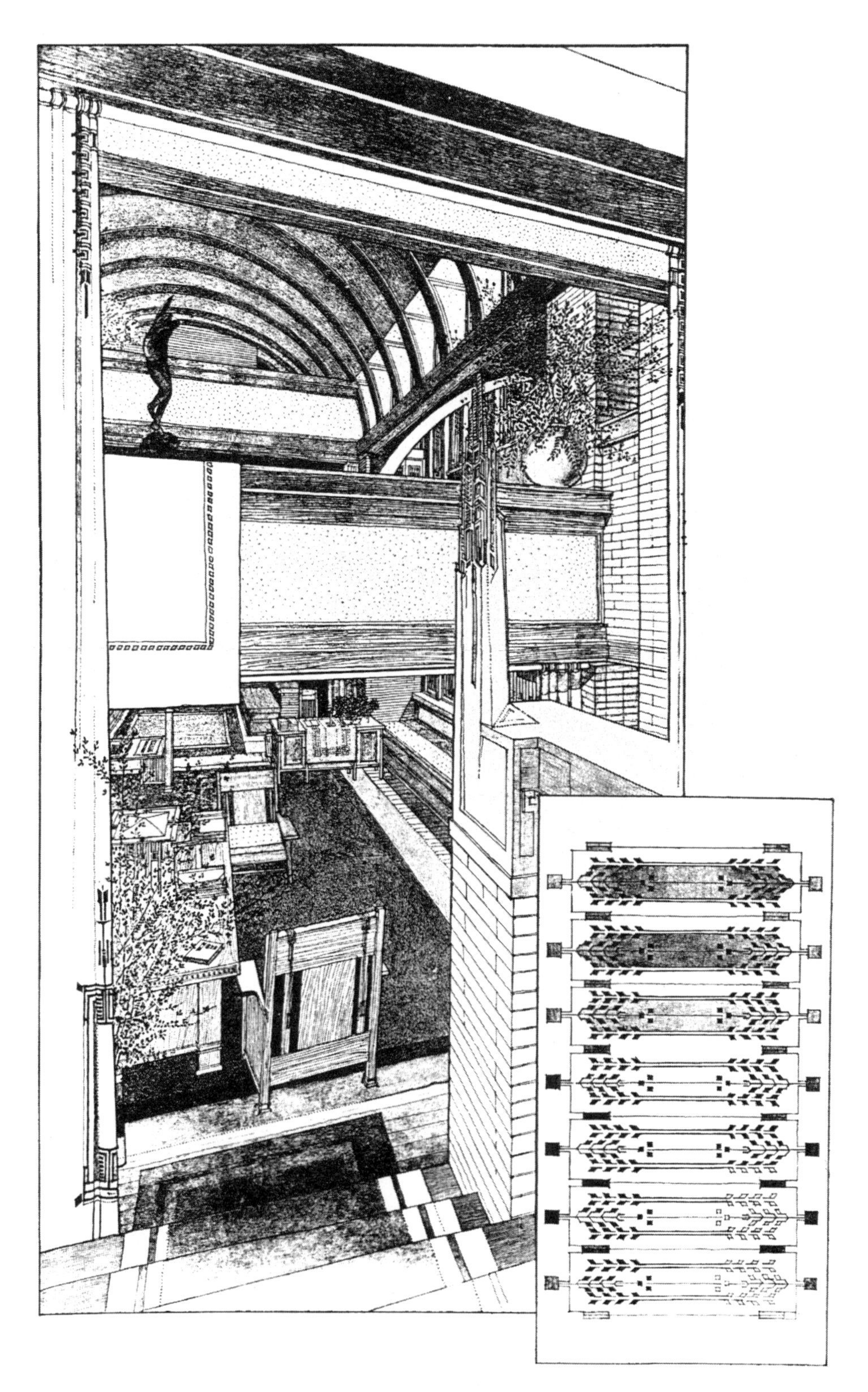

Interior perspective rendering of the Susan Lawrence Dana Residence (1902) at Springfield, Illinois. The drawing shows the interior of the two-story combined gallery (above) *and library* (below). *The sculpture is the work of Richard Bock. Drawing from Frank Lloyd Wright,* Ausgeführte Bauten und Entwürfe von Frank Lloyd Wright *(Berlin: Ernst Wasmuth, 1910).*

that a great portion of our architects and artists are shocked by them to the point of offense is as valid an objection as that of a child refusing wholesome food because his stomach becomes dyspeptic from over-much unwholesome pastry—albeit he be the cook himself.

We may object to the mannerism of these buildings, but we can take no exception to their manner nor hide from their evident truth.

The steel frame has been recognized as a legitimate basis for a simple, sincere clothing of plastic material that idealizes its purpose without structural pretense.

This principle has at last been recognized in architecture, and though the masters refuse to accept it as architecture at all it is a glimmer in a darkened field—the first sane word that has been said in Art for the Machine.

The art of old idealized a Structural Necessity—now rendered obsolete and unnatural by the Machine—and accomplished it through man's joy in the labor of his hands.

The new will weave for the necessities of mankind, which his Machine will have mastered, a robe of ideality no less truthful but more poetical, with a rational freedom made possible by the machine, beside which the art of old will be as the sweet, plaintive wail of the pipe to the outpouring of full orchestra.

It will clothe Necessity with the living flesh of virile imagination, as the living flesh lends living grace to the hard and bony human skeleton.

The new will pass from the possession of kings and classes to the everyday lives of all—from duration in point of time to immortality.

This distinction is one to be felt now rather than clearly defined.

The definition is the poetry of this Machine Age and will be written large in time; but the more we, as artists, examine into this premonition, the more we will find the utter helplessness of old forms to satisfy new conditions and the crying need of the machine for plastic treatment—a pliant, sympathetic treatment of its needs that the body of structural precedent cannot yield.

To gain further suggestive evidence of this, let us turn to the Decorative Arts—the immense middle ground of all art now mortally sickened by the machine—sickened that it may slough the art ideal of the constructural [sic] art for the plasticity of the new art—the Art of Democracy.

Here we find the most deadly perversion of all—the magnificent prowess of the machine bombarding the civilized world with the mangled corpses of strenuous horrors that once stood for cultivated luxury—standing now for a species of fatty degeneration, simply vulgar.

Without regard to first principles or common decency, the whole letter of tradition—that is, ways of doing things rendered wholly obsolete and unnatural by the machine—is recklessly fed into its rapacious maw until you may buy reproductions for ninety-nine cents at "The Fair" that originally cost ages of toil and cultivation, worth now intrinsically nothing—that are harmful parasites befogging the sensibilities of our natures, belittling and falsifying any true perception of normal beauty the Creator may have seen fit to implant in us.

The idea of fitness to purpose, harmony between form and use with regard to any of these things, is possessed by very few and utilized by them as a protest, chiefly—a protest against the machine!

As well blame Richard Croker for the political iniquity of America.

As "Croker is the creature and not the creator" of political evil, so the machine is the creature and not the creator of this iniquity; and with this difference—that the machine has noble possibilities unwillingly forced to degradation in the name of the artistic; the machine, as far as its artistic capacity is concerned, is itself the crazed victim of the artist who works while he waits and the artist who waits while he works.

There is a nice distinction between the two.

Detailed exterior view of the west facade of the Darwin D. Martin residence (1904) at Buffalo, New York, one of Frank Lloyd Wright's largest constructed Prairie Houses. Photograph by Robert S. McGonigal.

Neither class will unlock the secrets of the beauty of this time.

They are clinging sadly to the old order and would wheedle the giant frame of things back to its childhood or forward to its second childhood, while this Machine Age is suffering for the artist who accepts, works, and sings as he works with the joy of the *here* and *now!*

We want the man who eagerly seeks and finds, or blames himself if he fails to find, the beauty of this time, who distinctly accepts as a singer and a prophet, for no man may work while he waits or wait as he works in the sense that William Morris' great work was legitimately done—in the sense that most art and craft of today is an echo; the time when such work was useful has gone.

Echoes are by nature decadent.

Artists who feel toward Modernity and the Machine now as William Morris and Ruskin were justified in feeling then had best distinctly wait and work soci-

Interior view of the reception hall of the Darwin D. Martin residence. Note the mass and length of the arched masonry fireplace which becomes the focal point of this unique interior space. Photograph by Robert S. McGonigal.

The "Tree of Life" art-glass windows (with both zinc and copper cames) at the Darwin D. Martin residence. The scheme of the abstract geometric design for each of the windows shown is based on three flowers with seven leaves or branches. Photograph by Robert S. McGonigal.

ologically where great work may still be much miserable mischief.

If the artist will only open his eyes he will see that the machine he dreads has made it possible to wipe out the mass of meaningless torture to which mankind, in the name of the artistic, has been more or less subjected since time began; for that matter, [he] has made possible a cleanly strength, an ideality, and a poetic fire that the art of the world has not yet seen; for the machine, the process now smooths away the necessity for pretty structural deceits, soothes this wearisome struggle to make things seem what they are not, and can never be, satisfies the simple term of the modern art equation as the ball of clay in the sculptor's hand yields to his desire—comforting forever this realistic, brain-sick masquerade we are wont to suppose art.

William Morris pleaded well for simplicity as the basis of all true art. Let us understand the significance to art of that word—SIMPLICITY—for it is vital to the art of the machine.

We may find, in place of the genuine thing we have striven for, an affectation of the naïve, which we should detest as we detest a full-grown woman with baby mannerisms.

English art is saturated with it, from the brand-new imitation of the old house that grew and rambled from period to period to the rain-tub standing beneath the eaves.

In fact, most simplicity following the doctrines of William Morris is a protest; as a protest, well enough, but the highest form of simplicity is not simple in the sense that the infant intelligence is simple—nor, for that matter, the side of a barn.

A natural revulsion of feeling leads us from the meaningless elaboration of today to lay too great stress on mere platitudes, quite as a clean sheet of paper is a relief after looking at a series of bad drawings—but simplicity is not merely a neutral or a negative quality.

Simplicity in art, rightly understood, is a synthetic, positive quality in which we may see evidence of mind, breadth of scheme, wealth of detail, and withal a sense of completeness found in a tree or a flower. A work may have the delicacies of a rare orchid or the staunch fortitude of the oak and still be simple. A thing to be simple needs only to be true to itself in organic sense.

With this ideal of simplicity, let us glance hastily at a few instances of the machine and see how it has been forced by false ideals to do violence to this simplicity, how it has made possible the highest simplicity, rightly understood and so used. As perhaps wood is most available of all homely materials and therefore, naturally, the most abused—let us glance at wood.

Machinery has been invented for no other purpose than to imitate, as closely as possible, the woodcarving of the early ideal—with the immediate result that no ninety-nine-cent piece of furniture is salable without some horrible botchwork meaning nothing unless it means that art and craft have combined to fix in the minds of the masses the old hand-carved chair as the *ne plus ultra* of the ideal.

The miserable, lumpy tribute to this perversion which Grand Rapids [Michigan] alone yields would mar the face of Art beyond repair; to say nothing of the elaborate and fussy joinery of posts, spindles, jigsawed beams and braces, butted and strutted, to outdo the sentimentality of the already overwrought antique product.

Thus is the woodworking industry glutted, except in rarest instances. The whole sentiment of early craft degenerated to a sentimentality having no longer decent significance no commercial integrity; in fact all that is fussy, maudlin, and animal, basing its existence chiefly on vanity and ignorance.

Now let us learn from the Machine.

It teaches us that the beauty of wood lies first in its qualities as wood; no treatment that did not bring out these qualities all the time could be plastic, and therefore not appropriate—so not beautiful, the machine teaches us, if we have left it to the machine that certain simple forms and handling are suitable to bring out the beauty of wood and certain forms are not; that all woodcarving is apt to be a forcing of the material, an insult to its finer possibilities as a material having in itself intrinsically artistic properties, of which its beautiful markings is one, its texture another, its color a third.

The machine, by its wonderful cutting, shaping, smoothing, and repetitive capacity, has made it possible to so use it without waste that the poor as well as the rich may enjoy today beautiful surface treatments of clean, strong forms that the branch veneers of Sheraton [furniture] and Chippendale [furniture] only hinted at, with dire extravagance, and which the Middle Ages utterly ignored.

The machine has emancipated these beauties of nature in wood, made it possible to wipe out the mass of meaningless torture to which wood has been subjected since the world began, for it has been universally abused and maltreated by all peoples but the Japanese.

Rightly appreciated, is not this the very process of elimination for which Morris pleaded?

Not alone a protest, moreover, for the machine, considered only technically, if you please, has placed in artist hands the means of idealizing the true nature of wood harmoniously with man's spiritual and material needs, without waste, within reach of all.

And how fares the troop of old materials galvanized into new life by the Machine?

Our modern materials are these old materials in more plastic guise, rendered so by the Machine, itself creating the very quality needed in material to satisfy its own art equation.

We have seen, in glancing at modern architecture,

The Mrs. Thomas H. Gale Residence (1904) at Oak Park, Illinois. This design is an early indication of Mr. Wright's later use of sweeping horizontal lines and flat plane surfaces in the design of residences. Drawing from Frank Lloyd Wright, Ausgeführte Bauten und Entwürfe von Frank Lloyd Wright *(Berlin: Ernst Wasmuth, 1910).*

The Mrs. Thomas H. Gale residence (1904) at Oak Park, Illinois, is constructed of wood with plaster flat-plane surfaces. Photograph by the editor.

how they fare at the hands of Art and Craft, divided and sub-divided in orderly sequence with rank and file of obedient retainers awaiting the master's behest.

Steel and iron, plastic cement and terra-cotta.

Who can sound the possibilities of this old material, burned clay, which the modern machine has rendered as sensitive to the creative brain as a dry plate to the lens—a marvelous simplifier? And this plastic covering material, cement, another simplifier, enabling the artist to clothe the structural frame with [a] simple, modestly beautiful robe where before he dragged in, as he does still drag, five different kinds of material to compose one little cottage, pettily arranging it in an aggregation supposed to be picturesque—as a matter of fact, millinery [sic], to be warped and beaten by sun, wind, and rain into a variegated heap of trash.

There is the process of modern casting in metal—one of the perfected modern machines, capable of any form to which fluid will flow, to perpetuate the imagery of the most delicately poetic mind without let or hindrance—within reach of everyone, therefore insulted and outraged by the bungler forcing it to a degraded seat at his degenerate festival.

Multitudes of processes are expectantly awaiting the sympathetic interpretation of the master mind;

the galvano-plastic and its electrical brethren, a prolific horde, now cheap fakirs imitating real bronzes and all manner of the antique, secretly damning it in their vitals.

Electroglazing, a machine shunned because too cleanly and delicate for the clumsy hand of the traditional designer, who depends upon the mass and blur of leading to conceal his lack of touch.

That delicate thing, the lithograph—the prince of a whole reproductive province of processes—see what this process becomes in the hands of a master like Whistler. He has sounded but one note in the gamut of its possibilities, but that product is intrinsically true of the process and as delicate as the butterfly's wing. Yet the most this particular machine did for us, until then in the hands of Art and Craft, was to give us a cheap, imitative effect of painting.

So spins beyond our ability to follow tonight a rough, feeble thread of the evidence at large to the effect that the machine has weakened the artist, all but destroyed his handmade art, if not its ideals, although he has made enough miserable mischief meanwhile.

These evident instances should serve to hint, at least to the thinking mind, that the Machine is a marvelous simplifier, the emancipator of the creative mind, and in time the regenerator of the creative conscience. We may see that this destructive process has begun and is taking place that Art might awaken to the power of fully developed senses promised by dreams of its childhood, even though that power may not come the way it was pictured in those dreams.

Now, let us ask ourselves whether the fear of the higher artistic expression demanded by the Machine, so thoroughly grounded in the arts and crafts, is founded upon a finely guarded reticence, a recognition of inherent weakness or plain ignorance?

Let us, to be just, assume that it is equal parts of all three and try to imagine an Arts and Crafts Society that may educate itself to prepare to make some good impression upon the Machine, the destroyer of their present ideals and tendencies, their salvation in disguise.

Such a society will, of course, be a society for mutual education.

Exhibitions will not be a feature of its programme for years, for there will be nothing to exhibit except the shortcomings of the society, and they will hardly prove either instructive or amusing at this stage of proceedings. This society must, from the very nature of the proposition, be made up of the people who are in the work—that is, the manufacturers—coming into touch with such of those who assume the practice of the fine arts and profess a fair sense of the obligation to the public such assumption carries with it, and sociological workers whose interests are ever closely allied with art, as their prophets Morris, Ruskin, and Tolstoy evince, and all those who have as personal graces and accomplishment perfected handicraft, whether fashion old or fashion new.

Without the interest and cooperation of the manufacturers, the society cannot begin to do its work, for this is the cornerstone of its organization.

All these elements should be brought together on a common ground of confessed ignorance, with a desire to be instructed, freely encouraging talk and opinion, and reaching out desperately for anyone who has special experience in any way connected to address them.

I suppose, first of all, the thing would resemble a debating society, or something even less dignified, until someone should suggest that it was time to quit talking and proceed to do something, which in this case would not mean giving an exhibition, but rather excursions to factories and a study of processes in place—that is, the machine in processes too numerous to mention, at the factories with the men who organize and direct them, but not in the spirit of the idea that these things are all gone wrong, looking for that in them which would most nearly approximate the handicraft ideal; not looking into them with even the thought of handicraft, and not particularly looking for craftsmen, but getting a scientific ground plan of the process in minds, if possible, with a view to its natural bent and possibilities.

Some processes and machines would naturally appeal to some and some to others; there would undoubtedly be among us those who would find little joy in any of them.

This is, naturally, not child's play, but neither is the work expected of the modern artist.

I will venture to say, from personal observation and some experience, that not one artist in one hundred has taken pains to thus educate himself. I will go further and say what I believe to be true, that not one educational institution in America has as yet attempted to force the connecting link between Science and Art by training the artist to his actual tools, or, by a process of nature study that develops in him the power of independent thought, fitting him to use them properly.

Let us call these preliminaries, then, a process by which artists receive information nine-tenths of them lack concerning the tools they have to work with today—for tools today are processes and machines, where they were once a hammer and a gouge.

The artist today is the leader of an orchestra, where he once was a star performer.

Once the manufacturers are convinced of due respect and appreciation on the part of the artist, they will welcome him and his counsel gladly and make any experiments having a grain of apparent sense in them.

They have little patience with a bothering about in endeavor to see what might be done to make their particular machine mediaeval and restore man's joy in the mere work of his hands—for this once lovely attribute is far behind.

This proceeding doubtless would be of far more educational value to the artist than to the manufacturer, at least for some time to come, for there would be a difficult adjustment to make on the part of the artist and an attitude to change. So many artists are chiefly "attitude" that some would undoubtedly disappear with the attitude.

But if out of twenty determined students a ray of light should come to one, to light up a single operation, it would have been worthwhile, for that would be fairly something; while joy in mere handicraft is like that of the man who played the piano for his own amusement—a pleasurable personal accomplishment without real relation to the grim condition confronting us.

Granting that a determined, dauntless body of artist material could be brought together with sufficient persistent enthusiasm to grapple with the Machine, would not someone be found who would provide the suitable experimental station (which is what the modern Arts and crafts shop should be)—an experimental station that would represent in miniature the elements of this great pulsating web of the machine, where each pregnant process or significant tool in printing, lithography, galvano-electro processes, wood- and steel-working machinery, muffles and kilns would have its place and where the best young scientific blood could mingle with the best and truest artistic inspiration, to sound the depths of these things, to accord them the patient, sympathetic treatment that is their due?

Surely a thing like this would be worthwhile—to alleviate the insensate numbness of the poor fellows out in the cold, hard shops, who know not why nor understand, whose dutiful obedience is chained to botch work and bungler's ambition; surely this would be a practical means to make their dutiful obedience give us something we can all understand and that will be as normal to the best of this machine age as a ray of light to the healthy eye; a real help in adjusting the *Man* to a true sense of his importance as a factor in society, though he does tend a machine.

Teach him that the machine is his best friend—will have widened the margin of his leisure until enlightenment shall bring him a further sense of the magnificent ground plan of progress in which he too justly plays his significant part.

If the art of the Greek, produced at such cost of human life, was so noble and enduring, what limit dare we now imagine to an Art based upon an adequate life for the individual?

The machine is his!

In due time it will come to him!

Meanwhile, who shall count the slain?

From where are the trained nurses in this industrial hospital to come if not from the modern arts and crafts?

Shelley says a man cannot say—"I will compose poetry."

> *The greatest poet even cannot say it, for the mind in creation is as a fading coal which some invisible influence, like an inconsistent wind awakens to transitory brightness; this power arises from within like the color of a flower which fades and changes as it is developed, and the conscious portions of our nature are unprophetic either of its approach or its departure.*

And yet in the arts and crafts the problem is presented as a more or less fixed quantity, highly involved, requiring a surer touch, a more highly disciplined artistic nature to organize it as a work of art.

The original impulses may reach as far inward as those of Shelley's poet, be quite as wayward a matter of pure sentiment, and yet after the thing is done, showing its rational qualities, is limited in completeness only by the capacity of whoever would show them or by the imperfection of the thing itself.

This does not mean that Art may be shown to be an exact Science.

"It is not pure reason, but it is always reasonable."

It is a matter of perceiving and portraying the harmony of organic tendencies; is originally intuitive because the artist nature is a prophetic gift that may sense these qualities afar.

Exterior view of the Price Company Tower for Harold Price, Sr. (1952) at Bartlesville, Oklahoma. The art and craft of the machine was integral in the construction of the tower. Prefabricated copper wall units with built-in windows were used to enclose the spaces between the cantilevered floors of the building. Photograph by the editor.

To me, the artist is he who can truthfully idealize the common sense of these tendencies in his chosen way.

So I feel conception and composition to be simply the essence of refinement in organization, the original impulse of which may be registered by the artistic nature as unconsciously as the magnetic needle vibrates to the magnetic law, but which is, in synthesis or analysis, organically consistent, given the power to see it or not.

And I have come to believe that the world of Art, which we are so fond of calling the world outside of Science, is not so much outside as it is the very heart quality of this great material growth—as religion is its conscience.

A foolish heart and a small conscience.

A foolish heart, palpitating in alarm, mistaking the growing pains of its giant frame for approaching dissolution, whose sentimentality the lusty body of modern things has outgrown.

Upon this faith in Art as the organic heart quality of the scientific frame of things I base a belief that we must look to the artist brain, of all brains, to grasp the significance to society of this thing we call the Machine, if that brain be not blinded, gagged, and bound by false tradition, the letter of precedent. For this thing we call Art, is it not as prophetic as a primrose or an oak? Therefore, of the essence of this thing we call the Machine, which is no more or less than the principle of organic growth working irresistibly the Will of Life through the medium of Man.

Be gently lifted at nightfall to the top of a great downtown office building and you may see how in the image of material man, at once his glory and menace, is this thing we call a city.

There, beneath, grown up in a night, is the monster leviathan, stretching acre upon acre into the far distance. High overhead hangs the stagnant pall of its fetid breath, reddened with the light from its myriad eyes, endlessly everywhere blinking. Ten thousand acres of cellular tissue, layer upon layer, the city's flesh, outspreads enmeshed by [an] intricate network of veins and arteries, radiating into the gloom, and there with muffled, persistent roar, pulses and circulates as the blood in your veins, the ceaseless beat of the activity to whose necessities it all conforms.

Like to the sanitation of the human body is the drawing off of poisonous waste from the system of this enormous creature; absorbed first by the infinitely ramifying, threadlike ducts gathering at their sensitive terminals matter destructive to its life, hurrying it to millions of small intestines, to be collected in turn by larger, flowing to the great sewer, on to the drainage canal, and finally to the ocean.

This ten thousand acres of fleshlike tissue is again knit and interknit with a nervous system marvelously complete, delicate filaments for hearing, knowing, almost feeling the pulse of its organism, acting upon the ligaments and tendons for motive impulse, in all flowing the impelling fluid of man's own life.

Its nerve ganglia!—the peerless Corliss tandems whirling their hundred-ton flywheels, fed by gigantic rows of water-tube boilers burning oil, a solitary man slowly pacing backward and forward, regulating here and there the little feed valves controlling the deafening roar of the flaming gas, while beyond, the incessant clicking, dropping, waiting—lifting, waiting, shifting of the governor gear controlling these modern Goliaths seems a visible brain in intelligent action, registered infallibly in the enormous magnets, purring in the giant embrace of great induction coils, generating the vital current meeting with instant response in the rolling cars on elevated tracks ten miles away, where the glare of the Bessemer steel converter makes conflagration of the clouds.

More quietly still, whispering down the long, low rooms of factory buildings buried in the gloom beyond, range on range of stanch, beautifully perfected automatons, murmur contentedly with occasional click-clack, that would have the American manufacturing industry of five years ago by the throat today, manipulating steel as delicately as a mystical shuttle of the modern loom manipulates a

Detail of ornamental prefabricated stamped copper sheets used to clad portions of the exterior of the Price Company Tower. Photograph by the editor.

silk thread in the shimmering pattern of a dainty gown.

And the heavy breathing, the murmuring, the clangor, and the roar!—how the voice of this monstrous thing, this greatest of machines, a great city, rises to proclaim the marvel of the units of its structure, the ghastly warning boom from the deep throats of vessels heavily seeking inlet to the waterway below, answered by the echoing clangor of the bridge bells growing nearer and more ominous as the vessel cuts momentarily the flow of the nearer artery, warning the current from the swinging bridge now closing on its stately passage, just in time to receive in a rash of steam, as a streak of light, the avalanche of blood and metal hurled across it and gone, roaring into the night on its glittering bands of steel, ever faithfully encircled by the slender magic lines tick-tapping its invincible protection.

Nearer, in the building ablaze with midnight activity, the wide, white band streams into the marvel of the multiple press, receiving unerringly the indelible impression of the human hopes, joys, and fears throbbing in the pulse of this great activity, as infallibly as the gray matter of the human brain receives the impression of the senses, to come forth millions of neatly folded, perfected news sheets, teaming with vivid appeals to passions, good or evil, weaving a web of intercommunication so far-reaching that distance becomes as nothing, the thought of one man in one corner of the earth one day visible to the naked eye of all men in the next, the doings of all the world reflected as in a glass, so marvelously sensitive this wide, white band streaming endlessly from day to day becomes in the grasp of the multiple press.

If the pulse of activity in this great city, to which the tremor of the mammoth skeleton beneath our feet is but an awe-inspiring response, is thrilling, what of this prolific, silent obedience?

And the texture of the tissue of this great thing, this Forerunner of Democracy, the Machine, has been deposited particle by particle, in blind obedience to organic law, the law to which the great solar universe is but an obedient machine.

Thus is the thing into which the forces of Art are to breathe the thrill of ideality! A SOUL!

8 The American System Ready-Cut House

Now, in America, you understand that we have been, all of these years, borrowing bad forms. The result is that our buildings have no life, no meaning in them, and if we are ever going to have a living architecture again—an architecture in which there is really joy and which gives joy—we have got to go back to first principles. We have got to go beyond the "renaissance" to reality, to truth!

Introduction

In 1916 Frank Lloyd Wright made a major effort to apply the potential of the art and craft of the machine to the design of prefabricated or, in this case, precut housing for Arthur L. Richards, a Milwaukee, Wisconsin, area builder, and The Richards Company. Richards was a former client of Mr. Wright on the con-

---

Text of a speech reprinted in its entirety from Frank Lloyd Wright's "The American System of House Building," *The Western Architect,* Vol. 24, No. 3, September 1916, pp. 121–123.

Frank Lloyd Wright, circa 1916. Photograph by DeLonge Studio of Madison, Wisconsin, courtesy of the State Historical Society of Wisconsin.

struction of the Lake Geneva Hotel at Lake Geneva, Wisconsin, in 1911 and the unbuilt Madison Hotel project at Madison, Wisconsin, also in that year.

The Richards Company was organized on July 3, 1916, in Milwaukee, Wisconsin, with Richards as its president. Mr. Wright was not a company officer and it is not known whether he held any stock. The purpose of the company, outlined in its articles of incorporation, was to

> *buy, sell, manufacture and deal in all kinds of lumber and all kinds and classes of building material which may be used or employed in or about the construction of all kinds of buildings and structures; to buy and sell real estate for any and all purposes, especially, however, for the purpose of erecting thereon, or having erected thereon, so-called "Ready-Cut Houses."*[1]

The American System Ready-Cut Houses venture was short-lived because only one annual report of the corporation was filed with the State of Wisconsin (for the year 1916). The Richards Company was formally dissolved on August 6, 1917, having constructed only a few buildings in its short thirteen-month existence.[2]

As part of Richards' promotional effort for the American System Ready-Cut Houses a six-page booklet was printed in 1916 by The Richards Company, titled *The American System-Built Houses, Designed by Frank Lloyd Wright.* The following is the complete text of that booklet:

> *What is a house anyway? Did you ever ask yourself that question? It isn't just a pile of brick, stone, wood and cement. It is a place for joy and peace—a place about which should move soft-voiced women and earnest, thoughtful men. If you have any feeling about a home at all it probably gets deeper than just surface talk. It goes deep enough into your system to get hold of your desire for beauty, peace, sweetness in living. You want your home to have an air about it. You want to have something sound and right about the house in which you intend to live and raise*

---

[1] Corporation File L-975 in the Archives and Manuscripts Division of the State Historical Society of Wisconsin at Madison.

[2] Identified structures in American System Ready-Cut House design are a bungalow located at 1835 South Layton Boulevard, a small house at 2714 West Burnham Street, and four duplex apartment buildings at 2720 to 2732 West Burnham Street, all in Milwaukee, a small house located at 1165 Algoma Boulevard in Oshkosh, Wisconsin, houses located at 330 and 336 Gregory Street in Wilmette, Illinois, and a small house located at 231 Prospect Avenue in Lake Bluff, Illinois. The Arthur Munkwitz Duplex Apartments, also an American System Ready-Cut House design and once located at 1102 to 1112 North 27th Street in Milwaukee, were demolished in the early 1970s. More recently, however, Shirley DuFresne McArthur, in her *Frank Lloyd Wright American System-Built Homes in Milwaukee* (Milwaukee, Wisconsin: Northpoint Historical Society, 1985) identified another home in American System Built design at 104110 South Hoyne Avenue, Chicago. Henry-Russell Hitchcock has reported in his *In the Nature of Materials: The Buildings of Frank Lloyd Wright, 1887–1941* (New York: Da Capo Press, 1942 and 1975, p. 122) that "Mr. Richards built other houses and duplexes from American System plans at this time [i.e., 1916] in several other cities and towns, but cannot remember exactly where."

your sons and daughters. A man's house should be, in some way, the expression of all that is best and sweetest in the lives of the people who live there—it should be beautiful.

Now wait. Don't be afraid of that word "beauty." Perhaps you thought beauty was a thing that belonged only to the very rich. Is that the way you felt about it?

Well, there is reason for you feeling that way. We who have built and sold homes have not talked about beauty and solid fine work. We have talked price. We admit that.

It's a crying shame when you come to think if it—that men, real men, in this big free land should live their lives in houses not equal in beauty of the peasants' cottages in Europe.

Arthur L. Richards (1877–1955), circa 1904. Photograph courtesy of the Milwaukee County Historical Society.

Elevation of a one-story, single-family American System Ready-Cut House for Arthur L. Richards (1916), looking north from the intersection of South Layton Boulevard and West Burnham Street in Milwaukee, Wisconsin. This particular style, called the American Model-Cottage A in the American System Ready-Cut House line of designs, was constructed of plaster and wood. Photograph by the editor.

But things are going to change now. The genius of a really great man has been brought into the building trade in America. Frank Lloyd Wright, the greatest architect America has known is pouring his genius into the creating of this great AMERICAN SYSTEM of houses for the people. We want you to see the models of these houses. We want you to understand how the genius of this man has made it possible for every home builder to build beautifully without spending more to achieve beauty than he now spends for senseless ugliness.

Here is what Mr. Wright has done. As an American you ought to appreciate it. He has designed many types of houses, each of them beautiful beyond belief and each susceptible of infinite variation, and has worked out these designs so practically that they can be built by ordinary labor under ordinary conditions at from 10% to 20% less cost than the ugly houses we have all been building so long.

How did Mr. Wright do this?

It is really very simple. He has eliminated the ugly, meaningless furbelows. He has done away with the hideous twists and scrolls and other "fancy" work that has done more than anything else to make our house building so universally bad. He has used commercial engines to your advantage—used them for you, not against you.

A detailed view of the entrance to Cottage A. Photograph by the editor.

You see Mr. Wright is a really big artist as well as a big architect. He can afford to be simple and unpretentious. Think it over yourself.

Builders haven't understood the strength and beauty of swift, straight lines. They put on fussiness.

And fussiness isn't good home building.

Let us tell you a little about Frank Lloyd Wright. He is an American boy like you and me. And here is the first American architect whose designs have been studied in every great city of the world.

Why did the king's architect of one of the great old world empires say that he would be proud to have his son trained under this American?

Because Wright is basic, he is sound. He builds houses that stand on the ground that have music and meaning in them.

And this great Architect has devoted himself to designing the American System of houses; a system of house construction that can be used with infinite variety and effect without ugliness or waste.

He hasn't done it half way either. When he designs a house that is to cost you a certain sum of money that's all it costs you. There are no extras. You know what you are going to buy and it is delivered to you complete—key in hand—ready to live in.

And think what you have for your money. Not a hodge-podge but a really lovely home—one that you will be prouder of every day, one that will grow more and more beautiful and valuable as the years pass.

Today, there is American Architecture. An architecture as brave as the country. It is a pioneer work. Frank Lloyd Wright has cut fresh trails as did the early American. He has forgotten the time-trodden roads of the older orders.

America deserves an architecture. The English, German or French home is a part of the actual country, it belongs where it is built; it fits their respective styles of living. The Italian home built on the hill side becomes part of the hill. It grows out of it. The buildings express the life of their occupants, and are national in character. Consider, for example, the home in this country, built out of cement blocks with an imitation rock surface and an ornamental design, which is an exceedingly poor copy of what is really good in Europe. Such a house is not a genuine expression of our national feeling. Our buildings should reflect our life, mode of living and character. We do not want high walls, small windows or imitations of foreign designs. We want light, air, ventilation. We want utility, compactness.

No longer do Americans have to satisfy themselves with homes that ape old world forms, that were never intended for the New America. The AMERICAN SYSTEM House voices American feeling. It is the expression of a national spirit. It is fresh, buoyant, vital.

American Architecture has come naturally. It has sprung up from among us. It is big with power. There is nothing artificial about it. There is no straining for effect. An American House speaks to you. It says I am the beauty of perfect utility. The inner rightness of design and material finds utterance in my outward lines.

Only a man who was a world-character in his knowledge and an American in feeling could have done this.

In Frank Lloyd Wright the nation has found its interpreter. Through him America is no longer the copier. America is the originator. The American House is the creation.

The American System makes the house a lasting structure. Frank Lloyd Wright was an engineer before he was an architect. His houses have the outward symmetry indicative of inward strength.

Concrete; cypress, "the wood eternal"; water-proof, fire proof, cement plaster. The best classes of material—and the best grades in these classes.

American System design and materials make these houses the soundest of investments. If at any time you decide to sell you will find that the depreciation will be negligible. The upkeep is extremely low.

Quality materials—and larger sizes than most builders think necessary. You may have seen some of the old New England homesteads, standing firm after 150 or 200 years' use.

The American System of construction partakes of the spirit of the old Colonial builders, combining with it modern scientific knowledge of stresses and strains, of the strength of materials and methods of building.

A view of a small, one-story, single-family American System Ready-Cut House for Arthur L. Richards (1916) in Milwaukee, Wisconsin, called the American Model-Cottage B-1. Photograph by the editor.

Detailed view of Cottage B-1. Photograph by the editor.

For example, an American house is not cut to pieces to place the window frames. The studs run through from foundation to roof. No breaks except for the outside doors. The strength of the construction is unimpaired.

An American House is as sound from the engineer's viewpoint as a great bridge or a skyscraper.

Integrity of means to ends. Economy, beauty. Frank Lloyd Wright has no scorn of the practical thing. He seizes the convenient and permanent—and lets it express itself beautifully.

It is no exaggeration to say that an American System-Built House is more durable than any other frame house ever built.

The woman asks about the arrangement of American Dwellings. This is important to her as the arrangement of her husband's store, office or factory is to him. Whether she performs the household duties, or merely supervises them she demands convenience. She finds it in the American Dwelling.

Study the floor plan and you'll see. There are no unnecessary steps to be taken, no waste space, no dark corners.

Then you will look at the placing of the windows. Note the cross-lighting. Even the kitchens and roof spaces are ventilated.

The first day you enter an American House you find it generously equipped with furniture that is a unit with the structure itself. It is made an integral part of your home and harmonize with its lines and proportions. This furniture, depending on the design of the house, includes built-in wardrobe, kitchen cabinets, breakfast nook, living room bookcase, dining and living room tables.

A combined beauty and usefulness makes the American House a most satisfying home. It is not a mass of gaudy, stuck-on decorations—not a jig-saw puzzle of unrelated parts.

It speaks of sane, rational thinking.

It belongs to the fine, straightforward thing that American home life is at its best.

It is clean within and without, honest, without pretense, quiet.

In this booklet we do not go into all of the mechanical details Mr. Wright has perfected to get his American System of houses ready to offer the public through us.

He has really done what no other modern artist has even dared attempt to do. He has achieved the touch the old craftsman had—the beauty that cannot die, by the use of modern building material mills, modern labor and modern commercialism, the machine.

The thing you want to know is that you get a beautiful house at less cost than an ugly one. We will prove that to you.

Go to see our representatives. Talk to them. Look at the models of the houses.

And remember the big story. Any AMERICAN SYSTEM built house you get will be designed for you by Frank Lloyd Wright. It will be beautiful. It will be built only of the finest grade material from cellar to roof. It will come to you intact, complete as it should be and the key handed over to you. There will be no extras.[3]

Antonin Raymond, an apprentice who joined the architectural practice at Taliesin near Spring Green, Wisconsin, in the early spring of 1916 while Mr. Wright was working on the American System designs, made the following remarks:

The work he [Mr. Wright] performed on paper was tremendous, but actual building for clients was very scarce, practically nonexistent. We worked on a prefabricated scheme [American System Ready-Cut Houses] for small residences, which was a predecessor of so many projects done by others in later years. Although the work accomplished on this problem was prodigious, it never amounted to anything serious as far as actual execution was concerned. Wright visualized the component parts of the structure to be delivered on the job site, some pre-cut and some prefabricated. The module was three feet, an idea apparently originating from his experiences and observations on one of his previous trips to Japan. Two-by-four-inch planks, stucco and plaster were the basic materials. The prefabricated scheme shows Wright in the amazing capacity of combining the characteristics of [the] true artist with those of a shrewd businessman [Arthur L. Richards].[4]

Although no longer associated with Mr. Wright, Richards continued to pursue the construction of prefabricated or precut housing in the Milwaukee area during the later teens and early 1920s, based on another system designed by a local Milwaukee architect, Russell Barr Williamson. Williamson had worked at Taliesin as an apprentice at the time that the American System Ready-Cut House designs were under development. Williamson's system and its products strongly resembled Mr. Wright's American System as well as other Prairie-style houses by him and other Prairie School architects.

The following is the text of a talk that Frank Lloyd Wright gave before a body of Chicago businessmen in mid-1916 on the American System Ready-Cut House designs he prepared for The Richards Company.

---

[3] The Richards Company. *The American System-Built Houses, Designed by Frank Lloyd Wright,* Milwaukee, Wisconsin: The Richards Company, 1916.

[4] Extracted from Antonin Raymond's *An Autobiography,* Rutland, Vermont: Charles E. Tuttle Company, 1973, pp. 48–51.

The Speech

WRIGHT: I hesitated a long time before I decided that I would undertake a thing of this nature. It is something I have always believed could be done here in America better than anywhere else in the world. In all of my work from the beginning I have had faith in the machine as the characteristic tool of my times, therefore an artist's tool. I have believed that this tool put into an artist's hand could be a real benefit to our civilization. I believe that the architecture in America that fails to take into account the machine and modern organization tendencies is going to be of no great benefit to the people. Of course, I know that it is going to take a more subtle art within more severe limitations to build houses beautifully while utilizing the machine, but I believe this effort is the logical conclusion of my studies and my architectural practice.

I believe the world will find in the American System of house construction the only instance in the world today of a work which has absolute individuality due to a central idea which is the *organic* integrity of the work. If the whole organization of the plan by which the American [System] models are to be merchandised is worked out in a broad, healthy way, great things will come of it.

Naturally, I do not want it exploited like a "flash in the pan" nor do I want anything done that will make the plan seem an expedient of the moment. The idea back of the American System has been in my head for years. I have guarded it carefully. I wanted time to think in quiet of how the idea might be brought to the public without injury to the integrity of my own art. Any student of design will know that the designs of these houses are not architectural attempts at reform. They are developed according to a principle. They grow from the inside out, just as trees or flowers grow. They have that integrity. The difference between my work and the work of other men is all a difference in grasp and treatment of old principles.

A view of two 2-story, 2-family American System Ready-Cut Houses for Arthur L. Richards (1916), looking northwest from West Burnham Street in Milwaukee, Wisconsin. These two buildings were constructed of wood and stucco and termed "Two-Family-Flat-C" in the American System Ready-Cut House line of designs. Four buildings are known to have been constructed and all are at the same West Burnham Street location. Photograph by the editor.

I do not want any mistake made about this new system. These buildings are not in any sense the ready-cut buildings we have all heard of where a little package of material is sold to be stuck together in any fashion. The American System-built house is not a ready-cut house but a house built by an organization systematized in such a way that the result is guaranteed the fellow that buys the house. I want to deliver beautiful houses to people at a certain price, key in packet. If I have made progress in the art of architecture, I want to be able to offer this to the people intact. I think the idea will appeal also to the man in the street. Every man would love to have a beautiful house if he could pay for the tremendous amount of waste usually involved in building such a house. The American [System] plan you see, simply cuts out the tremendous waste that has in the past made house building on a beautiful scale possible only to the very rich and any integrity in the result possible only to the especially enlightened individual. Unlimited money has failed there most loudly.

Somehow in America, architecture has never been appreciated. We are perhaps the greatest nation of house builders in the world and the most slipshod nation of home builders. Architecture has, for the most part, been let go by the board because we have had to have buildings and have them quick. The result is that the old log cabin, built in the woods by the frontiersmen, is really much more beautiful than the modern house with all its affectation, fussiness, and ugly waste.

Now, I believe that the coming of the machine has so altered the conditions of home building that something like this American System was inevitable but I have not borne in mind purely the economical side of it. I would like to explain to you men some of the impulses [in] back of my work in this direction.

When I, as a young American architect, went abroad, I found many things that astonished me. I expected to find over there a great variety—great interest. I went from one city to another and for the most part found beauty in the very old buildings only. The Germans who really built German buildings and the Italians who built really Italian buildings built beautifully. I naturally came to the conclusion that much of the hideousness in the architecture of modern day was due to the academic "Renaissance" that Europe has so nearly standardized. To my mind, the Renaissance, although academic, never was *organic*. And for centuries architecture, like other arts touched by the Renaissance, had been divorced from life, divorced from any *organic* relation of cause and effect.

A detailed view of one "Two-Family-Flat-C" American System Ready-Cut House. Photograph by the editor.

Now, when we go back to the old architecture, we find something quite different. The Gothic, for example, was a *true* style. It was a real architecture. It was an *organic* architecture. In all my work I have always tried to make my work *organic*.

A view of two American Model J-521 duplex apartment buildings in the American Ready-Cut House line of designs for Arthur R. Munkwitz (1916), looking northeast from the intersection of North 27th Street and West Highland Avenue in Milwaukee, Wisconsin (both buildings were demolished in 1973). Photograph by the editor.

Now, in America, you understand that we have been, all of these years, borrowing bad forms. The result is that our buildings have no life, no meaning in them, and if we are going to have a living architecture again—an architecture in which there is really joy and which gives joy—we have got to go back to first principles. We have got to go beyond the Renaissance to reality, to *truth!*

And now there comes a thought which is really back of this whole effort and which to you businessmen, may sound like a highly sophisticated affair. You see, you in America have been led to believe that an artist is necessarily a queer fellow—one divorced from the life about him. The contrary is *true.* The perfect artist should be a better businessman than any of you here sitting before me and he would be if he had time and the need.

In America, the natural tendency of our times is away from the old handcraft [sic]. The railroad locomotive, the great electrical dynamo—these are some of our *truly* beautiful products—beautiful because of their perfect adaptation of means to ends. Now, I do not believe any architecture in the time of commercialism, of industrialism, and of huge organization can be real architecture unless it uses beautifully all of these great tools of modern life. And that is just what the American System of building houses proposes to do.

A view of the elevation of an American Model J-521 duplex apartment. Photograph by the editor.

Of course, I realized the danger in all this. I would not dare go into it if I did not believe I could, in the midst of industrialism and commercialism, keep on top with my art. In the designing of all these houses, I have kept close to first principles but I look with horror at what might easily happen in spite of all the care with which I have handled this matter. I do not want to lose sight of the central idea of using the machine and all modern industrialism to produce beauty. I asked you men to be patient with me if I sometimes insisted upon things that you do not understand the meaning of. Simply selling houses at less cost means nothing at all to me. To sell beautiful houses at less cost means everything. A beautiful house means a *truer,* better house in every way.

Frank Lloyd Wright, circa 1930. Photograph courtesy of The Capital Times, *Madison, Wisconsin.*

The Preassembled House

. . . a good machine is good to look at. There is no reason why a house should look like a machine, but there is no reason why it should not be just as good to look at as a machine, and for the same reason. That is an entirely new basis for architecture and for thought and for life.

Introduction

On Thursday June 30, 1932, Frank Lloyd Wright appeared before more than 600 delegates to the 25th Annual Convention of the National Association of Real Estate Boards held at the Netherland Plaza Hotel in Cincinnati, Ohio, to deliver a speech entitled "Lower Construction Costs for Homes." One reviewer noted the following of this Depression-era convention:

> *Absent from the convention this year was any note of whining about present conditions. Not that conditions were overlooked or ignored. The spirit of the convention was rather to face them squarely, to recognize that they are beyond the*

The text of the excerpts of this speech was edited and reproduced from Frank Lloyd Wright's "The House of the Future," *National Real Estate Journal*, Vol. 33, July 1932, pp. 25–26. A condensed version of this article also appeared as Frank Lloyd Wright's "The House of the Future," *National Real Estate and Building Journal*, Vol. 58, No. 10, October 1957, p. 43.

immediate control . . . and that the thing to do is to stop waiting for them to improve.[1]

As an answer to providing lower construction costs for homes, Mr. Wright's speech focused on a concept he termed "the assembled house," at which time he again discussed the application of the art and craft of the machine to the betterment of the human condition.

---

[1] "Cincinnati Convention Charts Course for '32", *National Real Estate Journal,* Vol. 33, July 1932, p. 17.

The Speech

WRIGHT: I shall call the thing the "assembled house." I do not think there is a big concern in the United States that has not been flirting with it, more or less, that has not done some research work along the line of a standardized, machine-made house.

At first, of course, the house itself is going to take on some of the characteristics that Henry's Model T took on when it was in Henry's hands, when it was in the inventor's hands. An inventor is not an architect. The house will be ugly in the beginning, but it will get into the hands of the creative architect or the artist who can evolve a scheme or a plan by which it can be made a harmonious whole. There is no reason why the assembled house, fabricated in the factory should not be made as beautiful and as efficient as the modern automobile.

You will see a few appearing and will turn away from them and say: "My God, anything but that." But that is the way everything that is new and effective has found its way into civilization. When we have established a few models that are usable, beautiful, and livable, there is no question but that the people will like them.

There will be a great difference between this new house and the old house as between the old caravel in which Columbus discovered America and a beautiful stream-lined rotor ship. You will see that a new element esthetically has entered into modern life by way of the very things that are now doing more to destroy that life than to make it. There will be a new simplicity, a machine-made simplicity. Now, a good machine is good to look at. There is no reason why a house should look like a machine, but there is no reason why it should not be just as good to look at as a machine and for just the same reason. That is an entirely new basis for architecture and for thought and for life.

Now in working out this assembled house we have already the bathroom as a single unit to draw upon. We will call it unit No. 1. You can now get a bathroom with a bathtub and the bowl and the water closet in one fixture, and all that is to be done is to make the connection to the sewer we have provided and screw it up. There it is.

Now, your kitchen has been worked out in many ways. I think there are at least five now available where you can get a complete and a more practical, a more beautiful kitchen than almost any architect could himself design—unit No. 2. And in connection with that unit you have the heating of the house—the heat which you use for your kitchen for cooking—an immense economy. All that needs is a single connection, screwing it up, and putting it together.

The appurtenant systems in any house are more than one-third of the cost of the house. As the cost of the building comes down, the proportion rises. Once we have those things completely established as certain parts are established in your car, and they have nothing whatever to do with the general effect of the house as a whole, we have established one very essential economy, and we have then something at last toward the building of this modern house.

Now, in addition to that, it is just as easy to standardize a bedroom unit which is ideal and which does not have the old stuffy closet. We do not have closets any more in the older sense. We architects, in spite of our impracticability, have seen the consequences of providing the housewife with a hole in which to chuck things. Our closet is not essential any more and we do not have it. We have the wardrobe instead, which is a ventilated affair, which can be easily kept in order.

Site plan of Frank Lloyd Wright's Ocatilla Desert Camp (1928) at Chandler, Arizona, shown in the August 1930 issue of The Architectural Record. *Photograph courtesy of the State Historical Society of Wisconsin.*

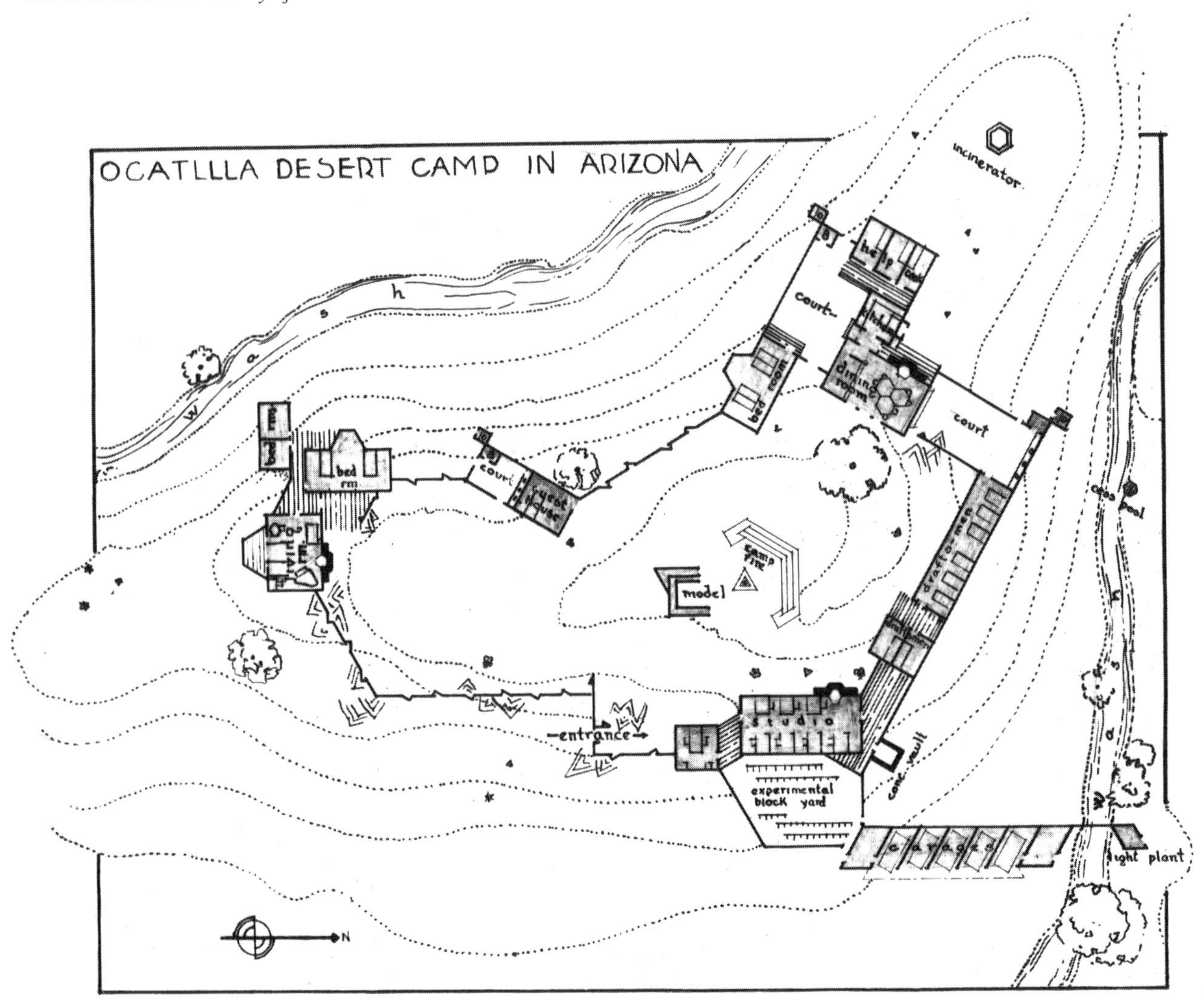

An exterior view of Frank Lloyd Wright's Ocatilla Desert Camp (1928) at Chandler, Arizona, looking northeast shows the cooking and dining structures (far left), *a sleeping room* (left), *the guest house* (right of center), *and sleeping rooms* (far right). *The camp is perched on a small desert-rock outcropping abutting a stream* (not shown). *The structures are constructed of boxboards 11-1/2 inches wide, 1-3/4 × 7/8 inch battens, and 10-ounce canvas, 4 feet wide, put together with nails, screws, hinges, and shop cord in a 4-foot modular unit construction system. Photograph courtesy of the State Historical Society of Wisconsin.*

An exterior view of Frank Lloyd Wright's Ocatilla Desert Camp (1928) at Chandler, Arizona, looking southwest from the entrance (far left of photo). *This view, taken inside the camp, shows the guest house* (right), *a sleeping room* (center), *and living room* (left). *The boxboards were painted a dry rose color, the canvas triangles of the gables were scarlet, and the other canvas areas were white. Photograph courtesy of the State Historical Society of Wisconsin.*

The bedroom unit can be in various sizes; it can be assembled in various ways with the other units.

Then we can have a living room unit of two or three sizes. In fact, all the features which are characteristic of modern life and modern living we can buy on some standardized scheme of arrangement. These can be laid out on a unit system so that they all come together in an *organic* style, and the design of these things in the first place can be of such character that in the final assembly no wrong or bad thing can happen.

In putting these units together according to your means, you may be able to have a three-unit house. You will probably have to have a bathroom, a kitchen unit, and a bedroom—three units at a minimum. Then you can go on and you can amplify that house until you have it surrounding an interior court. And this thing can all come knocked down to you in metal, metal slabs pressed on each side with some heat-resisting or cold-resisting insulation. In fact, you can have the slabs 10 feet or you can have them twelve feet long and eight to nine feet high in the knockdown shape and put together on the job with a BTU resistance equal to that of an eight-inch brick wall.

Now, in connection with this assembled house a man need not go so heavily into debt to own his house as he has to do now. He will not have to encourage the mortgage banker to quite such an extent. As his means grow and his family grows, his house can grow. And I can demonstrate to you with perspectives and models which are being prepared that none of these houses in any way you can put them together will be other than good to look at.

They are characteristic of the age. You can drive a car up to the door of one of these little houses, or big houses, however they may be extended, drive

An interior view of the studio situated at the eastern extremes of Frank Lloyd Wright's Ocatilla Desert Camp (1928) at Chandler, Arizona. The translucent canvas roof affords the diffusion of natural light. Photograph courtesy of the State Historical Society of Wisconsin.

An interior view of the architect's cabin or living room situated at the southeastern extreme of Frank Lloyd Wright's Ocatilla Desert Camp (1928), Chandler, Arizona. Photograph courtesy of the State Historical Society of Wisconsin.

into the garage, and it will all look as though it belonged together—as the costume of the modern woman as she is dressed today also belongs to that house and to that car. The man's costume does not [change] simply because the women won't let us change. We ought to have something simpler than we are putting on in order to be modern. We are dreadfully old-fashioned when we hook up about forty-three buttons and go through all our pockets, and finally take stock of the gadgets which go to make us complete. "Simplification" is the slogan of the machine age, a new significance for the car, for the house, for madame's dress, for monsieur, eventually, but we have got to fight for that freedom; it is not coming unless we do fight for it.

Well, now, I have laid before you a simple outline and the gist of this thing that we call modern. I have given you an outline here of the main characteristics and the thought behind modern architecture. It is not well to laugh at it, and it is not well to put it aside. You can't. I have seen it during the last thirty years which it has been my pleasure and privilege to try to build houses for people. I have seen it growing and growing, going abroad, becoming the characteristic thing in Holland, in Germany, in Switzerland, Czechoslovakia, Poland, and France. Our own country has been the only country satisfied with its own little plaster caverns, its own gadgets, its own little pretty things which it is willing to set up in some style or other and try to live in.

Now, it seems to me that the most valuable thing for a body of Realtors to get into their systems is the idea, first, that we have got to make spaciousness more characteristic of modern life. It is the *natural* thing for democracy to get space. The modern city works against it. All of you Realtors have worked against it all your lives. The finer you could get the thing, and the smaller the pieces you could pass around, why the more successful you were. That time has gone by, I believe.

There is a lot of ground in this country. In fact, if all the people of the world were put on the Island of Bermuda, they would not cover it standing up—I do not know about sitting down. And there are just about fifty-three acres, at any rate about fifty acres in this country, for every man, woman, and child in it if it were to be divided up on that basis. Now, it is senseless getting the thing in a heap, pig-piling, to pig-pile some more. Believe me, it is old-fashioned. It is not in the keeping of our modern opportunities. It is not in the keeping of our modern thought. It is dead.

Probably you do not even know now when you see the little gas station out there on the prairie that that is the advance agent of decentralization. Distribution is changing. Your telephone poles could be down tomorrow if it was not for the investment in them. The whole expression and guide of modern living has gained fluidity, spontaneity. What before took ten years is now spontaneous.

Have we got to go on building buildings, partitioning ground, setting up institutions along these dead old lines, and crucifying human life to make a little money? We are all where we are now, flat on our backs, gasping for a little sustenance—I guess we call it "cash"—just because we can't keep pace with the modern thought that is building the modern world. We have had before us a spectacle of what we call "depression. "I suppose we call it a depression to be nice, just the way the car people when they take your car call it "repossession. "But I do not believe that this is a depression. I believe that we are at the end of an epoch, and I believe that unless real estate men put their ears to their own ground and get this message — decentralization — reintegration — *organic* architecture—the use of our other resources—we are faced with a very serious situation. Those things seem insignificant, but God knows what they can do. Glass, steel, the automobile, mobilization of the whole community. Why, it has changed the entire face of civilization and the universe. And until we can grasp that, until we can interpret it, until we can capitalize it for the people, we have not got a civilization.

Frank Lloyd Wright speaks before a group of people, circa mid-1950's. Photograph courtesy of The Capital Times, *Madison, Wisconsin.*

10 The Marshall Erdman Prefabricated Houses

This still new engine called "prefabrication" is, of course, a dangerous engine. Anything vital, living, and competent has a dangerous side. There is nothing more dangerous than truth, nothing more to be dreaded if you are in the wrong.

Introduction

On Wednesday, January 22, 1958, Frank Lloyd Wright held a formal press conference in Chicago to introduce his designs for the prefabricated houses he had created for Marshall Erdman and Associates, builders of Madison, Wisconsin. Mr. Wright had designed four basic types of prefabricated housing—Pre-Fabs 1–4. Only Pre-Fabs 1 and 2, however, were ever constructed.[1]

Reprinted by permission of Hanley-Wood, Inc., from Frank Lloyd Wright's "America's Foremost Architect Speaks On Prefabrication and the Role of Creative Man in the Machine Age: 'Quality and Quantity Must Be Partners, Science and Art Must Live Together'—Frank Lloyd Wright," *House and Home,* Vol. 13, No. 4, April 1958, pp. 120–122.

[1] The six Marshall Erdman Pre-Fab 1 designs actually constructed were the William Cass residence, Richmond, New York, the Frank Iber residence, Stevens Point, Wisconsin, the Arnold Jackson residence (second design), Madison, Wisconsin, and later relocated in Beaver Dam, Wisconsin (see "Mid-'50s Frank Lloyd Wright Prefab House To Be Relocated," *Architecture: The AIA Journal,* Vol. 74, No. 3, March 1985, pp. 32, 37, and 42. for a complete account of this relocation), the Joseph Mollica residence, in Bayside, Wisconsin, the Carl Post residence in Barrington Hills, Illinois, and the Eugene Van Tamelen residence, Madison. Only two Marshall Erdman Pre-Fab 2 designs were actually constructed—the James B. McBean residence, Rochester, Minnesota, and the Walter Rudin residence, Madison.

The first Pre-Fab 1—the Eugene Van Tamelen residence—was constructed in Madison, Wisconsin, in October 1956. The first Pre-Fab 2—the Walter Rudin residence—was designed by Mr. Wright in late 1958 or January 1959 and was constructed in June 1959 (after Mr. Wright's death), also in Madison, in time for the Parade of Homes.[2] Briefly, Pre-Fab 1 was a one-story, three-bedroom structure that covered an area of about 2000 square feet. Pre-Fab 2 was a 2200-square-foot, three-bedroom house with two bedrooms on a second-level that projected into a two-story living room, fourteen feet high. Both Pre-Fabs 1 and 2 had attached carports and outdoor patio or terrace areas.[3]

During his press conference Mr. Wright not only talked about his new Marshall Erdman prefabricated housing designs but also reflected on "The Art and Craft of the Machine" speech he had delivered at Hull House in Chicago in 1901, almost sixty years earlier (see Chapter 7). The optimism Mr. Wright had displayed then about the potential of the machine to be used as an artist's tool was somewhat tempered during this 1958 press talk, but the optimism expressed in regard to his new Pre-Fab designs was even greater. The text that follows is extracted from the talk concerning those designs. One reporter who attended the press conference commented that Mr. Wright was "well groomed as usual in a herringbone tweed, a flaring pointed collar and puffed tie; Wright was in fine fettle."[4]

---

[2] See "Ready for Parade of Homes Here: New Wright Prefab Home To Be Marketed in Spring," *The Capital Times* (Madison, Wisconsin), February 9, 1959, and "At Parade of Homes: Wright House Draws Big Crowds at Show," *The Capital Times* (Madison, Wisconsin), June 22, 1959.

[3] For a detailed discussion and illustrations of Marshall Erdman Pre-Fab 1 see "Here Is Prefabrication's Biggest News for 1957," *House and Home*, Vol. 10, December 1956, pp. 117–121 and cover; and for a detailed discussion and illustrations of Marshall Erdman Pre-Fab 2 see "FLLW Designed This Big 'One Space' Prefab," *House and Home*, Vol. 16, August 1959, pp. 176–177.

[4] "Wright 'Unveils' Prefab Houses," *Chicago Sun-Times*, January 22, 1958, p. 3.

The Speech

WRIGHT: Way back in the days when Hull House was the cultural center of Chicago—say sixty-five years ago—William Morris, John Ruskin, and the Pre-Raphaelites were at the center of the stage in art and architecture. Handicraft societies were all over the United States.

Hull House had called a meeting to found a similar crafts society in Chicago. I was invited by Jane Addams to put forward at this meeting a minority report. The minority report was: "what is the use in getting behind doors and pounding your fingers trying to make things, when the whole world of production is stalled and missing inspiration that really belongs to the machine!"

In those days we hadn't reckoned with machines. We merely used them. The machine was new on the crafts horizon and it was murdering handicraft right and left. It had succeeded by way of Grand

Rapids in turning out machine carving as well as other hand work. I made a proposition at the meeting that we quit all of that study of the crafts.

I advocated the machine as an artist's tool and the machine, of course, meant prefabrication, reproduction, standardization. I suggested we go to work and investigate what it could do in Chicago, in the metal trades, what it could do with wood, what it could do with other building materials. But I was voted down and out. [The] Next day *The Chicago Tribune* published an editorial—I think Jane Addams wrote it—saying that for the first time in the history of art a Chicagoan had advocated the machine as an artist's tool.

Since then my lecture "The Art and Craft of the Machine" [see Chapter 7] has been translated into seven languages and gone around the world. It had long enough time to get around and come back and really nothing much has happened since.

The ability to envision and make practical the uses and purposes of machines—to get what inspiration we can from on high to quality the machine product in a new way, to new purposes—is still way behind the lighthouse. As a matter of fact, our architects are today building nineteenth-century buildings. We are still building the old steel frames. In other words, people who were accustomed to building lumber buildings now build them out of steel lumber. All our architects who are famous as modernists are still building steel-lumber buildings! New York's full of them, Chicago's full of them. They are all dying of arthritis at the joints because you can't insure the life of a steel-frame building by insuring the life of the joint with paint. As wood was born to rot, steel is born to rust.

That is only a little indication of our lack of education. I mention it here to show how slow it has been even to conceive the justice and the perfect common sense of the *nature* of materials and of making them beautiful in the way you work with them.

Now, that means today, prefabrication, because you can prefabricate nearly everything in a house that doesn't give it individuality. The bathroom doesn't give the house much individuality. You can prefabricate it, take it to the job, make three connections. The heating system I brought over from Tokyo—gravity heat I called it because heat rises as surely as rainwater falls—is now called radiant heat for some curious reason. That's mechanical and that's prefabrication. It can all be made and brought to the building.

Of course, anything done in the field has gone—laborwise [sic]—entirely out of all proportion. The cost of building used to be, for labor, about a third of the building's total. Today, labor is about one-half of the cost of the building. Architects—and they are all that is the matter with architecture, I assure you—have not given enough study to what can be done by modern machinery to the advantage of the well designed house.

Now where you live, the living rooms, these places of warmth, proportion, and charm, have gone by the board because no one is willing to pay for good design. Designs are something you get out of magazines. The magazines get them from boys who are looking to make a reputation somehow for something they have gleaned somewhere.

The so-called practical boys doing the housing now are not the real sinners. The real sinner today is education. Teachers have not placed the values in the right places and don't realize the value of good proportion and design. Without them there can be no real beauty in building except by rebellion.

Without *organic* consistency of method to purpose, man's tool, there can be no great beauty in housing. Without all these high-minded things, difficult to come by, we have only a stupid procession of empty technology. What could be technology is really not technique at all, it is here habituation and has come by way of the Realtor. Our nation is unfortunate in this respect. The industrial revolution—production-controlling consumption—is making a cinder strip of the whole

An exterior view, looking west, of the entrance area and carport of Frank Lloyd Wright's first constructed Marshall Erdman Pre-Fab No. 1—the Eugene Van Tamelen residence (1956) at Madison, Wisconsin, as it appeared in October 1956. This house is a prefabricated panel structure in which all walls and partitions fall within thirty-two-inch units or sixteen-inch half-units. The outside walls are faced with a slightly textured Masonite board. Photograph courtesy of The Capital Times, *Madison, Wisconsin.*

country, with little hot spots we call cities. Now, I don't think we were destined to wind up as an industrial cinder strip. I believe we were designed to give the beauty and freedom of the green earth as a heritage. Then came the Realtor, then came the developer—and God has not saved us from them. He won't, because He expects something of His children. He expects some intelligence on their part to stand up and say: "No, this is not living. This is not America. This is not sovereignty of the individual." All the freedom of life, and the beauty of it for the individual, is right there where you live, where your housing is.

In building homes we have the key to, and the cornerstone of, whatever culture our nation is capable of. By its buildings every great civilization is judged. And most of them passed away just as we are going to pass away, only we are going to pass away sooner. We are not going to last quite as long as most of them did because we can go faster and the faster we go, the sooner we finish. So it is high time to pause and take stock of the things that constitute the spirit of *true* building.

Good design is the spirit of man, the spirit of our times, the spirit of our nation made evident. There is nothing so valuable, nothing worth so much to a society, to its future, as the fine high quality of its living conditions!

Now, living conditions don't consist only of kitchens, bathrooms, and standardizations of rooms to live and sleep in. You can't prefabricate the thing that gives life to the building. That is something that has to come by benefit of clergy, so to say. So this prefabricated house here, which we have launched in order to save a third of the cost—probably without damage to its character or its spirit—still has something that I have just called benefit of clergy. This makes sure that the house belongs where it's built, that it is adapted to the site where you put it, that nothing can be done to mar or destroy the harmony of its features. The house cannot be distorted nor can the house be misplaced.

The sense of proportion is what put me into architecture in the first place. I was the man who declared that the human scale was the scale by which man should build. The old architectures were grandomaniac architectures and were intended to give man inferiority complexes. They did! But now we are entitled to give the American citizen something more in his own image, in his own right—in his own proportion, too. Something that came out of the everywhere to which he belongs and into the here in which he lives. Now that's quality.

Quality and quantity need not be enemies, necessarily. They can be partners and in the prefabricated house that's what they'll be. That's why they are and what they should have been many, many years ago.

Our trouble now lies mainly in lack of ground. There is no such thing as human habitation put on the ground; no such thing as human habitation placed center to center, blotting out the ground. Only if the ground space is developed into the spaces of the building and the building has enough ground space about it to characterize the building, and be characterized by it, have you got what we should dare to call American architecture.

We used to say that an acre to the family was enough. Well, it should depend upon environment. It will all depend on where and how the building is built. Now, much of the money that goes into the building should go into the place where the building stands. That is where your realtor has to come in for a drubbing. Because it is his habit to run out ahead of the crowd, buy up the land, put up his little advertising paraphernalia, and sell land in little pieces—the smaller the piece, the bigger his profits. Why do you take it? Why now when the automobile is here and we have a new time scale? We plan by time scale—five minutes, fifteen minutes, twenty minutes.

Now the automobile itself has changed everything in a building. We have made the car like a little horse and stabled it alongside the building where by *nature* it doesn't belong. If there is any companionship that is odious to a building, it is the motorcar of today. Gasoline, carbon monoxide, noise should be left outside somewhere. They are not fit for human companionship. And then if you look at the car itself, you can get an idea of what

An exterior view, looking southwest, of the entrance area and carport of the Eugene Van Tamelen residence (1956) twenty years after its construction (1977). This prefabricated structure has become an integral part of the man-made and natural landscape. Photograph by the editor.

happens to buildings in the way of design. Who designs those cars? No student of *nature*! Well, now you can't get designs from any other source than from a deep sincere study of *nature*.

What's the nature of our automobility [sic]? Is it that thing with fins sticking way up and out behind and all the rest of it like a raft or a ferryboat coming down the street gnashing its teeth at you? Well, now your houses are going in the same direction. You have your picture-window houses and you have all this glass you don't know what to do with. Perfectly indecent are most of these modern glassifications [sic] in subdivisions. I wouldn't be surprised if people began to commit suicide by the thousands on account of the way they have to live in their glasshouses!

Why shouldn't you stand up on your hind legs and say: "No, we don't want that sort of thing. We know this isn't the right thing and we refuse to be jammed into a box, no matter how big the hole is in front. We know there is plenty of ground room in this country. We know that's one thing the country is long on. We know we don't have to pile up on half-acre lots, twenty of us to the acre." We don't have enough sense of our own dignity! We don't know who we are, really. We lack respect because we give no respect. Have we lost sight of the main thing we're here to get?

There is no excuse for building poverty into the country as an institution as they've done in the big redbrick prisons of New York City. Those redbrick insurance investments, the money of the people put into building poverty into the nation as an institution!

An interior view of the living room taken from the dining area of the Eugene Van Tamelen Residence (1956) at Madison, Wisconsin. The living room, which measures twenty by twenty-four feet, opens onto a glass-enclosed terrace beyond the draperies. The battens on the natural one-quarter-inch mahogany walls form ornament within this space as well as in the other interior and exterior spaces of the structure. The furniture was not *designed by Frank Lloyd Wright. Photograph courtesy of* The Capital Times, *Madison, Wisconsin.*

If you can see freedom, if you can see green fields, if you can see children playing in the sun, if you can see buildings that have charm, what a man is, what a woman is, then you want something more than you are getting today. Now believe me—no man's home, notwithstanding prefabrication, need be so like another man's home as to cheat him of his *natural* distinction. Good design qualifies it by the things done to live in it. If the living room is there and the people are where they belong and the things round about where that house stands are different and the client's things are where he put them, individuality will come through notwithstanding such prefabrication as is advantageous.

Prefabrication and standardization are two different things and yet they belong together. They're going to stand together. We're going to have them together.

You can standardize almost anything but unless you know how to keep life in it by good design it will be more or less a quantity thing. Now a quantity thing is never going to take the place of the quality thing. But we know well enough now—I, as an architect, say this to you advisedly—to put quality into quantity up to a certain point. It can be done only by an inspired sense of design. It's not common and never will be. It's not in the magazines. It's not something you pick up in the street.

Good design is something you have to go in for carefully—not too sure of your own taste. Good design is something precious and rare. Of course, we're a taste-built culture. We have had no knowledge concerning taste. If you have been to a university or your children have been there, they have grown up in a haphazard environment. I think probably some regents should be taken out and

An exterior view of the Marshall Erdman Pre-Fab No. 2—the Walter Rudin residence (1958–1959) at Madison, Wisconsin. Pre-Fab No. 2, a 2200-square foot, three-bedroom house, has two bedrooms on a second level. The nearly square structure is eighteen feet high and is lighted by a band of windows under ornamental fascia panels two feet wide. The exterior was originally cream ocher with blue battens. Photograph by the editor.

shot just for their taste. University buildings were built by somebody's taste, nobody's knowledge.

You are likely to get into the same rut by taste. This still new engine called "prefabrication" is, of course, an dangerous engine. Anything vital, living, and competent has a dangerous side. There is nothing more dangerous than *truth,* nothing more to be dreaded if you are in the wrong. And here we are in our housing projects, the developers merry, ignorant of quality, desirous of quantity at so much per unit. But what of the human element—spiritual element—the element of the man himself? Look for it! Where do you find it? You won't see it in the big projects. It has been left out. Whose fault is that? It isn't the fault of the builder. It's the fault of the man who buys that project house and consents to live in it. He can groan and complain and think he might have had more for his money but there he is. It isn't how much house you get for your money, it's the quality of what you get. Now, if we could set that kind of thinking going we would really be what you might honestly call on an economic basis.

We boast of having the highest standard of living in this world. I'm afraid that when we say the highest we can only claim the biggest. Quantity is not the same thing as quality. You can have the highest standard of living when it isn't half so big. Now the question should be how do we improve the quality? How do we preserve and then how may we use quality?

Quality is a characteristic of the *free* man. Are buildings going to be subject to the deadly routine of conformity? The cheapest thing you can get in the cheapest way without consideration of quality and with no real knowledge of what constitutes quality? If so, then we are the biggest, shortest lived civilization in history. And the atom bomb—what do you call it now?—might as well drop because I don't see anything particularly admirable or desirable to stay here for. I think we might just as well kiss it all good-bye.

An exterior view of the two-story, twenty by twenty-four foot living room and projected dining room of the Walter Rudin residence, a prefabricated house constructed on a two by four foot module. Frank Lloyd Wright called it a "one-room house" because "when you walk into the building you see but one interior space." Photograph by the editor.

*An exterior view of the Marshall Erdman Pre-Fab No. 2—the James B. McBean residence (1958–1959) at Rochester, Minnesota. This view shows an attached carport (*left*), two-story, living room area (*center*), and protruding one-story dining room alcove. The dining room steps down from the living area. Photograph by the editor.*

There is only one thing that makes life worth living to an American and that is the highest, the bravest, and the best of everything there is available right down the line. Take no less, know what is the best, know what is really good, have knowledge.

Know why a house is good, know that the proportions belong, know that the building looks as though it belonged there where it is and couldn't be seen anywhere else and shouldn't be. Know a building's charm—the kind of appeal that good comfortable clothes have, the way good shoes fit you. That's the good house. That is the quality house. That's *organic* architecture and it means according to *nature,* to the essential intrinsic character of everything. Not just trees, flowers, and

A detailed exterior view of the two-car carport of the James B. McBean residence (1958–1959) at Rochester, Minnesota. The carport, with its flat roof and upper-story band of windows, lengthens the horizontal lines of the residence. Photograph by the editor.

out-of-doors but the actual inner life of everything. In man it would be *soul.*

Only as science becomes as one with the spirit of man can a culture or a civilization live indefinitely. Science can take things apart, but only art and religion can put them together again—to live.

This really is at the base and the very center of good design by prefabrication, which means the appropriate use of an enormously effective instrument, the machine as a tool to better the conditions of all human life. Our schools have to change their concept, training our architects to [do] deeper *nature* study. We can't blame the professions or the builders or the people who buy homes. The thing I am talking about has to come into society, has to come to us by way of a greater consecration to life itself, and by a deeper and more serious feeling for beauty.

Henry Mencken said: "Americans seem to have a lust for ugliness." Look at the poles and wires devastating our landscape. See the buildings we build violated by them. Everything we have sees no consideration for beauty nor much for life. We need to join together to make environment beautiful.

We have raised the flag to the spirit of man. Until science, vision and art become as one, there is no rest or peace for humanity.

Frank Lloyd Wright surveying a photograph of the Detroit skyline at the "One Hundred Years of Michigan Architecture" Exhibition before his talk to the Michigan Society of Architects in Detroit on October 21, 1957. Photograph by William E. Bradley, courtesy of American Commercial Photo, Detroit.

11 On Production

. . . architecture is something profound. It is something in the human spirit and the human soul and it requires poetry.

Introduction

On Monday morning, October 21, 1957, Frank Lloyd Wright spoke before the Michigan Society of Architects at the Ford Auditorium in Detroit. He had already addressed that Society a number of times (see Chapters 4 and 25). On this occasion he talked about quantity production and the lack of quality in it. More than fifty-six years earlier he had delivered his famous speech "The Art and Craft of the Machine" (see Chapter 7) in which he expressed optimism for the use of the machine as an artist's tool in production. In this speech in Detroit in 1957 his optimism in regard to the machine and man's application of it to improve the quality of human life seems to be absent. Mr. Wright scolds the audience, composed primarily of architects, for allowing quantity production to rise above quality and asks: "Where are the architects? What are they doing all these years? They have been running an institute called AIA (i.e., American Institute of Architects), interested in architects, not architecture, and that is the great trouble we have now."

Text of a speech reprinted from Frank Lloyd Wright's "Frank Lloyd Wright Townhall Lecture, Ford Auditorium, Detroit, October 21, 1957," *Michigan Society of Architects Monthly Bulletin,* Vol. 31, December 1957, pp. 23, 25, 27, 29, 31–32. Used by permission of the Michigan Society of Architects.

Eight days later, on Tuesday October 29, 1957, Mr. Wright appeared with Carl Sandburg and Alistair Cooke on *Chicago Dynamic,* a WTTW-Chicago, Channel 11 television program, to discuss the dynamics of the City of Chicago and the skyscraper.[1] In this conversation and the events that followed Mr. Wright chided the steel industry for the production of steel to construct buildings "just like the old log cabin . . . a box with steel for horizontals instead of lumber."

[1] For a detailed discussion of this program, its complete text, and the events that followed it see Patrick J. Meehan (Editor), *The Master Architect: Conversations with Frank Lloyd Wright,* New York: John Wiley and Sons, 1984, pp. 254–270.

The Speech

WRIGHT: I have just come from Washington with very little voice. I came back with the golden keys to the City of Washington and a bad case of laryngitis, the Queen and I, but she does not have, so far as I know, a case of laryngitis.

If I can be of any service and do myself a little pleasure, I would like to say what I think about the motorcars that these big boys, by their own choice, are feeding the American people by the millions. If ever there was an evidence of bad design, they are the present motorcars. I think in my life I have never seen such an ignorance of the nature of anything existing carried so far. You know, the thing is a ferryboat coming down the street, gnashing its teeth at you for no good reason, and it is more a platform trying to digest four wheels than it is anything mobile. To be frank, there is nothing mobile about it but the name and the engine. The engine is good. The American engine is all right.

But I don't know where these big boys—I guess they call them hotshots—ever got the designs for these things; I suppose from some little boy in the back room who has combed the magazines and has some ideas of peculiarity and idiosyncrasy which he calls beauty. Anyhow, they don't know the difference—the big fellows—and I don't think they would care anyway.

As things are, production is controlling consumption at the present time. Is the American public going to stand for that? You know, that is pretty serious. It isn't so light a matter as it seems at the present moment. When you look at those fantails on the cars, they look as though they were designed to fight each other in the street. A car is mobile. A school of fish is mobile, isn't it? You know, you have to get in and among a school. We say a school of fish. Well, we can say a school of cars. If a fish had all their corners extruded and lighted and emphasized and then guards for the lamps and the extrusions, they would all lie dead on the surface in a very short time.

What is mobility but something to be considered when you are designing the thing and putting it into effect? I suppose the progenitors and promoters of it in ancient times would be taken out and hung or shot at sunrise, but we have no such provision. They can do with us as they damn please. Now isn't that too bad?

It reminds me of Mr. [Louis H.] Sullivan. A lady came in to see him one day and wanted a colonial house. He said, "Madam, you will take what we give you."

We are taking what they give us all right and trying to like it.

What is the answer to all this? There is no study of *nature*. There is no study of the *nature* of mobility in a car. It is the old lumber wagon still trying to digest four wheels.

Have you ever ridden in a New York taxicab? Any taxicab anywhere? Why, it has no respect for you. It has no respect for the circumstance of its existence. It is trying to imitate the boss car on the basis of one and a half passengers per trip. And why? What is this thing at the root of this?

Somebody told me once upon a time they thought it was madam. They were trying to please madam. I don't believe they are. I don't think she is that bad. She can be diddled out of her eyeteeth but I don't think she is as foolish as that car would indicate that she is.

I am interested in buildings, in the quiet beauty of environment. You drive one of these things in there and it shrieks to heaven and it gives the house the back of the hand. It has no respect for anything. So why do you put up with it? Why do you buy the things? Why do you go on from here to there with your streets becoming more and more crowded and your cars getting bigger and bigger and no consideration ever given to the *nature* of the thing?

If I have any claim to respect from my own people, it is because I have been a profound, serious student of *nature* from the time I was born until now. When my mother, who is a teacher, put me down to the kindergarten table, there is where I started to learn the *nature* of *nature*, and ever since I have been working away at it, and it is now, standing here talking to you from this standpoint of the study of *nature*, that I am saying what I am saying.

Detroit is the head of the inequity of the motorcar. I don't suppose if the big shots ever wanted to hire anybody that knew anything about designing a car that they could find one, but I am not sure that they would want to if they could, so I can't do anything about it and neither can you.

Now America is in that state and that is what worries me, this drift toward conformity, conformity, conformity, whereas we, according to Thomas Jefferson, were expected to be the bravest and the best by way of the freedom declared by the Declaration of Independence. He thought education would qualify people for the vote and that mediocrity would not be rising into high places. But see how mediocrity is rising into high places. Mediocrity you see everywhere you go.

This is the thing we have been talking about in the motorcar. What is it? Mediocrity, the lack of the higher intelligence, the lack of the vision and the perception that makes quality instead of quantity. No democracy can live on quantity. We have had all that sort of thing in the world before. We have got it in communism now. If we can't distinguish ourselves by way of a love for quality and really believing it, not only believing in it but producing in it, we are gone too.

This drift toward conformity of the American people at the present time is an ominous thing. I can't think of anything in the history of civilizations—and there have been so many that have failed—that is anything nearly so tragic as this drift in America toward conformity.

Of course, a man can't be elected to office unless he gets the biggest vote, unless he appeals to them asses. It was a printer who made an error that time by shoving the "m" over to the "e" so that it read "them asses" instead of "the masses." I don't hear very much reaction to that. Why? For the same reason.

Mass is not the only consideration of democracy. Quality is. Distinction coming from actual experience and *nature* is the only salvation the common man has, and when he becomes jealous of it and when it becomes, as it is almost now in our country, unconstitutional, then it is time to protest.

And I think that protest should rise in this nation now.

There is no hope of its rising from the educational institution, and that is where Thomas Jefferson made his mistake on that. He thought that education would qualify the voter and make him fit to be free according to his own choice.

Well, now, here we are, and that is a serious proposition for an architect because an architect builds free for a free people if he is an architect. If he is a conformist and if he also is doing the fantail on the car down the street, he is doing all those things that are now characteristic of production when it controls consumption.

If consumption were in control of production, the people would have something to say about these things. The action of the intelligentsia would be registered and change the thing, wouldn't it?

Can you change the car?

Can you change anything in the car? No. And there isn't anything probably in our country anywhere in existence that you can change or have any effect upon now because we have the wrong end to. We have production in control of consumption.

In order to do that, and keep it up, we have to go to work before long. We have to drop an atom bomb in order to keep these boys satisfied and busy in this debt system under which we live. The day of reckoning has got to come. What is the day of reckoning? You can't pass a car on the street that is owned by the man that drives it except perhaps one in fifteen.

How are you going to get a house nowadays? How do you get them? Go and look at what you get, quantity production, quality gone, no distinction, no individuality, nothing of the sort that was declared by our forefathers to be the aim and end of the Declaration of Independence.

Well, why? Now what has happened? What is it that has happened? Why has mass and the trembling [sic—trampling] of the herd in education, in production, and everything else written down the level of intelligence and character and beauty of what is produced by the American people?

I came down here to say those things in connection with architecture—with the car and the car is architecture. There isn't a thing in connection with your lives that isn't architecture. Your clothes, the way you dress, the way you live, the way you sit down and eat and what you eat and the way you do it all is architecture. The car is architecture.

Where are the architects? What are they doing all these years? They have been running an institute called AIA [American Institute of Architects], interested in architects, not in architecture, and that is the great trouble we have now.

Well, all I could do about it I have done. Now why don't you do something about it? You sit there at home in your beautiful homes, luxury, not all of you, but most of you. You see the buildings that are built on this square. They are all in a mode. They are not built from the inside out. Architecture today is still nineteenth-century. It is still back there in the days when steel was discovered and they could do nothing with it but roll it into lumber. Don't you know what they did? We had steel beams like wooden beams and we put up posts and framed the beams and made a framework of steel just the way we would make it of wood.

There came a dispensation early in the twentieth century where steel was seen to be what it was as steel and stranded and made so you could build on it this way. You couldn't pull it apart. And its great economy and beauty was its tensile strength.

Then we got the Brooklyn Bridge, among other things.

And that element in steel has been neglected to this day, and the buildings you have across the street are what? They are that old steel frame by the nineteenth-century bridge engineer. They are not from the inside out. They are merely paperhanger's facades.

The building isn't built that way, and who cares how the building is built. If you hang a front on it that looks tasty, we'll say, and novel, that's all. But it is not enough for an architect. It may be enough for the car maker but architecture is something profound. It is something in the *human spirit* and the *human soul* and it requires poetry. The poetic principle is the heart of architecture, and if you are not inspired by the poetic principle to develop from the *nature* of the thing a beauty never seen before you are not an architect. You are not a poet, in other words.

The word beauty is something we use with discretion or we are sorry in our country. We have science galore. We have all the things that science can give us. Science can take anything apart but it can't put anything together to live.

That is why we have lost our art, architecture, and religion. Do you know we have no religion of our own now? The only thing we have left to go on after the Declaration of Independence was the declaration of Jesus who said: "The kingdom of God is within *you.*"

That, of course, is where we are as a nation by way of our Declaration of Independence. We have declared the sovereignty of the individual. Now what have we done to justify the Declaration?

We should be the light of the world today. We should be the light of the world in this innate expression of human *nature* we call art, and we should have a religion of our own. We shouldn't still be [a] gambling, quarreling aggregation of sects. We might have lots of fun by differentiating a thing, but still we should have a core of faith, faith in man, faith in our own Declaration, in our own way of life, and we should find its beauty and it should be more beautiful than anything this world has ever seen.

Well, is it? I think we have made some progress. I don't want to write this whole thing off because I know how earnest and how serious many of our people—most of our people, I will say—are in finding something good, something *true,* something that goes in and buttons back, something that really comes out from within with integrity, and it is that integrity that is lacking throughout the American fabric today and lacking in the car. There is no integrity in the whole performance. There is no integrity anywhere in the housing that you see built.

Frank Lloyd Wright as he appeared in discussion on June 8, 1956, at his Taliesin III (Spring Green) birthday party which took place a year before his speech to the Michigan Society of Architects in October 1957. Photograph by C.A. Thompson, courtesy of The Capital Times, *Madison, Wisconsin.*

Where did we lose this contact with integrity when we declared the sovereignty of the individual? Where? In education? Yes. Thomas Jefferson felt that we would qualify the vote, temper this great

Frank Lloyd Wright at his Taliesin III (Spring Green) birthday party on June 8, 1956.
Photograph by C.A. Thompson, courtesy of The Capital Times, *Madison, Wisconsin.*

unwieldy, unthinking, unfeeling mass by education. Well, look at the buildings first of all in which this education is administered. Has it any deep consideration and feeling for the impression that it would make upon the mind of the young by the integrity of its beauty and character? There is only one university in the United States that has an American campus and that is Florida Southern College [see Chapter 12]. Not one of the others has one that really represents the new thought, our thought, our belief in humanity. It is all handed to us as derelicts from the past, from civilizations that are either dead or doomed to die. Education has failed us, and it has.

This car shows us up. Everything we do shows us up, shows that we have never learned the vital necessity of going into whatever the *nature* of the thing we do is.

For instance, if you were to take the *nature* of a motorcar or the *nature* of the dwelling of the man without much money, what would the *nature* of the thing—if you yielded to it, developed it—bring you? If we really got into the *nature* of humanity and arranged things accordingly at the best level we could come to, what would we have? Would we have this Realtor? Would we have these cities we live in now? Would we have anything we've got which we practice as a leftover from the past?

We got production so easy and in such volume that it could wipe out everything else except production. Now where are these things being reckoned with? It is not in architecture.

John Roebling's Brooklyn Bridge in New York was completed on May 24, 1883. Wright: ". . . he was the first prophet of steel in tension. . . ." Photograph courtesy of the New York Convention and Visitors Bureau.

You know, this is an architect's job. The architect is the form giver of his people in his time in his nation and he hasn't been present in ours. He has been educated first of all at the Beaux Arts at Paris and we have those architects.

Then we got another kind, an import from abroad when the "Bah Houses" [Bauhaus] closed up, and now we are looking around to find out what really it is that has happened to us and what it is?

How many of you have really ever given it a thought? We have got to think. We have got to wake up. We have got to make of this country a great beautiful civilization or we will be the shortest one in history because our scientific advantages have been so exaggerated; they have so far outrun our spiritual interpretations and so far gone ahead of everything that we know or feel within ourselves that we don't know where we are.

We don't know what to do with the thing. It has got us. We haven't got it. We are not designing these things anymore. We are not building our buildings anymore. We are not designing our cars or designing anything anymore. Well, why aren't we? We, a free people—we, the people with the greatest gift of riches on earth, with the greatest expanse and beauty of ground—what have we done? It isn't a fair question. I'm sorry. I apologize. But I really haven't got very much to offer on the side of an apology.

We now have reached the point where everything is publicity. Publicity is managed. Publicity, publicity, publicity; names, names, names. And when you go to school, it is not the *nature* of the thing your attention is directed to. It is again comparisons, comparisons, comparisons. Now, the inferior mind learns by comparison but how does the superior mind learn? By analysis! The superior mind doesn't ask who is this and who is that and what is this name and that name and that name. It says: "What is the *nature* of this one? What is the nature of that one?" And it goes inside and comes out with something.

That is what is missing in our educational system. It is what is missing in our nation today. It is why these silly cars roam the streets. It is why these houses we live in are so lacking in harmony, beauty, and proportion. It is why your diet even, is a shame and not only a disgrace but it is practically going to destroy the nation if we don't do better than we are doing now.

All these things should be related to something we don't seem to have, and that is the integrity that comes from knowledge of *nature* and *nature* study.

What is *nature*? We don't mean horses, cows, streams, trees, or flowers only. We mean the *nature* of you, your *nature*—and other *nature,* the *nature* of this thumb of mine here. What is the *nature* of the thumb as compared with the other fingers? It means an interior sense of whatever is!

And this architecture I have devoted my life to we call *organic.* What does *organic* mean? It doesn't mean something in a butcher shop. Necessarily, it is that, but that is the lowest form of it. *Organic* means something that has entity. Only entity can live. So when you get that into a building, you have got it into civilization, and, when you understand the *nature* of the term *organic* and the *nature* of *nature* study as I am advocating it to you now, you have the center line of the civilization that can preserve itself, that can persevere.

Now, it is so near. Why don't we have it? What is the matter with these professors? What is the matter with these dignitaries? What is the matter with these big shots with millions to spend? They don't build that kind of building. They don't build that kind of car. They don't build that kind of life by way of their religion, etc. We haven't got the religion that presents it to the people as it should.

Now, architecture presents man to man. Literature tells about man, but here the most fundamental thing we can have in our life, young as it is as a nation, is a fine architecture of our own, and that means we have got to have some knowledge, some sense of what makes this thing virtuous, which gives it to us right side up, and we know little or nothing about it.

And if you ask me, if you were to go to the AIA and try to find out from them what I am talking about, they couldn't tell you and they are architects. I have never joined them and I never will because I think if they changed the name from American Institute of Architects to the American Institute of Architecture, I would. There is a difference. I think architects today are all that is the matter with architecture!

Gerald Stanley Lee, a preacher who was very much worth listening to in his day, said that: "the only trouble with goodness in America were the people that had hold of it." Well, the only trouble with the cars today is not the people who run them, or is it? Maybe it is. I dare say that we are missing something here and that these cars wouldn't be there in the foolish fashion they are in unless it was for you. It is your responsibility and so is all the rest of this.

QUESTIONER: [Mr. Wright, I would like to know if you designed the Arizona Biltmore Hotel?]

WRIGHT: This lady wants to know if I designed the Arizona Biltmore Hotel, and I did. I spent a whole year at it. There was a young student of mine who had the commission. He never built anything but a house, so they sent for me to help out and I helped out. So that is the Arizona Biltmore.

QUESTIONER: What kind of car do you drive?

WRIGHT: Shall I confess? I do not drive an American car.

A view of the front of the Arizona Biltmore Hotel (1927) in Phoenix, Arizona, designed by Frank Lloyd Wright and Albert Chase McArthur. This structure utilizes an economic, modular, concrete-block construction system with decorative patterns. Photograph by the editor.

I am building a house [the Maximillian Hoffman residence in Rye, New York] for the distributor of the Mercedes, Mr. Hoffman, and a beautiful house it is. And he had this car made for me in Stuttgart, the one I am driving, and brought over here.

We have one other sports model, so we have the two Mercedes which today are probably as good as the Rolls Royce. Now, will that satisfy you?

QUESTIONER: [Mr. Wright, should everybody design his or her own car?]

WRIGHT: Here is a do-it-yourself girl in the audience who wants to know if she should design her own car. That is rather an embarrassing question because I wouldn't know. It would depend on how good she was.

QUESTIONER: [What are the chances of building the Mile-High Illinois Skyscraper Project?]

WRIGHT: This man wants to know what the chances are of building the Mile-High [Illinois skyscraper] building in Chicago. I think that it is inevitable. I have no doubt whatsoever that the mile-high building will be built and the sentiment of the whole region is similar to mine.

You must understand the Mile-High to understand that it isn't spoofing. It is absolutely scientific, and it is a great economical project. It will end all this foolishness of skyscrapering [sic], you see. That is what I designed it for.

Going home on the train the other day—Chicago had a Frank Lloyd Wright Day recently and there was an exhibition, and the evening of that day one of my friends was going out to the north side on a late train, you know, eleven o'clock, and there were four workmen—this just indicates the grass roots—playing cards in the back of the car. He was listening. One of them said, "Why, that thing will

Frank Lloyd Wright presenting his design for the Mile-High Illinois Skyscraper Project at Chicago's "Frank Lloyd Wright Day" testimonial dinner on October 17, 1956. Photograph courtesy of The Capital Times, *Madison, Wisconsin.*

never be built. Tain't practical." Another workman stuck his hand in his pocket and pulled out a $10 bill and laid it on the table: "There ," he said, "there is $10 to say it will be built within three years." And there were no takers. That is the way I feel about it.

QUESTIONER: What do you think of the concrete shell medium in modern architecture?

WRIGHT: Concrete reinforced with fibers of steel is the body of our modern world in any form. Concrete with steel fibers embedded in it, which is very like your own structure or the structure of a tree or any structure *nature* indulges in, is going to be the body of our modern world. This old lumbering with steel, building these frames and idealizing a facade on the frame and hanging wallpaper on it isn't going to last. That is not twentieth-century architecture; that is the old nineteenth-century bridge engineer's architecture. And, as for me, to hell with it!

QUESTIONER: It has been said that music is architecture in a fluid state.

WRIGHT: Well, now, ladies and gentlemen, it is perfectly *true* that music and architecture flower from the same stem. The composer has his score. The architect has his modular unit system on which he works, and the minds are very similar, practically, the same. My father was a musician and a preacher. He taught me to see a great symphony as an edifice, an edifice of sound, you see. So when I listen to Beethoven, who is the greatest architect who ever lived, I never fail to see buildings. He was building all the time. He was a great, competent builder and so was a great composer also. So never miss the idea that architecture and music belong together. They are practically one.

QUESTIONER: What do you think about the interplanetary activity?

WRIGHT: It amuses me somewhat, and I think it is of no very great significance except to win a race or something or other. I don't think that is the matter with us or what we need or that it is going to do anything for us. I think the planetary race that we

Chicago's Mayor Richard J. Daley (left), *Madison's (Wisconsin) Mayor Ivan Nestingen* (right), *and Frank Lloyd Wright at Chicago's "Frank Lloyd Wright Day" testimonial dinner on October 17, 1956. Photograph by C.A. Thompson, courtesy of* The Capital Times, *Madison, Wisconsin.*

should run is one under our vest, one inside our own hearts and minds. And all this scientific competition, what does it amount to anyhow? Why such an excitement over it?

Suppose we go to the moon? What is the moon but a carcass, and what is all this thing to do for us in the end except to maybe make it foolish to go to war again, in which case it is very well done. But I doubt if it will accomplish that.

We are not in need of more science. We are not in need of more demonstrations of the ability of science. What we need now is some expression of the human heart, of human sympathies, of the human mind, of the poetic principles. The poetic principle is dying among us. If we let that die, we don't live, and that is *true*.

QUESTIONER: Who is more guilty, the people who buy these cars or the people who make them?

WRIGHT: That is a pertinent question. And the same with the houses. If the people aren't there, if they don't demand, if there isn't something in their own souls and hearts that says: we want something better and something right, you won't get it. And I don't think you can blame the big boys for putting it over on you. They will put it over on anybody.

What are they interested in, these big fellows? Promoting anything spiritual? Promoting anything that comes from the interior of the human soul?

No. They want the biggest and if it takes the best to get it they will give you the best. If they can get it cheap, they will get it cheap. They are not great crusaders for the soul of humanity, believe me. They may say they are. They may think they are. They will have to guess again one of these days and it is up to you to say what you will have and what you won't have.

The other day I was talking about a terrible housing project in the region of Madison. It was a disgrace. I said so. And a woman got up and said, "But Mr. Wright, that's all we can buy." And I said, "Madam, but you bought it, didn't you? You are living in it, aren't you?" She said: "Yes." Well, is that excuse enough? She could have bought a tent. She could have gone out with her babies and lived in a tent and said: "I will not buy one of those stinking things!"

That is the kind of spirit we need in America and that is the Declaration of Independence. That is the sovereignty of the individual. It isn't being herded. It isn't trembling in masses in universities and getting a lick and a promise of something in the future, being conditioned and sent home fooled, cheated, even worse than before.

QUESTIONER: Will you speak about your Baghdad project?

WRIGHT: Ladies and gentlemen, I don't suppose I should talk about my clients much, but the Middle East, Baghdad, has always been a romance to me, "The Thousand and One Nights," you know and Haroun el Rashid and all that.

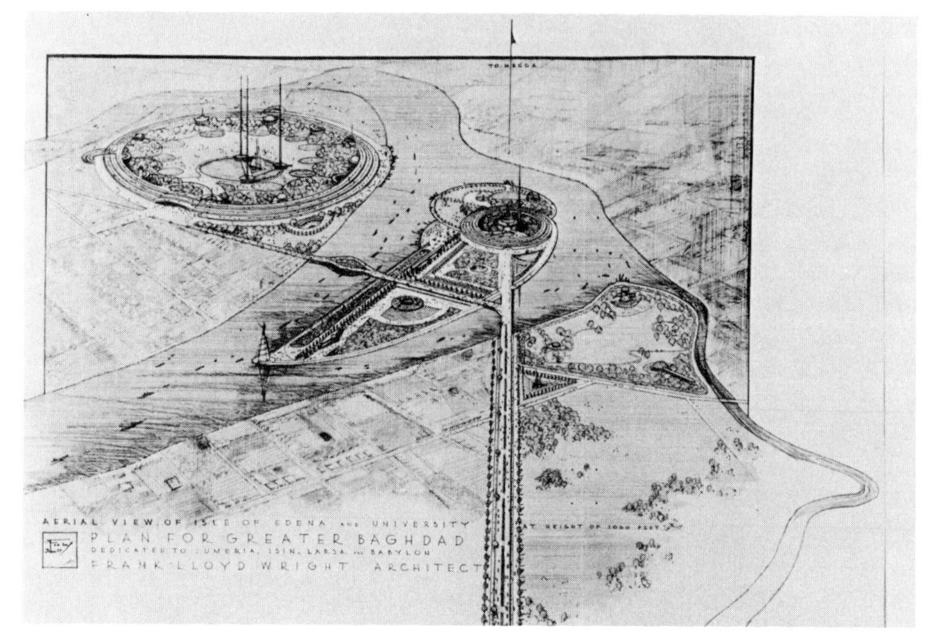

An aerial perspective rendering of Frank Lloyd Wright's Plan for Greater Baghdad Project (1957) in Baghdad, Iraq. His proposed Baghdad Opera House and Gardens appear at the upper right, his Baghdad University Complex and Gardens at the upper left, and the statue to the left of center is his design for the monument to Haron al-Rashid. Drawing from the May 1958 issue of Architectural Forum. *Drawing used by permission of Billboard Publications, Inc., 1515 Broadway, New York, New York 10036.*

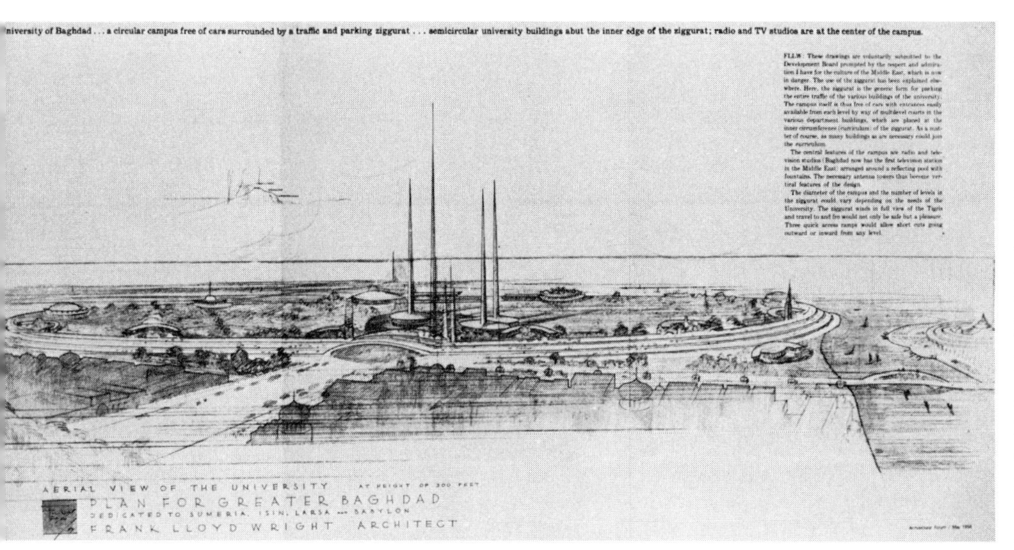

An aerial perspective rendering of the Baghdad University Complex and Gardens Project (1957), Baghdad, Iraq. The ziggurat form is an automobile ramp and parking lot used to help free the campus of the automobile. Radio and television studios are at the center of the campus and are arranged around a reflecting pool. The antennae towers are strong vertical features of the university complex design. Drawing from the May 1958 issue of Architectural Forum. *Drawing used by permission of Billboard Publications, Inc., 1515 Broadway, New York, New York 10036.*

So when it came to me to build the opera house for Baghdad, I was delighted, and I went over there enthusiastically and I have done an opera house which some day you will see. It is the Arabian Nights and it is Aladdin with his wonderful lamp and it is all that for Baghdad.

But, in general, I saw the little King [Faisal] when we were coming down [to] an island in the Tigris. It was about a mile and a half long and about three-quarters of a mile wide, and there was not a thing on it, and it was in the middle of the river. So I wondered. So I asked the Development Board what about it, and they said, "Well, we can't do anything about that, Mr. Wright, nothing at all. It belongs to the Royal Household."

Next day I was to meet the King, so I took with me a little sketch that I made showing what I wanted to do for Baghdad if I could have that little island to work on, and I told the little King about it. I say little—he is twenty-two years old now and he is going to be married next year. So he listened intelligently and appreciatively, and he knew what I was talking about. And when I finished, he stood up, pleasantly looked me in the face, put his hand on where I had been talking about and he said: "Mr. Wright, the island is yours."

Well, I was converted to monarchy right there. You know in a democracy what it would have taken to get that island. It would have taken fifteen years or more and "mine and yours" and "where do you come in" and "what do I get?" and everything else. So we have that island now and we are working out on it a project, a nine-year project.

And the Minister of the Development Board just left me. He was delighted with what I have done. I am reporting on the job. And you will see probably before very long what can be done with an ancient civilization that was the basis of all future civilization. You know, civilization was invented in Iraq. The Samarian civilization was the first and the idea of a civilization occurred there. The Garden of Eden is only sixty miles away, and the Tower of Babylon is only about forty miles away. So there is Mesopotamia, the very center of all that has happened since.

It is interesting to go back to a civilization and to the source of civilization with something as beautiful and strong in spirit as anything they ever had. That is what I am trying to do.

So, good-bye.

PART FOUR

In the Cause of Improving the Human Condition

Dr. Ludd M. Spivey (President of Florida Southern College from 1925 to 1957) and Frank Lloyd Wright inspect the red-square logo atop Mr. Wright's birthday cake at his birthday party on June 8, 1954, at Taliesin III near Spring Green, Wisconsin. Photograph by C.A. Thompson, courtesy of The Capital Times, *Madison, Wisconsin.*

12 An Adventure in the Realm of the Human Spirit

. . . look upon these buildings . . . here as engaging in an adventure. The greatest, most important of all adventures: an adventure in the realm of the human spirit, searching for a greater harmony, a greater truth of being, and with it comes, God knows, a more blessed richer life.

Introduction

The West Campus of Florida Southern College, which occupies about one hundred acres of a former orange grove overlooking Lake Hollingsworth in Lakeland, Florida, was designed by Frank Lloyd Wright over a twenty-year period, beginning in 1938. The campus, which contains ten designs by Mr. Wright, represents the world's largest single-built complex of his work. The idea of building the campus came in 1936 from Dr. Ludd M. Spivey, president of the college from 1925 to 1957.

Dr. Spivey made the following comments in 1952 to the editors of the *Architectural Forum* on the architecture of Florida Southern College:

Reprinted with editorial corrections from Frank Lloyd Wright's "An Adventure in the Human Spirit," *Motive*, Vol. XI, November 1950, pp. 30–31, and from the publication titled *An Address by Frank Lloyd Wright: In Connection With Founders Week* (Lakeland, Florida: Florida Southern College), 1950, pp. 1–5. Reprinted by permission of Florida Southern College.

When the college decided to use Mr. Wright's architecture, it didn't realize it was to benefit from a by-product of his buildings—student enrollment. This has long been a major problem with small private colleges such as ours, but the Frank Lloyd Wright architecture has made this college known all over America and much of the world. It has largely solved our enrollment problems . . . .

It is also interesting that college presidents from all over the country are coming to the campus in increasing numbers to see what the Frank Lloyd Wright buildings do to and for education.

I have seen a new spirit and a new attitude in the student body and the faculty since the coming of the Frank Lloyd Wright architecture. It took a little time for the buildings to make an impact but they finally did, and one on the inside of the college finds a new stirring of minds all over the campus.[1]

In 1952 also Mr. Wright made the following remarks to the editors of *Architectural Forum* in regard to his designs for Florida Southern College:

About fifteen years ago this spring [i.e., 1952], when Dr. Ludd M. Spivey, the presidential good-genius of Florida Southern College, flew north to Taliesin, he came with the express and avowed purpose of giving the United States at least one example of a college wherein modern life was to have the advantages of modern science and art in actual building construction. He said he wanted me as much for my philosophy as for my architecture. I assured him they were inseparable.

And ever since, owing to Dr. Spivey's unremitting efforts, this collection of college buildings has been in a continuous state of growth. Their outdoor-garden character is intended to be an expression of Florida at its floral best.

Study these buildings from the inside out if you would know something about the kind of building we call organic architecture . . . .

So, as for these buildings in which a *true* portion of America moves, studies, works and has its being, if you would honestly try to understand these Florida Southern College buildings and would really know what they are all about (whether you like them or not), something important to our country's future as a democratic nation will transpire. Because not only do buildings last long but in these buildings here and now you may see something of your own tomorrow that is yours today. Yes—and maybe the day after the day after that.

Because a preceptor in education like Dr. Ludd M. Spivey took thoughtful measure of his time and flew to Taliesin, you will see in these buildings now standing at Florida Southern College the sentiment of a *true* educational saga along the cultural lines of an indigenous architecture for our own country.[2]

Mr. Wright designed at least eleven structures for Florida Southern College between 1938 and 1958. These, of course, did not include the Florida Southern

---

[1] Extracted from "Florida Southern College Revisited for Glimpses of the Administration Group in Wright's Organic Campus," *Architectural Forum*, Vol. XCVII, No. 3, September 1952, p. 125.

[2] *Ibid*, p. 120.

An aerial view of the Florida Southern College Campus (1938–1958), designed by Frank Lloyd Wright at Lakeland, Florida. Lake Hollingsworth can be seen at the right. Photograph by Brad Beck, courtesy of the Florida Southern College.

College Development Plan of 1938 for an ultimate total of sixteen buildings on campus. Mr. Wright's ten constructed designs were the Annie Merner Pfeiffer Chapel (1938), the Carter, Wallbridge, Hawkins Seminar Buildings (now one building—1940), the T.R. Roux Library (now Buckner Building—1941), the Ordway Industrial Arts Building (1942), the Emile E. Watson Administration Building (1945), the covered walkways or esplanades that connect many of the college facilities (1946), the Science and Cosmography Building (Polk Science Building—1953), and the William H. Danforth Chapel (Minor Chapel—1954). He also designed a music building, never constructed. In 1939 Mr. Wright designed a house for Dr. Spivey for a site at Fort Lauderdale, Florida, but it was never built.

This chapter presents the text of Mr. Wright's address at Florida Southern College on Friday, March 3, 1950, in connection with the College's "Founders Week." It was a short talk, only about fifteen minutes, that covered his philosophy of architecture—organic architecture—as "an adventure in the realm of the human spirit, searching for a greater harmony, a greater *truth* in being . . . ." Four months later Mr. Wright was in England for the presentation of prizes to the students of architecture at London's Architectural Association (see Chapter 19). Chapter 13 contains the text of another speech delivered by Mr. Wright at Florida Southern College on October 25, 1951.

The Speech

WRIGHT: Ladies and gentlemen, we are gathered here together on this most auspicious occasion to do honor to one whom it is a delight to honor, the president of your college—a hard worker, and believe me, a wise one in the vineyard of the Lord.

Incidentally, we are to honor architecture and I think it's time we make some gesture, at least, in that direction because we're beginning to learn that the word of God is not something in books—we are beginning to learn that the highest and finest kind of morality is beauty and that there is no culture for a democracy, no culture for America until it has one of its own!

You can't live your entire life on borrowed ideas, borrowed knowledge, a borrowed culture. We must evolve something from within ourselves. And what you see in the good doctor's [Dr. Ludd Spivey] effort here, and in the aid that I've given him, is really a sincere effort to realize this thing you call "the word of God" from within ourselves—for ourselves—and, of course, building is the natural way to do it.

I don't see how we can consider ourselves as civilized, cultured people if we live ignorant of the *nature* of our environment; if we do not understand what we do to make it. Where the buildings that we live in are false, where they do not represent *truth* and beauty in any sense, where they are merely stupid or merely copying something that's not understood. Because, believe me, when you understand a thing you will not copy it. A copycat is a copycat because he does not understand. Now, understanding is love. If you don't understand, you don't love!

And, out of an understanding of the beauties of *nature,* using the word *Nature* with a capital "N" in its *true* sense, not just out-of-doors but the *nature* of everything—of a book, of this hand, of anything at all—*nature* in that sense studied. And you'll find there the greatest and highest form of ethics. Now, of course, ethics, morality perhaps, at the present time has very little in common with ethics. Morality is seldom ethical—but beauty is ethics—a high and fine kind of ethics and so is good architecture.

And, that's my message to you here today—that these little buildings on this campus are not extraneous to the thought of God, to the thought of good, to this thing you call religion.

We need a new religion in this nation—or, at least, not a new one—we need one, and we're going to get it by practicing this thing that we call the love of beauty. Now we don't find it—can't find it—outside ourselves. We've got to find it coming out from within ourselves to an outside that we've learned to understand as harmonious and *true* and beautiful, *true* to the *nature* of materials, *true* to the methods

The Carter, Walbridge, Hawkins Seminar Buildings (1940—now one building) at Florida Southern College in Lakeland, Florida. Photograph by Brad Beck, courtesy of the Florida Southern College.

of our day, *true* to the life of our time, *true* to the best of our sense of ourselves.

Now, you know most of us have never even met ourselves. We can meet almost everybody else on, perhaps, their own terms or our own terms, but mighty few of us have ever had a good look at ourselves.

Now, the type of architecture that you see standing around you can't mean much to you until you've had a good look at yourselves. Until you have tried to find within yourself what these buildings quite naturally represent—the laws of harmony, of construction, of rhythm, of all that is poetic and *true* to [the] best in human *nature.*

Now, that's the new architecture! That's what we're learning to call *organic* architecture today. And it's quite proper that we should confess to you that the world has seen very little of it as yet—even when the time when architecture was greatest and highest and most important to human life—very little of it. It's like a little green shoot in a concrete pavement trying to take root, trying to *be,* and depending upon people who are also trying to be for its existence.

I don't believe you can build beautiful buildings, that an edifice can rise, except as it comes from within a worthy source and that source is, inevitably, the human soul, the human heart.

In all America today, especially in our educational institutions, you won't find that architecture coming from within the soul of man. You won't find an architecture with a soul, not one with a heart! In other words, you won't find a genuine expression of that thing that we talk about so glibly and think that we love to think that we have—which is democracy.

Democracy needs a new gentleman—a new definition of a "gentleman." It needs a new alignment of ethics and it can get it by way of architecture because *organic* architecture has in it the principles; it is the center line of this thing which we would love to feel we had, were we a democracy.

Now, democracy ceases to talk or feel much concerning the life of the common man. As a matter of fact, is there a common man? Have you ever met one? And as for a common woman? No. There is you—there is me and there's the other

An exterior view of the circular T.R. Roux Library (1941—now the Buckner Building) at Florida Southern College in Lakeland, Florida. Photograph courtesy of the Division of Archives, History and Records Management of the Florida Department of State.

An interior view of the T.R. Roux Library at Florida Southern College. Photograph by Brad Beck, courtesy of the Florida Southern College.

An exterior view of the Ordway Industrial Arts Building (1942) at Florida Southern College. Photograph by the editor.

An interior view of the Ordway Industrial Arts Building at Florida Southern College. Photograph by the editor.

fellow, but I believe there is no common man, nor do I believe there is what we call a "public" either.

And, I think we've wasted in all our efforts a great deal on this common man and a great deal on what we call the public and we've not been sufficiently meticulous concerning this fellow that is ourselves. We haven't been willing to take a good look at ourselves, so how can we have an architecture that grows from within the individual for the individual as a creative act.

You see the cosmic ray hasn't yet reached us! The creative ray we don't yet know in our country, and until we do get in touch with it, until we do learn to understand its significance as we see it around us—by way of *nature* study, by way of getting inside, first ourselves and then what's around us—we aren't going to have a *culture,* we're not going to have an architecture—and without an architecture there is no culture.

How can you have a culture living in squalid, untrue, blind conditions? You can't. So here, on this little campus, your Dr. Spivey has planted a little green shoot in the realm of the spirit; something that is *true* to itself, something that is *true* to mankind, something that insists upon integrity throughout. It's not sufficient that it should stand up.

The Emile E. Watson Administration Building (1945) viewed from the pool area at Florida Southern College in Lakeland, Florida. Photograph by the editor.

The Science and Cosmography Building (1953—now the Polk Science Building) at Florida Southern College. Photograph by Brad Beck, courtesy of the Florida Southern College.

The Annie Merner Pfeiffer Chapel (left, *1938) and the William H. Danforth "Minor" Chapel* (right, *1954) at Florida Southern College. Photograph by Randolph C. Henning, Architect, used by permission.*

The Annie Merner Pfeiffer Chapel at Florida Southern College. Photograph by Randolph C. Henning, Architect, used by permission.

Anybody can put two sticks together and make a pile of building material that will stand up. But that which will stand there in accord with the *nature* of the circumstances which put it there and with all a grace of rhythm, a *truth* such as you see in your trees, fruits, and flowers—that is *organic* architecture!

And that is what this campus is going to proclaim more and more to those who want to understand it. I think it will be regarded in years to come as a missionary, as a thought along the line of a culture which we narrowly missed. We have missed it to date. It is not in our great universities; it is not in our great churches; it is something that was lost long ago—at least 500 years ago. And it is now being brought again to the front—for a free people and a free nation, and I don't see any smile on your faces when I make those two references. Are we a free people? Is this a free country? Can it be said to be so when it can't build anything for itself of its own? I don't think so. If we are free and we haven't built—well then there's something very serious in the way of an indictment that can be brought against us—isn't there?

Is it, perhaps, that we are all asleep—that we have never waked up to these things that we declare and that these things we profess and boast to profess? Have we never really had a good look at ourselves as a free people?

We had a foolish president not so long ago who boasted of the four freedoms. Well, the very boast is in itself a confession that we are not free. When you begin to count the freedoms on the fingers of your hand—one, two, three, four, you're merely confessing that you are not free! And that went around the world and no one challenged it. Well, so it is we are not free and we have no free architecture and we have no culture of our own.

And, you can go into the homes of this land from coast to coast—from border to border—and find

An interior view of the Annie Merner Pfeiffer Chapel at Florida Southern College shows the large pipe organ and balcony seating. Photograph by Brad Beck, courtesy of the Florida Southern College.

An Interior view of the Annie Merner Pfeiffer Chapel at Florida Southern College. The chapel seats approximately 1000 persons on two levels. The pulpit area (lower left) is beneath the choir loft (upper left) which is screened by an ornate concrete lattice. Photograph by Brad Beck, courtesy of the Florida Southern College.

The William H. Danforth "Minor" Chapel (1954) at Florida Southern College in Lakeland, Florida. Photograph by Brad Beck, courtesy of the Florida Southern College.

An interior view of the pulpit area of the William H. Danforth "Minor" Chapel at Florida Southern College illustrates its unique concrete-block construction. Photograph by Brad Beck, courtesy of the Florida Southern College.

so little manifestation of the *truth* of our own being—outside of the shops, outside of buying and selling, outside of eating and sleeping—that it's just pitiful.

Now, look upon these buildings and look upon this little college and look upon the wise doctor [Dr. Ludd Spivey] here as engaging in an adventure. The greatest, most important of all adventures—*an adventure in the realm of the human spirit,* searching for a greater harmony, a greater *truth* of being, and with it comes, God knows, a more blessed richer life.

Thank you.

AUDIENCE: (loud applause)

Frank Lloyd Wright's large red-square marker at Florida Southern College in Lakeland, Florida, bears the statement: "I believe truth *to be our organic divinity." Photograph by the editor.*

13 Quality and the Vision of the Superior Human Building

A prophet said: "Where there is no vision the people perish." I say: Where there is no vision there are no people.

Introduction

The following short speech was delivered by Frank Lloyd Wright at a service held in the Wright-designed Annie Merner Pfeiffer Chapel at Florida Southern College at 10 A.M., Thursday, October 25, 1951. Three weeks earlier Mr. Wright spoke before the Henry George School of Social Science in Chicago on the topic of arts and industry in a democratic economy [see Chapter 24]. This speech is short but to the point in that it addresses the need for a "spiritual quality" in architecture before *true* architecture can exist and has a religious aura that is manifest in the beautiful chapel in which it was delivered. Mr. Wright had always considered himself a deeply religious person, not believing necessarily in organized religion, but *truly* believing in God and God as na-

Reprinted with editing from Frank Lloyd Wright's "Quality, Not Quantity, Seen as Big Need by Mr. Wright," *The Southern* (Florida Southern College), Vol. 65, No. 7, November 23, 1951, p. 2. Reprinted by permission of Florida Southern College.

One of the three interior stairwells in the Annunciation Greek Orthodox Church at Wauwatosa, accented by an ornamental light spire. Photograph by the editor.

An exterior view of the rostrum or auditorium of the Unitarian Church (1947) at Shorewood Hills, Wisconsin. The prow or apex pointing north is a steeple. Photograph by the editor.

ture—nature was Mr. Wright's church. For this reason and its underlying belief Mr. Wright was able to design in a highly spiritual manner for many organized religions, evidenced by his prolific religious architecture. Once Mr. Wright commented: "If I belonged to any one church, they couldn't ask me to build a church for them. But because my church is elemental, fundamental, I can build for anybody a church."[1]

Mr. Wright designed or participated in the design of more than thirty religious-related buildings from 1887 to 1959, of which several were constructed after his death. The religious projects that were built to his specifications are Unity Chapel (with which he was intimately involved as an employee of Joseph Lyman Silsbee, architect), Helena, Wisconsin (near Spring Green), 1887, the Abraham Lincoln Center for the Reverend Mr. Jenkin Lloyd Jones (Mr. Wright's maternal uncle), Chicago, 1903, Unity Church, Oak Park, Illinois, 1905, the W.H. Pettit Mortuary Chapel, Belvedere, Illinois, 1906, the Annie Merner Pfeiffer Chapel at Florida Southern College, Lakeland, Florida, 1938, Kansas City Community Christian Church, Kansas City, Missouri, 1940, the Unitarian Church, Madison, Wisconsin, 1947, the Beth Sholom Synagogue, Elkins Park,

[1] See Patrick J. Meehan (Editor), *The Master Architect: Conversations with Frank Lloyd Wright,* New York: John Wiley and Sons, 1984, pp. 292 and 307.

An interior view of the rostrum or auditorium of the Unitarian Church (1947) at Shorewood Hills, Wisconsin. The prow or apex of the building provides a backdrop for the pulpit, which is made of stone with an oak cap. The angled roof and ceiling is supported by a series of transverse trusses that reaches from wall to wall; the largest span measures about sixty feet. Photograph by the editor.

Pennsylvania, 1954, the William H. Danforth "Minor" Chapel, Florida Southern College, Lakeland, Florida, 1954, the Annunciation Greek Orthodox Church, Wauwatosa, Wisconsin, 1956, the Pilgrim Congregational Church, Redding, California, 1958, and the First Christian Church and Bell Tower, Phoenix, Arizona, 1971 and 1978, respectively.

Mr. Wright's religious designs for buildings that have not been constructed are the Unitarian Chapel (also a Silsbee project), Sioux City, Iowa, 1887, the All Souls Building Project, Chicago, 1897, the Abraham Lincoln Center Project, Chicago, 1901 (this design differed from that of the building ultimately constructed), the Christian Catholic Church Project, Zion, Illinois, 1911, the Steel Cathedral for William Norman Guthrie Project, New York, 1926, the Memorial Chapel Project for an unknown location, 1930, the "Memorial to the Soil" Chapel Project for southern Wisconsin, 1937, the Methodist Church Project, Spring Green, Wisconsin, 1940, the Southwest Christian Seminary University Project, Phoenix, Arizona, 1951 (portions of this project were constructed as the First Christian Church, 1971, and Bell Tower, 1978, at Phoenix), the "Rhododendron" Chapel Project for Edgar Kaufmann near Bear Run (Connellsville), Pennsylvania, 1953, the Christian Science Reading Room Project, Riverside, Illinois, 1954, the Christian Science Church Project, Bolinas (Marin County), California, 1955, the First Christian Church Master Plan Project, Phoenix, Arizona, 1957, the Wedding Chapel for the Claremont Hotel Project, Berkeley, California, 1957, the

An exterior view of the Beth Sholom Synagogue (1954) at Elkins Park, Pennsylvania, a tripod form constructed of steel beams, faced with stamped aluminum, and rising to an apex one-hundred feet above the floor. The tripod carries a double wall of translucent panels of white corrugated wired glass outside and cream white corrugated plastic inside, with a five-inch air space between. The massing of the building is reminiscent of Mt. Sinai. Photograph by Robert S. McGonigal.

Detail of the exterior roof ornament of the Beth Sholom Synagogue. Shown here are two of the protruding Menorahs, the Seven Branched Candles of Light, which outline the pinnacle of the Synagogue. In the ancient Tabernacle the Menorah was a central symbol and at the Beth Sholom the Menorahs lift their arms as in prayer. Photograph by Robert S. McGonigal.

Trinity Chapel Project for the University of Oklahoma, Norman, 1958, the Unity Chapel Project for Taliesin Valley, Spring Green, Wisconsin, 1958, the Christian Science Church Project, Chicago, 1959, and the Greek Orthodox Church Project, San Francisco, 1959.

The Speech

WRIGHT: I want to congratulate you [Florida Southern College Choir] in the balcony. The acoustics are good. As Dr. Spivey [Dr. Ludd M. Spivey, president of Florida Southern College] said, the architecture speaks for itself, so I don't see why I should talk. How about it? This will be something like painting the lily or gilding the gold. When I stand here in my own work, is it necessary for me to say much?

I suppose you all want to know how to build a building? Want a prescription for a house? All for the price of one admission? You seldom get it because it can't be had that way. The common things that you pick up in the street are easy to come by. That is why they are common. A superior thing is difficult to get. We are finding it in this nation of ours in building a superior building. What do you have to have? A superior human being. A builder to build. That means difficulty. All kinds of things come along to disappoint you. After awhile, though, it will all come out, a thing of beauty.

This chapel [Annie Merner Pfeiffer Chapel] now is filled with flowers. Human beings in our buildings. It looks like buildings coming out of the people, people coming out of the buildings. That's new in the architectural world. For 500 years buildings have tended to make people feel inferior. Modify the human being. Buildings not built on the human scale. Buildings for human people that give joy to the occupants, simplicity in their own right.

Dr. Ludd M. Spivey, President of Florida Southern College, and Frank Lloyd Wright at the "Frank Lloyd Wright Day" testimonial dinner in Chicago on October 17, 1956. Dr. Spivey was the master of ceremonies on this occasion. Photograph by Carmie A. Thompson, courtesy of The Capital Times, *Madison, Wisconsin.*

Want me to give you the secret of architecture? Architecture has a language. It can't be put into words. People talk more because they found out they could do it more than anything else. Now that

The Byzantine-like symbol of the Annunciation Greek Orthodox Church (1956) at Wauwatosa, Wisconsin. The general theme of the Church design can be seen at its site in this monumental Greek cross, with its circular components, which signifies that the Church, like a circle, is endless. Photograph by the editor.

they found out they could talk they take it out on talking. They talk everything to death, talk the arm off of everybody. If I had to translate these buildings into talk and persuade you to take them, I would have a hard time because other people talk, too.

All you have to do is have a feeling about something in your mind. You have to learn it—it's a matter of the heart—a feeling that comes out as a matter of knowledge—then you can do something. When you started, you were mostly accidents. Personality is something you inherit, but by working on it and with help from your superiors you will perceive something which is you. You will become capable of seeing yourself as others see you.

I have always thought that going to school meant going to find out about ourselves—a technique which would enable that inner being to begin something fine—the architecture or spirit—that which we call the soul. That has to take place before you can recognize a building when you see it. Shakespeare said: "You can't make a silk purse out of a sow's ear." Architecture is subjective. The known architectural things in the world are subjective also. People are rare who can interpret and understand a building. Architecture is a blind spot in our nation. You may have a smattering of things but you will be left ignorant about architecture. The good doctor [Dr. Ludd M. Spivey] has fixed this for you. At least he has placed you in a position so that you can find out about it.

I would hate to start in now and have to ask you what it means to you. Word has come to me that some people have wept in here [the Annie Merner Pfeiffer Chapel]. Is there nothing in these buildings which sings to you or makes a note of spiritual quality which can't be defined? Something deep inside of you which needs response? That's what we call appreciation. If we had appreciation and knew what architecture really means, we would have architecture.

No one can refer to the buildings of colleges today as architecture. They are hangovers—no longer indicative of our times. That's why we are high and dry today. We must have a good feeling. We will talk of atmosphere. Here at Florida Southern College you will be educated in an atmosphere of *truth.* And if you can only see it, you have a better chance of growing into something fine spiritually as you are being educated in an atmosphere of *truth.* And if you can only see it, you have a better chance of growing into something fine spiritually as you are being educated in a good atmosphere.

Some would inquire: What is [this] thing to us? What gives me this feeling? What exactly has happened in this field of architecture? Appreciation of architecture as such is an awakening. Almost everyone is asleep who doesn't have it. Some people never cease talking and come out of these buildings never having said anything. Three-fifths of the boys and girls keep on talking and never see

A nocturnal exterior view of the Annunciation Greek Orthodox Church at Wauwatosa. The thin-shell concrete dome is 104 feet in diameter and rises to a height of forty-five feet in the center. The dome rests on more than 700,000 structural devices similar to ball bearings, and 325 hollow glass spheres encircle the lower part of the dome. The base of the dome forms the Greek cross in plan view on which the dome rests. Photograph by the editor.

*An interior view of the Annunciation Greek Orthodox Church at Wauwatosa shows the pulpit (*left*), iconostasion or icon screen, and the sanctuary. The iconostasion is the partition that separates the sanctuary (or Holy of Holies) from the nave and on which are placed icons that make more vivid to the faithful our Lord and His Life on earth and the role of the Saints. The icons are not intended to be realistic paintings but rather symbolic interpretations of the great spiritual values of Christianity. Photograph by the editor.*

First Christian Church Belltower (designed 1951, constructed 1978), Phoenix, Arizona. The tower is free-standing and constructed of native desert stone masonry with ornamental metal to match the construction materials used for the church building. Photograph by the editor.

An exterior view of the First Christian Church (designed 1951, constructed 1971–1972) at Phoenix, Arizona. The church lantern and stained-glass spire rise to a height of eighty-eight feet. Photograph by the editor.

An exterior view from one of two arbor areas of the First Christian Church at Phoenix, Arizona. The pattern of the structure of the building is reflected in the shadow pattern created by the lattice work. Photograph by the editor.

An interior view from the sanctuary, looking toward the chancel, pulpit, and baptistry of the First Christian Church at Phoenix, Arizona. The baptistry stands in front of the great stained-glass window titled "Regenesis," which rises symbolically from the baptistry and whose cross emerges from the traditional colors for sin, hate, and anger to the brown representing the earth. Photograph by the editor.

anything here. It is a difficult thing to see. You look and you get a certain impression but you look and don't see. In other words, you lack what is called vision. How to develop vision? A prophet said, "Where there is no vision the people perish." I say: Where there is no vision there are no people.

In other words, there is no life, no quality. What we need is quality—quality, not quantity. God, we have that running over. Where you can see quality, you can feel education is on speaking terms with culture. Students here will go out with a better sense of beauty than those at Harvard and Yale and other Gothic-designed colleges but it should be so, by all that's holy. The atmosphere in which you live and move and have your being; it should make quality. Quality is a matter of culture. Primarily, we start with a good animal, by way of environment, the most vital of all means by which we lift this animal to the spiritual. That is why I am so anxious to have better buildings built. I would not be a talker. So isn't this enough?

Mr. and Mrs. Frank Lloyd Wright, circa 1956. Photograph by Carmie A. Thompson, courtesy of The Capital Times, *Madison, Wisconsin.*

14 Building for the Sick

What is the nature of the hospital? First of all, it's a human problem. Disease is a human misfortune. . . . Out of your sense of humanity . . . as architects should come some great human beneficence for the desperate, for the ailing and the sick. . . . A hospital should be a blessing where sickness would seldom be seen, a place where you would never feel that a curse had descended upon your kind.

Introduction

The Southern Conference on Hospital Planning was held in Biloxi, Mississippi, from May 19 to 21, 1949, under the sponsorship of state chapters of the American Institute of Architects (AIA) from Alabama, Arkansas, Florida, Georgia, Louisiana, Mississippi, North Carolina, South Carolina, Tennessee, Virginia, and West Virginia. The purpose of the conference was to bring together architects

Text of a talk used by permission of WLOX-AM Radio, Biloxi, Mississippi, from a radio broadcast, dated May 20, 1949. The text of this talk was also published as part of the *Proceedings of the Southern Conference on Hospital Planning, Hotel Buena Vista, Biloxi, Mississippi* (Montgomery, Alabama: Southern Conference on Hospital Planning, February 22, 1950, pp. 105–114.).

in the southern states who were concerned with hospital design for a discussion of hospital-design fundamentals with certain persons in the hospital field.

Frank Lloyd Wright spoke as guest of honor to more than 300 registrants of the conference at the Buena Vista Hotel on Friday evening, May 20. Two months before his speech at this conference he addressed the American Institute of Architects in Houston, Texas, as the recipient of the AIA Gold Medal for 1948 (see Chapter 16). His talk in Biloxi was broadcast over the local radio station of WLOX-AM and published later as part of the *Proceedings of the Southern Conference on Hospital Planning. Hotel Buena Vista, Biloxi, Mississippi* (Montgomery, Alabama: Southern Conference on Hospital Planning, February 22, 1950, pp. 105–114). In addition, recordings of Mr. Wright's talk were made available to the general public by the sponsors of the conference. The text of the complete talk is contained in this chapter.

In 1948 Mr. Wright was interviewed by the editors of *Modern Hospital* for his thoughts on hospital design:

> *More people die of fright than for any other reason [in hospitals]. . . . Hospital patients should never be imbued with the idea that they are sick. . . . Health should be constantly before their eyes, and even injected into their dreams. . . . The psychology of the sick man has not been studied sufficiently by doctors or builders of hospitals. The psyche in which he finds himself should be attuned to health. In short, the emphasis in the new hospital should be on normality, not on the paraphernalia of abnormality. Death's head shows at once in the present hospital; grins there incessantly at any and every unfortunate victim. As a result, more people die of the hospital than of the illness they bring to it! Why is a hospital not as humane in practical, esthetic effect as it is humane in purpose?*[1]

The interview in this very popular magazine may have led indirectly to his invitation to speak in Biloxi in the following year.

Mr. Wright's speech was followed by an informal question-and-answer session, during both of which he not only talked about the architect's responsibility to design for the sick but also about the South, democracy, nature, organic architecture, *truth,* culture, and his own "Lieber Meister" Louis H. Sullivan, architect. He was well received by the audience and spoke at length throughout the evening. Mrs. Frank Lloyd Wright was at his side during the speech and question period.

On Saturday, May 21, 1949, the local Biloxi newspaper, *The Daily Herald,* reported the following:

> *Today the conference . . . will conclude with the dedication of a memorial to Louis Sullivan, late famed architect and one of the teachers of Frank Lloyd Wright. St. John's Church has been chosen as the church building where the memorial tablet to Sullivan will be placed. The memorial service and dedication will take place at 3*

[1] Extracted from "Frank Lloyd Wright On Hospital Design: A Modern Hospital Interview With the World-Famous Architect," *Modern Hospital,* Vol. 71, No. 3, September 1948, pp. 51–54.

P.M. Sullivan designed St. John's Church which was constructed 68 years ago. Sullivan was one of the outstanding architects produced by this country. His theories of design and ornamentations which he developed perhaps have influenced more architects than any other person, it was pointed out by officials of the planning conference.

On Monday, May 23, 1949, *The Daily Herald* added:

> *A simple ceremony at nearby Ocean Springs, Saturday afternoon in memory of the late Louis Sullivan, Mississippi architect terminated the three days of meetings. Moreland Griffith Smith, Architect of Montgomery, general chairman of the conference turned a spade of earth on the grounds of the Episcopal Church to mark the spot where a rose garden will be planted to the memory of Sullivan.*

The memorial plaque was reportedly designed by Frank Lloyd Wright.

Mr. Wright spoke again on building for the sick at Salt Lake City on Monday, April 27, 1953, before 1000 to 1500 members of the twenty-third annual convention of the Association of Western Hospitals. He again declared:

> *We need a hospital with an atmosphere that is benign, one where a man couldn't believe himself sick, one where he is not forever seeing crowds of sick people.*[2]

He reportedly added that "he hoped to find a hospital of the kind he advocated before he himself needed bedding down."[3] This attention brought Mr. Wright seven medically related projects between 1954 and 1958[4]: the Dr. Alfons Tipshus Clinic Project, Stockton, California (unbuilt—1954), the Karl Kundert Medical Clinic, San Luis Obispo, California (constructed—1955), the "Neuroseum" Hospital and Clinic for the Wisconsin Neurological Society, Madison (unbuilt—1955), the Kenneth L. Meyers Medical Clinic, Dayton, Ohio (constructed—1956), the Herman T. Fasbender Medical Clinic, Hastings, Minnesota (constructed—1957), the Lockridge Medical Clinic, Whitefish, Montana (constructed—1958), and the Dr. Jarvis Leuchaner Clinic Project, Fresno, California (unbuilt—1958).

[2] "Hospitals Taken to Task—Frank Lloyd Wright Declares Most Are Monstrosities," *The New York Times*, April 28, 1953, p. 30.

[3] "Wright is Right," *Newsweek*, Vol. XLI, May 11, 1953, pp. 97–98.

[4] Before this national attention was received, Mr. Wright had designed only one medical building—the Rockefeller Foundation Chinese Hospital Project of 1915 (unbuilt—location unknown to the editor).

The Speech

MORELAND GRIFFITH SMITH: We are now gathered together in the Buena Vista Hotel, Biloxi, Mississippi, to hear Frank Lloyd Wright and to share his message with others over Radio Station WLOX. We have conducted a student competition among students of the southern schools of architecture and you have seen the results of this in the lobby. Through this medium we brought the best thinking of our youth to bear on this most interesting and vital problem. It is, therefore, fitting that we now turn to the experienced, and there is no one we could more fittingly turn to than Frank Lloyd Wright. I believe this because the most permanent things we have in this material world are [the] ideas which we bequeath to those who follow, and certainly Mr. Wright exemplifies the most masterful architectural ideas of our time. For a long time I was of the opinion that one's name was the most important thing to guard and, second, to strive to gain prestige, and I have worked toward that goal. Today I am satisfied that the promulgation of ideals is more important.

It is proper and fitting when we are looking for [a] functional solution of hospitals that we look to the master architect of today for [the] establishment of ideas toward which we can work. Master of all architects in America—Frank Lloyd Wright.

WRIGHT: Gentlemen and your ladies, I've just received a wifely admonition: "Don't pick on the audience!" and I might have said: "I'm afraid that the audience will be picking on me before I finish" because I've always had the dubious pleasure of making a minority report. I'm not quite so clearly a minority now and I'm a little uneasy concerning the whole thing. I don't know what's going to happen. But forgetting all that, here we are in the warm-hearted South. The warm-hearted, tragic South. I never come South that my conscience—as a man of the North—doesn't trouble me. I'm never quite clear as to the justice of the victory of the North over the South unless, perhaps, the victory of the South over the North might have been even more tragic. Napoleon, the greatest of all advocates of force, spent the last weeks of his life walking the floor trying to understand why force never could organize anything, had never organized anything, concluding that force never would organize anything. Every time I come South the South to me seems, oh, so tragic that I am unhappy and hope to some day see it again justify its existence by a superior culture. I think, so far as our architecture is concerned—and it is basic—that the South will have less trouble, as my friend here to the left has just remarked, coming to a new philosophy because it hasn't had either the means or the time to fuss with the in-between. The South will come directly from the old to the new and so, I hope, therefore will be saved a great deal of fustian plus bad imitation and bad politics. I hope it will come directly into this new thought, this new basis of democratic life, which the philosophy of an *organic* architecture will make clearer to us all as time goes on.

We have just heard Louis Sullivan's name mentioned by our chairman. He was our great native genius. Primarily it was due to his thought that we are now on the track of a new life in architecture and a life to go with it which could be genuinely called democratic. I was reading the paper today, coming here on the train, to learn that our masterminds assembled in the East, upon being asked to define *democracy,* turned in eighty-five different answers, none of which agreed. So that is where we are in our international thinking on that subject. I don't believe the feeling—I think we only have the feeling for something that might be democracy—has ever come clear in our own thinking and certainly not in our recent politics or economies. So it would seem strange were we to turn to architecture to establish a center line for the democratic policies and thinking of our nation. But architecture could do just that for us because this search for the *nature* of things which it is, really and *truly,* is finding new form—although the form is so very old that it is now new—of, shall we say, *nature* worship. *Nature* study in that sense means that we are not going to be the gross materialistic nation we are now. It means that our architecture is not going to be the materialism it is now.

It means, for instance, that doctors are not going to regard their patients as merchandise and standardize that merchandise in the type of hospital that we have pretty much built all over the country today, buildings and more like the office building, becoming less and less humane—less and less considerate of those qualities that really make us what we ought to be if we are ever to be a democracy.

Now a democracy must live on genius. Democracy is the apotheosis of the individual as such; necessarily not mere personality, but the apotheosis of a gospel of individuality that means individual courage. That means no man [is] a coward. No moral cowardice can ever find, protect, or defend a democracy. It cannot disregard genius. I've always felt that Communism, Socialism, almost all the -isms and the -ites and all that went with them were cowardly, were the faith for cowards, while democracy was a challenge to the manhood of our race—the integrity of the world. I am now quite sure that if we should pursue that faith in mankind—if we have that faith in ourselves as individuals—we would have that faith in ourselves as a nation and I believe we would have no enemies. We would no more be scared by our politicians and huddle like a lot of sheep while they got from us anything they wanted to get. If we were properly agrarian according to the *nature* of our situation and opportunity instead of trying to give an imitation of a manufacturing island like England, for instance. If we would make the most of our agricultural opportunities in a great cultured agronomy, yes we would have no enemies. To keep going our present ideal of an industrial plutocracy we must continue to have war. We have to keep scaring the sheep. A politician today is that man among men who can scare them the worst and huddle them the fastest and the most, managing that way to get almost anything out of them. Now I don't know why it is so easy to stampede the American people. I don't understand just why it is so easy to scare us. What are we afraid of? Russia? I think that fear is utter nonsense. It is an affair of our own bad conscience, ladies and gentlemen. Yes, I am afraid fear of Russia is due to our own bad conscience. By now I think we have done nearly everything the forefathers we've lost sight of wished that we might

Wright: ". . . doctors are not going to regard their patients as merchandise. . . ." Exterior view of the Karl Kundert Medical Clinic (1955) at San Luis Obispo, California. Photograph by the editor.

At the medical clinic the patient is made to feel at home in a residential setting. An interior view of the waiting area at the Karl Kundert Medical Clinic at San Luis Obispo, California. Photograph by the editor.

never do, so I think we are in a position today where we could be justly blamed for going back upon the principles and the ideals which we originally held up to the world as democratic; we have sold them all down the river.

What we should call *organic* architecture is an attempt, a sincere attempt, to get them back again. To get ourselves back to the ground, to get us back to the source of inspiration by what is really our new reality and what has been called, and what we—in architecture—are calling today the new "romance. "Romance today is really the center line of a search for *reality.* The search for reality is now romance and the search for reality means the age-old search for *truth.* Unfortunately, today, the search for *truth* is dangerous. Genius today in our nation is much in the same position as criminality. A criminal gets the same consideration, is treated with the same care, and gets about the same break that a genius would get. Now, why? Louis Sullivan, himself, died penniless, alone, neglected by his profession, an outcast from a society, virtually, without a penny to his name, and that will pretty much be the fate of genius from now on unless something wakes up in the hearts of the American people to place appreciation where it belongs, to realize that no life can come to a people by way of democratic ideology without genius.

We are mostly here to consider the modern hospital, a typical example of, so it seems to me, the whole tendency of our national materialism. God knows we are the most materialistic of all modern civilizations on earth today. We are looking too much down along our own noses and so we don't see very far into the future. But we've soon got to realize that this materialism we're championing, living upon, and calling success is not bona fide. It can't last and won't result in the happiness or growth of the soul of the human being. It's temporal beyond all words, menial in culture beyond anything the world has yet seen. Unless something happens to allow that to develop in us which I believe is there, I have faith in, and I know it's in these youngsters sitting here in front of me now, we shall be the shortest lived civilization in all history. Young America may have it, but the present-day adult America—well, what has happened to it? I don't know. Something has gone wrong. It couldn't have been Franklin D. Roosevelt? No. It couldn't have been the leadership of any one man. I think it was chiefly the consequence of a false success ideal which the American people came to hold and it is that which has resulted in this terrific mercantile materialism, gross beyond anything Rome ever knew; more depraved, more selfish, more inconsequential where the soul of human life is concerned than any civilization that has ever happened. Haven't we made of all these so-called modern advantages a mere exploit—and so, a mockery? What have we today in all these great inventions from, well, we'll say, the internal combustion engine to the atom bomb, which is any guarantee at all of human usefulness and happiness, any guarantee of a great future for us as a united, happy people? Nothing! Speed is the new veracity, though the automobile is still a horse and buggy. The atom bomb is still in uniform. We haven't much to show for culture if we are serious and sincere with ourselves. If we do face ourselves, we haven't much of the spirit to travel into the problematical future. No, not much. And I think these hospitals of our nation, as well as most of the other buildings that we build are a confession of our tendency to regard everything in life as merchandise.

With us, everything is merchandise. I have been planning a mortuary, of all things, and listened to the promulgator of the enterprise referring to the corpse as the "merchandise."

AUDIENCE: (loud laughter)

WRIGHT: Well, you laugh, but tell me, where in all this nation is anything going on—going anywhere—that doesn't regard its subject matter as "the merchandise"? Not the hospital industry. No. Not the professional doctors, a few of them individually—yes, certainly. But always in between only is there this glimmer and the gleam that holds hope for a more humane future.

If you will look, by and large, at the present-day practice of any profession you will see a sordid picture. Absolutely a sordid picture. To stand up against any professionalism of this sort is the duty, the privilege, and the job of American youth because materiality is of the old—it is aged. When you once get its punctilio into your veins and therefore into your system you're old, you are aged. Yes, your life is done and you are finished. You may cling to your profits, you may even be, and probably will be, a great success, your name blazoned in lights or in the headlines in the daily newspapers. You may have all that they call success today and be really dead from the neck up! The best thing our harmful old Nicholas Murray Butler ever said—he was responsible for more ruination of men than he was for building men up: "Dead at thirty, buried at sixty." Do you remember that? Well, there is a lot of it in hospitals now by way of what we call "success." Now, in this idea of a hospital realm here tonight a new success ideal is absolutely necessary! In the building of our homes a new success ideal is necessary; in anything we do now, from now on. The architects know now we've got something we didn't have in our world before—we have a concrete, rational ideal. A new integrity has come into sight by way of the meeting of the philosophy of the Orient and of the West. It was Kipling who said: "these twain shall never meet," if you remember. But they have met in these new, old ideals of an *organic* architecture. They do meet.

At Taliesin we have Turks, we have Hindus, Japanese, we have Chinese, we have Egyptians, we have Irishmen and Frenchmen. We have an international accord there—a coming together of minds upon an ideal which seems to be becoming common to the whole world. Yes—we've got that accord. It's ours, it came from us, back again to us. It began with Louis Sullivan and is actually our own—something that the world could well expect of a democracy. Something due from us to the modern world. We have it in this ideal of an *organic* architecture.

Now, how much of *organic* architecture has ever appeared in our hospitals? How much has appeared in your houses, in your lives, or even in your own consciousness? Not much, but perhaps enough. A little is always eventually enough, but today I can see it extending all over this planet; around the coastlines of the whole world. These

Sign directing visitors to Taliesin West (1937 ff) at Scottsdale, Arizona. Photograph by the editor.

The ornate entrance gate to Taliesin West (1937 ff) at Scottsdale, Arizona. Photograph by the editor.

things we call *organic* buildings, here and there, and dotting the land more and more frequently everywhere you go, always with the countenance of a new existence for the individual as such. But it can go wrong. It's so easy for it to go wrong. It's so easy that I'm afraid it will always go wrong if you can't learn to differentiate between the individual and the mere person; between personality and individuality. These two terms are mixed in almost everything and anyone you meet or anything you can read. As a matter of fact, to get to the essential I—the individual—you must correlate three, five, or seven different people. All these in your own selves, yourselves becoming more and more mechanized—living a life as mechanized as a garage—especially in a hospital! All these people you are meeting, you don't know each other. But until they become one you are no individual. You're the usual number of personalities without *unity*. You're one thing in the morning, you're the next thing in the afternoon, and in the evening another person, and all of them, being expedient, can be bought. Until you have become, out of conflicting personalities, one unified individual, you are no democratic citizen. But when you are that thing, when you have honestly gone to work upon

This building is organically and completely integrated with the site and both become one. Taliesin West (1937 ff) at Scottsdale, Arizona. Photograph by the editor.

Taliesin West (1937 ff) at Scottsdale, Arizona, is constructed of native stone, concrete, wood, and canvas (the canvas roofing has since been replaced). Photograph by Randolph C. Henning, architect, used by permission.

An approach view of the terrace near the entrance court at Taliesin West (1937 ff), Scottsdale, Arizona. Note the integration of the building with the flora typical of the desert. Photograph by the editor.

A detailed exterior view of the terrace near the entrance court at Taliesin West at Scottsdale. Photograph by the editor.

The entrance court at Taliesin West in Scottsdale. Photograph by the editor.

*Broad steps lead to the terrace at Taliesin West in Scottsdale. Note the desert-stone wall that houses a small, open landscaped garden (*left*). Photograph by the editor.*

*A general view of the workroom terrace (*left and center*), the reflecting pool (*center and right*), and the gravel terrace (*foreground*) at Taliesin West, Scottsdale. Arizona. Photograph by Randolph C. Henning, architect, used by permission.*

*A detailed view of the workroom terrace and broad steps (*background*)·and the reflecting pool (*foreground*) at Taliesin West, Scottsdale. Photograph by the editor.*

A partial elevation view of the central portion of Taliesin West, Scottsdale, which houses the workroom (far left) *and loggia* (right). *Photograph by Kristine MacCallum and Daniel J. May.*

A small terrace fountain at Taliesin West, Scottsdale. Photograph by Randolph C. Henning, architect, used by permission.

Detail of the integration of the terrace, desert-stone wall, wooden roof structural elements, and canvas roofing material (now fiberglass) at Taliesin West, Scottsdale. Photograph by the editor.

you, yourself, and by way of suffering and sacrifice have cultivated your individual "I," then willy-nilly you have it.

Without that *unity,* [which] we should call *individuality,* you can't be trusted. You are really nobody. You don't deserve a good house; you can't deserve any position in authority; you won't deserve to be trusted because you can't be yourself. If a man can't be himself, who should trust him? Should anybody trust him? I say no! Until all of him comes together and becomes this individual "I" which is the unit in a democracy to build and build for—until he can trust himself and respect himself as himself, why should anyone trust him? You can't make the architect of a good hospital out of him. An architect is the pattern giver basic to any *true* civilization. It's *true* such as he [is]—that we must look for the civilization we haven't got yet because he's not been on the job! No, he, as all individuals, has not been on the job! He's gone to universities for an education where this doesn't exist. He can't get one out of books. We've all got to get it out of our own selves by way of our own honest experience with life itself. We have to face ourselves for it and no matter how it hurts us dig it out.

Sounds like mere language, does it? All right, I know that architecture in that sense is a gray-headed profession. It's something we boys begin, enter into; if we have the basic ideas, we grow. Each one will get his own technique in time only as he digs it out for himself. The technique that matters can't be given to you. The techniques of another man will never serve you more than possibly as an entry into something of your own. It'll never make you great or enable you to do great work. Every man for himself. You've got to find your own technique, but you've got to get the proper direction first. First of all the *meaning* of the thing.

What is the *meaning* of this thing we call the hospital? What is the *nature* of the hospital? First of all, it's a human problem. Disease is a human

An exterior view of the workroom (left)*, the terrace steps* (left of center)*, terrace* (foreground)*, and reflecting pool* (right) *at Taliesin West, Scottsdale. Photograph by Randolph C. Henning, architect, used by permission.*

An exterior view of the terrace at Taliesin West, Scottsdale. Photograph by the editor.

Decorative oriental artwork embedded in native desert stone at Taliesin West, Scottsdale. Note Frank Lloyd Wright's characteristic red-square tile to the right of the design. Photograph by the editor.

misfortune, isn't it? Out of your sense of humanity, then, out of your feeling for humanity and by way of your mastery of form and of ways and means as architects should come some great human beneficence for the desperate, for the ailing, and the sick. A hospital shouldn't be like an office building built downtown. A hospital should be a blessing where sickness would seldom be seen, a place where you would never feel that a curse had descended upon your kind. A hospital should be a comforting, joy-giving place. Yes—a happy place that you'd love to be in if you were well and not one to which you had been condemned because you were unfortunate. To me the *spiritual* side of this thing you call a hospital is the great and important side to build for, but it's lost sight of in anything I've yet seen built. We have one in our town of Madison [Wisconsin]; they're going to build another one in Madison probably even worse than the one they've got. Why? Just because that phase of a great, unsolved problem has not been touched upon by the creative artist and because they have instead consulted "experts."

Now, an "expert" is a man who has stopped thinking. He has had to stop thinking or he would be no expert. You can't call a man an "authority" who is growing and so changing his mind about things, can you? No, the expert has got to know or profess he knows. He's got to stand there knowledgeable! Well, too bad, because there is no such human except he be somewhat a phoney. Inasmuch as nearly everything in our civilization is more or less phoney for profit, the hospital is probably phoney and for profit, too. So I don't trust one much. When building the Imperial Hotel, it was my happy fortune or misfortune to fire seven experts. During my brief experience of building 549 buildings in fifty-six years of practice I have had the dubious joy of firing hundreds of experts. Most of them were code makers, too. Well, they say confession is good for the soul.

Now, as to Mrs. Wright's admonition: "Don't pick on the audience," I'm going to let this audience pick on me here, tonight. The best times in England, where we were lecturing not so long ago [see Chapter 19], came after the so-called lecture—the heckling period. The English love to heckle; they'll even get to heckling each other in heckling time before the evening is over. Often they forget all about the speaker and light into each other. Now, I like that. We don't often do it over here. It's awfully hard to get anything out of an audience in that way. Even some of those boys in Pittsburgh recently who wrote back to me—I did pick on the audience there, and that is why my wife is a little bit shy tonight about my picking on you—wrote back that they liked the amateur better than they did the professional. You may see that taking a gold medal from my profession [see Chapter 16] is going to have a bad effect.

Now, speaking of hospitals, the South is sick—my heart is with the sick South, although I was taught in my youth that it was a disgrace to be sick. I was so taught coming from a family of iconoclasts.

Unitarians they all were in a day when the Unitarian was the devil's own because he dared believe in the *unity* of all things, including himself, just as we now are coming to believe in the *unity* that is the individual as such; learning to regard him as the only basis for life or for a building or a cure for a disease. That basis is where we've got to begin here in the South.

The South must change over from the old, dead, meaningless heresies now. You know, gentlemen, and your ladies, that when our discipline is too long continued, discipline that has outgrown its usefulness and significance, it becomes a heresy and impedes blossoming time which is not yet and may not be for many years. To avoid that heresy is the *true* course for you now to pursue. We can't expect the gallant old gentlemen and their fine old ladies to throw aside everything that they once fought for and have held dear. We'll have to treat them and their belongings with patience and with consideration. We'll have to treat them all the more gently and I think the best way to do that is to let their old heresies die on the vine. Like Napoleon, I don't think you can destroy error by force. I don't think you should try. Let's admit that was a great mistake the North made regarding the South. They tried to destroy something by force that they might better have let die on the vine. Now, I'm sure that modern architecture is in the position right now where it can afford to let whatever opposition it has die on the vine.

We needn't fight much more. The fight, practically, is won. Nothing can now stop the feeling for this new thought in this new way of building, this new approach to any problem. Yes—either for a physician, an architect, or for anybody in the private ways of private life. It's the only ideal that has life in it now and thereafter, the only one that is of any consequence to the future. It's set against materialism; it's all for the spirit because it's all for that thing which really gives meaning and quality to a man as a man.

An exterior view of the Kenneth L. Meyers Medical Clinic (1956) at Dayton, Ohio. The brick building is perched on a hill and can be seen from the abutting arterial street. Photograph by the editor.

An interior view of the patients' waiting area at the Kenneth L. Meyers Medical Clinic, Dayton. The room is equipped with a massive fireplace and is furnished like the living room of a large house. Photograph by the editor.

SMITH: Mr. Wright, we thank you for bringing us this message. To all of us comes the opportunity of being in tune with the Master Spirit to some degree, lesser or greater, but very seldom in any generation do we have the opportunity of personally hearing a man who is in tune so completely with the Master Spirit as the one we have heard this evening. I believe that concludes the time on the air and I will mention here, because I think it is appropriate, we have made arrangements for the recording of this talk by Mr. Wright because we felt that we would have something that would not be possible for all of us to absorb at the time that we received it. We have made two recordings and the Executive Committee will decide which recording is the best and will make available reproductions of that recording to those who desire them. The price of reproduction will be announced later, and your orders can be given at your our discretion.

We have had a very gracious offer by Mr. Wright for an opportunity to have a little heckling, and we hope that you will respond to that opportunity. I would like to say, though, before we start, Mrs. Wright, I hope you won't hold him back too much. That's what we've got him here for. We believe here that, although we move slowly and sometimes talk indistinctly, we need a little jog every once in a while to get along, and we want you not to hold him back too much.

WRIGHT: Asking for punishment?

SMITH: Mr. Wright, would you like to get started now or should we have a rest before we ask you some questions?

WRIGHT: I feel very kindly toward this audience, so let's start. [pause] I don't want to be a hindrance to anybody. When an old veteran comes in from the

An exterior view of the Herman T. Fasbender Clinic (1957) at Hastings, Minnesota. Shown is the building elevation emphasizing the ground-hugging metal roof as viewed from the abutting arterial street. The building houses two levels (one of which is below the viewing grade). Photograph by the editor.

field, you know, it's a pity to let him get away without heckling him a little, isn't it?

SMITH: Have we any heckles ready?

WRIGHT: I seem to have oppressed my audience tonight.

SMITH: They do seem to be a wee bit embarrassed. Any questions? How about the students—after all, they always ask questions. Well, if the students won't start, let us start with Mr. E. Todd Wheeler from Chicago.

E. TODD WHEELER: I want to know why Mr. Wright is wasting his time designing a mortuary?

WRIGHT: Wheeler, I'm not wasting my time designing a mortuary because I have discovered that the proprietor of the merchandise wanted a grave digger, not an architect. And, I might add, that probably were somebody to ask me to design a hospital I should be careful to find out what the man really wanted. Or the committee. It's always the committee with a hospital, I believe. What the committee would probably desire would be one of these cellular office-building structures in which you could cram as much merchandise as possible and have it as convenient for the doctor as possible and to hell with the merchandise.

SMITH: We are just warming up here now. How about some more questions?

EARL L. MATHES [*Fevrot & Reid, Architects*]: Mr. Wright, I would like to ask you a question and I would like your candid opinion. Do you believe that modern architecture will come back to a time where we will have ornamentation? Not that we don't ornament the buildings now with steel, windows, or other various materials, but will we ever come back to a time when we will put on some ornamentation that is not needed structurally?

WRIGHT: My dear boy, you must have been a victim of what is called, for the lack of a better term—and a phoney term it is—the "International Style. "Isn't that it?

MATHES: Do you think we will ever come back to it?

WRIGHT: To ornament? I think that we have never left it. I am sure that *integral* ornament is as essential an expression of the human soul as music and I think that our buildings will never be lacking in that element once we better understand its *nature.* But we did have to pass through a period of negation because the whole thing became meaningless because it was overdone so badly. Ornament had lost all significance. So, we had to deny ourselves ornament for a time until we could get the meaning of it back again, until we could use it, intelligently and with feeling. Whenever you feel that way about ornament in designing your buildings you use it. It is coming alive again. No, [it] never was dead. I have written a little book coming out on the eighth of June [1949], so the publisher says, on the work-life of myself and [that of] Louis Sullivan called *The Pencil In His Hand* [Editor's Note: The book was actually published under the title of *The Genius and the Mobocracy,* New York: Duell, Sloan, and Pearce, 1949] and it's illustrated by the master's own drawings, none of mine—they aren't necessary. That will be an answer to your question, I'm sure, and, the answer to many another one who may feel that modern architecture has gone away from what is justly called *ornament.* It's only gone away from frippery. It's only gone away from lace curtains, looped as these usually are, and all that sort of flubdubbery [sic]. You see, architecture has—for a time—only gone away from the artificial, meaningless, exaggeration of something that was not really understood. When you get an understanding of ornament as such, you will use it with understanding, and discretion, as you would music. Yes—boy, use it! Everybody loves good ornament because it's a language of the soul, like the language of sound. When *true* ornament speaks, it's the music of the soul. No—we're not going to let it go. Never!

STUDENT QUESTIONER: In the beginning of the program you made some comments on competitions. Well, we've had some pretty stiff competition all the way through school and I would like to hear more about that idea.

WRIGHT: Well, my boy, all competitions are likely to be vicious in their results. If you can point to one single consequence of a competition that is admirable, I'll abdicate. Competitions have never yet given the world anything worth having. Let's point to the Lincoln Memorial. Let's point to that public comfort station to the honor of Thomas Jefferson. Well, what have you?

Point to anything down the line and see if you've got anything out of it. No! Now, the reason is this—one reason, this isn't the only reason, in every competition that goes through, the committee is first of all an average. The people or interests choose for committeemen those on whom the average can average. So your committee is an average to start with—excuse me, Ed [sic]. Then, the committee goes through the exhibit, picks out the best designs and the worst ones, and throws them out. Why? Because they can't get together on the best one. That one is always a minority report. You see? The best ones have to go. The worst ones have to go. Then there is the average. The average now proceeds to average upon the average, you see—and judges for what, for the average. So you have an averaging of averages for the average.

STUDENT QUESTIONER: Mr. Wright, how can the architect design for the client when the client does not know what is best for himself?

WRIGHT: If the client doesn't know that his own architect is the best thing for him, he's hopeless. Don't try! A client who doesn't trust his architect and hasn't selected him for his qualities because of his belief in him has no right to an architect. Let him take what happens to him. It won't be a good architect.

ARCH WINTER [*Mobile, Alabama*]: Mr. Wright spoke of the meeting of the two principal philosophies, Eastern and Western, and of the unity in architecture which might come out of that meeting. I would like to ask him to enlarge a little bit on that. Tell us what it might mean in the development of our *form* here in this country we would like to make democratic.

WRIGHT: That's a large order, sir, for one evening. I've devoted a lifetime trying to answer that question to my own satisfaction. It is a very pertinent one and one that requires and deserves some attention. This idea of how the meeting of the East and the West is going to affect the lives and the architecture of the buildings that we build. For instance, space as the essential *nature* of the building—not the walls, not the roof seen as the reality of building—this is Oriental. That was the contribution of Laotse, you call him Lao-Tse, I believe, the greatest of Chinese philosophers. That sense of space as the reality of the building was in my mind when I built Unity Temple in Oak Park [Illinois].

To realize the big rooms within as the reality of the building is what I was trying to do. I felt that the room was the great essence of the whole thing and didn't want the walls to conceal that fact. There was a great room there within which was merely defined by the features I arranged about it and put the ceiling on it so that when you were within there seemed to be no limitation to the spaces of the room itself. Well, now here was the West building something in a way that the East had uttered the philosophy of, oh, say 500 years before Jesus. That's what I mean by the philosophy of *organic* architecture. I don't mean a *modern* architecture; the term has become so confused, let's drop it. Let's say *organic* architecture. Well,

Wright: ". . . all competitions are likely to be vicious in their results. . . . Let's point to that public comfort station to the honor of Thomas Jefferson." The Jefferson Memorial in Washington, D.C., is a circular, domed structure surrounded by Ionic columns. The central memorial room houses a bronze statue of Thomas Jefferson by sculptor Rudolph Evans. Photograph by the editor.

there is the heart and soul of *organic* architecture. Now it is very simple. The whole sense of reality has shifted. It so used to be that when you'd ask someone what the reality of this drinking glass was they would say—they would look at the glass itself, wouldn't they? They would say that this thing the glass man did was reality. But not so now. We know that the idea of the thing is the great thing about it: that this space within, into which you put something, is the reality of this glass—all the life it has. You see, that's the change. In that is where the East and the West now come together in this ideal of an *organic* architecture because that is what *organic* architecture is trying to do. It's the idea of the thing that is the soul of the thing and therefore counts and constitutes its reality. You see! Reality no longer consists in the materiality of the thing. The reality of the thing is the idea of that thing. As our good chairman [Moreland Griffith Smith] said a little while ago, that he believed in the idea and it was the idea that was consequential and important and nothing else beside mattered so much. That's what has happened. That's where now we stand together—East and West—in this new idea of what constitute a good building, a good life, a good man. Does this mean anything to you?

WINTER: Yes, I think so, Mr. Wright.

QUESTIONER: I would like to ask Mr. Wright what does he anticipate will be the end result of modular coordination?

WRIGHT: Modular coordination, or coagulation if you like, is the material aspect of a great idea, and if the great idea is not clear, coordination will not take place. You cannot put technique before idea. There is the trouble with all our educational processes today. Boys go to get technique for something they don't understand. If they go and get the idea of the thing first by *nature* study and build themselves up in the idea by experience, they will find their own technique and we'll have an architecture. Until they do get modular coordination that way, we won't have one.

QUESTIONER: Mr. Wright, one of the things we're not taught in school relates to our dealings with our clients. The few that I have had seem to want to know how much a building is going to cost. It is one of the things I had admired most about the way you have handled your work and I have wondered how you always got around the cost.

WRIGHT: Or, how the cost got around me, you mean?

QUESTIONER: No, I mean how you got around the client.

Wright: "That sense of space as the reality of the building was in my mind when I built Unity Temple. . . ." Perspective drawing of the exterior of Unity Church (1905) at Oak Park, Illinois. Drawing from Frank Lloyd Wright, Ausgeführte Bauten und Entwürfe von Frank Lloyd Wright *(Berlin: Ernst Wasmuth, 1910).*

WRIGHT: We had a little dinner club in Chicago when I was a young fellow like you and they used to heckle me and want to know what I did to my clients—how I ever "sold" them, as they said, those crazy ideas. I told them that I didn't try to sell them anything at all. I never could sell anything. I think, if I wanted to, but there is something about the *truth* that's hypnotic. If you know and if you feel that thing to be right, you become master of that thing and you can present it in a masterful fashion. Your client will be your client, you'll not be just his architect. You'll convince him by virtue of your own conviction. That's the only way you have any right to a client. No man should ever work for a client who doesn't have faith in him, one who doesn't believe that he is the man of all men to do his building for him, and if there ever appears any question put on your hat and walk out of the office. Leave him sitting there.

QUESTIONER: Before I say this, I'd like to beg Mr. Wright's pardon, but ever since reading this book I have wanted to hear Mr. Wright on the subject of that great piece of American literature that Miss Ayn Rand wrote, *The Fountainhead.*

WRIGHT: Well, that's very simple and as easily disposed of. I'm sure of this, because I haven't seen this movie which is forthcoming. Miss Ayn Rand has apparently played house with the idea which I have just expressed to you here tonight, of the individual, per se, as such. She has absolutely mistaken and abused the privilege which she took to herself and is going to get people very badly mixed up if they are already in the gutter. But I don't think it is going to hurt anybody who isn't in the gutter already. So I don't think you or I need worry much about it. I suspect it's a hideous deformation from any standpoint of a great philosophy.

GEORGE J. WALLACE [*Alabama Polytechnic Institute*]: Mr. Wright, I would appreciate [it] if you would help me with my understanding of one term you use in most of your writings. You mentioned it here tonight but it is still floating around. It's your interpretation of *organic.* Is it structural growth or is it structure which makes the environment grow, or what is its *true* meaning? What inference do you put to it?

Interior view from a balcony in a corner of Unity Church Oak Park. Photograph by the editor.

WRIGHT: That's a good question. The man wants to know the *true* significance of my own use of the word *organic.* Well now, it might be used in a biological sense and you'd miss it. We use the word in a *spiritual* sense. We take the word from the realm of the body to the realm of the *soul.* That thing is *organic* which has entity, in which the part is to the whole as the whole is to the part, which is the condition of life in anything, even physically. Spiritually, it is the same. Only as the thing is complete as a whole and has the unity of part to whole, as whole is to part, have you got *organic* entity. That's the way the word *organic* is used by me in connection with architecture. Does that make it clear? If it doesn't, then ask me again because it's important that you get that straight. *Organic* architecture is a thing of the *spirit* and so it is a matter of the *soul.* Not necessarily although inevitable, I presume; also in the body it would be so and in the flesh [it] would also be *organic.* But that would be subordinate to the initial and a greater sense of the word *organic* that would get into the *nature* of the thing as a whole. You see as *organic* trees, flowers, and plants as growth from the soil, don't you? Well, they are organic but are so in a lower sense. Now, we want buildings as *organic* and as *true* to the *spirit* of man as those things are to the ground, you see? And have that same harmony, that same *truth* of *spiritual* being that you can easily see manifest in the physical world. So the word *organic* can't fail you if you use it in that sense of *nature.* Anyhow, it's a good thing to tie to. If you can't get into the *spirit* of it, why stick to its physiological sense and let's see what you do with it that way.

DR. D. V. GALLOWAY [*Jackson, Mississippi*]: Mr. Wright, I would like for you to comment, if you please, sir, gently if you can, upon what you think may be the effect of government on the design of hospitals designed under the direction of one of these government agencies. One of these hospitals might be mine, and I'm afraid government might have some influence on it and I've been thinking that most of us have been hoping it would be good if you can comment on the influence of government on hospital design.

WRIGHT: I can't be very gentle with that question! Because it's perfectly manifest, judging from performance, that government is unfit to handle anything in the realm of the *soul,* and a great building, any great enterprise in building, is nothing for government. Government is always ten years ago when it comes to anything in the performance we call building. Government is anterior to the next election. Government will never be just and has no *true* perception. Government, if it is good government, is executive. So, where are the ideas to be executed to come from? We've got into the habit of expecting ideas from an executive. How ridiculous! That's one of the abuses of democracy that's occurred and one of the bad things that's happened to us. Government executives have no business with ideas. They execute them but where do the ideas come from? Well, they have never come from organized government. What's more, here's a prophesy: they will never come from government because it is not in the *nature* of that animal.

DR. JUAN A. PONS [*San Juan, Puerto Rico*]: Because of that answer and the statement that was made, I would like to ask Mr. Wright what suggestions would he offer to take the place of the function of government as we understand it today in the development of an appropriate place for human suffering?

WRIGHT: I didn't quite understand.

PONS: I was wondering if Mr. Wright has any suggestion to make as to what might take the place of the function of government in building as we have it today?

WRIGHT: Bureaucracy cannot substitute for genius! When you build a hospital, you require genius. It must be so. If we are going to build hospitals in and for a democracy we cannot build dead or perfunctory buildings. We must build buildings that live for human life and that are the proper record of a civilization that is a great civilization. Government can't do that. It never has done it. It's a question for the democratic citizenry to nominate their builders and to do their own buildings and not expect or allow the government to do it for them the bureaucratic way. It's an individual matter—the affair of a good building, I mean.

QUESTIONER: I'd like to ask Mr. Wright how he keeps himself abreast of new materials, the inventions, and ideas that are created and built by other men in other fields and how he relates those to his architecture?

WRIGHT: Rather hind end to, son. Ought you not [to] put the other end around? [sic]

QUESTIONER: I would like to have Mr. Wright talk a little more about his relation between the *organic* or the *spiritual* in architecture and the material and how it works.

WRIGHT: Well, that's the heart of this whole matter of an *organic* architecture—hospitals for the unfortunate or dwellings for the fortunate. This young man wants me to go a little further into the relationship between *spirit* and *matter. Matter* meaning the materials with which you work and *spirit* meaning the way in which you work with them. You see! Does that answer you? It should, because that's the process. Now, when in the right *spirit* you work with the right materials in the right way, the result will be *organic.* When you are the master of the materials with which you work and that means you know their *nature;* when you thus know their honor, we say, and when your honor and the honor of the materials are one honor, you will have an *organic* result. Now, what is the honor of a brick? Hmm—what could be the honor of a brick? Being a good brick, wouldn't it? The brickness [sic] of the brick would be the honor of the brick, yes? Same with a board, wouldn't it? Same with anything—steel, glass, wood. How about a man? It would be his quality as an individual, wouldn't it? Well, now add that all up together and what have you got? What have you got when you add that all up?

SMITH: Now, Mr. Wright, we do not want to impose on your good nature; you've had a long trip down here to be with us.

WRIGHT: I am enjoying myself—just warming up. Go ahead, boys!

WHEELER: This time I wish to ask Mr. Wright a serious question on education. I'd like to hear him say that the *technique* is to follow the *idea.* How does he suggest that we give our thousands of architectural students the *idea* so we may encourage them to learn the *technique?*

WRIGHT: The answer ought to be very useful, very useful, indeed! Mr. Wheeler wants me to tell him how to found a university and that's all very simple. I tried to found one my way. I founded it on the farm, founded it on building buildings, founded it on really knowing what a design means because when you sit down at the drawing board and make it you get up and go out and execute it. That's what I think the university should be like. I believe you cannot grasp the idea without knowing the *nature* of the thing, and I don't believe you can know the *nature* of anything without getting into action with it. I don't think you can sit around on your fannies and study it much or get much of it from books. I think you've got to get in contact with it, get into it, and by way of such immediate experience comes some knowledge of the *nature* of the thing you want to do. There's no way to learn about building except by building. There's no way to learn about life except by living. There's no way to learn manhood except by being one. Experience is the only road. So, were I to found a university, I would close those that are now operating for at least ten years and I would have every student go back home and go to work trying to make his own neighborhood beautiful—more beautiful even—according to his way of thinking. I would have him pitch in and really build it up and he would build himself up thereby. It's a very distressing answer but I can't help it. My little wife hints that this is more than enough. She knows.

SMITH: Mr. Wright, we want to thank you for your graciousness.

WRIGHT: Oh, I have had a lot of fun, and please don't thank me. Good night to you all.

SMITH: We've had a great deal more and we appreciate it.

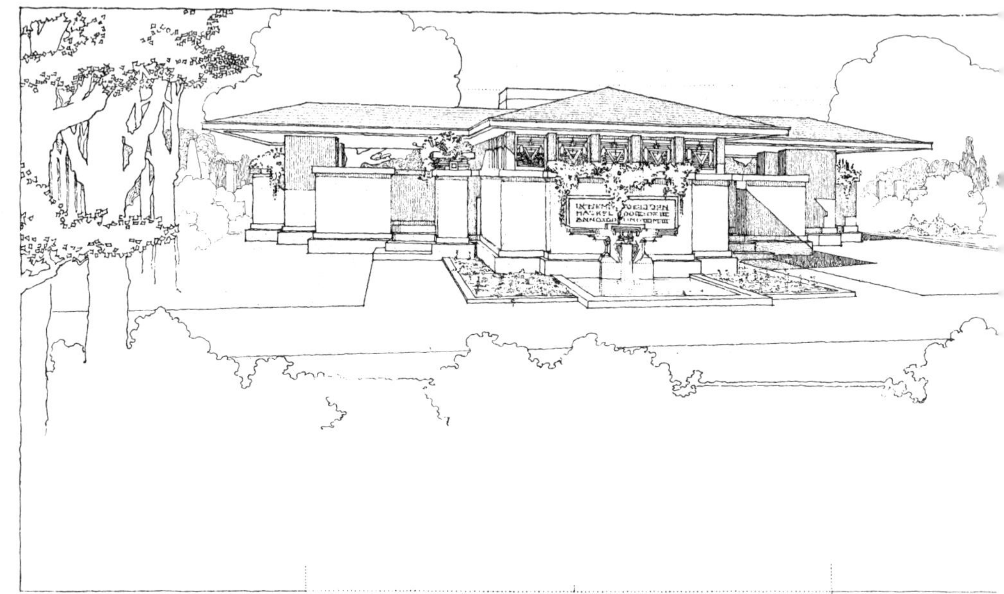

An exterior perspective rendering of the W.H. Pettit Mortuary Chapel (1906) at Belvedere, Illinois. This small chapel in a small Illinois town represents Frank Lloyd Wright's first known project that related to architecture of the dead for the living. Drawing from Frank Lloyd Wright, Ausgeführte Bauten und Entwürfe von Frank Lloyd Wright *(Berlin: Ernst Wasmuth, 1910).*

Wright: "Modern architecture declares this horizontal extension to be a better lead." Note the horizontal emphasis of the Prairie style in the design of the W.H. Pettit Mortuary Chapel at Belvedere. Photograph by Randolph C. Henning, Architect, used by permission.

15 Architecture of the Dead for the Living

I think these places we call cemeteries should be more pleasurable to the living as habitation for the dead—less dead to the living.

Introduction

This chapter presents Frank Lloyd Wright's speech to the Chicago convention of the Memorial Craftsmen Union of America which he delivered in late 1936 or early 1937. During his talk he discussed the design of cemeteries and memorials to the dead. This speech appeared in published form for the first time in Frank Lloyd Wright's "At Taliesin" column, written for *The Capital Times* of Madison, Wisconsin (Vol. 39, No. 70, February 26, 1937, p. 9.). A short excerpt appeared later in Frederick Gutheim (Editor), *Frank Lloyd Wright On Architecture: Selected Writings, 1894–1940* (New York: Duell, Sloan, and Pearce, 1941, pp. 209--210). An original draft is housed in the Frank Lloyd Wright Papers Speech and Article File-1936 in the Manuscript Division of the Library of Congress, Washington, D.C.

Throughout his career Mr. Wright designed only four projects related to the architecture of the dead: the W.H. Pettit Mortuary Chapel, Belvedere, Illinois (constructed—1906), the Darwin D. Martin Blue Sky Mausoleum Project, Buffalo,

Text of a speech reprinted in its entirety from Frank Lloyd Wright's "At Taliesin, "*The Capital Times* (Madison, Wisconsin), Vol. 39, No. 70, February 26, 1937, p. 9, by permission of *The Capital Times.*

New York (unbuilt—1928), the Memorial Chapel Project (unbuilt—1930; location not known to the editor), and the Nicholas P. Daphne Funeral Chapels Project (unbuilt—1948), San Francisco.

The Speech

WRIGHT: Concerning this business of dying and having to have "one of those things." I am glad you sent for an architect. You, Memorial Craftsmen of America, are chiefly occupied in distinguishing, or making distinguished, the houses of the dead, whereas the architect is busy—if he is busy at all—making the houses of the quick distinguished; some not so quick nor so distinguished; some "dead at thirty, awaiting burial at sixty."

I think these places we call cemeteries should be more pleasurable to the living as habitation for the dead—less dead to the living.

How to make them less dead?

Let's talk it over.

First, the first general curse on habitation for the living is placed there by the *Realtor.* It is the *lot,* the interminable row of *lots,* whereas an acre of ground to every house is [the] only sensible minimum now if it never was before. The Realtor comes first to the cemetery too—he seems to get everywhere first. The citizen alive gets a lot two by twice in some long row and dead he gets another—as long as he is tall and as wide as he is long—when he moves down and out or is moved out and down.

There is no sense in this Realtor's curse in either case, and I believe if the resting places of the quick and dead are ever to be made more beautiful—ground, and plenty of it, must be more

The Getty Tomb (1890) in Graceland Cemetery at Chicago, Illinois, was designed by the architectural firm of Adler and Sullivan. Louis H. Sullivan was Frank Lloyd Wright's "Lieber Meister." Photograph by the editor.

Frank Lloyd Wright's ancestral burial place—the tomb of ancestor John Lloyd Thomas (possibly his maternal great grandfather)—in England or Wales. Photograph by J. Thomas of Liverpool, courtesy of the State Historical Society of Wisconsin.

sensibly and generously used for that purpose. The matter of improvement begins right there and there is nothing much to do until the Realtors are rounded up and most of them taken out to be shot at sunrise.

Now, we have several accepted ways of caring for our dead and there is much to be said for all three of them. The first and simplest of all is the grave in native ground, made as attractive and beautiful as possible. The second and most pretentious is the mausoleum, wherein the body reposes in [a] marble casket, enshrined in [a] fine building. The third and most scientific disposition of the whole matter is cremation—burning the flesh, grinding the bones to dust, and committing the dust to memorial urns, storing them in some grandiloquent columnarium [sic]. You memorial craftsmen are concerned with all three ways, according to the temperament of the deceased or the families. One of these ways is usually selected.

Concerning the first and simplest—the grave—we have more than plenty of ground and more of it ought to be freely used for the living and also for the dead. This would enable us to use the horizontal headstone and the extended pavement of stone slabs inscribed or tableted [sic] with bronze and surrounded with appropriate gardening, appropriate flowers, trees, and shrubs. Make the city of the dead a proper memorial for the living. But where crowding has already taken place, I call to mind a design I made for the Martin family of Buffalo. I called it the Blue Sky Mausoleum because the sloping lot became a terraced series of marble sarcophagi, making a white marbled terraced pavement for the entire *lot.* And the pavement rose on either side of a central marble aisle to an exhedra [sic] or marble seat a half-hexagon in shape, in the center of which stood the family monument, suitably inscribed. The cover slabs of the concrete receptacles for the caskets, which made the terraced paving of the entire lot, were also inscribed, to be read from the central aisle. The whole structure thus rising in gentle elevations on the hill slope. Lead and sulfur made the joints waterproof. A small, tall group of conifers stood behind the exhedra to give relief and contrast to the white marble pavement of aisles; each slab was seven by three feet.

I mention this merely as a possible use of ground in already overcrowded cemeteries; a dignified way of making the accursed small lot more endurable. And, if monuments must be, why not now extend the monument horizontally, keeping it broad and low instead of pushing it upward to make the usual inane forest of stone posts? Modern architecture declares this horizontal extension to be a better lead.

*Frank Lloyd Wright was buried in this small country cemetery, located near Taliesin III down the highway from Spring Green, Wisconsin, from 1959 until 1985. His grave lay near the evergreen tree (*left*); (*right*) Unity Chapel (1887) was designed for the Lloyd-Jones family by Joseph Lyman Silsbee, architect, by whom Mr. Wright was employed at the time as a draftsman. Photograph by the editor.*

Frank Lloyd Wright's first resting place. A flat, native-stone slab and erect native-stone marker marked his grave from 1959 to 1985 near Spring Green, Wisconsin. In 1985 his remains were moved to Taliesin West at Scottsdale, Arizona. Photograph by the editor.

I believe the monument should give away now to the memorial. There is an essential difference where the living are concerned, and inasmuch as tombstones are really for the living instead of for the dead I believe the monuments should give way to a sensible memorial. Monuments are merely a form of grandomania and grandomania has gone so far with us now that we really should take steps to see that it is discouraged. Provincial vainglory and selfish pride should have small place in the hamlets, villages, and cities of the dead but I know of no place in our civilized arrangements where we show all these to such bad advantage in respect to these qualities as in these poetry-crushing cemeteries of ours. The same thing is going on there between the Smiths, Joneses, and Robinsons that goes on in the towns. These burial places show how little real feeling or creative imagination the living have to make these abodes at all fit for the living or, for that matter, for the dead either.

Wright: "Everyone has a last line in him or her and the headstone or the pavement or the marker is a good place for it." A detailed view of Frank Lloyd Wright's resting place from 1959 to 1985 near Spring Green, Wisconsin. His last line, set in stained glass, on the grave-site marker was: FRANK LLOYD WRIGHT, 1867–1959. Love of an idea is the love of God. Photograph by the editor.

I can imagine the ideal buryingground chosen for its natural beauty; that beauty heightened by parklike spacing of broad and quiet memory stones or tablets of bronze or both together; mausoleums like the Getty Tomb at Graceland or the Ryerson Tomb there, or the beautiful Wainwright Tomb in St. Louis; beautiful appropriate edifices designed by my beloved master Louis Sullivan. These places we call burying grounds should be places to which we might look with no repulsion or dread, a blessing, too, instead of a curse on life. And, believe me, this is all a matter of design; appropriate spaciousness in the first place; an intelligent use of materials in the second place. A fine sense of the whole, dominant. If we are to be regimented in rows fifty feet o.c. [on center] while we are alive, for God's sake give us enough room to lie in, gracefully, separate, and beautifully informal when we are dead. This in order to have little freedom to look forward to and a better sentiment toward death than we now seem to have; not that this would do us any good after we are dead but because it would do us all good while we are alive to see our loved ones better treated at last. Finally, shouldn't every one of us be allowed a last line? The last line would shed much light upon the living, be a certain come-back from the dead. I have in mind Dorothy Parker's epitaph—she designed it for herself:

"Excuse my dust."

Everyone has a last line in him or her and the headstone or the pavement or the marker is a good place for it. Humanize the cemeteries, you memorializers [sic]! Humanize the burial places of your kind! They are now so much more dead than the dead can ever be dead!

PART FIVE

Honors, Awards, and Medals

Frank Lloyd Wright addressing the 81st Convention of the American Institute of Architects (AIA) during his acceptance of the AIA's 1948 Gold Medal on March 17, 1949, at the Rice Hotel, Houston, Texas. Photograph by Bob Bailey, American Institute of Architects Archives.

16 The Gold Medal of the American Institute of Architects

I've heard myself referred to as a "great architect." I've heard myself referred to as the "greatest living architect." I've heard myself referred to as "the greatest architect who ever lived." Now, wouldn't you think that ought to move you? Well, it doesn't! Because in the first place they don't know! . . . What's the honor of a man? To be a true individual, to live up to his ideal of individuality rather than his sense of personality.

Introduction

In his architectural career of more than seventy years, Frank Lloyd Wright was the recipient of at least thirty-one prestigious honorary degrees, honorary memberships, awards, and medals:

1919 Kenchiko Ho (citation). Royal Household, Japan. Conferred by the Imperial Household, represented by Baron Okura.

Reprinted with editor-transcribed corrections from a surviving audio recording of the event from "Citation with the Gold Medal to Frank Lloyd Wright," *AIA Journal*, Vol. XI, April 1949, p. 163, and "Acceptance Speech of Frank Lloyd Wright Upon Receiving the Gold Medal for 1948, "*AIA Journal*, Vol. XI, May 1949, pp. 199–207. Reproduced by permission of the *AIA Journal*.

1927 Honorary Member. Academie Royale des Beaux Arts, Belgium. Conferred by the State.

1929 Extraordinary Honorary Member. The Akademie der Kunst (Royal Academy), Berlin. Conferred by the Reich.

1932 Honorary Member. National Academy of Brazil.

1937 Honored Guest of the Soviet Union to attend the World Conference of Architects.

1939 Honorary Degree. Master of Arts, Wesleyan University, Connecticut.

1940 Honorary Member. American Institute of Decorators.

1941 Honorary Member. Royal Institute of British Architects. Conferred by King George VI.

1941 Sir John Watson Chair, The Royal Institute of British Architects. An academic honor by the Sulgrave Manor Board.

1941 Royal Gold Medal for Architecture. Royal Institute of British Architects (RIBA). Conferred by King George VI.

1942 Honorary Member. National Academy of Architects, Uruguay.

1943 Honorary Member. National Academy of Architects, Mexico. Conferred by the State.

1946 Honorary Member. The National Academy of Finland. Conferred by the State.

1947 Honorary Degree. Doctor of Fine Arts, Princeton University.

1948 Honorary Member. National Institute of Arts and Letters, United States of America.

1949 Gold Medal of the American Institute of Architects (AIA).

1949 Gold Medal of the Philadelphia Chapter of the American Institute of Architects.

1949 Peter Cooper Award for the Advancement of Art. The Cooper Union, United States of America.

1950 Centennial Award. *Popular Mechanics.*

1950 Honorary Degree. Doctor of Laws, Florida Southern College, Lakeland, Florida.

1951 de Medici Medal. City of Florence, Italy.

1951 Star of Solidarity. City of Venice, Italy (one of Europe's most coveted awards given only once in one hundred years).

1953 Honorary Member. Akademie Royale des Beaux Arts, Stockholm, Sweden. Conferred by the State.

1953 Gold Medal for Architecture of the National Institute of Arts and Letters, United States of America.

1953 Frank P. Brown Medal of the Franklin Institute of Philadelphia (awarded in 1953 and presented in 1954).

1954 Honorary Degree. Doctor of Fine Arts, Yale University.

1955 Honorary Degree. The Technishe Hochschule of Darmstadt, Germany. Conferred by the nation.
1955 Honorary Degree. The Technische Hochschule of Zurich, Switzerland. Conferred by the nation.
1956 Honorary Degree. Doctor of Fine Arts, University of Wisconsin-Madison.
1956 Frank Lloyd Wright Day in Chicago, Illinois. Proclaimed by the City of Chicago for October 17, 1956.
1956 Honorary Degree. Doctor of Philosophy, University of Wales.

The Gold Medal of the American Institute of Architects, however, was the most elusive award of all those bestowed on him in his lifetime and was, indeed, as Mr. Wright said "a long time coming from home." In 1949 he had already been the reciplent of at least fifteen honors throughout the world for his architectural achievements and was approaching his eightieth birthday. Finally, on December 6, 1948, he received a letter from Douglas William Orr, then president of the AIA in which he was asked to accept the Gold Medal "in recognition of most distinguished service to the profession of architecture."[1]

Later, several regional and local chapters of the Institute voiced opposition to the Institute's selection by stating that "the qualification [sic] of Mr. Wright have been and still are subject to serious question." In the face of these protests Mr. Wright replied that "when a professional society dignifies itself by awarding the highest honor within its gift, regardless of affiliation, bias or rebellion, it shames noncooperation. My hat is off to the AIA."[2]

Finally, on Thursday evening March 17, 1949, the award was made at the Rice Hotel in Houston, Texas, at the Institute's annual convention dinner. This chapter presents the complete text of introductory remarks by the president of the Institute, the presentation to Mr. Wright, the official citation of the medal, Mr. Wright's acceptance speech, and audience responses to his remarks.[3]

Even after Mr. Wright's death in 1959 he continued to be honored. His posthumous honors include the following:

1966 Frank Lloyd Wright two-cent ($0.02) United States postage stamp.
1982 Architecture USA postage stamp series. A twenty-cent ($0.20) United

[1] See Bruce Brooks Pfeiffer (Editor), *Frank Lloyd Wright: Letters to Architects,* Fresno: The Press at California State University-Fresno, 1984, p. 211.

[2] See Sterling Sorensen's "Receipt of Architects' Award Is Highlight in Wright's Stormy Career, "*The Capital Times* (Madison, Wisconsin), Vol. 63, No. 81, March 10, 1949, p. 5.

[3] Mr. Wright's acceptance speech for the AIA Gold Medal appeared in print on three previous occasions known to the editor (none of which presents the entire award event). These are "Acceptance Speech of Frank Lloyd Wright Upon Receiving the Gold Medal for 1948, "*AIA Journal,* Vol. XI, May 1949, pp. 199–207, "The Speech of Acceptance," *A Taliesin Square-Paper: A Nonpolitical Voice from Our Democratic Minority,* No. 13, 1949(?), pp. 2–7, and, more recently, in Bruce Brooks Pfeiffer (Editor), *Frank Lloyd Wright: Letters to Architects,* Fresno: The Press at California State University, Fresno, 1984, pp. 217–223.

States postage stamp that features Mr. Wright's famous Edgar J. Kaufmann, Sr. "Fallingwater" residence (1935), Ohiopyle, Pennsylvania.

1983 American Arts Medallion (one-half ounce of gold).

Introductory Remarks, The American Institute of Architects Citation, and the Acceptance Speech for the Gold Medal of the American Institute of Architects

DOUGLAS WILLIAM ORR (*President of the American Institute of Architects*): It becomes my high privilege of my office tonight to introduce one who needs no introduction. Among the moving forces of the cosmos is mankind's urge to function as an individual; his yearning for freedom of mind and spirit—a constant quest for opportunity to advance a cause. These always have been attributes of man and without them he would have little. It is unwise to hamper or to destroy that individual initiative; to restrict individual freedom; to abolish opportunity for advancement. Perhaps there is no area in life's effort to which these *truths* are more germane than to architecture. Reliance on the security of forms of [the] past is just as deadening to progress as deadly as reliance on *security*—the ultimate goal of so many today. Through architecture, [it] has always been the expression of the social, economic, political, or religious idea of the time. For many years Frank Lloyd Wright has borne that urge to create; to find and follow *truth;* to carry forward alone the light struck by that brilliant group of Chicago architects of the last century. I present the citation for the award to Mr. Wright:

Prometheus brought fire from Olympus and endured the wrath of Zeus for his daring; but his torch lit other fires and men lived more fully by their warmth.

To see the beacon fires he has kindled is the greatest reward for one who has stolen fire from the gods.

Frank Lloyd Wright has moved men's minds.

People all over the world believe in the inherent beauty of architecture which grows from the need, from the soil, from the nature of materials. He was and is a titanic force in making them so believe.

Frank Lloyd Wright has built buildings.

Structure, in his hands, has thrown off stylistic fetters and taken its proper place as the dominant guiding force in the solution of man's creative physical problems.

Frank Lloyd Wright has kindled men's hearts.

An eager generation of architects stands today as his living monument. By precept and example he has imparted to them the courage to live an architectural ideal. They are reaching leadership in our profession, themselves dedicated to creating order and beauty, not as imitators, but as servants of the truth.

It is for that courage, that flame, that high-hearted hope, that contribution to the advancement of architectural thought that this Gold Medal, the highest award of The American Institute of Architects, is presented to Frank Lloyd Wright.

AUDIENCE: (loud applause)

WRIGHT: [A] Very fine citation! Ladies and gentlemen, no man climbs so high or sinks so low that he isn't eager to receive the good will and admiration of his fellowman. He may be reprehensible in many ways; he may seem to care nothing about it; he may hitch his wagon to his star and, however he may be circumstanced or whatever his ideals or his actions, he never loses the desire for the approbation of his kind.

So I feel humble and grateful. I don't think humility is [a] very becoming state for me . . .

AUDIENCE: (laughter and applause)

WRIGHT: . . . but I really feel by this token of esteem from the home boys.

AUDIENCE: (slight laughter)

WRIGHT: It has reached me from almost every great nation in the world. It's been a long time coming from home!

AUDIENCE: (laughter and loud applause)

WRIGHT: But here it is at last, and very handsome indeed. And I am extremely grateful.

I don't know what change it's going to effect upon my course in the future.

AUDIENCE: (laughter)

WRIGHT: It's bound to have an effect! I am not going to be the same man when I walk out of here that I was when I came in.

AUDIENCE: (laughter)

WRIGHT: Because, by this little token in my pocket, it seems to me that a battle has been won. I felt that way . . .

AUDIENCE: (loud applause)

WRIGHT: . . . [when] I was sitting in my little home in Arizona in '41 and the news came over the wire that the Gold Medal of the Royal Institute of British Architects had fallen to a lad out there in the Middle West, in the tall grass. Well, I felt then that the youngsters who have held, we'll say, with me, who have worked with me, who have believed and made sacrifices and taken the gaff with me had won a worldwide fight. But it hadn't been won at home. The Cape Cod Colonial—by the way, have any of you observed what we fellows have done to the Colonial? Have you seen it come down, and its front open to the weather, and the wings extend and have it become more and more reconciled to the ground? It has; you notice it.

Well, anyway, it is very unbecoming on an occasion like this to boast. But I do want to say something that may account in a measure for the fact that I have not been a member of your professional body, that I have consistently maintained an amateur status.

AUDIENCE: (laughter and slight applause)

WRIGHT: Long ago, way back in the days of Oak Park, I set up a standard of payment for my services of ten percent. I have consistently maintained it. I have always felt a competition for the services of an architect, who to me is a great creative artist, was a sacrilege, a shame, and pointed to history that proved nothing good ever came of it. And I think nothing good ever *will* come of it!

Also, I think that to make sketches for anybody for nothing, to tender your services, to hawk yourself on the curb—in any circumstances—is reprehensible.

Now, I know the ideals of this Institute very well. I took them to heart years ago, and believe me, with this Medal in my pocket, I can assert *truthfully* that never have I sacrificed one iota of those ideals in any connection whatsoever!

AUDIENCE: (applause)

WRIGHT: The man does not live who can say that I sought his work. And I remember in the very early days, when the children were running around the streets without proper shoes, and Mr. Moore, across the way, wanted to build a house, a fine house; a fine man; a great opportunity for a youngster like me. Well, I had these ideals at heart even then, and I never went to see Mr. Moore and I never asked anybody to say a word for me because who was there who could say an honest one? They didn't know anything about me.

AUDIENCE: (slight applause)

WRIGHT: So I glanced up one day through the plate-glass door—and, by the way, I *started* the plate-glass door!

AUDIENCE: (laughter)

WRIGHT: . . . there was Mr. and Mrs. Moore. Well, you can imagine how that heart of mine went

An exterior view of the Nathan G. Moore residence and stable (1895) at Oak Park, Illinois. Photograph by the editor.

pitty-pat. [They] came in and sat down opposite me.

"Now, Mr. Wright," he said, "I want to know why every architect I ever heard of, and a great many I *never* heard of, have come to ask me for the job of building my house?"

"Well," I said, "I can't answer that question, but I'm curious to know did Mr. Patton come?" Mr. Patton was the President of the Institute—that is, of The AIA at that time.

"Why," he said, "he was the first man to come!"

AUDIENCE: (loud laughter)

WRIGHT: "Well now," Mr. Moore said, "why haven't you come to ask me to build my house? You live right across the road."

"Well," I said, "you are a lawyer, aren't you, Mr. Moore? You're a professional man. If you heard that somebody was in trouble, would you go to him and offer him your services?"

"Ah!" he said, "I thought that was it! You are going to build our house."

Well it began that way, and it began to get noised about. The next man was Mr. Baldwin, who was also a lawyer, and wanted to build a house. Mr. Baldwin appeared several months afterward and laid a check on the table. It wasn't a big check. It was $350, but it would be $3500 now.

AUDIENCE: (slight laughter)

WRIGHT: And you can imagine what that did to me and he said: "Here's your retainer, Mr. Wright!"

Well, now, that's how it began, and it's been that way ever since, and I've never in my life asked a man to say a good word for me to another man who was going to build. Well, now, as a consequence, I've been sitting around—waiting.

AUDIENCE: (mild uproar)

WRIGHT: I've spent a good many years of my life hoping somebody would come and give me something to do. And every job I ever had hit me out of the blue on the back of the head. Now, that's *true*. So, this Gold Medal—let's forget all about design; let's forget all about contributions to construction and all the rest of it—I feel I can stick it in my pocket and walk away with it just because I sat there waiting for a job.

AUDIENCE: (loud applause)

WRIGHT: Now, of course, architecture is in the gutter.

AUDIENCE: (mild uproar)

WRIGHT: It is. I've heard myself referred to as a "great architect." I've heard myself referred to as the "greatest living architect." I've heard myself referred to as the "greatest architect who ever lived." Now, wouldn't you think that ought to move you?

AUDIENCE: (laughter)

WRIGHT: Well, it doesn't! Because in the first place they don't know! In the next place, no architect—in the sense that a man has now to be an architect—ever lived, and that's what these boys out in front of me here don't seem to know.

Architects as they existed in the ancient times were in possession of a state of society, as an instrument to build with. The guilds were well organized. The predetermined styles were all well established, especially in the Gothic period. An architect in those days was pretty well furnished forth with everything he needed to work with. He didn't have to be a *creator*. He had to be a sentient artist, with a fine perception, let's say, and some knowledge of building, especially if he was going to be . . . especially if he was going to engage in some monumental enterprise. But he didn't have to create as he does now.

Now we have an entirely different condition. We live by the machine. Most of us aren't much higher in our consciousness and mentality than the man in the garage, anyhow. We *do* live by the machine. We *do* have the great products of sciences as our toolbox, and as a matter of fact science has ruined us as it has ruined religion, as it has made a monkey of philosophy, as it has practically destroyed us and sent us into perpetual war.

Now, that isn't our fault, but where, I ask you, were these new forms of building to come from that could make full use of these advantages that have proved to us so disadvantageous? Who is going to conceive these new buildings? Where from? How come?

Now, it's a great pity that the Greeks didn't have glass. A great pity that they didn't have steel—the spider spinning—because if they had, we wouldn't have to do any thinking, even now. We would copy them with gratitude. No, not with gratitude. We wouldn't even know we were copying them! We would take it all for granted. We wouldn't have the least gratitude.

But now what must an architect be if he really is going to be one worthwhile, if he's really going to be *true* to his profession? He *must* be a creator. He must perceive beyond the present. He must see pretty far ahead. Well, let's not say that, because we can all do that, but he must see into the life of things if he is going to build anything worth building in this day and generation.

And, do you know, we ought to be the greatest builders the world has ever seen? We have the riches, we have the materials, we have the greatest release ever found by man in steel and in glass. We have everything, but. We have a freedom that never existed before. We profess democracy out of a *mobocracy* [sic] that is shocking, astounding, and arresting. But we have built *nothing* for democracy. We have built *nothing* in the spirit of the freedom that has been ours. No. Look at Washington. Look anywhere. You can even go out and see the Shamrock [Hotel].

AUDIENCE: (laughter and applause)

WRIGHT: And, by the way, I want it recorded right here and now that that building is built in what is called the International Modern Style.

AUDIENCE: (laughter and applause)

WRIGHT: Let's give the devil his due! Let's put it where it belongs. And, anyhow, while we are speaking of that exploit, why? It ought to be written in front of it, in great tall letters, in electric lights—W-H-Y—Why?

AUDIENCE: (loud applause)

WRIGHT: Well, Houston has it!

AUDIENCE: (laughter)

WRIGHT: And Houston is a good example of the capitalistic city, the pattern of the capitalistic city—great one single great broad pavement, skyscrapers erected at one end and, way out in the country at the other end—skyscrapers!

AUDIENCE: (laughter)

WRIGHT: In between, out on the prairie and in the mud—the people!

AUDIENCE: (laughter and applause)

WRIGHT: Well, now, we are prosecuting a cold war with people who declare with a fanatic faith that is pitiful in the *have-nots.* We declare a faith in the *haves,* when we act. We declare a faith in the union of something beneficial to both the *haves* and the *have-nots* when we talk. Now, when are we going to practice what we preach? When are we going to build for democracy? When are we going to understand the significance of the thing ourselves and live up to it? When are we going to be willing to sit and wait for success? When are we going to be willing to take the great will and the great desire for the deed?

Now, we can do it. We have got enough "on the ball," as the slang phrase is, to go on with in that direction if we will. But to me the most serious lack, the thing we haven't got—and if you look over the political scene, of course, it's obscene—of all this thing we are talking about. Honor? Nowhere. Now, what is the sense of honor? What would it be in architecture? What would it be in the building of buildings? What would it be in the living of a life in a democracy under freedom? Not mistaking freedom [for] license for freedom, not mistaking individuality for personality, which is our great error and which characterizes us as a *mobocracy* instead of a *true democracy.* Now, what would a sense of honor be, that sense of honor that could save us now? As science has mowed us down and

An exterior view of the Hiram Baldwin residence—second design (1905) at Kenilworth, Illinois. In 1904 Frank Lloyd Wright designed a house for Hiram Baldwin that was never executed, and somewhat earlier, in 1895, one for Jesse Baldwin at nearby Oak Park, also never executed. Photograph by the editor.

we are lying ready to be raked over the brink, what could save us but a sense of honor? And what would that sense of honor be? Well, what is the honor of a brick? What would be an honor of a brick? A *brick* brick, wouldn't it? A *good* brick. What would be the honor of a board? It would be a *good* board, wouldn't it? What's the honor of a man? To be a *true* individual, to live up to his ideal of individuality rather than his sense of personality. Now, if we get that distinction straight in our minds, we'll be able to go on. We will last some time. If we don't get it, we might as well prepare for the brink we're going over.

Now, I've been right about a good many things—that's the basis of a good deal of my arrogance. And it has a basis, that's one thing I can say for *my* arrogance.

AUDIENCE: (laughter)

WRIGHT: We can save ourselves. We're smart. We have ratlike perspicacity.

AUDIENCE: (laughter)

WRIGHT: But we have the same courage and that's what's the matter. I don't know of any more cowardly—well, I'm getting too deep in here and I cannot swear.

AUDIENCE: (laughter)

WRIGHT: Not tonight! But we are certainly a great brand of cowards in America. We've got all our great opportunities to live a spiritual life, with great interior strength and nobility of purpose, and minds go by the board. Why? I have asked myself all these years—why? You've all seen it. I am not telling you anything new. Churches—religion—what has it become? Philosophy—what is it? Education? What have you? Cowardice. What are the universities today? Overflowing with hungry minds and students. And yet, as I stand here now, I am perfectly willing to admit and to confess that it's not the fault of the universities. It's not the fault of education. None of this is the fault of the systems that exist among us. They are our *own* fault! *We* make these things what they are. We allow them to be *as* they are. We've got the kind of buildings we deserve. We've got the kind of cities that are becoming to us. This capitalist city, for instance, of which Houston is an example—we did it! It came to us because we are what we are and don't forget it. If we are ever going to get anything better, if we are going to come by a more honorable expression of a civilization such as the world is entitled to from us—we put ourselves on the hill here, in a highlight, we talk about the highest standard of living the world has ever seen, we profess all these things, and *we don't deliver!*

Now, why we don't isn't the fault of any institutions. It isn't the fault of any class. It isn't the fault of the big boys that make the money and make the blunders and shove us over the brink, like this out here that we spoke of a minute ago. No. How would they learn better? How is a man like Mr. McCarthy [Senator Joseph McCarthy] going to know any better?

AUDIENCE: (laughter)

WRIGHT: How is the architect who built the building going to know any better? How are they going to find out? They can only find out by your disapproval. They can only find out by your telling the *truth*, first to yourselves and then out loud, wherever you can get a chance to tell it. Now, we have got to find honor!

AUDIENCE: (loud applause)

WRIGHT: You know the old sayings—we dislike them now because they are a reproach. We don't honor the people, really, the men who came over here with an ideal in their hearts and founded this basis, as they thought, for freedom. They couldn't foresee but by the way of sudden riches and these new scientific powers put into our hands that we would be so soon degenerate! No.

Well now, I think if we were to wake up and take a good look at ourselves *as ourselves,* without trying to pass the buck, without trying to blame other people for what really is our own shortcoming and

(Left to right) *Frank Lloyd Wright, Mrs. Frank Lloyd Wright, Mrs. Edmund Purves, and Edmund Purves, Director of the American Institute of Architects, on March 17, 1949, at the 81st Convention of the American Institute of Architects, Rice Hotel, Houston, Texas, shortly after Mr. Wright had accepted the AIA Gold Medal. Photograph courtesy of* The Capital Times, *Madison, Wisconsin.*

our own lack of character, we would be an example to the world that the world needs now. We wouldn't be pursuing a cold war. We would be pursuing a great endeavor to plant, rear, and nurture a civilization, and we would have a culture that would convince the whole world. We'd have all the Russians in here on us, working for us, with us, not afraid that we were going to destroy them or destroy anybody else.

AUDIENCE: (applause)

WRIGHT: It's because of cowardice and political chicanery, because of the degradation to which we have fallen as men—well, a crack comes to mind, but I'll refrain.

AUDIENCE: (laughter)

WRIGHT: My wife knows what it is. I am not going to say it.

Well, now, that's serious enough, and that is all that I think I ought to say.

Now, I want to call your attention to one thing. I have built it. I have built it! Therein lies the source of my arrogance. Why I can stand here tonight, look you in the face and insult you—because, well, I don't think many of you realize what it is that has happened or is happening in the world that is now coming toward us. A little place where we live, with sixty youngsters—we turned away 400 in the past two years—and they come from twenty-six different nations. They all come as volunteers because this thought that we call *organic* architecture has gone abroad. It has won abroad—under different names. A singular thing. We will never take an original thought or an idea until we have diluted it, until we have passed it around and given it a good many names. After that takes place, then we can go, and we do go. Well, that has happened. This thing has been named different names all over the world. It's come back home and I use the word—I say come back home advisedly—because here is where it was born. Here it was born in this cradle—as we are fond of calling it—of liberty which has degenerated into license. Now, what are we going to do with it? Are we going to let it become a commonplace and shove it into the gutter or are we really going to look up to it, use it, honor it? And, believe me, if we do, we have found the centerline of a democracy. Because the principles of an *organic* architecture, once you comprehend them, naturally grow and expand into this great freedom that we hoped for when we founded this nation and that we call *democracy.*

Well, it's enough, isn't it?

AUDIENCE: (laughter and loud applause)

Frank Lloyd Wright relaxing in his study at Taliesin III, near Spring Green, Wisconsin, shortly before his birthday party on June 8, 1953—a little more than a week after his receipt on May 27 of the Gold Medal for Architecture of the National Institute of Arts and Letters in New York. Photograph by James Roy Miller, courtesy of The Capital Times, *Madison, Wisconsin.*

17 The Gold Medal for Architecture of the National Institute of Arts and Letters

Now, the philosophy of democracy is a search for truth and . . . this thing that we call architecture, the true basis of culture.

Introduction

On Wednesday, May 27, 1953, in New York, the National Institute of Arts and Letters awarded ~~their~~ coveted Gold Medal for Architecture to Frank Lloyd Wright at their annual ceremonial with the affiliated American Academy of Arts and Letters. Ten days before delivery of his acceptance speech on Sunday, May 17, Mr. Wright received national attention when he appeared in conversation with Hugh Downs on the nationally televised, now famous NBC program, *Wisdom: A Conversation with Frank Lloyd Wright.* [For a discussion of this broadcast and its complete text see Patrick J. Meehan (Editor) *The Master Architect: Conversations with Frank Lloyd Wright,* New York: John Wiley and Sons, 1984, pp. 31–56.]

The Gold Medal award of the Institute was, at that time, made twice annually for achievements in two different branches of the arts and had also been given for sculpture, music, history, biography, poetry, drama, and essays. Paul Manship, a sculptor and president of the Academy, presided over the presentation of Mr. Wright's medal. The actual award, however, was made by Ralph

Reprinted from the *Proceedings of the American Academy of Arts and Letters and the National Institute of Arts and Letters,* second series, number 4, New York, 1954, by permission of the American Academy and Institute of Arts and Letters.

Walker, an architect and vice-President of the Institute. Mr. Wright was elected to the Institute in 1947 and to the Academy in 1951. In conjunction with the presentation of this award a small exhibition of his work was mounted in the gallery of the Institute. This chapter contains the text of Ralph Walker's presentation of the medal and Mr. Wright's short acceptance speech.

The Presentation of the Gold Medal

RALPH WALKER: Frank Lloyd Wright, you are part and parcel of the wonder-making pioneer spirit of our people. It is difficult to say something new about you, for in your long eventful life you have been called many things: a Prometheus bringing the stirring flame of a new architecture, a Moses leading an eclectic benighted into the Promised Land of *organic* creation, and long since as a prophet well honored in his own country. Certainly you are not a shy cowslip to be gathered casually on a lower pasture in Wisconsin; nor have you been a recluse cloistered in a garden high on Taliesin; on the contrary, you have built not one but many Emersonian mousetraps and the world has enthusiastically beaten a well worn and widening path in merited appreciation. This honor about to be given you is just another leaf added to an already glowing laurel chaplet and will render but a further luster to a brow that was never bowed.

A *true* pioneer, you early set a course from which you have never swerved and along which as an octogenarian you still walk with the will and directness of youth. Your works, your thoughts ever soar above pedestrian paths. A blithe spirit, "with more Puck than of Ariel," you design your buildings as if they were to take their place in a happier world—one of light, of grace, of gaiety—and for human beings who are not burdened with fear, for humans who live in a world where what seems possible is actually so, and where the pioneer concept of democracy seems a reality. All your life you have denied the minimum and have reached for the stars; a free man in a free land, you have asked a drab society to compromise with you on the basis of your ideals.

You have created an architecture in which you have been thoughtfully aware of the powerful forces implicated in the new inventions, and though philosophically concerned with the machine you have never held that it should merely and heedlessly produce more machines or more machinelike objects, but that it should be used to make a world in which function may be controlled so as to emancipate enslaving form; and to increase the possibilities for new founded cities whose broad acres, as green as those beside the still waters, will furnish that beauty of life for which man has ever sought. In a world in which the architect is increasingly asked to sing in a guttural and meager Esperanto your voice is as warm and as native as *Oh! Susanna.* The National Institute of Arts and Letters here honors an American whose creative forces illustrate the anticipations of another great prioneer, Walt Whitman:

> *I swear to you the architects will appear without fail,*
> *I announce them and lead them.*
> *I swear they will understand you and justify you.*

The Acceptance Speech

WRIGHT: I had no idea how outrageously inadequate this introduction by Ralph Walker would be. Couldn't you do better than that?

You see it is not so easy. I myself wrote something for this occasion and came to feel that it was so wretchedly inadequate also that I abandoned it and decided to say very little, if anything.

As these honors have descended upon me one by one, somehow I expected each honor would add a certain luster, a certain brightness to the psyche which is mine. On the contrary, a shadow seems to fall with each one. I think it casts a shadow on my native arrogance, and for a moment I feel coming on this disease which is recommended so highly, of humility. So if this is to keep up, I am afraid that I am going to lose my usefulness to myself.

However, it is a very happy occasion for me to be welcomed at home—a home boy come back—you know, when [a] home boy makes good there is nothing quite so good, is there?

Perhaps, after all, there is something in an *organic* architecture that eventually will be understood, and all I have to say to you here today is simply this: of course the old Greek abstraction by way of our aesthetes, by way of aestheticism, by way of aesthetics has robbed us not only of an architecture but of all the things that go with it—all the things that should go with modern art. So let me say that if we are to have an architecture of our own that will be the basis of a culture of our own—if we ever have one—it will be based upon a sound philosophy. What we need now is that new philosophy.

Now, the philosophy of democracy is a search for *truth* and aestheticism is a matter of taste; it is a matter of seeing and feeling what you like as you like it. But we know very little; we know nothing of the fundamentals underlying this thing that we call architecture, the *true* basis of culture. A civilization we have. It is a way of life, and that is all it is. But a culture would be a way of making, ways of making that life beautiful, and we have not begun upon it. We live in an incongruity and an inconsistency that is positively disgraceful and I think it is not too much to endorse that saying of the English poet: "Where every man . . ." what is it?—

Where every prospect pleases
And only man is vile.

That is the office of architecture and of the architect. He is a poet—artists are poets or they are nothing, and it is poetry that is not valued as highly now as it should be. To say that you are a poet is to confess a certain measure of weakness, isn't it? To say that you are a poet and to lay claim to being a poet puts you rather in the backyard and out of things and the procession goes on without you. Now, we know that is wrong and we are not doing anything about it.

And here I, among my fellows today, ask their cooperation to set aside for some years to come the aesthetic and to try and think a little deeper and get our feet down on the ground, on something that we really can feel is the *truth*.

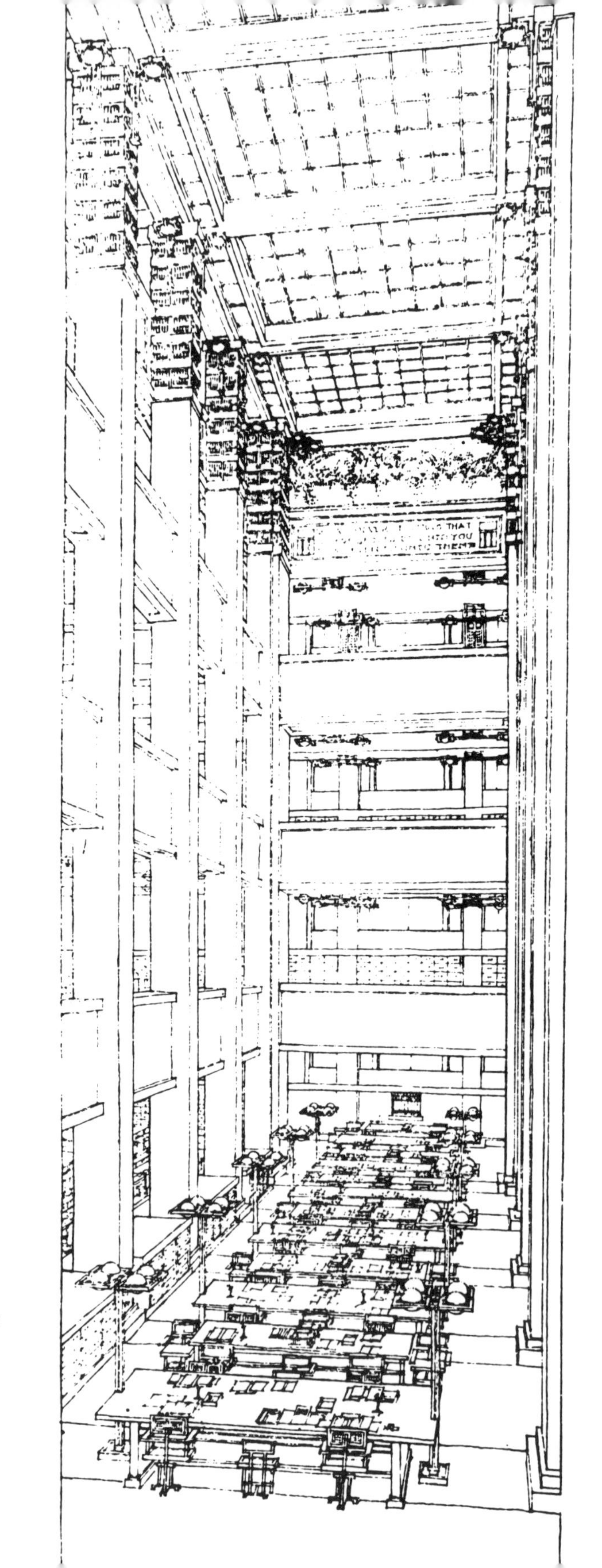

A drawing of a view of the interior work hall of the Larkin Company Administration Building (1903) at Buffalo, New York (demolished 1949–1950). This office building was the first to be equipped with metal furniture made in the United States and the first to be air-conditioned. Drawing reproduced from Frank Lloyd Wright, Ausgeführte Bauten und Entwürfe von Frank Lloyd Wright *(Berlin: Ernst Wasmuth, 1910).*

18 The Frank P. Brown Medal of the Franklin Institute

Now I believe architecture to be the humanizing of building. The more humane, the more rich and significant, inviting, and charming your architecture becomes, the more truly is it the great basis of a true culture. Unless it is true architecture in this sense, the less it's architecture at all.

Introduction

Frank Lloyd Wright was awarded the Frank P. Brown Medal of The Franklin Institute of the State of Pennsylvania on Wednesday, October 21, 1953; the medal was presented officially at the Institute's lecture hall in Philadelphia on Friday, June 4, 1954. Several days earlier, on Thursday, May 27, Mr. Wright addressed the Detroit Chapter of the American Institute of Architects on the subject of architecture in a democracy [see Chapter 25].

During his visit to Philadelphia, Mr. Wright also planned several meetings with Rabbi Mortimer J. Cohen and other members of the congregation of the Beth Sholom Synagogue. The purpose of these meetings was to discuss his

Text of the presentation and acceptance speech reprinted from "Presentation of the Frank P. Brown Medal," *Journal of The Franklin Institute,* Vol. CCLVII, September 1954, pp. 217–218, and Frank Lloyd Wright's "American Architecture," *Journal of The Franklin Institute,* Vol. CCLVII, September 1954, pp. 219–224, by permission of the *Journal of the Franklin Institute.*

proposals and plans for their new temple at Elkins Park, Pennsylvania, designed earlier in the year. The following is a brief account of Mr. Wright's arrival on June 4th to receive the Medal from The Franklin Institute:

> *Finally, the great day arrived [i.e., June 4, 1954]. Dressed for the reception and dinner at the Franklin Institute, the Cohens arrived to escort [Mr.] Wright from the Barclay [Hotel]. . . . When they called the Wright suite they discovered that the guest of honor had arrived safely, registered, and settled in but in the meantime had also disappeared. Where was he? Remembering that despite his energy and vitality [Mr.] Wright was a man in his eighties, the Cohens worried that some accident had befallen him. None of his entourage seemed to know what had happened to him. He had departed the hotel. Within the hour he was due at the Institute reception. As . . . the Cohens waited in the [hotel] lobby, consumed with anxiety, a taxi pulled up to the entrance of the hotel and the unmistakable figure of the architect emerged.*[1]

Mr. Wright had left the hotel to visit Oskar Stonorov, another Philadelphia architect, but he returned in time to receive the medal and address the awaiting audience.

The Frank P. Brown Medal was awarded to Mr. Wright for his extensive contributions to the field of architecture. It was founded by the Institute in 1938 and was awarded to inventors for discoveries and inventions that involved meritorious improvements in the building and allied industries.

---

[1] Extracted from Patricia Talbot Davis' *Together They Built a Mountain*, Lititz, Pennsylvania: Sutter House, 1974, p. 55.

The Presentation

S. WYMAN ROLPH (*President of the Institute*): Ladies and gentlemen, we will now hear from Mr. Coleman Sellers, a member of the Science and Arts Committee, who will tell us why the Frank P. Brown Medal should be awarded to our distinguished guest Mr. Wright. Mr. Sellers—

COLEMAN SELLERS: Mr. President, I present Frank Lloyd Wright for an award. Our candidate is without question the dean of American architecture. His influence on the architectural thought of our times has been great and far-reaching, both in this country and abroad. His career is unmatched, extending over a period of sixty years and still going on. Mr. Wright has always insisted on a return to *true* basic architectural principles. In that sense he is a *true* traditionalist. He has consistently hewed to his own line and refused to be submerged by the architectural trends of the times. Our candidate has shown remarkable foresight, imagination, and a brilliant romanticism of his own. He has always contributed the sensitivity of an artist to the architectural problems that he solved. In addition, he has always had a strong idea of what the technological advancements of our times have meant to architecture and he has used, with great

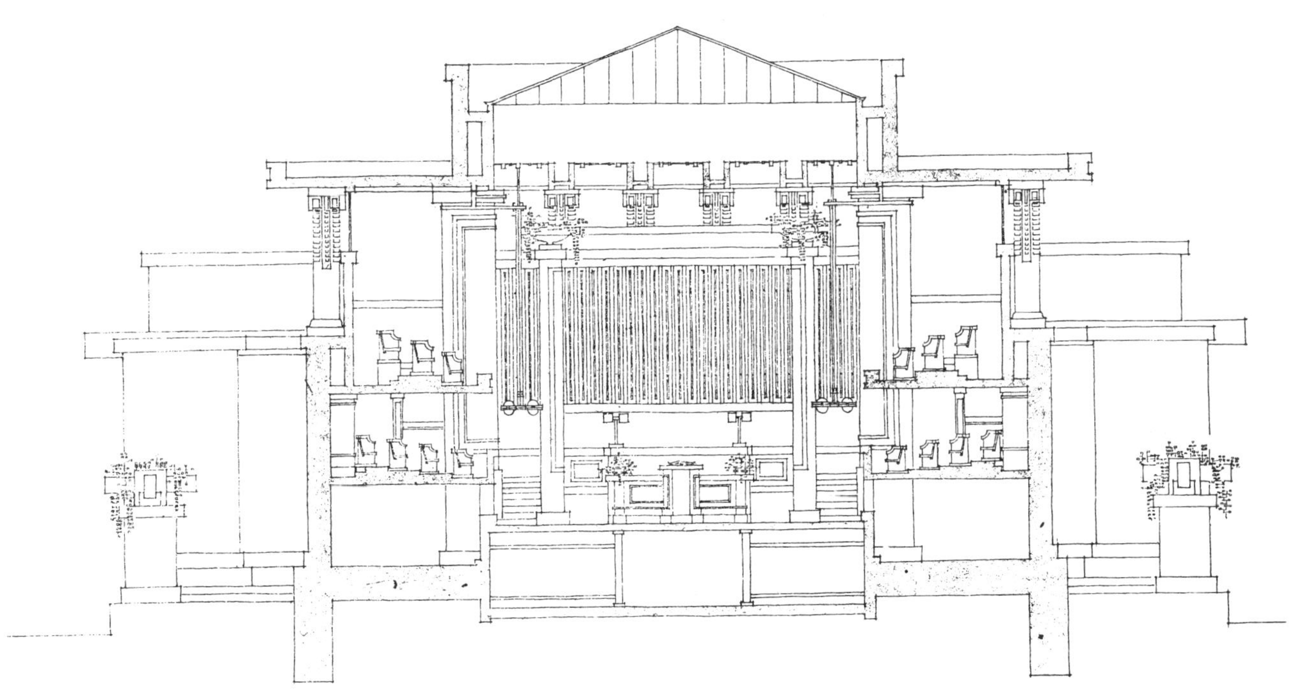

Interior sectional drawing of the main auditorium of Unity Church (1905) at Oak Park, Illinois, one of Mr. Wright's best examples of the "destruction of the box." Drawing reproduced from Frank Lloyd Wright, Ausgeführte Bauten und Entwürfe von Frank Lloyd Wright *(Berlin: Ernst Wasmuth, 1910).*

discernment, the many new inventions available in the field.

The work of Mr. Wright is probably most generally known by his homes. He has designed buildings, however, of all types, including commercial, industrial, and civic. All have shown great originality. For instance, the Larkin Building in Buffalo, [New York], built in the nineties, a contemporary of the Flatiron Building in New York, had many advanced features for that time. In the first place, it contrasted sharply with the architecture of that period, which was tending more and more to elaboration. This office building was designed in the terms of straight lines and flat planes. The heart of the building was the many-galleried court, lighted from above and from windows on the sides that were sealed from dirt and noise of the nearby railroad yard. The furnishings and filing systems were built in of steel. This building had many firsts: the first metal furniture made in the United States, the first air-conditioned office building, the first use of magnesite as architectural material, the first metal-bound, plate-glass doors and windows, and so forth.

Unity Temple, built in 1905, in Oak Park, [Illinois], was a Unitarian Church which was quite remarkable. Both outwardly and inwardly it went entirely contrary to anything ever constructed. Mr. Wright provided a quiet, simple, well lighted room, which gave the effect of a happy cloudless day as he predicted. This building was the first concrete monolith in the world. That is, it was the first building designed for and completed in the wooden forms into which the concrete was poured. Walls, roof, and floor were all made of this comparatively new building material.

One of Mr. Wright's most famous buildings is the Imperial Hotel in Tokyo. It was built to withstand

An interior view of the long promenade on the second level of the Imperial Hotel (1915) in Tokyo (demolished 1968). The hotel's floating foundation allowed it to survive that city's great earthquake in 1923. Photograph courtesy of the State Historical Society of Wisconsin.

earthquakes and went through the terrible quake of 1923 unscathed while practically all of Tokyo was in ruins. This was no mere chance, for the architect studied his problem most thoroughly and decided he would not fight the earthquake but make his building so that it could ride out the waves of the earth which he found were produced during quakes. Test borings showed him there were eight feet of topsoil resting on sixty to seventy feet of liquid mud. By carefully making concrete test piles and loading them with pig iron, he determined how much load they would support in various locations. The entire hotel was then designed on supporting piles about eight feet long.

Mr. Wright has been the recipient of many honors and medals. Among these are the highest awards of such organizations as the American Institute of Architects and the Royal Institute of British Architects. He has had similar awards from a dozen different countries. I take great pleasure in presenting Frank Lloyd Wright, of Taliesin, Wisconsin, as a candidate for the Frank P. Brown Medal, in consideration of his very extensive contributions to the entire field of architecture over a period of more than half a century, by means of countless and varied buildings, by reason of his many writings and lectures, and through his Fellowship at Taliesin, Wisconsin.

ROLPH: Mr. Wright, on behalf of The Franklin Institute of the State of Pennsylvania, I present to you this Frank P. Brown Medal . . .

WRIGHT: [holding the medal up] So you can all see it.

ROLPH: . . . and this certificate goes with the medal and the report which also accompanies the medal.

WRIGHT: What is this for?

ROLPH: We are very happy to make this award to you, sir, for the reasons which Mr. Sellers has given to us.

WRIGHT: A very fine medal indeed, Mr. Rolph!

ROLPH: Now we hope, Mr. Wright, that this fine unusual audience which expresses its admiration for you . . .

WRIGHT: Extraordinarily intelligent!

ROLPH: . . . will have the pleasure of hearing more of your wit and wisdom, sir.

WRIGHT: I don't know about the wisdom and I'm never sure of the wit!

The Acceptance Speech

WRIGHT: Ladies and gentlemen, this is a serious occasion. I was blamed for recently accepting, with lightness, and, I thought, some grace—a similar honor from the American Institute of Arts and Letters [see Chapter 17]. The comment upon the reception of the medal at that time was that mine was a cranky and cocky acceptance. I am not cranky now and I am not cocky. I am seriously gratified to have science thus recognize one in the field of art, which is, after all, rather low down at this time in the history of our world. So, I am glad to find myself here, a mere artist, in the presence of all that America knows anything about in the way of progress—in culture or anything else—and that is to say, science. You know very well, just as I know from a lot of experience during sixty years past, that science has given us all a magnificent toolbox full of splendid tools that we don't yet know how to use. Now, it is *true* that if we are ever going to learn how to use them it isn't going to be science that is going to teach us. At least, we are beginning to wake up to that fact and I suppose that here tonight an artist among scientists is something like a lady among lions—or is it a lion among ladies?; anyway, a terrible thing; I think I should owe what I do owe of distinction on this occasion to the fact that science is here awarding the medal to an artist. So I accept this token of honor in that unique spirit because I believe it is—it must be—unique.

A civilization, ladies and gentlemen, what is a civilization? There have been so very many but where are they all now? You see—a civilization is only a way of life—that's all it is. And you'll have to forgive me for now reminding you of the fact that that's all we have—*a way of life.* A *true* culture would be one where religion and art come in together, hand in hand—as they must. It is the way of making that way of life *a beautiful* way of life. Have we begun on it? Look about you. It isn't necessary to point out our buildings, they are growing more and more negative and desolate and inhuman. What have *we* emphasized as the *beautiful* in our way of life? What have we in it all that we can point to with pride as an awakening of an indigenous culture of our own? Now—as I am—wouldn't *you* too be put to it to answer? You wouldn't say painting, would you?

You see in me one of the few gray heads you'll see today that ever had the benefit of Froebel's wisdom when he was a youngster of six, seven, etc. Now it was Froebel's idea that no child should be allowed to draw directly from *nature* until he had mastered the rudimentary forms and elements of the various elemental forms in *nature*: the square, the triangle, the spheres, the circle, all forms that are basic to *nature*—primitive. Here is the square—symbol of integrity, the triangle—symbol of aspiration, the sphere or the circle—infinity—all forms in one dimension, the flat dimension. Then the forms go into the third dimension. Out of the circle you get the sphere; out of the square you get the cube; out of the triangle comes the tetrahedron. Well, that significance is merely a little indication of their importance in creation. We haven't time to talk much about this thing, but I've touched upon it to show how the elemental basis of thought in creative architecture goes back to these primary things, primarily. As a result, when I learned these things thoroughly, I didn't care to draw from *nature,* or to boondoggle with the surface-effects of anything at all. I wanted to combine, construct, to build, to create with these simple elements, and I believe that's where creation must begin in education.

I cannot believe that you can make an artist creative the same way that you make a scientist or a businessman. I do not think that we as a people—I won't say as a culture but as a way of life—understand the difference between the artist and the scientist or art and science. Radically, they occupy different worlds at the present time, as always. But some day the synthesis will be made between them; and I believe that synthesis is one thing a great institute like this should be busy with and might accomplish. Perhaps, beyond any other thing that synthesis would be *the* missing synthesis. Standing before you here tonight speaking to you in this scientists' hall from this scientists' rostrum, that is one of the hopeful signs I can be cheered by, this evidence that science is awakening to the fact that although it can take things apart it can never put them together again without the creative artist. Now the more you think about it the more you'll see that in that missing synthesis is where our civilization is today. We worship this god science and not with un-reason. But with un-reason we have neglected art and religion, those two essentials which always have and always will constitute the *soul* of a civilization. Now, a scientist does not know how to draw the line between the curious and the beautiful. That's where your creative artist comes in and that's where our culture as a nation must come in when we really have one. Until we as a nation know how to draw that line between what is merely curious and what is *truly* beautiful we haven't a culture of our own and without that discrimination you're not cultured beings yourselves.

It matters little how much education you've received in the backward and forward of our times or how much you may have been *conditioned* by favorable or unfavorable conditions or by the accepted educational conditioning of the mind; you are ignorant of that essence which is the only thing which can save a civilization as a culture for the future—if it is unknown to you. These are strong words, I suppose. You haven't heard them often. Why? You haven't heard them because all the education you know and all the educational systems established in our country today are based upon some scientific thesis of this or that and expounded by talk by men largely themselves—shall I say—mere scientists?

We have largely imported the German ways of thought. The German idea of living things is essentially scientific, seldom or never deeply artistic; never can be creative in artistic sense because the German self wasn't born that way—Goethe and Beethoven excepted. Nor the English. But we Americans were born in so many different ways. All the ways there are. We are a *mongrel* civilization. Aren't we? There is no definite trend of thought which we have inherited outside the British and—God help us all—all we ever got from the British was the British dormitory town; we call it Old Colonial. No, we didn't get the beautiful old England. For instance, we didn't get the best of what England got from France—much of it. The Old Colonial, of course, we did get from England. Where did England get it? From France. And where did France get it? From Italy. Music still speak Italian. What is the Italian word *chiaroscuro*—painting speaks it. You know that it was Italian? So it goes. There was the great Dante, the great liberator of what we call literature. He, too, was Italian, wasn't he? Well, also from Italy, from the Italians came the *soul* this art we call "architecture" ever has had.

Now it is the greatest of tragedies 500 years old now, at least, that the Italians thought art could be restated in the old Greek terms and then got what they called the Renaissance and we got this rebirth from them. If you go to Europe with love in your heart now, you'll see how all the great thought and feeling of the Middle Ages recorded there in stone, brick, and mortar was desecrated, yes demoralized by the academic sense of the old pictures made by Greek architecture made new. That, too, is when the painter first came in to curse architecture wherefrom we got the idea that a painter could see a building. He really cannot. Much less can he do one. But then and there Michelangelo gave us the symbol of authority—the dome in air on posts—then in common with other nations, we have adopted, which is, of course, completely bogus from any structural point of view—or standpoint with integrity; utterly phony—an arch up in the air on columns, on posts, a very fancy picture but nonsensical construction. Yet an anachronism became the symbol of authority for the whole world. And you can see how little *organic* thinking and how little deep feeling has gone into this matter of building if it is to be a quality in the life inhabiting that building. We might call that quality *integrity*? Now, it is that simple *integrity* that's lacking in our lives today—*integrity* and *soul*—no *depth* of feeling.

We have developed insensate voracity by way of speed to a point dangerous to the future of our civilizations, such as it is. Science has aided and abetted the circumstance without conscience. By way of science we have all the means of rapacity, speed, and destruction. Where is salvation coming from?

Well, we must again have recourse to those things of the spirit which have always borne the name art and religion. The two are as one. They work together or we cease to work at all, as a culture. No future. As a civilization—pretty close to the end.

Now, who built the first city? I myself have just learned from Rabbi Cohen today. How many of you know who was the originator of what we call the modern city? Ladies and gentlemen, please speak up! Do you know? I didn't know. It was Cain, the murderer of his brother. He built the first city. He was the author of urbanism. In urbanism isn't Cain still murdering his brother? Who then is going to do something about that? Science? No. Science can keep on building these great inimical blocks of nonentity, these great negations of the richness and the joy of the humane life of the American individual; these great masses of what? They are built by the insurance companies of America—bless *your* money. The people's savings are entrusted to these merciless magnates, "safely" spent to be paid back in time of need. That's why I never would take out a dollar's worth of insurance! And do you know—sotto voce—I recommend to you the same thing. If that's the best insurance companies can do with money, then let's put an end to so-called insurance and pay for our own impotence or carelessness in our own way—every man responsible for his own mistakes and he be the profiteer of his own virtues. I'm just paying now for one of mine.

Last spring I started a dried-grass fire at Taliesin with only one of my boys in sight. We hadn't yet opened the buildings. Suddenly—the wind changed and blew the well meant grass fire up against the building. We lost our theater. We also lost ten rooms and lost our dining room. There was not a dollar of insurance. But we are gradually making it much better now. The neighbors came, enjoyed the scene; they all came and sat on the grass and watched it—as they might—with pleasure? It wasn't costing them anything. There was no insurance.

Pardon this poignant—perhaps pointless—digression. The point I came here to make to you tonight concerned science *versus* art. Until we—the people—make the needed synthesis between them and these two become as one—yes—until the religionist and the artist and the scientist can stand up, understanding each other to work together, the one unwilling to proceed without the other, then only will we have a culture worthy the name. Then only will we be somebody in our own right. We will not then be political in the nonsensical sense that we are now political—I'm from Wisconsin. So I think that the situation in which our America finds itself at the present time, though bad enough architecturally, bad enough artistically, is politically a profanity.

Yes, ladies and gentlemen, this is a serious occasion. Here you come upon matter more serious than you may imagine. Here you really have come to put your own finger upon the center of our fault and upon the very center, too, of our hope. Because we do have hope in this nation today, although our hope has been superficially assumed and often mistaken, too often run off as some fashion in this or that direction or run off as a silly faction in that or another direction—still—I say, we do have the centerline of a *true* democratic culture in what is properly called *organic architecture*. That philosophy is something you may now learn to know.

You have seen what is now called modern architecture. That is merely contemporary. It isn't *truly* modern, that is to say most of it isn't; very little of it is *truly* modern. Most of it is merely contemporary along the lines of prevalent fashion. Most of it, too, is going to disappear and be hateful tomorrow, generally speaking—even the better class of residence made in that vein is already hateful as those red groups of prison buildings in New York City, Los Angeles—I guess you've got them in Philadelphia, too—or soon will have them if you buy insurance. Hateful as they are and inhumane.

Now I believe architecture to be the *humanizing* of building. The more humane, the rich and more significant, inviting, and charming your architecture becomes, the more *truly* is it the great basis of a *true* culture. Unless it is *true* architecture in this sense, the less it's architecture at all. May I ask you what those qualities in a building are that make that quality of humanity a possibility or probability? Certainly it would have nothing in common with what we call "housing," would it? It certainly would have nothing in common with anything we could properly call a "style. "The Colonial style, of course, is not really a style, but it was colonial. *Truth* to say, it was Italian architecture Frenchified by English adoption and came over in the Mayflower to our shores. We got it as inheritance. So far, so good. Why not? We had no culture of our own whatsoever. It was the best thing we could get, probably, certainly the best thing we could do at the time. But why now? As a prosperous nation we have been "in business" some 160 years; isn't it time we got something finer, deeper, more characteristic, more *truly* democratic than the hangover of an old aristocracy? America must build and *democracy* must build if America builds.

Now democracy has already started building. An *organic* architecture is ours. If you'll take time to study the centerline of the philosophy of an *organic* architecture, you will find you've got the centerline of the democratic faith and spirit of this nation. See how many of you know it already. But you are going to know more of it and you're going to know it soon. Knowledge of its principles must break into the ranks of education—somehow, somewhere. Now this may not be in our great universities. It may be that we'll have to take architecture away from the universities, even take it away from the professional architects, and turn it over to boys that really know how to build something—the contractors? Then God help architecture!

Well, ladies and gentlemen of Philadelphia, I am extremely gratified—I was about to say honored but that word is of dubious origin. I won't use it. As an *artist,* I am pleased by this token of esteem by way of *science.* As an *architect,* I want to raise my hand to salute the memory of a great man—*Benjamin Franklin*!

Frank Lloyd Wright in London for the annual prizegiving of the Architectural Association on Friday, July 14, 1950. Photograph courtesy of Dr. S.E.T. Cusdin of London, England.

19 To the Students of London's Architectural Association

In the giving of prizes it is just as it is in any competition. First of all, the judges are selected from amongst those . . . who . . . can agree so that you get the average of an average, and then they always go through them and throw out the best ones and the worst ones, and then they get together and average upon the average, so that the prize or the result of the competition is an average of an average of averages.

Introduction

Frank Lloyd Wright visited London's Architectural Association (AA) in 1939 and again in 1950. During these visits his talks with the students and faculty of the institution were recorded. Section I of this chapter presents his 1939 talk to the

Section I of this chapter was edited and reproduced from "Mr. Frank Lloyd Wright at the AA," *The Architectural Association Journal* (London), Vol. 54, May 1939, pp. 268–269. Section II of this chapter was edited and reproduced from "Dinner to Mr. and Mrs. Frank Lloyd Wright," *The Architectural Association Journal* (London), Vol. 66, August/September 1950, pp. 44–46. Section III of this chapter was edited and reproduced from "Annual Prize-Giving: Presentations by Mr. Frank Lloyd Wright," *The Architectural Association Journal* (London), Vol. 66, August/September 1950, pp. 32–37. Reproduced by permission of The Architectural Association of London.

AA and Sections II and III contain two talks given in 1950, at which time he was to assist in awarding prizes to the architectural students as part of their annual prize giving.

In 1939 Mr. Wright was able to visit the AA in conjunction with the Watson Lectures, a now famous series given at the Royal Institute of British Architects on May 2, 4, 9, and 11, 1939, in London, at the invitation of the Sulgrave Manor Board.[1] The council of the AA invited Mr. Wright to be present at their general meeting on Tuesday, May 2, 1939, and to be the guest of the principal, staff, and students at a luncheon on Thursday, May 4. On that morning Mr. Wright showed a color motion picture film of his work to an interested AA school audience. After the lunch on May 4, Mr. Wright visited the school studios and later addressed the students. The complete text of this address is contained in Section I of this chapter.

Mr. Wright returned to London to meet with the AA in the early part of July 1950 and to present prizes to students on the annual prize day of the AA School of Architecture. During this visit he spoke at a dinner in his honor on Friday, July 7; the text of this dinner talk appears in Section II of this chapter. He spoke again on Friday afternoon, July 14, under a large marquee in Bedford Square, London; the text of this presentation speech to the prize-winning students is reproduced in Section III of this chapter.[2]

Reflecting on Mr. Wright's 1950 visit to the AA, Robert Furneaux Jordan (one of the hosts on that occasion) made the following statement shortly after Mr. Wright's departure[3]:

> *I think his visit was a symbol; he came perhaps because in the first half of this century he—in his way—went through just the same sort of fight with men and traditions that the young architects of today will—in their way—have to go through in the next half century. It will of course be a very far cry from the London of, say, 1990 to the Chicago of 1890; the conditions will be vastly different socially and technically, but it is evident that if a new visual and physical environment is to*

---

[1] These famous lectures have been published as Frank Lloyd Wright's *An Organic Architecture: The Architecture of Democracy,* London: Lund Humphries and Co., 1939, 1941, 1970, and later republished by The MIT Press at Cambridge in 1970.

[2] In addition to the reproduction of this speech in *The Architectural Association Journal* (Vol. 66, August/September 1950, pp. 32–37), the text has also appeared as "AA: Frank Lloyd Wright, "*The Architect's Journal* (England), Vol. 112, July 27, 1950, pp. 86–87, as "Frank Lloyd Wright Addresses the Students of the Architectural Association, "*Architectural Design,* Vol. 20, August 1950, pp. 219 and 232, and as "AA 125 Echoes from the Past: Frank Lloyd Wright—The Annual Distribution of Prizes—1950, "*Architectural Association Quarterly,* Vol. 5, No. 1, January/March 1973, pp. 46–47.

[3] Edited and excerpted from Robert Furneaux Jordan's "A Great Architect's Visit to Britain: Robert Furneaux Jordan on Frank Lloyd Wright," *The Listener* (London), Vol. XLIV, September 28, 1950, pp. A15–A16. Portions of this article also appeared later as "Lloyd Wright in Britain: Mr. R. Furneaux Jordan's Radio Talk," *Builder: An Illustrated Weekly Magazine for the Architect* (England), Vol. 179, No. 5653, November 24, 1950, p. 540. Both articles cited here were transcribed from the BBC radio program titled *Third Programme,* broadcast on September 21, 1950. Text reprinted here by permission of Mrs. Robert Furneaux Jordan.

be created in our cities that the same old battle against obscurantism, philistinism, commercialism and academicism will have to be fought all over again.

It is true that we, at the AA School, invited Frank Lloyd Wright to England for the same reason as one might have invited, say, William Morris (had he been alive)—not only for what he had done but for what he had stood for. In the end, however, it will be the charm and the kindness that remain as a memory. Interwoven with the charm, or perhaps they are really the ingredients, are other qualities—an insatiable curiosity, an incredible vitality and an altogether delightful vanity. From the moment of his arrival in this country there was nothing about people or agriculture or the economic system about which he did not want to know the answer. Of the Queen Elizabeth *and its human cargo he held, on the whole, a poor view (as any man is entitled to do), and of the customs shed, its construction and organization his critical eye missed nothing. On the road from Southampton he noted the material of every cottage, the species of every cow and every piece of woodland, and then—at the end of a long day—he pushed all the furniture around to his better liking.*

His vanity might take some such innocent form as setting off to St. James' Street to buy top hats—in the plural. On the other hand, the experience of a lifetime was reflected in the self-assurance with which for two hours he gave the Chief Architect to the LCC a criticism of the Royal Festival Hall. He did not want to climb ladders, the drawings and models were good enough: "My boy, I can tell from those drawings what your building is like to the last gnat's heel." And at one point someone said, "So you fear, Mr. Wright, that we might get a little too much reverberation," he replied, "Fear! I don't fear, I know. I'm telling you. Sullivan and I built twenty-six concert halls and I know." In spite of his criticism, at the end came the smile and he asked for a box on the opening night of what, he admitted, would be a very great building. But he told me afterwards that that criticism, a detailed technical analysis of a great building, had tired him more than anything else on his visit.

With his Wisconsin and Arizona background it was difficult to make him realize fully the physical planning problems created by a population of fifty million in this small industrialized island. Finally, however, one did maneuver him in front of the great wall map of Greater London at the County Hall: "My God!" he said, "My God! What a morass!"

It is in the potentialities of bare wood, of granite and stone, of the Japanese way of extending house into garden, of the vast open hearth, of the organic linking of building and site or in such romantic conceptions as the translucent canvas roofing of the Arizona studios that he has found his main inspiration. It is this feeling for the organic and the romantic, I think, that explains his ecstatic response to the English Cotswolds. This was certainly not just the response of the American tourist to bogus Tudor, it was the stone walls of the sheeplands [sic], the barns, the simpler cottages and smallest churches that excited him—these and the humanized English landscape.

His dislike of the Renaissance sometimes led him to extremes; his comment while dining in the Goldsmiths Hall in the City—with its Corinthian columns, gilded ceiling and glass chandelier—"I acknowledge the dignity of this hall, but I deny that it has

Frank Lloyd Wright visited the Cotswolds in South Wales in July of 1950 with representatives of London's Architectural Association. Pictured in the top row (left to right)*, Mr. and Mrs. S.E.T. Cusdin, Mrs. and Mr. Frank Lloyd Wright, Robert Furneaux Jordan, and H. Calvin; bottom row* (left to right)*, Cadbury Brown, H. Goddard, and H. Dysillus. Photograph courtesy of Dr. S.E.T. Cusdin of London, England.*

a soul"—fair comment, perhaps, but the slightest classical twirl on an Elizabethan doorway would also bring down fulminations upon foreign intrusions. He never saw that there was an Anglicized Renaissance no less native to us than the barn roof. I once said to him that Shakespeare, whom he loves, was part of that *Renaissance, but his only comment was "Almost."*

However, his incurable romanticism, his love of the vernacular, the native and the organic must not be confused with any sham antiquarianism. In a Cotswold valley, he saw one of the loveliest of the smaller early manor houses together with the collections that may one day surprise the nation. This shook him a little—so clean outside the realm of ordinary tourism—but afterwards he had his comment: "There's medievalism, my boy, dead on your chest." His excitement returned when he got back to reality and to our welfare state at work; he went to see his ancestral Wales, and in Wales an industrial development area—new factories, new housing, new schools. This was real as well as romantic, and it belonged to the future, not to

Frank Lloyd Wright talks with Mrs. Wright (center), *Dr. S.E.T. Cusdin* (left), *and Robert Furneaux Jordan in the Cotswolds, South Wales, in July of 1950. Photograph courtesy of Dr. S.E.T. Cusdin of London, England.*

the past—it was more, it was his own decentralization at work, getting men out of dead cities. The factories and the houses might be good or bad, but here in the Welsh mountains where men had rotted in the 'thirties something was really happening, as real and practical as the Cotswold barn had once been—and FLW was really excited at last.

And so back to London and to the students. They did not all understand or approve of what he was driving at. From his grandfather who preached hellfire a hundred years ago in those same Welsh valleys he has derived a messianic touch, and when a man has been preaching his philosophy for so long a good many of the thought processes, essential to the argument, tend to get jumped. But he understood the student. He must have done, for he has written of them when he wrote of his own youth when his grandfather had already given him the motto "Truth Against the World"—has written of himself as "the young sentimentalist in love with the truth!" And he added, "Is there a more tragic figure on earth—in any generation?"

Section I: At the AA on May 4, 1939

G.A. JELLICOE: Ladies and gentlemen, I feel we are extraordinarily honored to have Mr. Frank Lloyd Wright to address us. As I said in my talk to you this morning, I consider him to be the finest exponent of his particular approach to architecture in the world. He has held that position for a great number of years and I hope that he may continue to maintain it for a great number more. Mr. Wright is young in mind—perhaps he is younger than anyone of us here today.

WRIGHT: I see you are ladies and gentlemen. Where I come from you would be just boys and girls. Well, I hope you will live up to it. I do not know what to say—talk is cheap, there is a lot of it, and by way of talk I have not seen very much happen in my time. What is needed is action, and with so many young architects sitting in front of me—oh, my goodness, how many!—I hope you will take *heed.*

Were architects always creative; were they always animated by love of principles! If they knew the principles of building and did not care so much about types, shapes, and styles of buildings! What you need is no poring over scrappy styles, but to know a little more of the inside, what's going on, and not what circumstances have thrust upon you. After all, we are concerned with culture; architects should be the centerline of culture. You chaps and girls, too, are going to be the interpreters of your time. You are going to have to put things together. You have to form something suitable, for what we have—and, boys and girls, believe me—is like nothing that existed before. Concrete, steel—a few of the things—are the mixture of life that is changing its principles. Drive a motorcar up to the door of your style house—Tudor of what-not Georgian—what happens? That is what is happening in life every day. Cities, towns, built and established for conditions which are no longer there. Congestion, muddle, force of circumstances of herding together as we do for convenience of living. Where are we now? The more we get together, the more we destroy the whole.

You have to interpret by way of new ideals, new character, new thoughts in building. What we call modern architecture is a change in that thought back to the basis of building. It isn't a change in styles of building or form by way of somebody's taste as it used to be, although it is still an aestheticism. I think you will see in Le Corbusier the statement of an aesthetic that is working itself up about machines, but if you take only that it is fatal. Now for a long, long time this thing we love called *architecture* has been pretty sick; for 500 years at least.

Principle went out of architecture; I think the Renaissance was a confusion that principle had left and the realm of aestheticism had begun. After

Frank Lloyd Wright presents a point to representatives of London's Architectural Association in July of 1950 at the Cotswolds in South Wales. Photograph courtesy of Dr. S.E.T. Cusdin of London, England.

all, the Renaissance is something out of life, not of it, and I presume you might say, because life was lacking, that building was lacking. They had no coherent sense of direction, no real culture of their own, and so the hybrid mass came about.

Perhaps at the present time, having no clear idea of things, no clear idea as to where we are going, perhaps you think you can strive with all this and make good things and adapt and adopt. May be, but I do not—no—do not believe you can do it. I think you suffer from this congestion, this tastelessness, that is put upon you by these conditions of life, this hangover of today. It is up to youth to devise and put into effect better things, and where are you going to learn about them—not from books, not from others or armchairs, as the armchair itself is tired of this affectation. You've got to see how work is being done—off the hard pavements. Get a place out in the country, get a plan for building something to work, function, and live, and get down to work and build it yourself. Conscript nature. Nature study, believe me, is the proper study for an architect and not what other people are doing or have done. It may help, maybe, looking at others, but it may also hurt. You see, when young minds are seeking the way out, to show them another man's way out is likely to hypnotize and disturb rather than to inspire. You can all look at the work of the past; if you study those expressions in relation to the times existing they may be just too bad, like the baroque or the rococo, all bad and superficial. You may have learnt from them, but it is best to throw them overboard. Get down to trees, flowers, and plants; how things are made and grow, how they establish character, and how they develop individuality, and how building must do these, too. The real life of the building must develop a form and character, taking into account the nature of the materials.

Things which are to be governed by machines have become a basis for a new eclecticism, all an exploitation with no understanding of [the] prin-

Mrs. and Mr. Frank Lloyd Wright relax under a large tree while visiting the Cotswolds in South Wales in July of 1950. Photograph courtesy of Dr. S.E.T. Cusdin of London, England.

ciples of life. That is what I object to, myself. It is the weakness of them. The era has bred a new influence which from my point of view has no creative characteristic and is by way of taste. I wish there were some way of heading you off from this practice of life or architecture. Of course, they have aesthetic principles, but until they have their feet on the ground—a good term that—they cannot get their heads in the clouds; and with their feet on the ground it is quite sensible [that] they should aspire. But before that they must create understanding, seeing it together; to think that landscape architecture, engineering, science of building, should be three separate things—it is ridiculous in itself. The architect we need is a master builder who will make a perfect welding between his building, trees, and life as well. This architecture I am talking about is *organic* architecture. Modern architecture is anything built today. Any building built now is modern, but you should learn to say *organic* if you are going that way.

So it is rather a big old world you are getting into—I think you ought to get together and draw up some plan, some idea of what you are aiming at. Finally, there are masters like Mr. Jellicoe who will have to prune you and weed you thoroughly, perhaps five to one. I think architecture is going to have the master builder and sham architecture must go overboard.

Well, it is a long subject and I could go on and on for a long time; but I did not know what to talk about and so there you have a few random thoughts.

G.A. JELLICOE: We have heard a great address from a sincere master builder and a sincere man. All of you should weigh his words carefully, for the future of architecture in this country is concerned with what he has said this afternoon.

At lunch I gathered an impression from Mr. Wright on the only point on which I would dare cross swords with him. He feels England is in rather a bad way at the moment [May 4, 1939]; but I think you will agree with me, I can tell him *right now* we are not. I propose a hearty vote of thanks.

Section II: At the AA on July 7, 1950

DR. S.E.T. CUSDIN (*President of the AA*): It is my pleasure to extend a very sincere and heartfelt welcome to our distinguished visitors. In Frank Lloyd Wright's decision to come here at our invitation I think that we can recognize the evergreen and indomitable courage of the pioneer.

Apart from my pleasure, I confess that I am extremely nervous—so nervous, indeed, that I might repeat the error of the student who, called upon to pay a tribute to another great man, said of Oliver Cromwell that he was a man with an iron will and a large red nose, and that underneath it was a deeply religious feeling, and that he won the Battle of Worcester on the anniversary of his death. For consolation I turn to Sir Eustace Peachtree's book *The Dangers of this Mortal Life,* in which he recalls that amongst the most noble dicta of ancient Rome there was the fancy that when men heard thunder on the left the Gods had some special advertisement to impart, and then the prudent laid down their affairs to study what Jove had intended. Though we no longer believe in these divinities, I hope that we shall be able to invoke a gentle peal from my right for our pleasure, instruction, and delight.

WRIGHT: You will get more thunder from the left!

CUSDIN: Since you were last here, sir, architecture has suffered a severe reverse, and I can now report that it is just recovering. After all your battles with

Mistress Architecture, we are looking to you for wisdom and guidance.

WRIGHT: Not for a good spanking?

CUSDIN: Maybe that as well, sir. No one who has read—and who has not—his autobiography will have failed to recognize the tender and devoted affection that Mr. Frank Lloyd Wright has for Mrs. Frank Lloyd Wright, and it is now my pleasure to ask our hostess to present a bouquet to Mrs. Frank Lloyd Wright as a token of our great respect. The response to the news of Mr. Frank Lloyd Wright's arrival here has been overwhelming, and Mr. and Mrs. Frank Lloyd Wright have a very full program in front of them. I do not intend that they should be overburdened tonight, the first night of their stay in London, with a lot of speeches. It gives me great pleasure to propose [a toast to] the health of Mr. and Mrs. Frank Lloyd Wright.

ROBERT FURNEAUX JORDAN (*Principal of the AA School*): I shall have other opportunities during the week, in the presence of the students, of saying more about the greatness of Mr. Frank Lloyd Wright and the honor which we receive by his visiting us here, so that all I want to do tonight is to remind you that the AA has a department called the school, and that about a year ago Mr. Frank Lloyd Wright, in Houston, when he received the AIA [Gold] Medal, said that that medal was bound to affect his future [see Chapter 16]. He was right because shortly after that I decided that it was really time that the AA Prize-giving was adorned by a great architect. There was only one great architect in the world, and so 500 students of the AA sent him a cable demanding his presence here this week, and here he is. He is extremely welcome as a very great architect, as a very great example in teaching, and as a symbol of what we want to do in the way of building and humanizing architecture and taking architecture back to nature and to the realities of humanity and to all that Mr. Frank Lloyd Wright has stood for.

With those few words on behalf of the school, I give Mr. and Mrs. Frank Lloyd Wright a very hearty welcome. It is indeed a great honor to have them and I only hope that we shall not work them too hard.

WRIGHT: Your Chairman asked me if I would say a few words. I should like to say a great many, and I thank you all. I remember a very charming occasion here when I sat over in the center of the room, how many years ago? It must be twelve years ago. I came over and did not have time then to discover America, but I have come this time really to discover America and England. It is a shame how we have abused time and how little we have done.

Almost everything that there is anywhere in the country that I have seen lying around here has an establishment. Here we are with a new idea which we call democracy, which has never got any further in our own minds than a love of freedom; and if you were to ask most of us what we mean by freedom you would see that we mean license.

I come over here and I find all this establishment, and what impresses me in your London is this feature and fact of establishment. To me it is amazing and I do not see how you ever get out from under. I think that if I had been born here in London you would never have heard of an *organic* architecture. I begin to feel that way when I look around and see how established everything is, how richly you have been done.

But it is admirable in a way. I myself have enough of the British in me to be proud of your tenacity, to be proud of what you have done with your back to the wall—and I guess that that is where you should always see a Britisher, with his back to the wall.

There was one that I met coming across. I had always thought that the Britisher had good manners. I boasted of the companionship of a cultivated Britisher; I thought it was the finest company in the world. But there was my lord on the ship coming over. The purser was indiscreet and invited some of us to a little party in his cabin. It was a great big ship, so big that it effaced the ocean travel; you do not know that you are on the ocean and you do not care if you are. Here was this Britisher—"Britisher" was an honorary title, because in fact he was from Canada, which, of course, modifies the circumstance. He was also very rich; he was a mercantile lord—I suspect you have lots of them now. He monopolized the purser, who was giving this party. We were all sitting round the room, and my lord stood with his back to us, managing the purser in conversation the entire evening. All that we could see was the smoke rising from his cigarette over the purser's head. Well, now, is that English? Is that good manners? No, I do not think it is. I never saw anything like that when I was here; it must be just what happens coming over on the Queen Mary or the Queen Elizabeth from the other side. You will forgive me for this slam. I thought he deserved it. I shall not tell you his name and anyhow I do not know what it is.

It is lovely to be here again. I enjoyed myself immensely in England when I was delivering the lectures for the Sulgrave Manor Board. People used to come to Mrs. Wright and ask her whether it was *true* that these lectures were extemporaneous and she assured them that it was. When they were brought to me by the old court reporter who had taken them all down I had nothing whatever to do to correct them; it was amazing and was the only time when a speech that I had made did not sound like the ravings of a drunken man. He had it straight and I had very little to do to it, and so it was published, when the bombs were falling on London, in one of the nicest little books I have seen.

That was the souvenir of my last visit to London in 1938—or was it 1939? At that time, I think, Chamberlain was in Munich with his umbrella and you were posting the town here with appeals to join up with Russia—"Sign up with Russia"! Do you remember it? It was all part of that visit, and that visit is for me a beautiful memory.

A few years after that we were sitting in our little home—that is not so little—in Arizona and listening to the radio, and in came the news that the Royal Institute of British Architects had recommended to the King that he should hand over the Gold Medal [of the Royal Institute of British Architects] to a boy out there in the tall grass of the western prairie, which he forthwith did, so that that was added to the color of this previous experience.

Now I am here again. I do not want to let you down, and least of all do I want to let myself down, and so I want to tell you, before I get through with this, what has happened since I was here before and how the hopes that I had concerning my influence in Britain have been rather damped by what I have seen, particularly in the replanning of London. If I had been successful, wherever a bomb hit you you would have planted grass. Instead of that you have rebuilt London wherever there has been damage and wherever a hole has been punched in your establishment. You cannot let go of that establishment. Now the time has come when the city is a dated circumstance, and I suppose—I cannot prove it, I can only invite your attention to it—that the finest gesture which could ever be made by Great Britain on behalf of its future and to ennoble its own *nature* would be to plant grass wherever a bomb fell. I do not care where it fell, even if it was on Buckingham Palace—plant grass!

That is, of course, spoken by an advocate of decentralization. Now, decentralization does not mean giving it all up; it means keeping it all in a better way for a better time and a better place. There are fifty million of you ganging up here in this establishment. To what end? What is your future? Have you a future? I wonder. Have any of us a future along the lines of this ganging up? Gangsterism is government now; the gang is in the saddle everywhere on earth. It is gang against gang. Where is the individual? Where is this thing that we profess, this democracy? In what does it consist? Are you democrats or are you democratic? Is Great Britain a democracy? Is the United States of America a democracy? I wonder. I think not. I do not believe that we know the meaning of that word; if we do, we are certainly renegades and traitorous in our attitude to it and in

*Mr. Robert Furneaux Jordan (*left*—Principal of the Architectural Association School), Frank Lloyd Wright, Dr. S.E.T. Cusdin (President of the Architectural Association), and Mrs. Frank Lloyd Wright in Bedford Square London, for the Association's annual prizegiving, Friday, July 14, 1950. Photograph courtesy of Dr. S.E.T. Cusdin of London, England.*

all that we have done of recent years, because if we have not betrayed democracy then democracy is not worth living for.

But can you betray something that you do not know anything about? Can you betray something of which you are unaware, which you thoughtlessly destroy? You cannot be called a traitor when you do a thing like that—or can you? No, I think that to be traitorous, to betray, you have to know what it is that you are betraying and sell it down the river consciously. For that you can be hanged, but for this thing that we have done there is no punishment except victory—and it seems that victory is about the most terrible punishment that can be administered in modern circumstances.

Architecture would seem to be extraneous to this circumstance and beside the mark in these circumstances. It is not. In the idea of an *organic* architecture we do have an interpretation of democracy; we do get nearer to the *nature* of it. This interpretation is the centerline of our future development; it means going from within outward, instead of gathering everything and putting it from the outside in, which is what we have been doing all over the world. We have been doing it especially in America, to such an extent that a Frenchman said that we were the only great nation that had proceeded from barbarism to degeneracy, with no civilization of our own in between. There it is, it is *true*. You laugh, and, of course, you English may laugh; but we Americans laugh, too. Why should we laugh? It is too *true*!

By this ideal of an *organic* architecture, the building of the thought and the feeling of a nation into sustenance with rhythm, poetry, charm, *truth,* we shall get to this thing that we call democracy because the principles of an *organic* architecture are the centerline of a democracy. When they asked the United Nations for a definition of democracy—as they did not so long ago; I do not know whether it got into the papers here—the United Nations returned eighty-five different answers, no two of which agreed. Speaking to President Harry Truman a little later, I said: "Don't you think, Mr. President, it's high time that at least we, the American people, tried to define ourselves to ourselves and know what we are all about?" He laughed and said "Yes," and that was all there was to that and it is all that there ever will be to that.

But what is this thing we call democracy in terms of actual performance? How are you going to actualize it? Great Britain has not got it. It does not lie in the direction of socialism or in the direction of communism or in the direction of any -ism or any -ist or any -ite. It is right within us, and that is where the ideals of an *organic* architecture are found—within us; the innate, integral actualization of human life and human *nature,* not pretending by way of some symbolism, not pretending by way of some effects, but that is it because it *is* it. It is something that comes out by way of *nature* as an innate expression of the human soul and do not be mistaken: there is a human soul. Notwithstanding all that we have seen and lived through, notwithstanding all that we see in the *nature* of establishment, there *is* a human soul, and that human soul survives, no matter what happens. There is a little something there which transforms it from one failure to the next failure, and then to the next failure, until ultimately the human race is going to succeed, and it will succeed.

That is the message that *organic* architecture has to bring; but we cannot deal with it all in one evening, and so, good night, everybody!

Section III: At the AA on July 14, 1950

DR. S.E.T. CUSDIN (*President of the Architectural Association*): Once again we have a prize giving and frequently this ceremony, marked by too many backward glances, takes on a funeral air. I hope that I can disperse any lingering wisps of depression by declaring the end of the old academic year and, with the regal formula, continue with "Long live the new!"

For your greater pleasure, I shall not indulge in any of the usual platitudes or old boys' stories, but it is necessary that I should express, on behalf of the council, our profound satisfaction at the achievements of the school and our gratitude to the students and to the teaching and administrative staff, with particular emphasis on the part played in that achievement by the principal, by his wise leadership and incredible scholarship.

To add to our delight we have with us today Mr. and Mrs. Frank Lloyd Wright, whose company confers upon us a great distinction. To them and to all our guests we extend a most sincere and hearty welcome.

ROBERT FURNEAUX JORDAN (*Principal of the Architectural Association School*): A few months ago some of us on the AA [Architectural Association] staff listened to the speech which Frank Lloyd Wright made in Houston when—better late than never—he got the Gold Medal of the American Institute of Architects [see Chapter 16]. I sent him a cable next day saying that five hundred students demanded that he should be here this afternoon. If I didn't get permission from quite all the students to do this, I hope they have forgiven me. Anyway, back came the reply "Will be with you in the summer," for, after all, there wasn't much else that he could say.

When he got that medal, Frank Lloyd Wright remarked that "it was bound to affect his future." And how right he was, for as you see it has brought him half across the world to Europe—the kid from the Middle West. May I add that I haven't all that much use for medals and, with it or without it, he would have had to come and would have been just as welcome.

Well, here he is with a lifetime of experience, and here I am, feeling very humble and supposed to say a word about the AA School. Frank Lloyd Wright and the AA—what can they have in common? Away over there is Taliesin, with sixty boys from a dozen nations, working under one master, building their own studios deep in the spaces and colors of the desert; and here are we, a hundred yards from Oxford Street, our students converging every morning from 400 square miles of London's conurbation to cram themselves—somehow—into our four Georgian houses and a tin hut.

However, Taliesin and the AA have at least three things in common. First and foremost, I hope, is a love of architecture. Second, Taliesin is called a *fellowship* and I should like to think that the AA was not just a school but a fellowship, where the minds of staff and students can work on each other in enthusiasm, like two cogs in a fast running machine. That isn't always easy, either for bewildered students or busy staff, but it is the only way that we shall ever get anywhere at all with architectural education. I said, however, that there were three things to link together the AA and

Mr. and Mrs. Frank Lloyd Wright in London for the Architectural Association's annual prizegiving, Friday, July 14, 1950. Photograph courtesy of Dr. S.E.T. Cusdin of London, England.

Taliesin; a love of architecture, a sense of fellowship—and then there is a third.

Frank Lloyd Wright, ladies and gentlemen, is here this afternoon not only as a very, very great architect indeed—though that, too, of course—but as a symbol of something in our policy, a symbol of the fact that architectural students must build, make things with their own hands and their own sweat as well as with their own brains. We are going to do something about that, for neither the brains nor the hands are either of them much use without each other.

A year ago I dared to say that if ever, in the context of our own time, we are to build as gloriously as our forefathers, then architectural education must change beyond recognition. We don't want revolution for the sake of revolution, but the architect in this century has ranked as a mediocrity, and there seems to be little or no basis for a defense of the status quo. One day, I hope, in years to come, the AA may be seen as having been an instrument in this change.

The general direction of the change must, I think, be away from the drawing board toward *true* technique of building, toward an understanding of man and of the whole fabric, urban and rural, of man and the visual world. Only thus can architecture once again take its place in our so-called culture.

True, modern building technique is so complex that the precision drawing must remain one of our principal media. Never can there be golden ages, never can we dream William Morris dreams of new Lavenham towers and Chartres portals, but we must, we simply must, find our own equivalent.

We shall never find that equivalent in a system which, however much style and context may have changed, is still basically that of the Ecole des Beaux Arts, a system wherein recognized formal solutions to formal problems are presented on the drawing board for the hundredth time. To say this is not to flog a dead horse, and it is not merely a matter of being modern—it is very much more radical than that. Technically, perhaps, we have to put the clock on a hundred years, where aeronautics and biochemistry have got to; but emotionally and professionally we have to put it back 500 years to where the masons of Kings College Chapel were.

Not an easy job, not a matter of curriculum, site work, or courses of lectures. These are part of it, but if the thing happens it will be partly through a whole series of such changes through many years, but mainly, I think, because the AA—graduate and postgraduate—can on a very big scale and in an English context be a Taliesin Fellowship. Our context is so different that our problems may not be those of Taliesin Fellowship, but the love and understanding of men and of real building—something far, far greater than a mere diploma to practice—are things that our *fellowship* can have too. All the forces of orthodoxy and common sense may be against us. Every profession is to some extent a conspiracy against the laity; every profession always was, but today those conspiracies have been crystallized into statutory forms. They never let Lethaby train architects; Gropius was thrown out of Germany and rejected in England. They were dangerous men. The AA *fellowship* might be more difficult to stop. No one ever stopped Frank Lloyd Wright. If all the rebel fire of the AA students of the 'thirties—some of them are helping to run the place now—which was sublimated then into the Spanish War and all that went with it, was sublimated now into architecture, anything might happen.

The AA should, in my view, be a place where those who are going to be concerned with design and with building—architects and builders—can share together a liberal education; second, it must be a laboratory where students learn to experiment with form, color, structure. Some mistakes on paper, en route, matter comparatively little. Students should, of course, emerge with a sound and sensible outlook upon orthodox building, but not even that if the excitement, sensual enjoyment, curiosity, or poetry of the native mind and heart are blunted in the process. Thirdly, the AA must be a place where the designer is concerned with the real world; unlike the painter and the poet, the architect cannot live in an ivory tower. Not only has he to face the social and technical implications of his world, he has to seize upon them and transmute them into real building. And this, like experiments in form and color and structure, must also be a part of a graduate's training.

In some ways, to me at any rate, this has been a rather fantastic year at the AA. I have known the AA for twenty years and more, and I can honestly say that never has the school—staff and students—worked so hard. There have been moments when I have found it almost terrifying, but that does not mean that I am not grateful—far, far more grateful than I can ever say, let alone explain in a short speech—to every single person concerned. Whether the hard work has been justified by the results is not for me to say. So far as we are concerned we are now planning and looking forward to a new session.

Finally, on these occasions someone usually tries to define what a good architect should be. These definitions never get us very far. This afternoon, however, I have a pretty good one. The Welsh word "Lloyd" means "honest or undefiled"; let us put it between two Saxon words—Frank and Wright—of which we all know the meaning, and you have your definition—"a free and honest maker of things"—Frank Lloyd Wright. That is not such a bad definition of a great architect!

CUSDIN: Though we were so slow in giving formal recognition to Frank Lloyd Wright, he has now become a legend. It is now my privilege to introduce you to the legend—Frank Lloyd Wright.

WRIGHT: I have had experience of a great many imports in my own country, but I stand here today an import, by way of the AA, and a very happy thing I find it. It is a very nice thing to be an import as an architect, and I hope that all of you young people will some day grow up and be imported yourselves.

I have seen a great deal of London this time. I came here before to deliver the Sulgrave Manor Board lectures. That was in 1939, just as the bombs were about to drop on London. I saw very little of London then, but this time I have seen a great deal more, thanks to Brother Jordan and our president, Mr. Cusdin, and I have been down in the country, where things were simple and natural and of the heart, unspoilt.

Some of the young people who are starting out to practice architecture are receiving prizes today. In the giving of prizes it is just as it is in any competition. First of all, the judges are selected from amongst those upon whom the circumstances, whatever they may be, can agree, so that you get the average of an average, and then they always go through them and throw out the best ones and the worst ones, and then they get together and average upon the average, so that the prize or the result of the competition is an average of an average of averages. It does not matter if they throw out the best ones, but it is important that they should throw out the worst.

You are coming into this field of architecture. I do not know what else to call it; I do not like to call it a profession because I think that the profession of architecture in our country—and it is probably the same in all other countries—is no longer the refuge of the great in experience and of really developed individuals which it was once upon a time. Perhaps the handing out of tickets to little boys to sit around for four years studying and reading about architecture may have something to do with it—a degree, I think they call it, saying that they are fit to practice architecture. That was the first blow that our profession got in our country, and another blow was that it is now considered a very nice occupation for a gentleman and the favored sons of fortune are barging in. I should like to see the profession, as a profession, honorably buried with due ceremony and the field left more open to youngsters who are willing to make the sacrifices that are essential to practice architecture.

The architect is the form-giver of his civilization, of his society. There is no way of getting culture into shape except by way of this worker that we call an architect. It is essential, then, that the very best material we can find we send into the ranks of the architects. It is the blind spot of our civilization, the blind spot of our culture. No one knows anything about architecture; the thing is so confused. For 500 years the thing has been going downhill until it is all mixed and so much a matter of habit that I think no one knows a good building from a bad building. That must be, so long as it is a matter of taste, a matter of fashion, so long as we have the fifty-seven varieties to choose from and never do a thing for ourselves.

Now it is my fear, as I stand here today before you, that the little prophetic insight into the *nature* of building which *organic* architecture represents, having produced effects at the beginning of an era which was ushered in, I think, by Mr. Louis H. Sullivan and alongside him, myself, may become, by way of these effects which were produced, another effect, another fact. I think that you can see all over the world today indications of a new style. But we do not want another style; we have had enough of styles in architecture. We want a new reality; we want to face reality.

What would reality be in a civilization committed to the ideals of a democracy? What would it be? A style? No. That commitment would be a commitment to the ideal of freedom, would it not? Freedom in architecture—what would it be like? Every man for himself and the devil take the hindmost? No, that would be license. Where does this freedom come from that we profess as the normal aim of our democratic life? It comes from within you. It is not something that can be made for you, that can be handed to you, but it is something in which you can be allowed to develop and in which you can be protected, and that protection is what we need now for the individual.

I think you will realize now that when you speak of individuality you are not speaking of personality. That distinction is usually missed. Our personalities we have nothing to do with; they are accidents. It is by what we do to develop our personality into a *true* individuality that we begin to differ from animals and become really manlike, really human beings, capable of being. Democracy is the championship and the protection of the individual per se, as such. That means that *organic* architecture is of the individual for the individual by way of individuals. There is lots of room for error, lots of room to go astray, very little to go upon except inner ideas, except that from within the *nature* of everything must come whatever you do in the way of making a form or making a plan or whatever you do as an architect.

Comes now the *nature* of materials, comes now the *nature* of the being inhabiting the building and the *nature* of the society and the circumstances for which the building is created in a free spirit. The most difficult thing of all is to keep the spirit free, not to imitate, not to copy, not to follow unreasonably and blindly and unthinkingly, but whenever you see an effect which appeals to you to get behind and inside that thing to try to find out why it is as it is; and, knowing that, from the inside out, you become a competent member of the society in which you live, and that should be your authorization to practice architecture.

Now, of course, this inner ideal, this sense of what is within being projected into a harmonious and beautiful exterior as a circumstance, is, I suppose, a religion, is it not? I was talking to the boys over here the other day, and, as I was going out, one of the little boys said: "Mr. Wright, you believe this, that a good architect has to believe in Jesus?" Well, I knew what he meant, but he did not get what I meant. I said: "Yes, he must," but I added "but I do not know where he is going to find out about Jesus, how he is going to find out what it was that Jesus represented." What Jesus really represented has been lost by the Church and has been lost by modern practice. You will have to go back into that thought of Jesus from which we can say that we got our ideal of *organic* architecture—the Kingdom of God is within you!

From within comes everything that you will ever have. From within comes that development which will make all the difference between you and an animal and therefore the core, the essence, of the new architecture for democracy. Up-to-date democracy has built nothing. We have talked about it and pretended to be democratic, but I do not think that any of us have looked that definition in the face or made one for ourselves; so let us say that democracy is the highest form of aristocracy that the world has ever seen because it is innate, it is of the individual. It cannot be transmitted; it cannot exist by privilege; it is the gospel of the doer and the be-er [sic].

Well, that is the new architecture; that is the spiritual basis of the new forms and the new life that we may gain when we have had enough of and become sick enough of the superficial pretence which surrounds us in the rubbish heaps in which we live, and we try to clear the decks and really live like men and women, like individuals, not mere personalities.

That sounds rather heavy as a program, does it not? It insists on freedom, and will not stand the imitator. You cannot get to the goal which we are setting for ourselves now by way of imitation; you can get there only by yourself becoming something. You cannot get the kind of architecture that democracy needs now out of a cheapskate, out of a pretender, out of a coward—and especially a coward. It is cowardice, I think, which ruins most of our efforts. The imitator is always a coward. I have heard it said that imitation is the sincerest form of flattery, but I assure you that by its very nature it is an insult. It is not flattery; it is only a confession on the part of the imitator that he did not understand; he admired, and he lost the significance of the thing that he admired. That is where most of us are today.

First of all, let us have the human being capable of bossing himself around. To get that let us make use of the best material that we have in our social fabric today, and I think you will all agree with me that it will be none too good. Then let us work upon it by working with it, by not trying to teach it anything, by merely opening the doors and windows, with what vision we have, so that we do what is possible by way of encouragement; but only in one way can we get this thing which is so essential to the life of a democracy, and that is by experience—experience that you see, experience that you hear, experience that you feel.

You can do it only by way of *nature* study. The books have a little of it; read the books and throw the books away. They cannot help you now—not along this road that we are going—because it is not in the books; it is out in the fields, in the trees, in the *nature* of things. That is another thing that you youngsters should bear in mind. When *organic* architecture speaks of *nature*, it uses the word with a capital "N. "It does not mean out of doors; it means the inner *nature* and meaning of the thing as it exists. We might say that we use the word *nature* in a philosophic sense or differently from the use of the old word.

Two words in this new religion which we are calling architecture are badly used—no, three. The word *organic* is another because ordinarily you use the word *organic* when speaking of something that you might see in a butcher's shop, something physical; but we use the word *organic* to mean imbued with that quality which can live, in which the part is to the whole as the whole is to the part, the entity—that is what we mean.

Then there is *individual.* By that we do not mean a person; we do not mean personality; we mean that which you can develop by way of your work upon your personality. You will see that the meanings which we are after now are not those in the dictionary. They are interior interpretations; they come from the spirit; they are of the spirit. They mean *freedom.* All of that has to be learned.

I stopped at St. Paul's as I came by and saw the effigy of Lord Kitchener, I think it is. I went inside and saw other mortuary relics, but I did not see anything in that building that was really genuine, that was really significant, that really portrayed from within the *nature* of the human soul. I do not know that the human soul is worth portraying, but, if it is not, what is the use of talking about architecture and why should we build? I believe, however, that it is essentially sound and coming to England now. I see how little effect all this messing up with bombs has had and that it has not mattered very much. I do not think wars have ever mattered very much as compared with getting hold of this inner thing by way of which we can have life in abundance, more life, *true* life, without war; for war could be no objective, war could be no circumstance if from within we got the individual, and, having the individual, we could build.

Well, thank you very much. Usually the boys get up at the end and put questions. There are so many of you here today and not one of you will dare. The other day, over at the school, I was trying to show a smart youngster the *nature* of this new sense of space which characterizes the new architecture, which is a sense of the interior as the reality in which we live and which must give us the grammar and the forms of the new architecture which we desire. He put a pencil in my hand and said: "Mr. Wright, I cannot understand it. Everything in life that is worth knowing can be demonstrated mathematically." It is not much use trying to do anything with that; that is the exterior, it is—what is the word I want?—science? That is science speaking. Now science can give us the toolbox and the tools in it—and leave us there. We can have all the science that the scientists of the earth can for centuries bring us and have everything to live with and nothing to live for. That is where we are with regard to science. Let us forget science except as a mere technique to achieve the ends of the spirit; only the prophet, the poet, the philosopher can help us now. We want architects who are that, primarily, as a basis.

Well, this cannot go on forever. I should add, however, that there is an exhibition here, and you might as well see it. It is not, believe me, of *organic* architecture, but something on the way to it!

[Editor's Note: Mr. Robert Furneaux Jordan then read the list of awards for 1950 and introduced the prizewinners to Mr. Wright, who presented the prizes. At the end of the prize giving Mr. Jordan added: "That, ladies and gentlemen, concludes the award of the prizes."]

WRIGHT: And that is the first time that I have ever participated in anything of the kind!

CUSDIN: I have now great pleasure in calling on Mr. Anthony Chitty to propose, and Mr. John Ambrose to second, a vote of thanks to Frank Lloyd Wright.

ANTHONY CHITTY: Frank Lloyd Wright mentioned that five hundred years ago affairs in our profession started to go downhill in certain ways, but I would remind him that something else happened 500 years ago. Five hundred years ago there were persons in this town who were so ignorant that they thought the world was flat. To them the world was Europe. Europe spreading outward from the Mediterranean, a world with England at its outer fringe and beyond only mists and the stormy seas,

*Mr. Robert Furneaux Jordan (*left*—Principal of the Architectural Association School), Frank Lloyd Wright, Dr. S.E.T. Cusdin (President of the Architectural Association), and Mrs. Frank Lloyd Wright in Bedford Square London, for the Association's annual prizegiving, Friday, July 14, 1950. Photograph courtesy of Dr. S.E.T. Cusdin of London, England.*

stretching out to the edge of the world, where the waters went over and down into hell. However, when they did reach that horrible point in the sea where the waters went over they found, not hell, but America. Discoveries such as that, sudden, overwhelming, must at the same time have seemed fantastic and quite inconceivable, though now we look on them as orderly stepping-stones in the stream of history.

In our small world of architecture it was with something of the same feeling of cataclysmic discovery that the works and ideas of Frank Lloyd Wright became known to the architects of my generation when we were students here in this square in the 'twenties and 'thirties. No single man had more effect upon us. At that time we were deep in the European study of overabstract ideas, but he showed us a new world, a world of materials and their effect upon design. He taught us his special ideal, the integration of building with landscape, of material with the scene. He taught us these things not by words but by his works, by his example.

There is nothing new to say about Frank Lloyd Wright; it has all been said before, and in any case it could not be repeated in the space of the five minutes allotted to me. I shall therefore confine myself to one thought only, and it is this. Let us thank God for great men, for their vision and imagination, for the color and excitement that they lend to drab days, for their honesty in an age when plain, good words have many meanings, for their courage and rebellion, for being different when all men are alike, and, in the case of this particular great man, for his long and fruitful life.

I wish to propose a vote of thanks to Frank Lloyd Wright for his presence here today, and in doing so I will ask this distinguished company to join with me in giving thanks not only *to* Frank Lloyd Wright but also *for* Frank Lloyd Wright.

JOHN AMBROSE (*Chairman of the AA Students Committee*): It has been remarked before now that, by comparison with his counterparts in Oxford and Cambridge, the London student is not vociferous. I do not think that we are ever actively discouraged from being so; it [is] due rather to genuine diffidence on our part to exhibiting in public, and, especially in London, students play a very small part in the life of the city. This is, in any case, the first time that I have ever been asked to speak in public, and the event is made pleasurable but slightly worrying for me on that account. On the one hand there are the students, who expect me to expound architectural theory to you, and on the other hand I have had the very good advice, which I propose to follow, to "keep it short."

This occasion is doubly rare. It is rare indeed for most of us to hear a speech from Mr. Wright, and secondly it is a rare thing to listen to a forerunner, to a man individually unique in his day. Such individuality may well become more rare in the future because it is an effect of mass education to produce the mass individual, with nothing to distinguish from one another.

On this point one is able to recognize, I believe, the real value of the AA in giving the individual a chance to develop. Fully to appreciate this, you must set the new student against his proper background of the school on the one hand and the forces, with their enforced discipline, on the other. In place of this enforced discipline, the school encourages the voluntary restraint of the artist, the craftsman, and the engineer. Perhaps those go to make the architect; I do not know. Therefore, while having the keenest pleasure in seconding the vote of thanks to Mr. Frank Lloyd Wright, I am determined that this opportunity shall not pass without thanks being paid to the AA staff—thanks on behalf of all the students here and especially those who, like myself, are leaving today.

[Editor's Note: The vote of thanks was then put by President Cusdin and carried by acclamation.]

WRIGHT: I am sure it is a great thing to thank you and very heartfelt. We are leaving tomorrow and I hope that we shall see you all in America some time—over there where the water goes over the edge!

PART SIX

The Truth About Education

Frank Lloyd Wright awaiting the receipt of his Honorary Doctorate of Fine Arts degree from the University of Wisconsin at Madison, Wisconsin, on Friday, June 17, 1955. Photograph courtesy of The Capital Times, *Madison, Wisconsin.*

20 Education and Art in Behalf of Life

I believe now there is no school worth its existence except as it is a form of nature study—true nature study—dedicated to that first, foremost, and all the time. Man is a phase of nature, and only as he is related to nature does he really matter, is he of any account whatever, above the dust.

Introduction

The following, although not a speech per se, was recorded by the editors of *Arts in Society* (a publication of the University of Wisconsin, Madison) at Taliesin near Spring Green, Wisconsin, on Tuesday, June 18, 1957. In this talk Frank Lloyd Wright discusses his views not only on education in general but also on universities, his early educational experiences, nature, God, and Lao-tse. Although he never completed his college education, he, nevertheless, was the recipient of eight honorary degrees, of which seven were doctorates and one a master's degree as discussed and listed in Chapter 16. One of his doctorate degrees was in Fine Arts from the University of Wisconsin, Madison, bestowed upon him on Friday, June 17, 1955, two years before the talk reproduced in this chapter was delivered.

Text of a talk reprinted from Frank Lloyd Wright's "Education and Art in Behalf of Life," *Arts in Society*, Vol. 1, No. 1, June 1958, pp. 5–10 by permission of the University of Wisconsin-Extension, Madison, Wisconsin.

The Honorary Doctorate of Fine Arts degree of the University of Wisconsin is bestowed on Frank Lloyd Wright in a ceremony at Madison, Wisconsin, on Friday, June 17, 1955. Photograph courtesy of The Capital Times, *Madison, Wisconsin.*

During his long architectural career Mr. Wright designed at least twenty-two education-related facilities, eleven of which were constructed. Among these buildings are the Nell and Jane Lloyd Jones Hillside Home School, Nos. 1 and 2, near Spring Green, Wisconsin (1887 and 1901, respectively), the Jiyu Gakuen Girls' School, Tokyo, Japan (1921), the Taliesin Fellowship Complex near Spring Green, Wisconsin (1933) and, later, Taliesin West, Scottsdale, Arizona (1937), the Florida Southern College Plan of 1938, Lakeland, which included three seminar buildings (1940), the Ordway Industrial Arts Building (1942), the Science and Cosmography Building (1953), and several other collegiate buildings (see also Chapter 12), the Wyoming Valley Grammar School, Wyoming Valley, Wisconsin (1956), and the Juvenile Cultural Study Center for Wichita State University, Wichita, Kansas (1957). In addition, he designed at least eleven other education-related facilities which were not constructed: for example, a schoolhouse for Crosbyton, Texas (1900), the Avery Coonley Kindergarten for Riverside, Illinois (1911), the Kehl Dance Academy with shops and residence for Madison, Wisconsin (1912), a schoolhouse for LaGrange, Illinois (1912), the Aline Barnsdall Little Dipper Kindergarten for Los Angeles (1920), the Rosenwald Foundation School for Negro Children for La Jolla, California (1928), the Florida Southern College Music Building for Lakeland (1944 and 1958), the Southwest Christian Seminary University for Phoenix, Arizona (1951), the Florida Southern College Outdoor Amphitheatre also for Lakeland (1955), the Baghdad University Complex and Gardens for Baghdad, Iraq (1957), and Building B of the Juvenile Cultural Study Center for the University of Wichita at Wichita, Kansas (1957).

Mr. Wright's comments on education, contained in this chapter, were made to the editors of *Arts in Society* only about three weeks after completing an assignment as Bernard Maybeck Lecturer in architecture at the University of California, Berkeley, in late April, 1957.[1] Six weeks later, on Tuesday, July 31, 1957, he returned to California to speak before the Marin County Board of Supervisors which had awarded him the contract to design the Marin County Civic Center (see Chapter 29).

[1] For a discussion of these important lectures and their complete text see Patrick J. Meehan (Editor), *The Master Architect: Conversations with Frank Lloyd Wright,* New York: John Wiley and Sons, 1984, pp. 185–228.

The Talk

WRIGHT: What is education without enlightenment? It's a mere conditioning. And what is mere conditioning but maintaining mass ignorance, the poisonous and poisoning end of what we call *civilization?* There is nothing more dreadful, more dangerous, nothing to be more feared in this world, than plain or fancy ignorance. We can see this today in the drift toward conformity. We can see it in the education of modern mass-society.

You can blame education for much of this because education has not seen what we have needed as a free people. It has not provided enlightenment. It has provided conditioning instead. Conditioning by way of books, by way of what has been—the past—by all habituations of the species to date. American education has not taken into account the views of men of vision capable of looking beyond today. But only such enlightened individuals can save the mass from itself.

If our education—called conservative—is ever going to do anything for us it has to provide enlightenment by means of art, religion, and science. But until art, religion, and science stop disregarding each other, until they realize their interest is one and the source of their inspiration is one, and realize that they can't live apart, that union will not be possible. We teachers must teach men to seek enlightenment by means of the poetic principles of art, religion, and science. We must manifest these to them as spiritual guideposts, as *true* measures of understanding. That is what these youngsters thronging our campuses—teen-agers going from pillar to post—need to know.

Now, what does *university* mean? Our state university is chiefly a trade school. You go down there for some specialized training. You are there just in line to learn to make a living. You don't go to the university to learn about the verities of *nature,* the *truths* of the *universal* for which *university* is the name. *True* education is a matter of seeing *in,* not merely seeing *at.* Seeing *in* means seeing *nature.* Now, when popular education uses the word *nature,* it means just the out-of-doors; it may mean the elements; it may mean animal life; it means pretty much from the waist down; whereas *nature* with a capital "N"—I am talking about the inner meaning of the word *Nature*—is all the body of God we're ever going to see. It is practically the body of God for us. By studying *that Nature* we learn who we are, what we are, and how we are to be.

I walked out of the university [the University of Wisconsin, Madison] three months before I would

Frank Lloyd Wright accepting the Honorary Doctorate of Fine Arts of the University of Wisconsin at a ceremony in Madison, Wisconsin on Friday, June 17, 1955. Photograph courtesy of The Capital Times, *Madison, Wisconsin.*

have graduated as an engineer. I got nothing. I studied all the things that were necessary—or so they thought—for an engineer to know. But through all my years none of that has been worth a dime. And education today is still very like that.

My mother wanted an architect for a son; so, naturally, I wanted to be an architect. Never thought of being anything else. Never had to choose. My mother—she was a very wonderful woman—used to send me as a boy up here to help Uncle James on his farm. Her favorite brother was Uncle James. You see, my grandfather came here when the Indians were still around, and my uncles and aunts owned practically this whole region. I learned a lot out there in the pasture with the cows. I never would put on a pair of shoes—except Sundays—from the middle of April until about the middle of September and I used to really work hard on the farm. That's where I learned most from age eleven to eighteen on the farm, from the poets, and Louis Sullivan.

I believe now there is no school worth its existence except as it is a form of *nature* study—*true nature* study—dedicated to that first, foremost, and all the time. Man is a phase of *nature,* and only as he is related to *nature* does he really matter, is he of any account whatever, above the dust. Otherwise he is offensive, vulgar. He may stink.

It's about 2000 years now since Jesus said that the Kingdom of God—He meant the kingdom of *nature's* apprehension and application—was at hand. He meant it was in man's capacity to know this Kingdom of God. He was a prophet, a real poet, the greatest one. But our world got Him all wrong, doesn't preach Him, doesn't take His teaching—never did. The Christian religions got Him all balled up by way of disciples and we are no nearer to His Kingdom today than we were in His own time, are we? We go to war, we kill, we steal, we make a profession of all those things and other wholly artificial ones.

The real body of our universe is spiritualities—the real body of the real life we live. From the waist up we're spiritual at least. Our *true* humanity begins from the belt up, doesn't it? Therein comes the difference between the animal and the man. Man is chiefly animal until he makes something of himself in the life of the Spirit so that he becomes spiritually inspired—spiritually aware. Until then he is not creative. He can't be. But education doesn't better him in that connection. It confuses him, tends to make him more of a thing than he really is, keeps him on the level of a thing instead of permitting him to become more a divinity. What makes man a divinity rather than a mere thing? Not only his intelligence, but his apprehension of what we call *truth,* and passion in his soul to serve it. That passion is what the universities should cultivate—culture of that sort instead of education. Isn't that it?

An exterior view of the concrete-block and wood constructed Wyoming Valley Grammar School (1956) at Wyoming Valley (near Spring Green), Wisconsin, the only elementary school building ever constructed from a Frank Lloyd Wright design. Photograph by the editor.

An interior view of a classroom at the Wyoming Valley Grammar School, Wyoming Valley. Photograph by the editor.

*An interior view of a multipurpose room with a central fireplace (*left*) at the Wyoming Valley Grammar School at Wyoming Valley. Photograph by the editor.*

To enlighten the young education must at least teach philosophy. Without a *true* philosophy there is no understanding of anything. Without your own philosophic resolution and analysis of pretended knowledge, as applied to life, what and where are you? Philosophy is the only realm wherein you can find understanding. Religion and the arts are all part of philosophy. There has never been a creative artist or poet, for instance, who wasn't deeply religious. Walt Whitman, the only poet we have who gave us anything in the way of poetry fit for the sovereignty of the individual—the theory of our democracy—was a deeply religious man. He believed, as Jesus said, that "the Kingdom of God is within *you.*" Jesus was a poet/philosopher. Every great creative artist who ever lived was a poet and a philosopher. What there is good about me, and may remain, is my philosophy. My work is only great insofar as its philosophy is sound, and if my philosophy is unsound my work will not endure. The fact that it has endured, and now has a chance to continue beyond any lifetime, is simply due to the fact that the philosophy behind it all was a sound one. If that philosophy didn't inspire my work, it wouldn't exist very long.

Lao-tse is the great philosopher [born 604? B.C.]. He revealed the reality of the nature and the life of a building. Lao-tse declared that the reality of a building consists in the space within—the space to be lived in—not the walls and the roof. I think you can see this *truth* by holding up a drinking glass. What is the real glass? What is the reality of the drinking glass? It's the space within in which you can put something, isn't it? Space that you use. That's the *real thing* about the glass, its *reality*. That is also the secret strength of *organic* architecture and where I come in as an architect. My philosophy concerning a building is that of Lao-tse. The same principles apply to you, as to me, in everything. Just as a building is a space within to be lived in, a man is a space within, in which a philosophy lives.

What is really lacking in man today? He lacks the certainty that comes of a creative life. He plays no

An exterior view of the Juvenile Cultural Study Center at Wichita State University (1957), Wichita, Kansas. The building is constructed of cast concrete and metal. An ornamental spire and lattice work decorate the two-story courtyard. Photograph by the editor.

creative role in life but by way of art, religion, and science. Lacking that inner certainty of life, he feels insecure. We all walk and talk in insecurity. The condition of freedom is insecurity. Yet no man is free who is afraid. Only a creative life can make man really free. If the man is man, in the sense of a good philosophy of *nature,* he is inevitably creative; he can't exist unless he is. But then his inspiration is not only for him. It has been to him a gift to be realized and exercised in behalf of life itself. He is absolutely an apostle of life because he sees *nature* for life. If an artist is thus for life he is for the individual, and if he is for the individual he is not alone and never will be. His work will then be of consequence. He will be for democracy and democracy will be for him.

21 To Princeton: Mimic No More

I have the same nostalgic love for Princeton as for the great founders of our Republic, and yet I believe that were all education above the high school level suspended for ten years humanity would get a better chance to be what humanitarian Princeton itself could wish it to be.

Introduction

On Wednesday and Thursday, March 5th and 6th, 1947, Princeton University marked its 200th year with a conference called "Planning Man's Physical Environment" to which about sixty of the foremost architects and planners of

---

Reprinted with minor editing from Frank Lloyd Wright's "Planning Man's Physical Environment," *Berkeley—A Journal of Modern Culture,* No. 1, 1947, pp. 5, 7, and from Frank Lloyd Wright's "Mimic No More," *A Taliesin Square-Paper: A Nonpolitical Voice from Our Democratic Minority,* No. 11, March 6, 1947, entire issue (four pages). This speech was reprinted later as Frank Lloyd Wright's "Let Us Go Now and Mimic No More: An Address by Frank Lloyd Wright at Princeton University," *The Capital Times* (Madison, Wisconsin), Vol. 60, No. 65, August 17, 1947, editorial page, p. 1.

Like the Robie residence almost fifty years earlier, the Dorothy H. Turkel residence (1955) in Detroit, Michigan, is an excellent example of Frank Lloyd Wright's work in an urban setting The Usonian automatic concrete-block system of construction, developed by Mr. Wright, was used to construct the Turkel residence. Photograph by the editor.

*Fifty-eight of the foremost architects and urban planners of the time, pictured here, attended Princeton University's 200th anniversary conference titled "Planning Man's Physical Environment," March 5th and 6th, 1947. Bottom row (*left to right*): Ralph Walker, John E. Burchard, Robert O'Connor, J. V. Hudnut, Adelbert Ames, Jr., Richard Neutra, Henry S. Churchill, Walter Gropius, Arthur Holden, José Luis Sert, Arthur E. Morgan, Alvar Aalto, George Howe,* Frank Lloyd Wright, *and Sherley W. Morgan. Second row (*left to right*): Liang Ssu-Ch'eng, Jean Labatut, Francis A. Comstock, Walter Baermann, Lawrence A. Kocher, Howard P. Vermilya, Fred N. Severud, Theodore M. Greene, Walter A. Taylor, Gyorgy Kepes, B. Kenneth Johnstone, Konrad Wachsmann, Marcelo Roberto, Leopold Arnaud, and Kenneth Stowell. Third row (*left to right*): Henry L. Kamphoefner, G. E. Kidder Smith, A. Gordon Lorimer, Ernest Kump, Theodore T. McCrosky, Thomas Creighton, George Grey Wornum, William Roger Greeley, Serge Chermayeff, Talbot F. Hamlin, Siegfried Giedion, A. M. Friend, Jr., Louis Justement, William Wilson Wurster, George Fred Keck, and Roy Jones. Top row (*left to right*): Kenneth S. Kassler, J. Kendall Wallis, Aymar Embury, Henry A. Jandle, Frederick J. Adams, Carlos Contreras, Morris Ketchum, Philip Johnson, Wells Ira Bennett, John Knox Shear, William F. Shellman, and Walter T. Rolfe. Photograph from the April 1947 issue of* Architectural Forum. *Photograph used by permission of Billboard Publications, Inc., 1515 Broadway, New York, New York 10036.*

the time were invited to talk: Ralph Walker, Richard Neutra, Walter Gropius, José Luis Sert, Alvar Aalto, George Howe, Gyorgy Kepes, Konrad Wachsmann, G. E. Kidder Smith, Serge Chermayeff, Talbot F. Hamlin, Siegfried Giedion, George Fred Keck, Philip Johnson, and, of course, Frank Lloyd Wright were among them. The seven sessions held covered the physical possibilities and limitations of design and the visual, social, philosophical, and psychological aspects of the environment from city and regional planning perspectives to the perspective of the design of buildings and other small objects.

Regarding the conference, *Architectural Forum* (Vol. LXXXVI, April 1947, pp. 12–14) reported the following:

> *Princeton had done its scholarly best to assist the architects in pinning down their racketing Physical Environment to a feasible point for two days' discussion. It had distributed mimeographed lists of "axioms and assumptions." It had, with professional zeal, put mimeographed questions. . . .*
>
> *Princeton had also invited as talkative and brilliant and opinionated group as had ever sat down together. (Among them it had distributed honorary degrees: Alvar*

Aalto and Robert Moses got them, Frank Lloyd Wright did not arrive in time for the award.) Most regarded the occasion with an appropriate solemnity. Even the unimpressionable Mr. Wright told the group that he had prepared a manuscript for the first time in many years and he read it without interpolations.

Frank Lloyd Wright was the recipient of the Honorary Degree of Doctor of Fine Arts from Princeton University in 1947. This chapter presents the complete text of his address before the Princeton University "Planning Man's Physical Environment" conference delivered at a dinner in Proctor Hall, Thursday, March 6, 1947 at 8:00 P.M. The conference concluded with Mr. Wright's address.

The Speech

WRIGHT: My favorite university is Princeton. Memory of pleasant times here long ago while delivering the Kahn lectures [1930] brings me from Arizona—desert to Princetonian revels of intellectual fellowship. I have the same nostalgic love for Princeton as for the great founders of the Republic, and yet I believe that were all education above the high school level suspended for ten years humanity would get a better chance to be what humanitarian Princeton itself could wish it to be. Our thinking throughout the educational fabric has been so far departmentalized, overstandardized and so split that like a man facing a brick wall, counting bricks, we mistake the counting for reality—and so lose or ignore the perspective that would show us the *nature* and wherefore of the wall as a wall.

As a people we are educated far beyond our capacity.

And we have urbanized urbanism until it is a disease—the city a vampire—unable to live by its own birthrate, living upon the fresh blood of others, sterilizing the humanity for which you, Princeton, have always stood. And now this cataclysm, the atom bomb of science, has thrown us off our base, undoubtedly making all we have called progress obsolete overnight. Prone to our own destruction, we may be crucified upon our own cross! To me, an architect, the hide and seek we have played with, this further revelation of the nature of the universe we inhabit as parasites or gods—it is up to us—has been a ghastly revelation of the failure of our educational, economical, and political system. The push-button civilization over which we were gloating has suddenly become a terror. But, instead of the agony appropriate in the actual circumstances, we are even more smug and heedless than usual. A little flurry—that's all. The military mind is a dead mind—so no surprise to find that reaction as it was. The journalistic mind, a reporter's mind, left to the humorist the only real attempt to arouse the people to reality: not an explosive bomb only, but a fantastic poison-bomb that made their habitation in cities no safer than an anthill beneath a ploughshare in a field.

So, my Princeton, I say, let's pause and consider this lack of vision that not only hides from us the better nature of ourselves but makes us unable to see further than our own furrow. Weighed down by our own armor, insatiate with this voracity we call speed, huddled the more—though not suitably in panic, it is conceivable that the country we now call ours may go back to the Indians. Escaping the bombing—the probable apex of our civilization, as they will, they might easily come and take it back again quietly in the night; proving that barbarism is, after all, better suited to human life here on earth than what we have too carelessly called civilization.

In this fearful emergency the state as such has proved utterly unworthy of the allegiance accorded it by the sons and friends of American education. Politics, in any perspective afforded by this insensate clamor and clash of power seekers, is sadly in need not only of the brief recess of ten years or more but utter abolition of the State Department and the Presidency as it now exists. We should strip the Capitol from the periphery of our nation and plant it nearer the heart of the country. We must realize that there can be no real separation between religion, philosophy, science, and the great art of building. They are one or none. But in this petty partisan particularly now everywhere so prevalent we find education the more divided into petty specialties, and those most advantageous to the ignoble profit and party system we have so foolishly made the very core of our Republic life.

So let us rise for a moment from the furrow to take the view, and soon, with disgust, we will dismiss petty politics for the prostitution it really is. Instead, let us view excess urbanism—this pig piling or human huddling we call the city. It is *true* that to every man the city is a stimulus similar to alcohol, ending in similar degeneracy or impotence—no city can maintain itself by way of its own birth rate, and a glance at history shows us that all civilizations have died of their cities. To others like our good old Doctor Johnson the city is a convenience because every man is so close to his burrow. But read "hole in the wall" now for "burrow." Nevertheless, American cities were dated for our humanity long before the cataclysmic poison-bomb of the Chemical Revolution appeared on the horizon.

Then, how now? Are not concentrations of humanity madness or murder? We might remember the Hindu proverb, "A thousand years a city and a thousand years a forest." [The] UN [United Nations] is, of course, the present hope for escape and survival. [The] UN itself has taken refuge in a New York skyscraper. Can it make good?

And we must view education, wherein this salt and savor of "work as gospel" is gone out. The gymnasium has taken its place. The higher education is busy taking everything apart and strewing the pieces about in the effort to find what

One of the great Usonian houses, the John C. Pew residence (1939) at Shorewood Hills (near Madison), Wisconsin, is oriented diagonally on a lot a mere seventy-five feet wide on the north shore of Lake Mendota. The house is well integrated with the sloping site and natural woodlands. Photograph by the editor.

Another great Usonian house, similar to the Pew residence, is the Gregor Affleck residence, first design, (1940), at Bloomfield Hills, Michigan. The house is sited in a sloping natural ravine. Frank Lloyd Wright designed a second house for the Afflecks in 1952 which was never constructed. Photograph by the editor.

makes it tick; failing to put it together again, it cannot make it click. It cannot because it cannot or will not go back with the *organic* point of view to begin anything at all. Education, like the city planning of short-haired experts for short-haired moles, is either a splash in the middle of something—or else, like some tangled skein of colored worsted, seeking any desired strand, it comes out only a short piece of any particular color. Continuity and unity? They are gone. So education is almost as helpless to confront this ghastly emergency we are blindly refusing to face as is the state.

Next, if not in order, let us view our ethics. Men born free and equal? Before the law, yes, perhaps—but the coming man does not believe that all men are born free and equal because he cannot. As a millennial aspiration? Yes, but it is fanaticism here on earth. Such a world implies total death. Struggle makes our world what it is—not struggle for equality but for supremacy. That struggle is the process of creation: inequality is the very basis of creation. In the brain lies the chief difference between men. Only a state politician out for reelection at a Fourth of July picnic could say we are all born with the same brain power.

Let us now glance askance at our own production. Naturally, everybody, everywhere, cannot be taught to love, appreciate, and assimilate art or religion. It is impossible to impact to any man one single grain of *truth* unless he has the undeveloped germs of it within him. Buddha said, "A spoon may lie in the soup for a thousand years and never know the flavor of the soup." Only when the heart is open is it fit to receive teaching quick with life. Eyes must be there and be opened first. Eyes must be there as well as ears and be opened first before illusion, superstition, or prejudice may be expelled. Architecture, the great Mother Art, is in itself the highest knowledge in action of which we have any knowledge and cannot be bought or even acquired from books. One good look at an actual building and a man has found what no reams of writing or years of teaching could give him—provided he has eyes to see.

And what of our buildings? Education and two wars have all but killed this germ of creative thinking. And so creative work for us—especially in building—is all but destroyed. This amazing avalanche of material we call production seems to have its eyes shut to all but destruction. The standardization it practices are the death of the soul, just as habitation kills any imaginative spirit. So within this welter of the misapplied wealth of knowledge with so little realization—wherein consideration and kindness are so rare—why not develop a little *integral know-how?* Only spirit affords that.

Now come our GI's devastated by war to be further devastated by four more years of education. Why send more GI's, by way of government money they will themselves repay or their children will repay, to school? Why not subsidize land and transportation for them to relieve intolerable immediate pressures instead of sending them back to hard pavements, to tramp or be trampled upon further by the herd? Why not get the boys out where they can get in touch with and be touched by their own birthright: the good ground? Give each man an open chance to make his own environment beautiful, if possible, and restore to him what he most needs: the right to be himself. If, owing to the false doctrines of artificial controls or of economic scarcity—making and maintaining black markets now, they are unable to build, why not throw natural roads open to immigration from countries where the skills have not been cut back by ignorant labor unions emulating still more ignorant employers? The only requirements for immigration to our democratic society should be common decency and trade skills. Then not only would the GI learn from them and by the natural working of [the] law of supply and demand have a home, but all Americans would soon have better ones and have them by their own efforts.

No, no assembly line is the answer either for him, for you, or for me—and that means not for our country. Decentralization of our American cities and intelligent utilization of our own ground, making natural resources more available to him, in his road, yours and mine, to any proper future as a democracy for which we may reasonably hope. Essentially, we are a mobocracy now. Our present extreme centralization is a bid to slavery all down the line, a bid-in by a shortsighted, all too plutocratic industrialism.

But the right to strike still belongs to the American people as well as to American labor unions. The time has come for that strike. I find it increasingly hard to believe that a free people can be so blinded to the *nature* of their own power as our people have been by their own foolish credulity. Do they want to keep their eyes shut? Perhaps so.

The remedy? No remedy will be found in more statism. That is more static, *truly*. No, the remedy is more freedom—greater growth of individuality—more men developed by the way of self-discipline from within the man. Today, especially, the most cowardly lie disseminated by the congenital cowards among us, as well as by the church, school, and state, is this lie that "I, the state, am the people!" In a democracy where the people means the people, the people do not understand the state any more than the superstition that the people call "money." In a *true* democracy the people are bound to suffer the state as against their own customs and natural rights. Democracy cannot love government! Government is its policemen, privileged by the people themselves to obstruct, expropriate, or punish. Under the watchful care of the people themselves, government must take its place down *under*, not up above the right of the individual to be himself. Let us mimic no more!

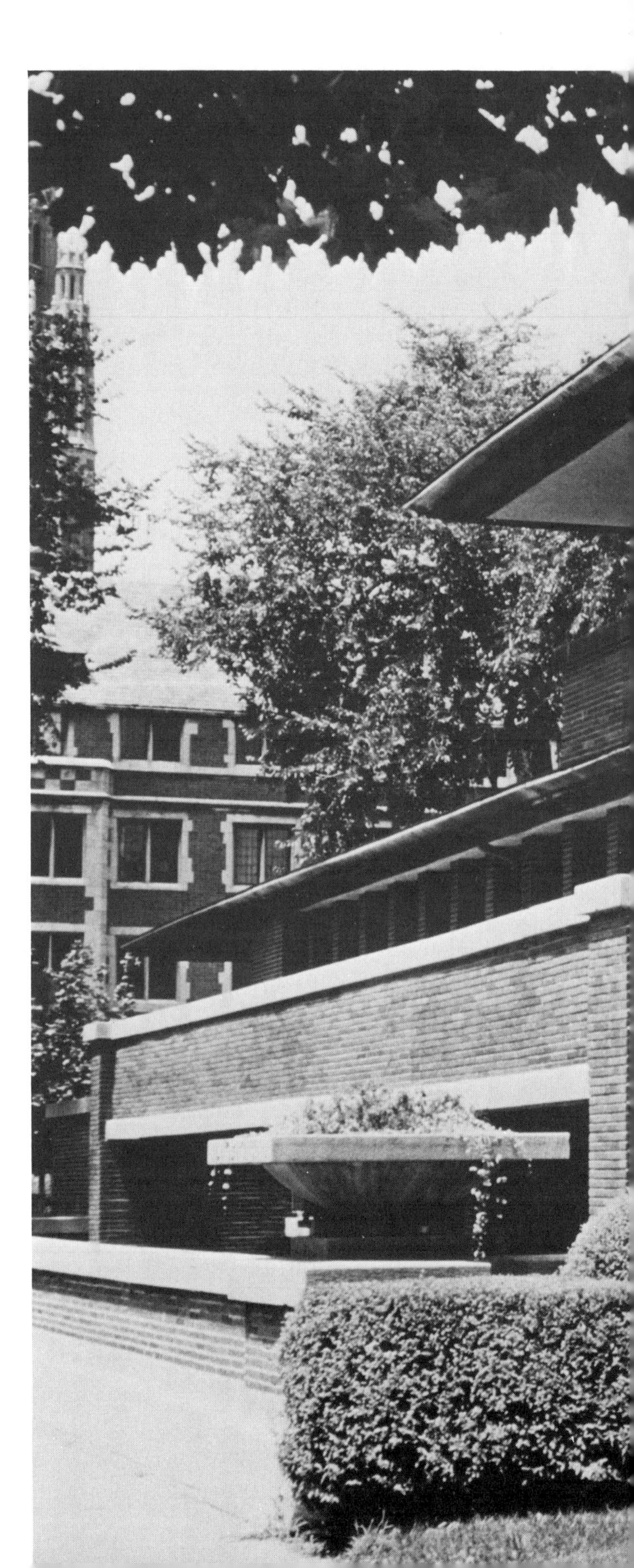

The Frederick G. Robie residence (1906) in Chicago, Illinois, is a massive brick masonry structure with dynamic sweeping horizontal lines and cantilevered roof eaves along a single-plane axis. Horizontal masses of the building appear to be suspended, yet are at one with the ground plane. The Robie residence represents an excellent example of Frank Lloyd Wright's work in an urban setting. Photograph by the editor.

The Anderton Court Shops (1952) at Beverly Hills, California, are another example of Frank Lloyd Wright's elimination of the box. A ramp, which winds its way upward, serves as the main entrance to this structure. Photograph by the editor.

22 Progress in Architectural Education

As no stream can rise higher than its source, so you can give no more or better to architecture than you are. So go to work on yourselves to make yourselves be in quality what you would have your buildings be.

Introduction

At the 84th Annual Convention of the American Institute of Architects (AIA) held at the Waldorf-Astoria Hotel in New York City on Wednesday, June 25, 1952, Frank Lloyd Wright addressed about two hundred student members of the student chapter of the AIA for a symposium titled "Progress in Architectural Education." Seven weeks earlier he addressed a similar crowd of architectural students and faculty, also on the topic of education, at the School of Architecture of the University of Oklahoma, Norman.[1] The following is an account of the 84th Annual Convention of the AIA and of Mr. Wright's speech to its student chapter, reported by the editors of *The New Yorker*[2]:

Text of speech excerpts reprinted with editing from Frank Lloyd Wright's "Progress in Architectural Education," *Line Magazine,* Vol. 2, No. 1, 1953, unpaginated (six pages).

[1] For a discussion of this speech and its complete text see Patrick J. Meehan (Editor) *The Master Architect: Conversations with Frank Lloyd Wright,* New York: John Wiley and Sons, 1984, pp. 169—184.

[2] Edited and reprinted in its entirety from "Fighting the Box," *The New Yorker,* Vol. 28, July 5, 1952, pp. 16–17. © 1952, 1980, The New Yorker Magazine, Inc. Reprinted in its entirety by the specific request of *The New Yorker.* Reprinted by permission.

We dropped in on the eighty-fourth annual convention of the American Institute of Architects, at the Waldorf one morning last week and, after receiving a program of events from an A.I.A. hostess, joined a knot of men whose lapel badges proclaimed them to be Arthur C. Holden, Wallace K. Harrison, William Lescaze, and Grosvenor Chapman.

"If I go on the public-housing projects tour this afternoon, will I miss the U.N. tour?" Mr. Chapman asked.

"No," said Mr. Harrison.

We asked Mr. Lescaze what he was up to.

"I'm busy with a hush-hush project," he said.

We asked him what the convention was up to.

"The usual talk is going on," he said. "Architects don't like to see the government bureaus doing too much building. They want to do it themselves."

We wandered into the Basildon Room, where exhibits of Plexiglas, Arcadia Sliding Glass Doors, Aluminum Company of America aluminum, and Minneapolis-Honeywell regulator products abounded.

"This is our latest electronic humidity control," a Honeywell man said to us. "The usual humidistat has blond hair, which absorbs moisture, but for a really sensitive control—for use, say, in a newsprint factory, where you have to control the humidity of paper—we use as a sensing device a gold-leaf grid embossed on a plastic base and treated with a special salt."

"Must the hair be blond?" we asked, going back a couple of phrases.

"Yes," said the Honeywell man firmly, and added, "Preferably female."

We consulted our program in search of something more comprehensible and hit on a students' symposium, in the Empire Room, at which the chief speaker was to be Frank Lloyd Wright. Thither we repaired, arriving in the latter stages of a speech by Morris Ketchum. "We are a team," he was saying to an audience of several hundred young people. "You and I, the engineers, the legal lights, the real-estate lights, and other experts. You have to know not just architecture but the art of getting along with people." The next speaker, Bonnell Irvine, a student at Pratt Institute, brought up the problem of the Negro architect. Then Kenneth K. Stowell, who was presiding, said the Institute drew no color line and asked Ralph Walker, a former president of the Architectural League, for a word or two. "I'm glad to see a large sprinkling of young women here," said Mr. Walker, in part. "We have a very charming girl in my office. I first saw her crossing Forty-second Street with a portfolio, and thought, what a charming girl! Later, I saw her in my reception room. She is now a very vital part of our organization." Mr. Walker sat down amid tumultuous applause.

A mirrored double door at the back of the room opened, several flashlight cameras flashed, and Mr. Wright, a fantastically distinguished figure at eighty-three, silver maned, erect, and sporting a golden-brown suit, a modified cowboy hat, a flamboyant bow tie, a pink silk handkerchief, and a Malacca cane, strode down the aisle. All rose. Mr. Wright doffed his hat, twirled his cane, and, gaining the platform, shook hands with Mr. [Kenneth K.] Stowell, who said, "You all know Mr. Wright." All sat down.

"Boys," said Mr. Wright, ignoring the large sprinkling, "how do you do? I am going to talk to my heirs here this morning, believe it or not, like it or not. I started war on architecture as a box. A box is a containment; I tried to abolish the box." Mr. Stowell handed him a piece of chalk, and he drew a box on a blackboard. "Now, you see, boys, there is the box," he said. He went on talking, the while demolishing the box with strokes of the chalk and smudgy erasures made with the handkerchief, which Stowell also gave him. "I had the feeling that the space within was the reality of a building," he said. "No longer the walls and the roof. Well, in Unity Temple I dealt with that problem. You will find a sense of space, not walled in. The walls become screens. What is the roof? An emphasized, splendid sense of shelter, a beneficent spread overhead; it doesn't shut you in. Of course, the box is a Fascist symbol. I felt it to be Fascist, undemocratic, and absolutely anti-individual." By this time the blackboard box had disappeared.

"I have had a curious and very interesting time fighting the box," Mr. Wright went on. "Organic architecture is the architecture of democratic freedom. What is spiritual, boys?" No one answered. Mr. Wright explained what spiritual is, at some length, and held up a glass. "What is the reality of this glass, boys?" he asked.

"The space within," someone said.

Mr. Wright beamed, devoted another twenty minutes to talking and to answering questions from the floor ("The architect is the pattern-giver of civilization. . . . You know, I think to be an architect is much more than being a preacher of the gospel or a man who makes billions because it involves quality. . . . Wasn't Jesus the first advocate of an organic architecture when he said, "The Kingdom of God is within you"? He was. . . . I think democracy is the highest form of aristocracy the world has ever seen. . . . Efficiency has become a hateful word to me. . . . Now think of this. When is a thing too big? When it's out of human scale. . . . I've heard about city planners recently. Who are they? Can a city be planned? I don't think so. . . . This country was never intended to become a great manufacturing nation. England had to be. We're a stooge of England"), concluded with a resounding anecdote censuring England and America alike, seized his cane, clapped his hat on his head, and began marching up the aisle. All rose and applauded. The great man went through the double door, followed by photographers and autograph seekers.

The text of this chapter represents excerpts from this speech. Later, in 1953, a three-record set of 33-1/3 RPM, long-playing sound records titled *Frank Lloyd Wright Talks To and With the Taliesin Fellowship* was pressed by Columbia Records for the Frank Lloyd Wright Fellowship and was released for national distribution for a price of five dollars. Record three of this set included a much revised reading by Mr. Wright of this address at Taliesin in September 1952, about three months after the initial delivery of the speech to the student chapter of the AIA on June 25, 1952, in New York. Still later, another excerpt from this speech appeared as "Address at the Meeting of the Student Chapter Members, the American Institute of Architects," in William A. Coles and Henry Hope Reed, Jr. (Editors), *Architecture in America: A Battle of Styles* (New York: Appleton-Century-Crofts, 1961, pp. 350–351.).

The Speech

WRIGHT: As you see it going on today in universities, our education in architecture is far too easy. The education we practice takes things by choice from on the surface, passes them around upon ourselves—not within ourselves. Teaching today seldom gets down to the elemental bottom—the *truth* of anything. Why? Well, because teachers were taught facts, which is what they teach instead of *truth.*

I am quite sure there is not a boy here today who could have told me what the corner window meant in architecture when he first saw one, except that it was an odd effect. As you all too well know now, architecture—modern architecture especially—is still chiefly concerned with effects. Effects are charming or they're ugly or they're desperate or despicable, but why? But, boys, why linger with effects you don't really understand? Education today is, as are all our rights and privileges—nearly everything that we have had or made—concerned with mere effects. Seldom is the endeavor of our day and time concerned with principles. They are concerned with causes but seldom, except in science—in art, never.

Young artists aren't taught to ask *why.* You can ask what, when, and maybe where, but never *why!* That cannot be *true* education. Along that line of eclecticism you are soon educated far beyond capacity. There is no *truly* educated man who does not ask that question *why,* either to himself or aloud, immediately when anything arises to him unusual. The first thing he should want to know is "well, yes but *why?*" If you ask that of your professors you might embarrass them because they never asked the question at the right time of the right person in the right way, either. It is time that you did ask that question and keep it uppermost in what you call your *minds.* This will probably make of you a terrible nuisance whoever you are because you will find very few willing or competent answers.

Now, here today I am giving you good answers. Let's go back with our profession of democracy to this simple little diagram of the box. [Editor's Note: Mr. Wright stands before a chalkboard drawing an illustration.] On stilts, yes. [The] Elimination of the box is the fact and figure of a building [and] is the *true* basis upon which the democratic spirit we covet could possibly flourish as genuine architecture today. The affirmation of this negation is flourishing more or less here and there. But more so abroad than here at home. Why? No basis at all for our own architecture today is this hanging from skyhooks by one's eyebrows without understanding why we should so hang or what it is we're hanging there for. Back of all this simple *organic* revolt in world architecture today comes another and much deeper sense of what constitutes *truth:* the constitution of *principle.* Principles are, yes always, *spiritual,* my boys! Science only concurs. Principle is always important; [it] is the *soul* of architecture—the great art of beautifully building beautiful buildings. Principle is especially important to you now.

Do you think *spirit* is something you may see way up there? Do you really believe that *spirit* comes down to you this way [Editor's Note: Mr. Wright gestures] from above and that the more you are able to detach yourself from earth the more *spiritual* you become? Do you think so? I don't like to believe you are so foolish, but there is much evidence against you. As for me, I have never seen anything but human confusion as a result of that belief. We are in it—as Christianity—now. But no *truly* great art has ever or could ever flourish by way of that sentimentality. Only such superficial architecture as we now have and have had for 500 years could have come of it. But that sentimental realm is where most of us are still living in art by way of our emotions, taking for granted the mistaken tokens of the life of Jesus we call, for lack of a better name, Christianity; a subdivision of

The art-glass windows of the William G. Fricke residence (1901), Oak Park, Illinois, suggest an opening up of the interior space to the outdoors. Photograph by the editor.

truth into various tokens of thought. We hang over earth from the sky by skyhooks by way of this mistaken idea of God which most of us wear as eyebrows. Now isn't that imagined elevation by detachment what they mostly mean by religion?

Well, I have sometimes been called an "earth son." I plead guilty to the soft impeachment. Guilty, because I believe that only by having your feet firmly on good ground, that by way of your love of the stars [and] your love of great life, growth will come to you from within upward. If you would ever achieve spiritually in your architecture, that is to say, great good building, if your work ever represents the *true* spirit of you the man, it will be because your feet are firm there and within you has developed a sense of *beauty* [that is] no longer confused with the curious, to be achieved as an innate sensibility. A sense of what is God. By that simple but direct aspiration you will see the only God you will ever see. Your own *ideal!* Now, that is what *organic* architecture sees. That innate faith in the self-God is the core of it.

Whenever you try to detach yourself from reality, say reality like this reality of the building which I've been trying to show you here—yes, we now know it to be the reality of any building we may call

An interior view of the Frederick C. Robie residence (1906) in Chicago, the most famous of Frank Lloyd Wright's "Prairie" houses. The Robie house is an early example of the elimination of the box which Mr. Wright pursued throughout his long architectural career. Photograph by the editor.

"architecture"—you will find that it goes as well all down the line of human thought and experience. Even as, in this glass of water standing here [Editor's Note: Mr. Wright points to a glass of water on the table near him] you have an instance. Here the familiar illustration—I hold up this glass of water before you and ask, what is *reality* here? Where does reality come in here boys? In the glass? In this? [Editor's Note: Mr. Wright taps the glass] No! With the lesson in mind I've just given you, you should see the answer. You do see, don't you? Well, again, just what is reality here in this so familiar object we call a drinking glass? The answer is *the space within into which you can put something!* In other words, the *idea.* And so it is with architecture; so it is with your lives; and so it is with everything you can experience as *reality.* You will soon find out yourselves if you begin to work with this principle in mind. Things will open to you. They will develop you and to you. You will soon see that many "grapes of wrath" have grown where none need have grown before. Therein lies the secret of the great peace missing in our western civilization as of today.

Here now, I have divulged to you, my heirs, what seems to me the very simple but both fundamental and top secret of power in your profession. By intentional destruction of the box as architecture we open the road to a great future architecture. This secret is not my secret. It is simply the age-old philosophy of individuality; the entire core of the creative self; the entire spiritual world which you may enter only by way of the love of it which is the great understanding. Who then, think you, was the first great promulgator of an *organic* architecture? He was an architect because in His ancient day they called the carpenter, architect. Wasn't he Jesus—the first advocate of *organic* architecture when He said, "the Kingdom of God is within *you*"? He was. Now be both patient and wise and you can't miss the integrity of this innate thing. See it operating in nature everywhere! Go afield! Go along with or go against your fellow men. Go anywhere you please with eyes open to *see.* Ask this troublesome question *why,* and if you have a sincere wish to learn—it is a kind of prayer—you will get somewhere. But to go along the paths of book knowledge as earmarked for youth today by way of popular education—you will get nowhere. Is that blunt enough?

As I am here with you today, boys, I would like to talk with each of you with illustrations by way of drafts on a blackboard more directly. Because

A view from the west bedroom of the Edgar J. Kaufmann, Sr., "Fallingwater" residence (1935) in Ohiopyle, Pennsylvania. The corner windows eliminate the box effect, extend the interior space to the outdoors, and bring the outdoors into the interior. A quarter-circle cutout in a bedroom desk (right) *allows the casement window to open, thus further integrating the outdoors with the interior and its built-in furnishings. Photograph by the editor.*

every boy, every man, every other person living is an entity, as we ourselves are. The *individual* means a *soul.* His great misfortune today is that no matter who he is, how good he is, what he has to give to his fellow man, he might enlist the entire press of these United States, add radio, put in television, and write books about almost anything above the belt and never get anywhere at all. So it is with this *spiritual* principle concerning, fundamentally, the state of a great work of architecture. Why has this so happened to us in America?

Having lately been abroad in Italy, Switzerland, and France, I have heard it said that America was too big for a democracy. Is it *true*? I am beginning to be afraid that there is too much *truth* in it. Mr. Big and the big thing which is a consuming desire to be big and our tendency to respect mass—the thing that is big just because it is big—this will ruin us as a democracy. It has mortified our great profession, too! Don't you think that probably Mr. Big is what is the matter with Usonian architecture as well as democracy today? Isn't he automatically the enemy of both when perhaps he desires to be a friend? At least you are never a *true* friend when you are ready to cash in on friendship, are you? So let's try for quality not quantity. Let's beware of being too big. Let's not give lip service to Mr. Big. Remember the sign that used to appear along the country roads: "Quality Knows No Substitute." You see it nowhere any more. Why? These merchant boys have probably grown too big. Quantity now is what counts with them now; not quality now. Both democracy and architecture die on that mobocratic platform! Both die because both are founded upon quality. Quality is always some form of individuality. The *nature* of individual worth is always the basis of the thing of quality. Whenever mass enters into the soul of anything, quality disappears. So the big thing has seldom been or can ever be the living thing we need in an indigenous *culture.* Is there such a thing as a *true* culture not indigenous? The big thing cannot be the democratic thing anywhere above the basis of a bare civilization.

Now what then is democracy? Have you ever thought about it for yourselves? Democracy is, I think, the highest form of aristocracy this world has ever seen. Why do we miss it as such? Well, for one thing, all the old aristocracies were founded upon privileges given to the overprivileged, most of whom hadn't earned them. But in democracy the form of aristocracy is innate. Nothing of it can be

Detail of a corner window at the Howard Anthony residence (1949), Benton Harbor, Michigan. The vertical window-framing element has been omitted where the two panes of glass are butted at the corner to allow an observer an unobstructed view of the site's natural surroundings and to open up the interior space to the outdoors. This corner window represents Frank Lloyd Wright's continued efforts to eliminate the box as an interior space. Photograph by the editor.

The main entrance to the Solomon R. Guggenheim Museum, which fronts on Fifth Avenue in New York. The upper four spiral ramps of the main gallery are shown on the right. Photograph by the editor.

An interior view of the Solomon R. Guggenheim Museum (1956) in New York, looking down from the seventh ramp of the main gallery. Photograph courtesy of the New York Convention and Visitors Bureau.

inherited. All has to be of the thing, not on it. Privilege is of the people for the people not on the people by way of somebody who has power and authority. So democratic or *true* aristocracy should be, and is, a cultural matter and affair of quality. Democracy is not to be ruined by any ambition for quantity. That ambition would be changed to *mobocracy*.

So what are you incipient architects going to do about this new type of aristocracy? How do you feel about *big* housing, *big* buildings, *big* business? A little boy came to me out of the sticks some years ago and said, "Mr. Wright, I want to learn how to build *big* buildings." He had me. I didn't know how to build a big building except by learning how to build a little one well and then by making it big. Well, now we know that that psychology is, of course, not universally applied. But, it is still growing there in our midst. This element of size, the *big* thing, the *big* listing, the hope of vast quantity production—because of that—we're really now all under the heel of the *big* man with the *big* machine. Efficiency has, therefore, become a hateful word to me.

One thing more, boys: consider that you, as young architects, are to be the pattern givers of American civilization. There can be no other pattern givers than its architects. So, if we in America ever do have a culture of our own, *you* must be the way showers. A *civilization* is only a way of life. A *culture* is the *way* of making that civilization beautiful. So culture is your office here in America. As no stream can rise higher than its source, so you can give no more or better to architecture than you are. So go to work on yourselves to make yourselves be in quality what you would have your buildings be.

PART SEVEN

Democracy

Frank Lloyd Wright seated at his drafting table (February 1947). Photograph courtesy of The Capital Times, *Madison, Wisconsin.*

23 Building a Democracy

. . . our greatest lack as a civilization is the beauty of organic integrity and that beauty itself is the highest and finest kind of morality.

Introduction

This chapter presents the text of a speech delivered by Frank Lloyd Wright at the second session of the Fifteenth Annual New York Herald-Tribune Forum on Current Thought in the ballroom of the Waldorf-Astoria Hotel, New York, at 5:30 P.M., Tuesday, October 29, 1946, in which he spoke not only of an *organic* democracy but of freedom and the right to be one's self—especially in relation to architectural design.

The Speech

WRIGHT: Democracy and architecture, if both are *organic,* cannot be two separate things. Neither can democracy nor architecture be enforced in any sense. Both must come from within,

Text of a speech reprinted with minor editing from "Building a Democracy," *A Taliesin Square-Paper,* No. 10, October 29, 1946, pp. 1–4; "Wright Calls for Organic Architecture to Match Growth of Democracy," *The Capital Times* (Madison, Wisconsin), Vol. 58, No. 150, November 10, 1946, p. 11; "The Right To Be One's Self," *Husk* (Mount Vernon, Iowa), Vol. XXVI, December 1946, pp. 37–40; "Frank Lloyd Wright On the Right To Be One's Self," *Marg* (Bombay, India), Vol. 1, No. 2, January 1947, pp. 20–24, 47; and "Building A Democracy," *Albright Art Gallery, Gallery Notes* (Buffalo Fine Arts Gallery, Buffalo, New York), Vol. 11, June 1947, pp. 14–18.

An exterior view of the F. F. Tomek residence (1907) at Riverside, Illinois, a Prairie-style structure of wood and plaster. Photograph by the editor.

spontaneously. In architecture, as in democracy, this *organic* way is new to us only because the interior *nature* of man is still new to mankind and democracy is still a search for *organic* form.

Democracy is not so much a form—even were we to find it—or a policy—even were we to make it—as it is [an] abiding faith in man's indivisible right to himself as himself. That faith is the natural essence of manhood and is therefore the only safe foundation for creative building. Insofar as the state is concerned, it is the same. It is only the man with self-respect who has any respect for others, and so is capable of faith in mankind and thus of constructing a government. Lacking this sound human foundation, no government can rise above servility and secret hate. Collective security without this foundation *first* is merely illusion. Internationalism without this foundation *first* is coercion.

Man-made codes come in to obstruct, expropriate, or punish only when we lose sight of the way to live naturally as we build and build naturally as we live.

An exterior view of the masonry-constructed Henry J. Allen residence (1917) at Wichita, Kansas. Photograph by the editor.

Unfortunately for us, and the *nature* of democracy at this moment as well, the way of our literate official architecture is, owing to academic education, utterly inorganic. It is by code, and our way of life therefore is no longer free nor inspired by principle. How can a man's life keep its course if he will not let it flow from within. The democratic code must be designed to *complete,* not to *prevent* the man.

The mass to which we belong calls itself "democracy" while betraying the courageous idea that the

The view from an elevated terrace overlooking an interior garden court (foreground) *at the Aline Barnsdall "Hollyhock" residence (1917) in Los Angeles, California. Note the influence of the ancient architecture of Mesoamerica in this spectacular design. Photograph by the editor.*

An exterior view of the Charles Ennis residence (1923) at Los Angeles, California, which utilizes Frank Lloyd Wright's revolutionary modular textile concrete block as an organizing and construction material. Photograph by the editor.

soulful source of all inspiring life flows from the individual. The other mass is obsessed by the cowardly idea of taking cover under a State supreme, with no individual responsibility whatever.

To overcome false ideas, bad work, or violent men democracy has only to mind its own business, stand its own ground, build its own way, the natural or *organic* way.

Were we genuinely a democracy, this violent division would be resolved and there would be no adversary.

The structure democracy must know is the living kind, and that kind of structure is of life at its best for the best of life itself. In itself, *organic* character is sound social foundation. Integral or *organic* structure grown up from the ground into the light by way of the nature of man's life on earth, the method of building to show man to himself as nobly himself. The *true* architecture of democracy will be the externalizing of this inner seeing of the man as Jesus saw him, from within—not an animal or a robot, but a living soul. *Organic* life cannot grow from anything less than the independence of the individual as such—the independence of the individual, his freedom to be *true* to himself! And since that cannot be enforced it cannot even be standardized.

Force is futile. It can organize nothing. Nor can science help us now. Science has put miraculous tools in our toolbox, but no science can ever show us how to use these tools for humanity. It is only natural or *organic* architecture, interior philosophy, and a living religion, not the institutionalized kind—I am talking now about the heart and the deep-seated instincts of man—it is these three alone, *organic* architecture, interior philosophy, and a living religion, that can make life again creative, make men as safe as is good for them, or ever make government tolerable. These three need each other at this crucial moment as never before. In the light of these three *organic* inspirations, revived and alive, we could build an *organic* democracy.

Here in America, if we will only discover what our vast good ground is good for, and use it to build with and build upon, a native culture would come to us from loving our own ground and allowing our ground to love us. A great integrity! The integrity we lack!

We have no good reason here in America to give an imitation of a little industrial nation confined to a small island like England, whose only way out is manufacturing. Our entire nation from border to border and coast to coast is still just a neglected backyard, while we have this cinder strip here in the East. A marvelous range of individual expression waits us as a people when we do discover our own ground. Why are houses alike all over America? Why do we think they have to be so? Why are we as a people inhibited so early? Because we build by code. Sometimes I think we were born, live, and die by code. Give us freedom!

Let inspiration come to us the natural way. Why plant more Oxford Gothic on the plains of Oklahoma? Let us mimic no more. If we build in the desert, let the house know the desert and the desert be proud of the house by making the house an extension of the desert, so that when you're in the house the desert seems the house's own extension. The same thought, in the same feeling, goes for whatever we build, wherever we build it. *Organic* buildings are always of the land and for the life lived in the building. They are not merely on a site, they are of it! Native materials for native life where such exist are better than plastics which have to be brought in. According to circumstances, both may be equally desirable.

And this idea that seems to have invaded our country from somewhere that architecture is one thing, landscape architecture another, and interior decoration a third is absurd. In *organic* architecture all three of these are one.

Whether a structure be life, a building or a state, why buy more monstrosity?

Look at Washington. Is there a single-minded democratic, that is to say, *organic* building there, one sincerely devoted to the nature of its purpose? Bureaucrats are there to work. How can they work in these miles of stone quarries erected to satisfy a grandomania as insatiable as it is insignificant?

Not satisfied, look at Moscow. The case is much the same. A new civilization, unable to find a way of building that is its own, slavishly reproduces the buildings of the culture it overthrew. It overthrew the great high ceilings, high chandeliers, pornographic statues playing on grand terraces. Only now they want the ceilings higher, five chandeliers where there was one before, and they want it all everywhere, even in the subway!

Not liking Moscow, see London! The greatest habitation on earth sunk in its own traditions, unable to see daylight anywhere—part of its charm, of course.

If you see within at all, you will see the same degradation in all. You will find them poisoned for democracy, one and all militaristic, their columns marshaled like soldiers menacing the human spirit, their opposing major and minor centerlines of classic architecture—the *true* crucifixion.

A democratic building is at ease; it stands relaxed. A democratic building, again, is for and belongs to the people. It is of human scale for men and women to live in and feel at home.

No wonder we were bound as things were and must struggle to be unbound as things are.

Were we to build a building for the United Nations, we could not build for an incongruous idea anything but incongruity. The attempt of the nations now to get together is a hopeful sign. All this struggle is good. I have a feeling—it is only a

An exterior view of the David Wright residence (1950) at Phoenix, Arizona. Originally Frank Lloyd Wright called this design, done for his son, "How to Live in the Southwest." Photograph by the editor.

An exterior view of the Norman Lykes residence (1959) at Phoenix, Arizona. This house, which is constructed of desert-rose-colored concrete block, rises elegantly from the mountainous desert landscape. Photograph by the editor.

hunch—that we have to make some mistakes; we can't come upon the ideal thing right side up all at once.

I do know that when the home of the United Nations is built it must be a modern high-spirited place of great repose, an unpretentious building, abandoning all spacious symbolism, having the integrity of the *organic* character in itself, an example of great faith in humanity. Let the assembly room be a place of light as wide open to the sky as possible—that influence is auspicious. Make it no screen to hide ignoble fears or cherish native hypocrisy cultured anywhere by any tradition. Like the human being it would prophesy—its basis the earth, its goal the universal.

If the United Nations is to be a success, it is all up to each of us right where we now are, in the citadels of democracy, our own homes. We love to call them our own. We wish to live there the life of brotherly love and creative sensitivity with full individual responsibility. But we want to live as potent individuals craving immortality, believing in ourselves, and therefore in each other, as with worldwide hospitality we strive for the things that seem more fair to live with and to live for.

When the *organic* architecture of democracy is allowed to build for democratic life the *organic* or natural way, we the American people will recover nobility. Our creative sensitivity will then learn from right-minded architecture to see a man noble as man, a brick that is a brick, see wood beautiful as wood not falsified by some demented painter. We will wish to have a board live as a board and use steel as steel—a spider spinning—and we want glass to be the miracle life itself is. We will see, by means of it, the interior space come alive as the reality of every building. We will learn that our greatest lack as a civilization is the beauty of *organic* integrity and that beauty itself is the highest and finest kind of morality. When democracy builds, it will build the *organic* way and every man's building—his chosen government no less—will be *benign.*

If we love democracy, the way to *do* is to *be.* I can see no fight for freedoms. In a democracy there is only *freedom.*

24 The Arts and Industry in a Democratic Economy

Now, truly, democracy can only be one thing—the gospel of individualism.

Introduction

This speech which was followed by a short question-and-answer period, was delivered by Frank Lloyd Wright at the First 18th-Year Commerce and Industry Luncheon of the Henry George School of Social Science, held on Thursday, October 4, 1951, in the Wedgwood Room of Marshall Field and Company, Chicago. In his remarks, Mr. Wright discussed his ideas on democracy from an *organic* perspective, as in Chapter 23. In this chapter, however, he uses the work and ideas of Henry George as exemplar. Mr. Wright was introduced to the luncheon guests by Mrs. Paul S. Russell and their questions were read by C. Bayard Sheldon for Mr. Wright to address. These questions and Mr. Wright's answers to them are included in this chapter. Three weeks later Mr. Wright visited Lakeland, Florida, to speak on the subject of quality and the vision of the superior human building at the Florida Southern College (see Chapter 13).

Text of a speech and questions and answers reprinted with editing from the published Frank Lloyd Wright's *The Arts and Industry in a Controlled Economy*, Chicago: The Henry George School of Social Science, October 1951, pp. 1–7. Reprinted here by permission of The Henry George School of Social Science.

Frank Lloyd Wright seated at home in Taliesin III near Spring Green, Wisconsin (circa late 1940s or early 1950s). Photograph courtesy of The Capital Times, *Madison, Wisconsin.*

The Speech

WRIGHT: No man ever deserves much praise usually. No matter how good he may be, he's never as good as he thinks he is, possibly, but he's twice as good as other people think he is after all.

I'm here today on this auspicious occasion because I believe in any man who has an *organic* basis for his thoughts, and the man we're honoring today has that basis for his thoughts and his actions. The word *organic* isn't very familiar. Certainly not in architecture. We live in the huts we live in and the way we live in them because we have no concept of what constitutes an *organic* thing. Now, when is a thing *organic*? When can you say that a building is *organic*? When it's natural, properly appropriate to whatever end it's put; where the part is to the whole as the whole is to the part. When you grasp the significance of that word *organic* and learn to apply it to life, to building, to what you do—then I think you have something in common with Henry George.

I think that Henry George had that quality, the only quality that I honor in a human being. It's a most rare quality also. If it were a quality of government today, we wouldn't be at war with anybody and nobody would want to be at war with us. We would have our feet on something and we'd be going somewhere in the direction everybody would recognize as right, as normal, as natural, as belonging to the better aspirations of the human race.

When the depression of 1929 fell on us and the architects, I didn't have a nickel to get from where I lived to where I had to go to get a job offered me. Nobody had anything. Nobody could do anything. There wasn't a hammer ringing in the State of Wisconsin.

There was an idea for a school building and a place to which to take young people and condition them for building buildings and being

An exterior view of the Melvyn Maxwell Smith residence (1946) at Bloomfield Hills, Michigan. This house, an Usonian design, is constructed of brick and cypress wood veneer. Photograph by the editor.

something in their own right. So I got together about forty or fifty working men and their families in the poorhouse. I made an agreement with them to give them what money I could that had already come through and was brought in at that time to apply on their wages, and then we made an agreement that they should have their wages when I got the building that went with them. It went along all right for a couple of years and we were getting toward something when America went on relief, and all these men figured out that they could do better by two dollars a week by not doing anything at all. So we lost all except three.

That isn't all. In Wisconsin, under LaFollette, they passed a law that no person had a right to sell his labor and go without pay for longer than two weeks. So I became a criminal. And all these men began standing around waiting for me to pay up. But what was I going to pay up with? Well, anyhow, that's the kind of thinking that we have been victims of.

Now that's when I began to sit up and take notice of economics. I thought, my God, if an individual has an idea and he can't get that idea into effect by sharing with his fellowmen who are as desperate as he is and who have no more than he has and whose families are starving, what's the matter? Well, I'll tell you what's the matter. It's because we had no *organic* basis for our economic system. We had never listened to men like Henry George. We had never put the thing on a sound basis for human endeavor. We had never made any arrangement which was *organic* by way of which men can grow, by way of which human beings can come together, *free* to exercise their faculties and to prosecute their ideas by way of their own endeavors. It can't be done today. It *can't* be done today.

We have all sorts of organizations, all sorts of insanities at once, all debating, debating, and doing nothing. I won't accuse *this* society of doing nothing because I don't know whether it's doing anything or not. But I'm speaking of societies formed for—what do we call it—advancement? The public good? Well, what have you? Anyway, they're doing nothing. [Editor's Note: Mr. Wright mentioned a book titled *Equitable Commerce* by Josiah Warren, recently called to his attention. He chided the audience on their unfamiliarity with the book and the author and went on to suggest that the Henry George Society republish that book. He was equally aghast at the audience's apparent ignorance of Robert Dale Owen, a contemporary of Josiah Warren.] Now, you know, Henry George was one of a great group who had preceded him and whose thought and feelings he carried further and made more sound. Now here are two of the men who preceded him and were in his class and not a member here ever heard of either one of them!

Well, that's what's the matter with the whole thing—just ignorance! I don't believe there's enough intelligence concerning the thing we call democracy in the nation today. Who can give us a good definition of what constitutes democracy? What do we have today? What is democracy anyway? I had a half-hour with President Harry [Truman] last year. I had read in the papers the day before we met that the UN asked for a definition of democracy and that they turned in eighty-five different answers, no two of which agreed. So, I said to him, "President Harry, don't you think the first thing this country ought to do, you fellows down here running the show, would be to get together and find out what we're all about?" Well, you know it is difficult to define the mess we're in because if you judge us by our actions you get at it wrong-end-to. You can't judge us by what we're doing or what we've done or what it seems likely we are going to do. You've got to go back to the days before apologies. You've got to go back before Henry George. For the nexus of this thing we called democracy in the day of Madison you've got to go back to the men who framed an instrument which is probably the greatest and most effective protection for the growth of the individual in society—our Constitution. We've lost it.

Now, I'd like to pursue this by trying to find somebody in this audience who can tell me what democracy really meant to him. Now, *truly,*

An exterior view of the Herman T. Mossberg residence (1948) at South Bend, Indiana. Like the Melvyn Maxwell Smith residence (1946) in Michigan, this house also is constructed of brick and cypress wood veneer. The pitched roof is clad with cedar shingles. Photograph by the editor.

democracy can be only one thing. A thing that would enable a man like Henry George to have had some effect in his day. Democracy is, of course—is inevitably—the gospel of individualism. It is the supreme encouragement and protection of the individual per se as such, first of all. And that's what the men who came over here and framed this document meant to embody in it. This document has been tampered with and fooled around with and almost destroyed when they made the Fourteenth Amendment to let the states languish so far as individual responsibility is concerned—you know—and federalized the whole thing, and made a hero of the president. Now democracy can't afford heroes. Democracy can't afford anything it's indulging in at the present time—not if it's genuine.

Now, whether President Harry knows this or not there's no means of knowing. But surely this government must know, and we've got to take a stand on the side of the thing in which we believe! Now it's almost impossible, as I have myself found, for anybody in this country to believe that a man will do anything because he *loves to do that thing.* Now that's not democracy. Because in a democratic state of thought in society that's the very basis upon which a man puts in his efforts. Because he *loves* that kind of thing and that's what he's going to do. But have we got it? Have we got anything resembling it? No. Quite the contrary. We have unions. We have big shots. We have a capitalist system, we say—but we haven't got one. We don't have a capitalist system. We've got a system where capitalism has got its apex on the ground and its base in the air and all these artificial props to hold it there. But to get it over with its base on the ground we'd be in production way beyond anything required for war. If we skip the fact [that] the country's bankrupt, we would have everybody in this nation working his head off at something he was proud to do. We would be subscribing one hundred billions for a hundred years to assist the backward nations, the backward countries of this world, when they wanted it and asked for it. We wouldn't go and be murdering them to try and get them to believe as we believe. And on that basis capitalism would be *true* capitalism. It would be a great benefit to the world and out of It would come peace that we don't really want.

Why don't we want it? Why don't we want peace? Well, it's a simple answer. We don't want peace because peace doesn't pay. With the system we've set up we've got to have more war—we've got to have orders to consume these goods that are so—so manifestly a surplus. We can't face it and we won't face it. We're afraid of it. And we've got so that fear is the characteristic thing in our midst today—fear in our position, fear in ideas—because we can't define our own. Well, hatred required cheered talk and denouncing your neighbor as a public virtue. Now what is that but Fascism, Hitlerism, Stalinism, and what a silly thing for the country to have started out attacking an ideology, attacking communism. We can't lick

An exterior view of the Mrs. Clinton Walker residence (1948) at Carmel, California, perched on the shore above Monterey Bay. Construction is stone and copper. Photograph by the editor.

communism by democracy, so far as we've got it. But we could put Stalin out of business—we could put the abuses of communism out of business—if we really knew what we were all about and really meant what we have set up and if we understood where we were.

Now it's perfectly *true* that in a democracy, where genius is neglected or feared—I don't think it's so much neglected as feared—fear seems to be the characteristic condition of mind of everybody that's got anything. Now, to have a "to-have-and-to-hold" religion on the basis of fear is contemptible. The profit motive on any basis of fear is contemptible. Without courage, without the resolution to be free, and without the endorsement of freedom as a great motive, well, what are we? I'd like to have somebody give me a sufficiently descriptive slogan. Well, I don't know that I'm going to get anything for the Henry George Society by trying to get down to the basis of anything. But this should be the place for it—with the men who honor this man who had *organic* character in his thought. The preface of his principal work is one of the finest things in the English language, and every child in school should be taught to recite it by heart so that the words and what it meant might sink into his little mind—and when he grew up, he would become a champion of the *organic* character in whatever might appear.

Now, money, of course, is an abstraction, ladies and gentlemen. Civilization is an abstraction. You know what an abstraction is? You know the difference between abstraction and a definite picture of something? Well, now, an architect, an *organic* architect, has to know. Abstraction means essence. The essence of the thing is the proper abstract of that thing. What is essential, made evident as a pattern, is an abstraction in architecture. We need that type of thinking in government, we need that type of thinking socially, we need it educationally. We don't have it. We send these children of ours, good plums, to

An exterior view of the James Edwards residence (1949) at Okemos, Michigan. Construction is brick and cypress wood. The roof is clad with asphalt shingles. Note that the house stands on the side of a hill in a wooded area. Photograph by the editor.

colleges and universities and we get back prunes. They're all . . . the freshness and the vitality and what you might call the juice in the plum is gone, and what we get back is unable to give us this thing we want. This thing we call *democracy* is killed right there.

Well—so what? What are you going to do about it? What are we going to do about it as a nation? What are we as a people headed for with our ugliness—our ugly cities, our ugly cars, our ugly houses, the ugly way we live in them? We're not even aware of it. And that's the pity of it—so little do we know of what goes on in our own selves. Now I always thought that a young man was sent to college, for what? To learn about himself. "The proper study of mankind is man." That was said long ago. But he doesn't learn anything about himself at all. And very few men today, if they're in any degree successful, know anything at all about themselves. There's their personality, which was an accident. None of us is responsible for the shape of our heads, the ears, nose, our eyes, or the way we move, maybe. That we couldn't help. Personality was a gift or a curse to us. But, now, what do we do with it when we go to work upon it intelligently, ourselves—to produce something by way of our own thought and feeling in ourselves—then only are we fit subjects of a democracy.

Now democracy is the highest and finest ideal. Men like Henry George knew what it meant and fought for a basis for it. It's the highest and finest ideal on earth today or in the mind of man because it is predicated on the basis of freedom.

Now freedom is an interior thing. It isn't something Franklin D. Roosevelt hands you, nor Harry Truman, nor the senator you send down to Washington. It's something you've got and by way of which you send him and for which you send him. And if you haven't got it, you're going to have the kind of government we've got today. And it's because you haven't got it that we haven't got the government.

And as for our houses and the pig piles we live in, the same to you!

AUDIENCE: (laughter)

WRIGHT: You've got them because you don't know any better. Now you don't learn better when you go to school. Why shouldn't you? Why shouldn't education be taking this thing in hand and conditioning the minds of these young people for freedom, teaching them to build upon themselves and from out [of] themselves that sense of responsibility and individuality which can stand up against anything that's not *organic* and not right?

Well, where were we? There was a question and answer period after this, wasn't there? Anybody want to ask any questions? I don't think so.

AUDIENCE: (laughter)

WRIGHT: Will you read it to me? What is it?

C. BAYARD SHELDON: Here's one, right off the bat. Have you any comments, Mr. Wright, on building codes as an example of controls?

WRIGHT: Well, of course, a democrat doesn't like controls from the outside. He likes to be put upon his own sense of honesty and responsibility and that's the difference between a Nazi and a democrat. You can illustrate it very nicely in this fashion. The difference between a democrat, generally, and a Nazi or a Communist or any of the other "ists" and "isms" confronted by the code—he would finger the pages of the code—the Nazi, the Communist, the Fascist—and he would say, "Well, I don't see this in the book. No, we can't do anything for you. No, this is wrong. No, we can't help you." And you go out to die.

A democrat, fingering that code, would say, "Here, of course no rule, although it's made to be foolproof, can ever be more than a rule for fools. Here's a case that really was not considered and was overlooked. The rules don't apply." Throws it on the side. Says, "All right, you go ahead. That's the right thing to do and a good thing." Now there's your democrat!

Now, how much of that have we got in this three million population of bureaucracy that we're up

An exterior view of the Richard Davis residence (1950) at Marion, Indiana. The American Indian teepeelike (almost monumental) structural form houses the massive concrete block fireplace and living room. Construction is painted concrete block with redwood trim. Photograph by the editor.

An exterior view of the William Palmer residence (1950) at Ann Arbor, Michigan. This house blends with its natural topography and is well integrated with its site. Construction is brick and cypress wood. Photograph by the editor.

against? Codes, of course, are made by fools for fools. Like an expert. What is an expert? An expert is a man who has stopped thinking. *He knows!*

AUDIENCE: (laughter)

WRIGHT: That's *true.* It's an architect speaking—I ought to know!

AUDIENCE: (laughter)

WRIGHT: For fifty-nine years I've been practicing architecture and been absolutely all of the time and in every instance up against the codes. And yet I've built the buildings. So I ought to be good on codes. Anybody else?

SHELDON: Would you like to see stricter licensing laws for architects?

WRIGHT: I would like to see no licensing laws for architects whatever.

AUDIENCE: (applause)

WRIGHT: I think these controls and licensing laws for architects have put the inferior product in the field on a par with the better product and not one of them has to be an architect at all. All he has to do is hang out his shingle and say he's one. Well, that's not good enough. In a democracy you have to prove your case. You have to be the thing you pretend to be or you don't get a job. But that's all out now. So controls from without are, like the controls visited upon any individual in any society in any place anywhere, undemocratic. So—got another one?

SHELDON: What effect, if any, do you expect on civilization with most women working out[side] of their homes? Is that progress or retrogression?

AUDIENCE: (laughter)

WRIGHT: I should say that it's ultimate damnation.

AUDIENCE: (loud laughter)

WRIGHT: There's a reason for that, too, ladies and gentlemen. What is home today? Is home democratic? Is home a democratic institution? And in a democracy the home is the unit upon which not only government but society is based. And anything depreciating the quality of the individual home and the individuals in it—well, it spells the end of anything democratic. Now what's good for the home is good for democracy and vice versa. I think we should build better homes, happier homes, houses where there would need be no division, where the man and the wife working together, feeling life together and understanding each other, could really do a great work at home.

Well, you see the condition in which we live is ugly because it's sick. There seems to be very little health in this great new experiment in the direction of freedom. What has become of the vitality, what has become of the integrity of the individual in this great experiment, even at home? Especially at home. If it existed at home, it would be everywhere in the country. And I've wanted to build homes of the people rather than these public buildings, rather than great buildings for the public, because I believe that that's where culture, if it ever comes to us, is going to come from. A witty Frenchman has said that we were the only civilization, the only great nation on record, to have proceeded directly from barbarism to degeneracy with no culture of our own in between.

AUDIENCE: (laughter and applause)

WRIGHT: Now I've been working on that line. I've been trying to give our people a culture of their own, and I know it begins with architecture. Basically, it is architecture we have to have. If we're ever going to have a culture of our own we'll have an architecture of our own. Now we started it. It's well on the way. I could hang gold medals all over the front here talking to you because America at last said something out of the freedom that foreign nations are bound to respect as culture. That's why I believe it could be done and I believe it would pay, it would pay out, I believe it would lick Communism. I think it would lick every other faith on

A detailed exterior view of the Donald Schaberg residence, second design (1950), a house of brick and wood at Okemos, Michigan. The roofing is cedar shake. Frank Lloyd Wright did an earlier, but aborted, design for Schaberg, also in 1950. Photograph by the editor.

earth if we only took it to our bosoms and had the courage to practice it. If we'd make some sacrifices for it. We won't. That all?

SHELDON: Here's one I found on the table when we came up here. I understand that Frank Lloyd Wright homes have low ceilings.

AUDIENCE: (laughter)

SHELDON: Before air-conditioning, did this low ceiling result in poor air when a number of people were in one room, such as a party?

AUDIENCE: (laughter)

WRIGHT: No.

AUDIENCE: (laughter)

WRIGHT: The infiltration was always something to be overcome.

AUDIENCE: (laughter)

WRIGHT: We couldn't build windows and doors tight enough to keep the air out. Ever since we discovered floor heating we can raise the ceilings, but before that time we had to keep them down in order to keep warm up north. We couldn't have a high ceiling and really be comfortable. Not only that, but the homes that I have built and the buildings I have built have high ceilings only as a dramatic contrast to the high one which follows very soon. It's a little trick, ladies and gentlemen, as well as economy. It's an artistic subterfuge if you want to call it that. Why not call it a refuge? Call it a

An exterior view of the entrance to the J. A. Sweeton residence (1950) at Cherry Hill, New Jersey. In the foreground is the driveway; a dynamic cantilevered roof forms the carport canopy. The house is constructed of concrete block and wood. Photograph by the editor.

poem. Because, after all, before we began building buildings to human scale the old classic idea was to mortify the individual—give him an inferiority complex—that was the first aim they had. That's why they built great high ceilings and high columns and made you rattle around in space you couldn't use.

AUDIENCE: (laughter)

WRIGHT: Well, any more?

SHELDON: Here's one. Do not people produce more and/or better when enslaved? For example, Michelangelo as "prisoner" of the Pope produced the murals of the Sistine Chapel.

WRIGHT: Oh, he was no . . . that's all history that is garbled or distorted. Michelangelo was never anybody's slave, least of all the Pope's. There may have been some reason why the Pope wanted Michelangelo's services completely to himself. I don't know. Probably so. But Michelangelo was no slave of the Pope. The man that hurled the Pantheon on top of the Parthenon was nobody's slave. He made *us* all slaves!

AUDIENCE: (laughter)

WRIGHT: There isn't a thing done since in the name of authority that hasn't had that goddamned dome!

AUDIENCE: (prolonged laughter)

SHELDON: We're very pleased to have had Mr. Wright with us. It's been very wonderful. I'm sure all of us are going to grab our economics textbooks and find out about those two fellows he mentioned.

AUDIENCE: (laughter)

Frank Lloyd Wright, circa mid-1950s. Photograph by Carmie A. Thompson, courtesy of The Capital Times, *Madison, Wisconsin.*

25 Architecture in a Democracy

Now, democracy can only live by way of its own genius. Democracy cannot live on anything borrowed.

Introduction

Mr. Wright spoke before the Detroit Chapter of the American Institute of Architects and the Michigan Society of Architects at the Masonic Temple in Detroit on Thursday evening, May 27, 1954. Shortly after tickets went on sale it was reported that: "Tickets to the Wright lecture are being sold rapidly, even before there is any promotion to speak of. Large blocks of tickets are being bought and . . . it is evident . . . the lecture will be sold out far in advance."[1] Before his appearance on May 27 the editors of the *Michigan Society of Architects Monthly Bulletin* reflected upon Mr. Wright's past visits to Detroit[1]:

> *On one of his former visits to Detroit the architects arranged a press luncheon for him at the Detroit Athletic Club. Everything was set, newsmen were present, and the cocktails were enjoyed—but no Mr. Wright. Next day one Detroit newspaper, whose editor didn't love Mr. Wright, front-paged the headline, "Two wrongs don't*

Text edited and reprinted from "By Frank Lloyd Wright," *Michigan Society of Architects Monthly Bulletin*, Vol. 28, June 1954, pp. 9, 11, 13, 15, 17, 19–21, and 23. Used by permission of the Michigan Society of Architects.

[1] "Frank Lloyd Wright Lecture," *Michigan Society of Architects Monthly Bulletin*, Vol. 28, May 1954, p. 17. Used by permission of the Michigan Society of Architects.

produce a Wright," and the article went on in disparaging terms, concluding that "your guess is as good as ours as to whether he will even show up for the lecture."

The feat was accomplished, the place was mobbed, even by bobby-soxers—the kind who swoon for their favorite crooner—and when they had to be turned away they were asked why they didn't go down in the lounge and hear him over the public address system, they would say, "We want to see HIM." Had everything gone according to schedule, there wouldn't have been nearly the news value.

Thinking to get some expression about our architecture and city planning problems, a reporter asked Mr. Wright what he thought of Detroit. His answer, "must I think of it?" This is somewhat typical, as he generally gets attention by insulting his fellow architects—but in a way that they like it . . . Mr. Wright is no stranger to Detroit where he has many friends.

Chapters 4 and 11 present two other speeches delivered by Mr. Wright in Detroit—one on March 22, 1945, and the other on October 21, 1957.

Mr. Wright did appear for his May 27th speech. He talked long on subjects that ranged from culture to McCarthyism but most of all on democracy and what it should mean to a free country and especially to the architecture of a free country. Mr. Wright's lengthy speech was followed by a question-and-answer period in which the audience participated. Several days later, on Friday, June 4, Mr. Wright delivered a speech in Philadelphia in acceptance of the Frank P. Brown Medal of the Franklin Institute (see Chapter 18).

The Speech

WRIGHT: Ladies and gentlemen, I have a feeling at this occasion that it is badly out of scale—I don't see that architecture is entitled to any such spaciousness as this or any such audience. I don't believe you are all interested in architecture. It is hard to believe it.

AUDIENCE: (laughter)

WRIGHT: Architecture is the blindest spot of our culture. We know a little music now—not much. We know a little painting; we can see that that has practically been demoralized and is practically gone.

AUDIENCE: (laughter)

WRIGHT: Sculpture—who refers to sculpture as a culture nowadays? Anybody?

You see, the arts in our nation are in a bad way. Somehow in previous cultures art and religion have been the soul of those cultures.

We have a way of life that is called a civilization but lacking a culture, which is the way of making that way of life beautiful. Of course, we don't know much or hear much about the arts, with a capital "A."

When we do have a culture of our own, architecture will be basic to that culture. As a matter of fact, what is wrong now with painting and with sculpture, chiefly, is that architecture being dead, with what they call the Renaissance lying moribund for 500 years, painting and sculpture took a little shovel full of coals and started little hells of their own and they haven't been able to make it. And they won't be able to make it until that great synthesis comes again, which once existed in the world, from all the arts with architecture fundamentally there.

Let's put it the other way around because architecture, of course, is the greatest of all the arts when it is understood. We don't understand it because anybody can plan a house or build a fire, and a house is a piece of property anyway, isn't it?

We are very careless about it, and what we see in our own nation is not a great congruity but a great incongruity, and, of course, it's a disgrace, provided we were a culture. Now, I don't mean *culture* as the Germans use the term at all. I mean *culture* as the Dutchmen used the term when they took the little flower out of the garden—the larkspur.

That beautiful little thing. What a charming pattern it has! They didn't educate the larkspur; they didn't try to teach it anything. It was there. But with patient experimentation they found out what that little flower liked best, and then they gave it that. And it grew and grew—bigger. Then they gave it more, until finally what have you? You have the queen of the garden, the delphinium, out of the little larkspur. Well, now, that is culture.

All we have had is what you call education. You cannot get the artist—an architect because an architect must be fundamentally a great artist—you cannot get one by the same methods you produce a scientist. You can't get one by the same methods used to produce a businessman. There is some confusion, I think, in the minds of the American public as to whether this creature we call an architect is a hybrid. I don't know what they think he is. I have been a practicing architect for sixty years myself and I don't know. There seems to be some confusion of ideas of what he is, really—who he is, how he is.

Certainly the way they are trying to make them in our universities would seem to indicate they don't know much about it, which is an indictment I think I am entitled to bring because I am trying to do something about it. I believe that if we are going to have young men worthy of this great opportunity and a new civilization where time, place, and man are all in changed circumstances and nothing of the old philosophy of architecture—which really wasn't a philosophy at all—remains useful to us, we are at the point where we have to start practically from scratch.

Steel and glass came in and you know the Greeks didn't have those two miraculous materials. Glass, to keep air in. Steel, the spider spinning. The ancient Greeks were never able to build buildings

The Dr. Maurice Greenberg residence (1954) at Dousman, Wisconsin. This brick masonry and concrete structure was built into the side of a wooded hill. Photograph by the editor.

on which you could pull this way [Editor's Note: Mr. Wright gestures with his hands]. They'd all come apart and fall down. Now, we have this great element of tenuity, steel, an entirely new principle in construction.

The principle has enabled the cantilever to come into being. You all know what a cantilever is, being here interested in architecture, and I shouldn't have to explain it. But I think I will have to and say to you it is merely an extended lever.

This would be a cantilever, resting here [Editor's Note: Mr. Wright again gestures with his arms], and the distance that it projects over, it lists in this direction, so that a cantilever system enables the reduction of great spans and puts the support directly on the load. Now, that opportunity never existed in the world before.

Let's get down to the simple structural basis of a thing. The old architecture has gone. You see, the old architecture was a box and the corners of that were the supports. This will probably bore you, but never mind—you may learn something!

AUDIENCE: (laughter)

WRIGHT: When you have to span from corner to corner, you see, you have a very big span to cover. It was very expensive. But, when we got the cantilever and the principle of steel, you could move those supports in and have the corner free, and the cantilever is created by that; reduced the spans, broke out the corner of the box, and let you look out where you never looked out before.

Now, when that happened, the walls began to disappear. The walls were vanishing. Now, when the corners go and the walls vanish, what have you got? You certainly have a new freedom, haven't you? You have got a chance now to build buildings that are for a free life within the building; where the life within the building becomes more aware of and part of the outside world and the outside world can be used at convenience from the inside.

So your walls become screens, and the box form is now the old thinking and the old thought, and what you hear of as the International Style is, of course, the old box with its face lifted. You make the box walls of glass and you look into the box. Has the thought changed? Never! The same old thought; no real dissidence.

That is not modern architecture, that is only contemporary. There is a distinction I wish you'd remember because it's a valid one and it's a genuine basic structural reason for what we call *organic* architecture.

Now, little things—and those are not little things—but that is the type of thing that has changed the civilization of the world. It has sometimes destroyed them. It has sometimes made them.

By way of our Declaration of Independence and what we call *democracy* this gives America a chance to build a culture unparalleled in the history of the world. We don't have to follow the Greeks. We don't have to follow anybody. We have a new freedom that will enable, eventually, an architecture to appear that will astonish and delight the Greeks if they ever get a chance to see it. They would think: "How foolish and how silly we were to do what we have been doing all these years."

But we have been doing it. We have been standing columns up just for the sake of columns. A bank didn't have credit unless it had columns up in front!

AUDIENCE: (laughter)

WRIGHT: To do honor to a great democratic president with columns we built a public comfort station to the greatest statesman we ever had with columns. We go back to the Greeks for dignity and honor. How long do you think a free people are going to stand for that? We have stood for it ever since we began.

I hope you are aware of the fact that nearly everything we have got that could be named architecture or culture, or has been so named, came to us third hand. The French got it from the

Italians, the English got it from the French, and we got it from the English. If we had only taken the best of it, we would have been better off. What we got is what the dormitory towns took from it; the big towns in London, for instance. We got a very much bastardized edition of original Italian architecture in what we call the Old Colonial.

Now, I have given you the history, which is valid. You can't evade it. We are mongrel people and have borne with a mongrelized culture for how many years—a hundred and how many?

The Declaration of Independence was unique, wasn't it? It was the first time in the history of the world that people stood up on their own feet and said: "Hell, let's be ourselves. Let's have individual responsibility as the basis of our personal freedom."

We got democracy and that is where we are. Here we find ourselves doing everything we declared in that day and time we would not do and doing it for what? To save our own faces. Because we are scared, I guess, because we are congenital cowards; is that it? Well, why? Why have we denied and gone against every fundamental principle that we found our forefathers—or would have found if we studied it—declared as freedom? I can't understand it, unless it is that all our standards are so mixed, like our blood, that we have lost sight of anything straightforward, clean, *true* and original.

Now, democracy can only live by way of its own genius. Democracy cannot live on anything borrowed. We have got a new work to do in the way of a new culture.

We have gone about it in a way that is unthinkably disastrous. We send our young people now to learn

A view of the Harold Price, Jr., residence (1953) at Bartlesville, Oklahoma, taken above the driveway. Photograph by the editor.

A view of the elevated terrace of the Harold Price, Jr. residence (1953) at Bartlesville. Photograph by the editor.

how to characterize this freedom and this new life and to prophesy the individual as our forefathers claimed and desired would come *true.* We send them to these old rattraps—these old buildings—their own selves perfectly debased as far as culture is concerned; they are nothing. They form line associations with those buildings and they come back to us conditioned.

Well, now, education in our country has become a kind of conditioning instead of enlightenment. Enlightenment is one thing; conditioning is another. We, as a people, are being conditioned. When you start looking a thing in the face for what it is, you will be just as displeased and shocked.

I used to be angry about it. I am not anymore because I know it can't be helped, but it's there. We are not fundamentally ourselves. We are not fundamentally paying attention to the basis of our real democratic existence.

When I was in Italy last year—or a few years ago—when this Italian show was on [Editor's Note: Mr. Wright's "Sixty Years of Living Architecture" exhibition], I talked with many Italians and, believe me, the Italians are the most intelligent artistically of all the people of Europe today, as they have always been. They said:

> *Mr. Wright, your attempt at democracy is going to fail because you have not provided anything to prevent the rise of mediocrity into high places. Your design was to be ruled by the greatest and the best. How are you going to accomplish the greatest and the best when mediocrity can become your rulers?*

What is the answer? I wish you'd tell me.

Our forefathers didn't care for it when they made a vote conditioned upon a stake in the country. You had to have something of it that you were in for and could protect and call your own before you could vote. But they destroyed that.

Now, I don't think there is anything standing between our democracy—our freedom and our architecture and our life as a great culture—and destruction unless we can do a little thinking along with voting. A lot of us thought that when the women got the vote that would change things. Well, it didn't. The balance of power remained precisely as it was. You know that, don't you? It has been ascertained perfectly that when women got the vote nothing changed at all. But you might have expected that when she did get the vote culture would get a little better break. Finding that it hasn't worked that way, I decline to be booked to women's clubs to speak.

AUDIENCE: (laughter)

WRIGHT: When I didn't have a nickel to my own name, I went to an agent and became one of his trained seals. He said, "Mr. Wright, we want to bring lectures back. I want you to take your dress suit." I didn't have one but I got one and went out over the country. He put a joker in it. At the last lecture of the series I found myself in Richmond, Virginia, and I thought I was going to the Art Institute [of Chicago]. This was the last lecture of the series and he put one over on me. He booked me for the Richmond Women's Club. I got there and it was a handsome place. There were handsome women serving tea. The richest women's club in the world and there I was. Well, it was a great opportunity for revenge.

AUDIENCE: (laughter)

WRIGHT: I told them why I didn't want to talk to women's clubs, because what was the use? There was no use at all. I went on at some length and explained why.

After the lecture I was coming down into the audience to get out the back way and out comes a very handsome, tallish lady, beautifully dressed, with a beautiful young daughter on her arm. She slipped her arm in mine and said, "Now, are you real?" and pinched my arm. She said, "I never expected to live to see the day." Well, it was Cissie Patterson herself. She herself had had troubles culturally, I guess.

Why are all you women here now in this audience? Do you feel any individual responsibility toward the cultural side of life that your children are going to live hereafter? Now, when you got your foot on the bar rail and a cigarette hanging from your lip, you felt that was progress, I dare say! Well, it worked just the other way. You haven't progressed; you are now a liability rather than an asset. The question arises: What in the name of heaven are we going to do with you?

Look at the magazines, television, radio, everything—is there anything from the belly button up? No, it's all from the belly button down. That is what you have done to us. What good did it do to let you have the vote? I think we ought to take it back!

AUDIENCE: (laughter and applause)

WRIGHT: Now, of course, it is easy for me to stand here in this great vacuum and mention these unmentionable things. There is some satisfaction in just that, but not enough. I wouldn't have come down here just to mention these things unless I thought that by mentioning them, by calling your attention to them—and being an old veteran practicing architecture for sixty years, 647 buildings, and seeing some of you at home and in company—I have attended these cocktail parties, than which there is no worse ever, standing around with drinks, gassing away about nothing, and I tell you that the artistic sensibility of our people has practically gone to pot. Yes, it has and I don't see why it wouldn't be fit and meeting [for] our women's clubs to do a little something about it. And what are they doing about it?

As for the men, well, in America it is a weakness to talk about the beautiful for a man who can really make money. Making money is the basic art, next to advertising—we'll have to cut that in—in the whole nation.

We are a juvenile civilization, with our feminine angle, now able to drink and smoke, and where is our culture as a nation? What are we doing? How many of you here would know a good building from a bad one? How many would know why it was good or why it was bad? You can take a handful of you, say fifteen or twenty of you out there, if that many, and then you might be mistaken.

But there is something elemental; there is something fundamental; there are principles in this life of ours. We don't see much of them. We don't hear much of them.

You can get an angle of what we have by [the] trial that is just going on here by this mobocrat from Wisconsin. He used to be called [Senator Joseph] McCarthy. I have got another name for him, but I wouldn't dare mention it here tonight. But that is where we are. I spoke a little while ago about democracy arising into high places. There you have it. This man is a mob. There isn't anything there but McCarthy. That is enough for him. It is what the Germans invented a word for. Do you know that word?—to "Schriben" [sic]? You Germans know it. It means "written dead." In other words, let it drop—with a dull and sickening thud.

Well, let's get back to architecture. See if it works. Another sad thing is that we don't get the good

View of an exterior elevation of the lobby (left) *and the auditorium/rostrum* (right) *of the Unitarian Church (1947) at Shorewood Hills, Wisconsin. Photograph by the editor.*

material in architecture that we used to have. The men we had building buildings when I was a youth came in the hard way. They made their reputations by sheer performance. They didn't get a little pink slip from a college and go out and practice architecture. They had to show something on the ball, what they were and had, and what they could do; and they did it. At least they were men.

When I was a youth in Chicago, the Art Institute was built. When it was built, they wondered who was going to go to it and who would patronize it, if anybody. But they found a use for it. When papa and mama made a boy that was no good and they couldn't do anything with him—he wouldn't work and he wouldn't do anything—the cure for that was to send him to the Art Institute. And that is how the Art Institute was filled up. It was filled with that type of material. If he is no good for anything else, he might make an artist.

That is where we are now, and that is why architecture is where it is—one reason. We don't have the men and it is because it has become useless, in a civilization as juvenile as ours is, to really become a great artist.

How can you? They are not made, they are born—and they grow by encouragement. They grow by the opportunity to become great. Where are they going to get it now?

Well, this is all very encouraging, but what I am driving at is this: It is time, high time, that you American women—and even you American men—woke up to the fact that a great civilization without a great culture is in great danger. It can commit suicide overnight. Science has driven us to a brink. All it would take would be an H-bomb or two and a black satchel with some insane person to drop it and the whole world would go to pieces. That is what science has done for us. Science can take things apart like that. What can put things together again? What? Science? No. Science can't even put together again what it takes apart.

Creative art, the creative mind—the creative individual is the only one that can save this civilization from itself. That is not an overstatement. Isn't it time, instead of trying to make artists the way we make businessmen and the way we make chauffeurs and truck drivers, that we paid a little attention to the best way of getting something out of what we have? I think we have got it, and I believe it lies not with this generation that I belong, certainly—that is practically gone—nor to the generation after me—because that is entirely gone—nor the generation after that—that is going—but to the children that are now in high school. I get letters from those children all over this country, children in high school:

> *Dear Mr. Wright:*
> *We have selected you for our thesis. Would you kindly send us some material?*

So I'm getting out a form letter. The secretary is going to send it when they write in, there are so many of them.

Now, what occasion is there to awaken interest in a culture that is indigenous? I am at a loss; I am really asking you because I am sure I don't know. But it is there. I think it is there because I think it is time. You know, there is a right time in all this sort of thing. It goes down; it is like the weather, more or less, and it's on the grand average. In [the] course of time things come right side up. In [the] course of time the bad will subside and the good will arise. So there is hope in the young.

Then, too, if you go far west, out to the far-western towns and cities like Barstow, California, or Phoenix, Arizona, the new ones where things are new, there is hope. You see, these middle-western towns like your town here and other towns grew up at the very worst possible time. They are, of course, now unable to overcome that period. But if you go where things are new, you see what we call modern architecture characterizing the whole place. You see people waking up and taking an interest. They are really very attractive, beautiful places. Then you come back to a middle-western city and what do you find? Well, you know. You live here.

Now, that shouldn't be the case. You see, the Russians got one great break over us. When they started to build a great city, Moscow, do you know what they did the first thing? They blew up squares; they blew up old blocks. When I was there in 1939 I saw them going up in the air. I don't know how they did it. They must have had the H-bomb then.

But they cleared out the whole center of Moscow, except the Kremlin, and then they planted the tall buildings far out. The further out they went, the higher up they could go. But they couldn't come down to the center. That is what we call decentralization on a grand scale.

We can't do that. Our property is too precious for us to ever do anything like that. We have got to hang onto it or die, if we don't look out. The owners of the city aren't going to let go voluntarily. They are going to build more and more, and higher and higher, and they are going to build great streets—great freeways that are going to enable you to get away from the city after a while. That is really what they are for.

So there you are now and there is your opportunity. How many of the best people live in the cities now that you know of? Not many can get away and get out. How many great firms are inhabiting the city now? Aren't they going out?

I built a little church in Madison. It was a Unitarian Church. They wanted to build it downtown. I persuaded them to go out into the country, so we went out about five miles, I think it was, or maybe four and a half. We thought it was far enough. Before we got the church finished the city was all around it, and Madison isn't growing very fast.

So I think that to decentralize today you have not only got to go out as far as you dare go but five times as far. And the city then will get you before it passes away unless the blast released with the H-bomb happens along. Sometimes, don't you think that would be, perhaps, merciful?

AUDIENCE: (laughter)

WRIGHT: It would give us a chance to start all over again. You know, it wouldn't hurt. We wouldn't know it happened at all. Even if it were to drop tomorrow, I don't suppose any of us would suffer a pang—we'd just disappear. That is not a gloomy thought altogether, but still we don't want it to happen.

When we were talking about architecture, and if you don't think this is architecture you are very much mistaken because architecture today, the central principle of it, is decentralization; now there is where the women could come in. Do you know what keeps the city alive, chiefly, today? It is the women. The women really are for the city, and they are going to keep the city alive until the last gasp. Why? For one basic reason—it is the best hunting ground there is!

AUDIENCE: (laughter)

WRIGHT: I think that eventually it is going to be a great house of prostitution. It will also be a gambling center and a place where you will find—well, let's change the subject.

We can't get too flippant tonight. The occasion is too outstanding. I prefer the little gatherings so you can all get together and see each other, talk about things, and have fun. You can't have fun tonight!

AUDIENCE: (laughter)

WRIGHT: But here is something we must realize as a people—and this is serious. If we do not realize the *nature* of architecture as basic to culture and waken to the fact that we don't have one worthy of a free people, that we are living the lives of cowards in more than one sense, and reach for something even if it's a stiff drink, it will give us a little courage. That is what we lack.

Now, I have often tried to figure out why we are so cowardly. What scared us so? What is it that has put us back on our haunches for nothing, no reason at all? Is it a bad conscience? Is it because we have lost all sense of proportion? Is it because we gave the women the vote? Could be. It could be a lot of things. I haven't been able to figure it out, and I don't think you will either, so let's drop it.

Let's go forward to something where we can all realize that life is only worth living if you can make it more beautiful than it was when you found it. That is *true*. That is the only real life worthy of a man, and I have found in my own personal experience that what pride I have is where I have tried to make the life around me and the life of my people and my own life in connection with it more beautiful than it was. How do you do that? It's the only thing that is worth your time.

We talk about the payoff. Everything in this country revolves around the question: Will it pay? What is the payoff? Where do I come in? All that sort of thing.

Well now, cowardice is the death of all these things I am talking about. There is no beauty in cowardice and there is no beauty for cowardice. It is the very antithesis and death of the beautiful in every sense. It takes courage. It takes blood. It is only out of the heart that this thing comes of which I am talking about, not out of the hand. Architecture is a scientific art but primarily architecture is of the heart. It is here [Editor's Note: Mr. Wright places his hand over his heart]. It is love for the beautiful, for the *truth*, for integrity, for strength and purpose.

Now, art and religion are the soul of a civilization. Science is nothing but the brains and the toolbox. When you are low on heart and low on religion, don't talk about a culture.

You know, I believe too that it isn't much use to talk about manhood or womanhood either, because if that is not present and you are not aware of it and you are not cultivating it and you are not fighting for it and it isn't the most precious thing to you that is imaginable; you are not free. You are not individuals. You are not anything in your own right at all—you are just things. And you can be a thing to a certain extent. You can be conscripted and go to war and get killed or come back a hero, and what good is it? What good is any of it except that thing wherein you have the feeling in your heart that you are contributing, that you are developing and making this world a better place for those children that you caused to come into this world to live and their children, too?

Now, there is where we got a culture and that is what culture means. That is why it is. That is why a civilization isn't good enough.

Why, the Indians had a civilization. God knows, how many hundreds of them there were. Look how many have come and gone. What did they die of? Why did they die? Why aren't they here now?

Where are the Romans, for instance? We are the modern Romans, of course. We put the razor on the scruff of our necks, expose our heads behind the ears, where there is no expression whatsoever, as the Romans did. Why do we do it? Because the Romans did it. We don't do it for any good reason that we know of. You get your hair cut today as the Romans got it cut, and God knows they were the ugliest people on the face of the world!

The Greeks were a little better. The Greeks didn't have their hair cut. The Greeks were personable citizens, they were handsome. They were Negroid—they were black, brown and yellow—but they were good to look at and they dressed beautifully.

The Greeks had great sculpture but they had no architecture. They again were degenerate where architecture was concerned, and that is something we have had to learn—I mean unlearn. The whole world has had to unlearn that.

Another damage which is done to us continually, that we have had to unlearn, that a painter cannot make an architect, and a painter damages architecture. The greatest painter who ever lived, Michelangelo, did the most grievous error an architect ever committed when he did St. Peter's. Now, why? You all think that is your answer—that arch up in the sky standing on posts. Did you ever think what an anachronism it is? Did you ever think how false it is to construction? Did you ever learn that it would have fallen—great chunks of it were falling—and the call went out to all the blacksmiths in Rome to make a great chain to put around the base of it to

Wright: "That is a great big box . . . it makes no sense . . . it is utterly undemocratic in spirit. It is not free, nor is it fault free." The United Nations Secretariat (1951—1952) in New York, designed by Wallace K. Harrison and Associates. Photograph courtesy of the New York Convention and Visitors Bureau.

hold it there, and it is there now? Otherwise, St. Peter's would have been down and out.

We went on copying, we didn't care. Now, we build it with iron plates bolted together and imitate an arch. And there it is, sitting up on cast-iron pins purely a false form, purely an anachronism. Do any of you know it? No. Did the English know it when they copied it in St. Paul's? No. It has become the symbol of authority the world over, and that symbol of authority is essentially false.

It is like the UN Building in New York City. That is also false in the same way. That is a great big box, a crate in which you could ship any number of people to here, there, and back again. It makes no sense except Fascism, Communism, and all the other -isms—it is utterly undemocratic in spirit. It is not free nor is it fault-free.

Now, all these things you must know and you must know the reason why these things I am telling you are so. I am not going to answer it, and you must look into this thing a little deeper and you must get hold of something you don't have hold of now. I suggest that women's clubs of this country take it up and study it.

Well, now, usually when I come in out of the field and I am still working—working hard—there are people in the audience who really want to know something that I could tell them. There are questions that I could answer, and the question and answer period when I was in England was really good. It was the best part of the evening, and I enjoyed it and they did, too. They got to heckling me to the point where they got to heckling each other, and the thing would break up almost in a row. But you don't get that out of an American audience and I don't know why. You won't fight. You won't come back. Why shouldn't you? I am not going to say things to you that are not very pretty. There may be another side to this that I don't understand and I am very willing to listen. So, now, you go on. Let's hear from the audience. Has anybody got a question?

The Questions and Answers

QUESTIONER: Have you ever designed any low-cost houses, Mr. Wright?

WRIGHT: I never designed anything else!

QUESTIONER: Let me restate the question then: Have you ever designed any homes that would be available, say, to quite a few people, say, within the $10,000 to $15,000 bracket?

WRIGHT: Yes, plenty of them.

QUESTIONER: You have designed plenty of them?

WRIGHT But not lately.

QUESTIONER: That is very fine, sir, and I know you did. I have seen pictures of the homes you designed quite a few years ago in the $10,000 to $15,000 bracket, which I imagine now would cost $30,000 to $40,000, but I don't know.

WRIGHT: $30,000 to $35,000.

QUESTIONER: Unfortunately, there aren't too many people in this country who can afford homes like that.

WRIGHT: They should wait. I don't think they should expend themselves in unbecoming ways just because they haven't got the money.

QUESTIONER: That is very fine, but a lot of people would like to have them while they are still living!

AUDIENCE: (applause)

WRIGHT: I don't see why they should have them while they are still living if they don't deserve them. That is what is the matter with architecture now, largely. People want something they can't afford, they get it, it is unsightly, they live in it, and they are degraded by it.

QUESTIONER: For a man who doesn't seem, to my mind, to think very much of businessmen you seem to think that the only man who deserves that type of home is the successful businessman or the one who has made enough money so he can afford the right type of home.

WRIGHT: On the contrary, sir, such people don't come to me. I don't see the successful people. I am for the upper middle third of American life. I wouldn't build for the rich and I don't build for the very poor.

Questioner: "Have you ever designed any low-cost houses. . . ?" Wright: "I never designed anything else." An approach view from the driveway, looking south at the Loren Pope residence (1939) in Mount Vernon, Virginia (relocated from its original site at Falls Church in 1965). Its cost in 1940 was $8000. Photograph by the editor.

The west portion of the exterior south elevation of the Loren Pope residence (1939) at Mount Vernon. Photograph by the editor.

QUESTIONER: I understand that, sir, but it seems to me that you are talking about success right now in a certain term which I don't feel that you agree with.

WRIGHT: I don't agree with your disagreement with me.

QUESTIONER: I didn't think you did, sir, to tell you the *truth.*

WRIGHT: I think that what you are driving at is all right. I believe we should have ways and means by which young people can get together and get married, whether they deserve to be or not or whether they have got the wherewithal or not, just because they want to be. But is that a good enough reason?

QUESTIONER: To get married? Well, can I ask you a question?

WRIGHT: Yes.

QUESTIONER: Why did you become an architect? And, if I may, I'd like to answer the question at the same time. I believe you became an architect because you wanted to become an architect.

WRIGHT: On the contrary, I had no choice whatsoever.

QUESTIONER: That is the same reason a few of us feel that we get married—because we had no choice whatsoever!

AUDIENCE: (applause)

WRIGHT: That isn't why you get married. You just get married because you want to be married, that is all.

I became an architect because my mother was a teacher and she wanted an architect for a son. Tell me, why? I don't know. She felt that she was going to have a son, and so in the room where I was born, around the walls, were nine wood engravings by Timothy Cole of the cathedrals of England. She sent me down to the kindergarten table when I was six, she saw it at the centennial—it came over here from Germany [Editor's Note: Mr. Wright is

An interior view of the living room from the short entry at the Loren Pope residence (1939) in Falls Church. Note the sectional wooden seating and the perforated, patterned window boards or frames. Photograph by the editor.

speaking of the Froebel kindergarten toys]—and I am one of the white heads, perhaps the only one, that you know that had kindergarten training. My mother wanted an architect for a son, and my goodness, I never had a thought that I would be anything else.

QUESTIONER: It happens that I read your *[An] Autobiography* and I found it very interesting.

WRIGHT: I am glad to hear you say so.

QUESTIONER: But, sincerely, getting away from the point . . .

WRIGHT: What point?

QUESTIONER: It may be a dull point, but it is a point, nevertheless. It is the very fact that, after all, you are just telling me and telling the rest of the audience that we are a by-product of our environment. I believe that is what you are telling us.

WRIGHT: No.

QUESTIONER: I thought that you said that you became an architect . . .

WRIGHT: Our environment is a dreadful by-product of ourselves. We got just exactly what we earned and what we deserved.

QUESTIONER: I happen to like it, as far as that is concerned.

WRIGHT: You are welcome.

QUESTIONER: But I would also like to live in one of your homes.

WRIGHT: You are not entitled to it, I'm afraid, if you like what you are in now.

QUESTIONER: I'm in life right now and I happen to like it. I would like one of your homes; I would appreciate it very much. However, if I can't have it at the present time, I am not going to drop dead over it.

WRIGHT: I don't think you need to. I think you have a makeshift, poor fellow. I'd like to help you but I can't.

QUESTIONER: Well, I didn't ask you this question because I wanted you to feel sorry for me, Mr. Wright, because I don't feel sorry for myself. The only thing I wanted to state is that I think everything you say is absolutely wonderful.

WRIGHT: I don't think it is, but still . . .

QUESTIONER: That is a difference of opinion. I happen to think it is.

WRIGHT: Good.

QUESTIONER: And I'd like to see everybody—not who deserves it but everybody who feels for it—to be able to take advantage of it.

WRIGHT: I wouldn't.

QUESTIONER: That is another difference of opinion.

WRIGHT: I think you have to earn these things. I don't think you are entitled to a thing just because you want it. I don't think I was entitled to fame as an architect just because I want it—I had to earn it, and I think we have to earn everything in this life that is worth having. I think that the people today, young people, get too much for nothing. They expect too much.

AUDIENCE: (applause)

WRIGHT: How many boys come and want me to take them in and educate them as architects, and have a wife and babies, and I have to take the whole damn family in order to get them? They want to be married. Now, how many people that you know want to have their apple and need to eat it, too? Do you know anybody such?

QUESTIONER: I know quite a few.

WRIGHT: Maybe you are one of them!

QUESTIONER: Maybe I am.

WRIGHT: Anyway, that is a great failing. It has put us where we are. We are all reaching way ahead of what we are entitled to. Most of us are living way beyond our means. I don't mean in just dollars and cents. We are living way beyond our means spiritually. We don't pay our way as we go. We don't want to put that wherewithal on the dotted line because it costs more than any money can pay for. It costs something here [Editor's Note: Mr. Wright points to his heart].

An interior view of the dining room showing the plywood table and chairs at the Loren Pope Residence (1939) in Falls Church. The furniture was specially built for this house. Photograph by the editor.

QUESTIONER: Was Mr. Kaufmann, in Philadelphia, more worthy of the house you built for him than your mother?

WRIGHT: I don't see the connection. This man wants to know if Mr. Kaufmann was more worthy of his house than my mother?

QUESTIONER: That is what I am asking. Was it because he had the money to buy it?

WRIGHT: Mr. Kaufmann's having the money to buy the house was a fortunate incident to both him and me.

QUESTIONER: Mr. Wright, may I ask a question? Can you hear me?

WRIGHT: Isn't this a vast place?

QUESTIONER: I have the feeling, as you talk, that you were talking to the average man and woman, and you said that a creative person is the person who is going to help us out of all of this.

WRIGHT: Yes, certainly.

QUESTIONER: If you are talking to the average man and woman, then, generally, in that field, there are a lot of rules and regulations that are generally given to the artist for the architect to follow. If you are speaking to the average man and woman, they have no rules to follow because they don't, for instance, go to college to study. So, from that I can only gather that there must be something beyond the rules and regulations that is necessary and creative, and I wonder if these rules taught in books are really necessary or is there something else basic?

WRIGHT: I really didn't understand it. But I think what she is maybe saying is that there is an average person who is in betwixt and between opportunity

The Edgar J. Kaufmann, Sr., "Fallingwater" residence (1935) at Ohiopyle, Pennsylvania, taken from Bear Run looking east during the summer. Photograph by the editor.

of all kinds, who lives—I don't see why—and how is that person going to get this thing that I am talking about as a creative individual?

QUESTIONER: That is right.

AUDIENCE: (applause)

WRIGHT: Well, I'll tell you, my dear lady, that if she doesn't get it there is something the matter with her, not me. You see, this thing comes from the inside; the answer isn't on the outside. It is inside.

QUESTIONER: Pardon me, I disagree with that.

WRIGHT: There are many ways of getting this thing, as many as there are individuals on earth. My way wouldn't be your way; your way wouldn't be his or her way. But there is always a way, just as sure as can be.

QUESTIONER: Why is it that we are not allowed to build something on property we own and pay taxes upon because it doesn't conform with the neighborhood?

WRIGHT: You mean, my dear lady, that the rules and regulations are all against human beings having the things that they really ought to have or want to have. As an architect, I have found that the code and rules and regulations are all made by people who seem to have put them there to prevent progress, and I think that is the way they work.

Godfrey [sic—Alfred] North Whitehead, one of the really good men Harvard ever had, said that in a democracy codes were justified only if they were fearlessly, continuously revised. It is the hardest thing in God's world to get one of our codes revised. They become laws and thousands of people are living under them. And by way of their enforcement and sustaining them to keep them in force and effect you deprive hundreds and thousands of people of their livelihood if you break the codes. So, the codes become an incubus. They become monstrosities. They defeat the very purpose for which they were made because, in the first place, they are made by experts.

The Edgar J. Kaufmann, Sr., "Fallingwater" residence at Ohiopyle, from Bear Run overlooking the stream. Note the extended cantilever structure. Photograph by the editor.

Now, who is an expert? What is an expert? An expert is a man who stopped thinking. Why? Because he knows. He is finished; he doesn't have to think anymore.

AUDIENCE: (applause)

WRIGHT: So, experts will eventually be the death of the very thing they were intended to preserve, just like the letter of the law. The minute you begin to interpret the law according to the letter of the law that law will kill the very thing it was intended to conserve. That is going on all through the country today. The interpretation of the law according to the letter instead of the *spirit*. It is only the *spirit* of the law that counts. It is only the *spirit* of the code that counts.

But we can't elect people to interpret those codes and laws according to their spirit because we are afraid they will be dishonest and they probably will be. So, there you have it. What is the answer? I was bringing it up a little while ago. Mediocrity is always dishonest. You may not think that is a *true* statement, but let's go it the other way around and say dishonesty is always mediocre.

QUESTIONER: Mr. Wright, I think you can probably hear me. I am a schoolteacher in charge of forty-two kids. I saw your church you built in Madison, Wisconsin, the Unitarian Church. It was inspiring enough to me to make me want to join the church and I have never regretted it. I just want to know if you can interpret for me and the rest of the audience what it was in that structure that you conceived that provided the inspiration for not only me but others who have seen it to go away with that feeling.

WRIGHT: Well, that is the thing I referred to when I was talking about getting away from the city, out into the country. What do you want to know about it?

QUESTIONER: What in that building combines the inspiration which is in your architecture which is not found in these ordinary boxes that you have been talking about? Can you interpret for me what it was in this building that you have been expressing in bricks and stone and steel, that is not provided in these ordinary monstrosities?

WRIGHT: I must have failed or he wouldn't be asking this question!

AUDIENCE: (laughter)

WRIGHT: You see, I am a Unitarian myself. I come of a long line of preachers, way back. My people were Unitarians. Now, Unitarian means what it says. The unity of all things is the thrill Unitarians get out of life. Thomas Jefferson was a great Unitarian. Nearly all the founders of our nation were Unitarians.

Every Unitarian believes in that essential principle of oneness—overallness [sic], we would say. Here's a little building for that type and kind of society. Now, what would best express that feeling of oneness, of unity, of an overall sense of things and at the same time be reverential? In my kindergarten days I was taught that this meant reverence [Editor's Note: Mr. Wright puts his hands in prayer position]—an attitude of prayer. It does, instinctively. So I made a little building in that attitude that had an overall shelter for the secular and the religious performance of life. A oneness, the unity of all things, a building that had unity for its purpose—and it was at the same time in an attitude reverential. That was what I had in mind. I don't know if I got it.

QUESTIONER: You did.

WRIGHT: If I got it, you probably wouldn't be asking me this question.

QUESTIONER: I'm glad that you interpreted it for me. Thank you.

WRIGHT: Thank you.

QUESTIONER: Mr. Wright, why is your faith in America increasing?

WRIGHT: My faith in America is increasing and my understanding of America is improving. I know now what my America needs most. I never knew until I was of age. Now I am beginning to find out.

There is nothing the matter with America except America itself. America is juvenile, not grown up. We don't have the adult mind in our country in politics, in business, in architecture, in anything. That doesn't mean that we are done for and we are going to bust and fail. It does mean that we need to wake up to what things are essential.

Now, here we are like a kid with a pistol in his hand,

The interior of the auditorium/rostrum facing the pulpit at the Unitarian Church (1947) in Shorewood Hills, Wisconsin. Photograph by the editor.

loaded, and he doesn't know it's loaded, and he doesn't know what to do with it, and he runs around with it. What for? That is where we are as a people right now. We are just about as intelligent. We are just about as responsible as that boy would be who got hold of a gun he wasn't entitled to and didn't know how to handle.

Now, does that mean that I don't believe in America? It means that I have a very deep concern for America, and that I am trying to understand America—and I think I do. If I don't, well, it is just too bad for me.

QUESTIONER: Mr. Wright, you said you think you understand America and you have been very critical. You are probably the outstanding exponent in the field. What is your constructive criticism of America? What do you have to offer to these people who are willing to invest $15,000, who have only $15,000 to invest, and who believe in you and need you? You can't let it go by just saying that Mr. Kaufmann had the money? How about telling us what you would do for those of us who are only within that $15,000 bracket, and no more, at today's valuation? What can you give us that we need?

WRIGHT: He is pleading with me for a $15,000 house!

AUDIENCE: (laughter)

WRIGHT: Let me say this: I have given it to him and he doesn't know it. I have given it to him in what I call the Usonian Automatic, where the union has been eliminated; where masonry at twenty-nine dollars a day is out, where there are no plasterers at the same rate, where there are no carpenters at all. It is a block house.

I did it for the GI's. The GI can go in his back road—he's got sand there—get himself some steel rods and cement, make the blocks, and put the blocks together. You can see two of those houses standing in Phoenix now. One is a very expensive one that cost $25,000. It would have cost $75,000.

I have done that thing. Don't you know it? You can build your own house! You can go to that plan—we call it the Usonian plan—and you can buy the cement, the steel, and the sand somewhere and build your own house.

The T. A. Pappas residence (1955) in St. Louis, Missouri, features Usonian Automatic concrete-block construction. This view shows the living-room terrace. Photograph by the editor.

A detailed view of the Usonian Automatic concrete-block construction of the T. A. Papas residence in St. Louis. Note how the windows are organically integrated with the construction of the concrete block; more than 500 blocks with integral glass form the envelope of this building. Photograph by the editor.

Wright: "I started this . . . system of construction. We called it the textile block system, and it is earthquake-proof. It will stay there hundreds of years." Shown is a detail of this concrete block, which was used extensively in the design of the Charles Ennis residence (1923) in Los Angeles. Photograph by the editor.

Now, what is the consequence? I had to devise electrical lighting for that house that could go into it ready made, where the owner could turn up a connection and that would be all because the union wouldn't work on it. Then I had to design a bathroom for the house that made only three connections. The bowl was over the foot of the tub and the closet right beside it. It was all one fixture and all you had to do was connect three connections in order to make it. The union couldn't stop me. I expect to be shot from ambush one of these days just for that. And you don't know about it! Well, is that my fault?

QUESTIONER: Where can you find out more about it, Mr. Wright?

WRIGHT: There has been a lot printed about it in *The Christian Science Monitor* and, let me see, *The Milwaukee Journal,* and a half a dozen other papers around the country. Where have you been all this time?

QUESTIONER: Send a reprint to Lillian Jackson Braun and we will get it.

WRIGHT: I started this back in 1921—this system of construction. We called it the textile block system and it is earthquakeproof. It will stay there hundreds of years. It is a masonry house—fireproof and verminproof.

I am a salesman now. I didn't come down here to sell you anything. I am surprised, I supposed everybody knew about it and was just too lazy to go to work at it. Well, I think that is enough.

AUDIENCE: (applause)

PART EIGHT

Broadacre City

An oblique view of one-quarter of the model of Broadacre City (1934)—the civic, educational, and institutional section. This particular portion represents an area of land that measures only one US Public Land Survey Section or one square mile. The total model, in plan, measured four square miles. Photograph courtesy of the State Historical Society of Wisconsin.

Another oblique view of the civic, educational, and institutional section of the Broadacre City model (1934). Photograph courtesy of the State Historical Society of Wisconsin.

26 A New Freedom for Living in America

. . . all true forms are born of some inner struggle.

Introduction

This chapter presents the text of a speech delivered by Frank Lloyd Wright on radio on Monday, April 15, 1935, at Rockefeller Center, New York, at the opening of the Industrial Arts Exposition of the National Alliance of Art and Industry. The text of this speech was published as "A New Freedom for Living in America" in *Taliesin I,* No. 1, October 1940, pp. 35–37. Mr. Wright's models for his Broadacre City were seen for the first time by a national audience at this exposition. His speech was intended to explain his new concept of the American democratic metropolis of the future.

The Industrial Arts Exposition had an impressive presidential opening. By pressing a gold telegraph key in the Oval Room of the White House at 8:30 P.M. on April 15 President Roosevelt activated an electric impulse that set off 120 flashbulbs in the forum of Rockefeller Center, turned on fifty floodlights, started a siren, dropped an American flag, and turned on the current on an electric organ, all of which officially opened the exposition.[1] In its arrangement the National Alliance of Art and Industry emphasized beauty of design in objects of mass production intended for the average consumer. The display re-

---

Text of a speech transcribed from a radio broadcast dated April 15, 1935, which originated from Rockefeller Center, New York, on the occasion of the opening of the Industrial Arts Exposition of the National Alliance of Art and Industry.

[1] As reported in "Arts in Industry Glorified in Show," *The New York Times,* April 16, 1935, Section 1, p. 23, column 1.

mained at Rockefeller Center from April 15 to May 15. At that time Mr. Wright was reported to have commented:

> *A tragic breakdown stares us in the face. American leadership was too ignorant or is too blind to be entrusted with the might we got by way of machine success. Now, an architect, at least, should see life as a structure, taking outward forms from interior conditions. In official America, there is yet no such organic form. We live in economic as well as esthetic and partially moral chaos.*[2]

The main model of Broadacre City measured twelve by twelve feet, eight inches and was constructed of wood at a scale of one inch to seventy-five feet. This represented four square miles of land or, as defined more traditionally, four US Public Land Survey sections for a total of 2560 acres. This four-square-mile area, reportedly, would accommodate about 1400 families or dwelling units.[3]

Mr. Wright believed that Broadacre City, as the inevitable community of the future, was compelled by three major inventions—the automobile, electric-communication and power-transmission facilities, and standardized machine production. Significant elements of his plan included the correlated farm, the factory from which smoke and gases were eliminated by burning coal at the mine to create electric power, prefabricated housing, decentralized schools, home offices, safe traffic flow, and simplified government that retained the county as the only local governmental unit. Transportation at Broadacre City was shown on the model as a great arterial highway, which consisted of many lanes of traffic above, monorail speed trains in the center, and truck-related traffic on its lower lanes. Also within the structure of these highway facilities was storage space that eliminated unsightly accumulations of all raw materials.

Land at Broadacre City was to be redistributed by the state by allotting at least one acre to childless families and more to larger family units, although Mr. Wright felt that the architect should be the agent of the state in all matters affecting its disposition.

The philosophical and design themes established at Broadacre City recur throughout his subsequent architectural, urban planning, and literary works. In the 1950s he was to return formally to the Broadacre City concepts of the early 1930s and further refine them (see Patrick J. Meehan's *The Master Architect: Conversations with Frank Lloyd Wright,* New York: John Wiley and Sons, pp.117–152, for further discussions by Mr. Wright of his Broadacre City concept).

---

[2] *Ibid.*

[3] The 1400 total family figure was reported in "Architect Models New Type of City," *The New York Times,* March 27, 1935, p. 16, column 1. Later, on September 12, 1981, the Frank Lloyd Wright Foundation reported in a limited publication titled "The Living City: An Introduction to Broadacre City, Frank Lloyd Wright, Architect" that the total estimated number of dwelling units represented by the 1935 model of Broadacre City was 761. The more recent figure (1981) was developed in the Foundation's study of the surviving Broadacre City model (then housed at the Taliesin Fellowship Complex on the grounds of Taliesin, near Spring Green, Wisconsin) and of the historic photographs of that model.

The Speech

WRIGHT: Upon an occasion like this to say that I love America and her ideal of democracy is to set myself down as the usual sentimentalist or as a mere politician. Nevertheless, I say it. It is my first line, as I believe it will be my last sentiment. But even if the first forefathers of our democracy could have foreseen the kind of success we were to have by way of the machine they could not have set up the necessary mechanism needed to defend their ideal of democracy. Let us admit it—our forefathers lacked the technique. Nor have the statesmen with the needed fundamental technique and the necessary nerve yet appeared.

Meantime, what hope of democracy we have left to us goes from bad to worse, until almost no one now believes it practical. Here we are, an enormous nation of -ites, -istic with all the -isms which make the also-ran, busily inventing new -isms—tragic breakdown staring us in the face. The present success-ideal proves to be a bad one for all but the few.

Now an architect should at least see life continually as [an] *organic* form. His work should take shape according to the fundamentals of human *nature* and *nature* otherwise. As an architect I can see no such *organic* form in the life of our people today, but I can see forces working together or separately in that direction. As everyone knows, we live in economic, aesthetic and moral chaos for the reason that American life has achieved no *organic* form. As our civilization moves on, it becomes more of an agonizing economic struggle than a happy realization.

But this architect knows, too, that all *true* forms are born of some inner struggle. So far as our struggle has been, and is, sincere, we may hope to find the forms, architectural and economic, that will finally let democracy come through to us.

Out of an experience somewhat extensive in getting *organic* forms evolved in our architecture it is with the great hope to make clear an *organic* form for the democratic city of the American future that I have tried to grasp and concretely interpret the whole drift of great change taking place in and around us in order to help create a human state more natural than the one that present cupidity and stupidity will allow. This means, of course, that through these models we have set up you may see a new success ideal for your own America.

In Broadacres you will find not only a pattern for natural freedom for the individual as individual. You will find there structures based upon decentralization of nearly everything big business has built up to be *big,* and you will find an economic groundstructure aimed at more individuality and greater simplicity and at more direct responsibility of government where human individuality is not concerned. So, Broadacre City is no mere back-to-the-land idea but is, rather, a breaking down of the artificial divisions set up between urban and rural life. By a more intelligent use of our developed scientific powers we establish a practical way of life that will bring the arts, agriculture, and industry into a harmonious whole. And I believe that there are harmonious elements in any city that really has a democratic future. Whether we yet know it or not we are about ready to throw away the costly but ugly scaffolding of which present urban life is the worst example and let the horizontal city appear together with a system of creation and distribution corresponding more to the natural conditions to our life here on earth. Naturally, the new city will appear because of, and by way of, the great development in science that we have so dearly bought as the physical basis of our present life. We ought now to use that basis for the purpose of a greater freedom instead of our growth being hampered and our souls enslaved by its consequences.

So here, in the entrails of final enormity, Rockefeller Center, New York City, you may see concrete ideas

Wright: "Many months of devotion on the part of the Taliesin Fellowship—the young men and women who unselfishly made them—have brought the models here, where their worth for the future may be judged." Taliesin Fellowship apprentices at work on the early Broadacre City model (1934) at their temporary headquarters at La Hacienda in Arizona. Photograph courtesy of the State Historical Society of Wisconsin.

of a fresh way of life—man staying with the ground, his imagination creating new forms firmly based on the ideals that were intended to found this country in new freedom as a democracy.

Certainly, the new forms that Broadacres proposes do represent a new success ideal, but the forms are not mere invention. By anyone inclined to patiently study them they will be found to be conservative interpretations of actual circumstances today. I do not say that Broadacre City is the ultimate form. But I say it might well be that if we could honestly call our lives our own we are going forward to the freedom of which the forefathers well dreamed.

Great *nature* mocks man-made efforts, throws the man aside to take a little here and a little there to go on with her work. I could point to history to prove that to work with her is wisdom, to go against her is failure or, even worse, catastrophe. And it no longer requires a seer to realize that America now knows the punishments that are the result of going recklessly against *nature*. Broadacre City not only perceives that failure but, with the belief that quantity can never be a satisfactory substitute for quality, gathers together the net result of our best world efforts to this time and goes forward to a new cultural form, a form more firmly and generously based upon enlightened human egoism than any yet conceived. Superficially you will see it as a form of architectural order, but you may see it as inherently a safer basis for our democratic society than the substitute for civilization we have achieved in our quite complete commercialization of life.

It is high time that some fundamental radicals among us gathered together the loose ends of opportunity lying waste all about us, and instead of laying more by means of them project some such sensible plan for life as our forefathers hoped and believed would be ours. It is some *organic* sense of the whole seen as entity that is now the greatest social need.

Because the psychological moment is here, the models are here to show you the future that is now. Really to grasp the significance of our work on this cross section of our civilization requires considerably more intelligent and unselfish application on your part than most of you will yet be either prepared or be willing to give. But the making of these models required just that kind of application for a lifetime and also the fruit of a lifetime of experience. Many months of devotion on the part of the Taliesin Fellowship—the young men and women who unselfishly made them—has brought the models here where their worth for the future may be judged.

Frank Lloyd Wright strolling at Taliesin III, circa early 1930s. Photograph courtesy of the State Historical Society of Wisconsin.

27 Mr. Wright Talks on Broadacre City to Ludwig Mies van der Rohe

Only as we can plan to take advantage of the law of change in process of growth can we do justice to human nature. Through the law of cause and effect we must proceed to interpret the present in terms of the future.

Introduction

On Wednesday, September 8, 1937, Ludwig Mies van der Rohe famous German architect, wired Frank Lloyd Wright at Spring Green, Wisconsin to ask if he might visit Taliesin. He expected to be in Chicago on Thursday, September 9.[1] Permission was given for the visit and van der Rohe and an American architect who spoke fluent German and acted as translator arrived on Friday morning, September 10. Mies stayed with Mr. Wright until Monday, September 13, when all drove back to Chicago.[2] During his visit to Taliesin van der Rohe viewed

Reprinted from Frank Lloyd Wright's "Mr. Wright Talks On Broadacre City To Ludwig Mies van der Rohe," *Taliesin*, Vol. 1, No. 1, October 1940, pp. 10–18.

[1] A copy of this telegram appears in Bruce Brooks Pfeiffer (Editor), *Frank Lloyd Wright: Letters to Architects*, Fresno, California: The Press at California State University, 1984, p. 98.

[2] An account of Ludwig Mies van der Rohe's September 10 to 13, 1937, visit with Mr. Wright is documented more fully by former Frank Lloyd Wright apprentice Edgar Tafel in *Apprentice to Genius: Years with Frank Lloyd Wright*, New York: McGraw-Hill Book Company, 1979, pp. 69–80.

much of Mr. Wright's work, which included the model of Broadacre City. This chapter presents the text of a talk Mr. Wright gave on this occasion. He later had this to say:

> *As the . . . matter went along it was translated into German for Mies van der Rohe, the distinguished European architect now in charge of the Armour Institute of Architecture at Chicago. Many young architects were gathered together about the [Broadacre City] model listening as many thousands have listened from first to last—eagerly and intelligently as subsequent questions would show.*
>
> *But, each time I attempt to put the scheme for Broadacres into words a new aspect of many details not considered before occurs to me. So no two discourses concerning the future have all in common. There is more between the lines still than appears in the lines.*[3]

[3] Wright, Frank Lloyd, "Mr. Wright Talks On Broadacre City To Ludwig Mies van der Rohe," *Taliesin*, Vol. 1, No. 1, October 1940, p. 18.

The Talk

WRIGHT: I am sorry, Mies, that we have no time to do more than touch upon the few features that may happen to come into my mind at this moment because we have here before us in these models a complete cross section of our entire USONIAN civilization as it might easily and soon be—I might say as it is going to be. The model section is taken at a typical county seat of government. This design presupposes that the city is going to the country and assumes the country to be a characteristic four square miles of some future American county where the hills come down to the plain and a river flows down and across the plain. As you see here in the model there is some high ground running down to the plain. A river or stream cuts its way across the plain. This, being fairly characteristic topography, is chosen to model the development you see here of a typical section of an American—or USONIAN—county. The ultimate Broadacre City would be made up of these counties as they are now but grouped into states; the counties and states would all be federated then just as they are now. Broadacre City is the entire country and predicated upon the basis that every man, woman, and child in America is entitled to own an acre of ground so long as they live on it or use it, and every man at least owning his own car or plane. So the portion we see here as a whole is really only a minute part of the future Broadacre City which eventually would include these United States. But in this small part you may find most of the ideas at work that would eventually shape the whole and hold it all together.

Like every other architectural scheme which is real, Broadacre City as here presented is a transitional scheme. All genuinely great building is transition building. Only as we can plan to take advantage of the law of change in process of growth can we do justice to human nature. Through the law of cause and effect we must proceed to interpret the present in terms of the future. So this is not intended to be an ultimate pattern but one so free of major and minor axes as never to become the usual academic fixation and always to have sufficient reflex to accommodate inevitable *organic* change. In other words, it is not "classic." It is *organic.*

Here the agrarian, the industrialist, the artist, the scientist, and the philosopher meet on the ground itself. It may not be logical. But is the rising sun logical? It is natural and that is better. What Broadacres proposes is psychological and natural—now. The social forces of mankind have been dammed up long enough to see what must be coming.

All government services come from the county seat, from which postal deliveries are made and the necessary official distributions effected, direction and protection being given by aerotor from the official field nearby the town hall; public utilities, like gas, light, water, and gasoline, conducted in channeled roadways, are available by meter at the curb. As to other utilities—telephone poles and telegraph wires are obsolete; our airplanes are still splendid stunts, our system of building utterly unscientific, and the poor old railroads out-of-date. We have had to find new ways to do what they did. The railroad is not adapted to the fluid traffic that is now a characteristic of modern life. So we have taken the railroad right-of-way, it belongs to the people anyway, and have made architecture out of its double-track, central speedway from coast to coast express traffic—a great triple-lane, two-way automobile highway, paralleled on either side by county highways connecting every half-mile with the countryside. Cars go one way only, in one portion; trucks go two ways lower down, one way in one portion but can take on or off every half-mile. These ideal hard roads without ditches or gutters support speeds up to one hundred miles per hour. At county seat intersections we find stations for aerotor [helicopter] takeoffs and every half-mile you may see pass-overs and cross-unders for the main county crossroads. Beneath this road construction—probably federal—there is vast space for the continuous storage and delivery of building materials, fuel, etc. This main artery—the converted railroad—connects the counties of the states and the states themselves into the ultimate Broadacre City. All, of course, are owned and operated by the people's government.

Now, the counties of the USA average from thirty to fifty square miles each—and each already has a county seat. No need to change the location of these county seats nor change much that of the railroads nor change much from the locations of the state and federal capitals. But we do abolish minor village governments to cut down minor officialdom. Government will be more highly centralized, the county government being more closely knit with federal administration, but there will be far less of it needed. State government still serves as an intermediary but becomes less and less needed as the process of government control becomes more *organic* because life is so. What is now the policeman is here automatic. Otherwise through this emphasis or government centralization of the common needs this is a decentralization of all man-made concerns, based upon the modern use of materials, glass, and steel, mobility, and electrification—all owned or controlled by the general people whom they serve.

In determining the spacing of the city, we assume every man is to have a car—or two or four or five. So we can build one-car houses, two-car houses, or five-car houses. The space scale therefore has changed throughout, changed in the ground allotments as in the dwellings themselves. The planning norm has ceased to be a man on his feet or a man seated behind a horse in a buggy. A mile to our man with the motor or ten miles in the air makes only a moment's distance. Space can be reckoned by time rather than feet and inches. But as this particular model is laid out we are still space-crowded.

On the basis of spacing shown here, the whole population of the USA could be accommodated in Texas alone. So let us consider this as a congested area, compared to what might actually take place. The fact is that the model shows here a condition not too unlike the development already taking place in the regional fields of our great cities themselves, except that the haphazard of that

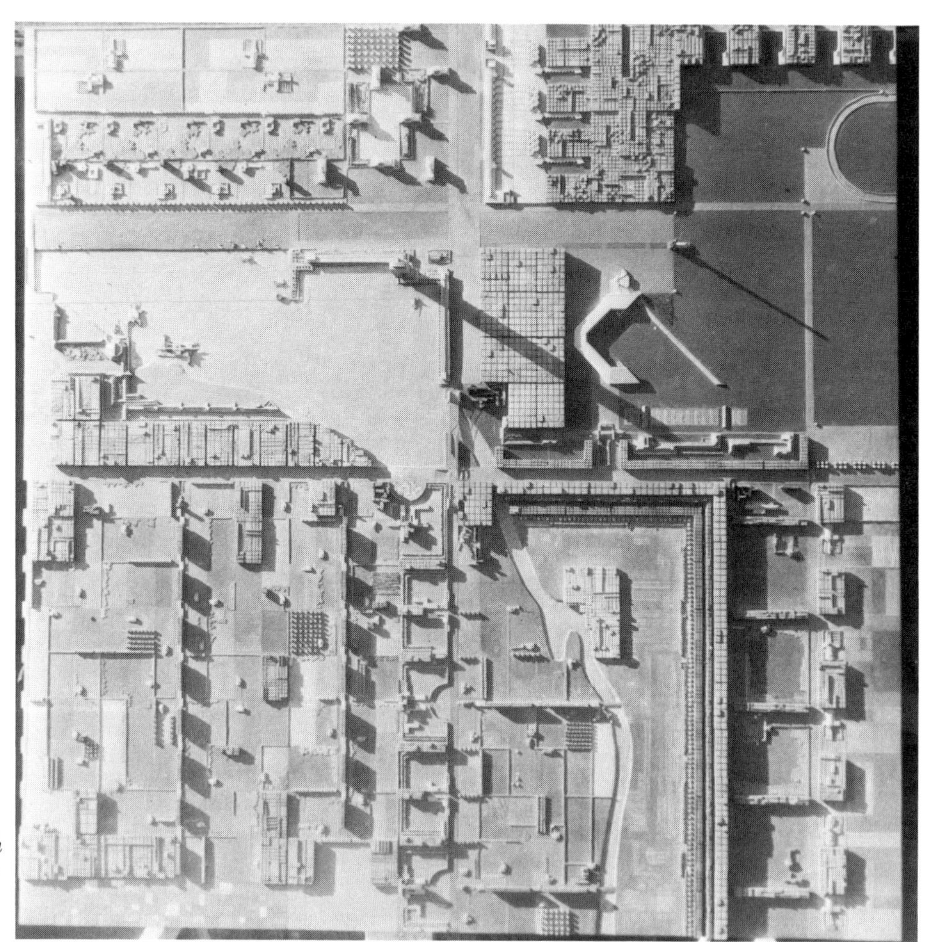

A plan view of a model of one square mile of an urban section of Broadacre City (1934). The model shows the civic center and neighborhood park and lake. A tower is located in the upper left quarter of the model. Photograph by M. E. Diemer, courtesy of the State Historical Society of Wisconsin.

circumstance is here correlated and completed.

To allow for growth of population we reserve at the beginning certain tree-covered areas, trees being valuable crops subsidized by state government. The government by setting aside, say, one-third of the tillable areas takes care of future growth by providing more ground to work, the trees being cut down as crops when needed, to provide for growth.

These tree masses are a great landscape feature of Broadacres. Many kinds of useful trees—fine woods or nuts—all suited to the climate, may be planted by the acre. The ground thus conserved coming back into tillage when and as needed. Tilled ground could be returned to wooded area in this same way. In our model the tree areas bear too small a relation to the whole area because we want to show as many features as possible in the small space at our disposal. So you will see more taken up in houses and gardens than would really be necessary in actual development.

In every society in Broadacre City there are certain special functions like the arts, art crafts, and small household manufactures such as weaving and dyeing and other small utilities. These are carried on in small factory units where the workers live.

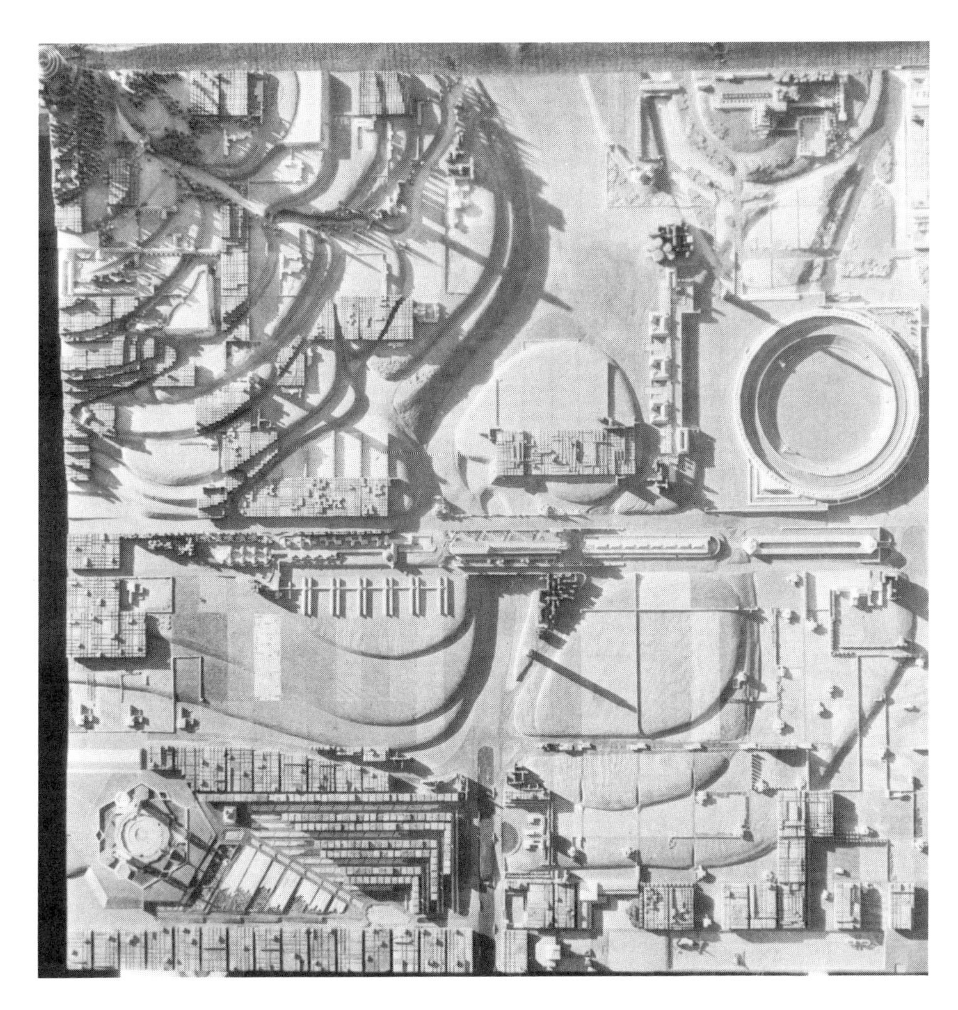

A plan view of a model of one square mile of the civic, educational, and institutional section of Broadacre City. The round structure located in the upper right quarter of the model is the proposed stadium and circus area for the county fair. Photograph by M. E. Diemer, courtesy of the State Historical Society of Wisconsin.

An oblique view of a model of a major highway interchange at Broadacre City (1934). The overpass provides for uninterrupted traffic flow. Photograph by M. E. Diemer, courtesy of the State Historical Society of Wisconsin.

A detailed oblique view of a model of a major highway interchange at Broadacre City (1934). The design calls for steel cables in tension to form a suspension bridge over the major arterial highway below. A high-speed monorail and low-level warehousing can also be seen underneath the bridge. Photograph by M. E. Diemer, courtesy of the State Historical Society of Wisconsin.

Everyone may live where he works if he wishes to do so. The function of education—now more devoted to *true* culture than the acquiring of information—is still found in what we call the new university. Radio is one of the city's active assets. But radio is built into Broadacres as one of the assets controlled by the people themselves. Related to the new university, a decentralized unit, are the arboretum, aquarium, and zoo. All phases of *nature* are to be collected here for special *nature* study. The university, as you will see, has changed its character. A "classical" education would be worse than useless, even more so than it is now. Instead, man studies man in relation to his birthright—the ground—and man in relation to men.

He starts his earthy career with his feet on the ground, but his head may be in the clouds at times. When he is conceived in his mother's womb his place is ready here, as much ground as he can use is being reserved for him. Broadacres follows Henry George in the belief that a man should not only hold his land by way of his own use and improvements but dedicate himself to it in the best sense of the spirit. There can be no absentee ownership of land. But meantime we cannot expect everyone to become bona fide tillers of the soil, particularly not the citizens of such urbanized population as we have at present. So we have made provision for the people who have been divorced from *nature* by excessive urban idealism and parasitic living. As I said, this must be a transition scheme because we must provide for people whose education and way of life have unfitted them for the more rounded life planned for here.

Understood rightly, industry, art, science, and agriculture all have a common basis. We have not seen in our age that common basis with any constructive vision. If we have seen it, we have not acted upon it. No sense of the whole is anywhere evident in our modern life; thus not only are all the many USONIAN industrial and social activities uncorrelated but every aspect of our activity there is a wasteful to and fro, relentless without purpose. Senseless concentrations are everywhere exaggerated. Concentrations are just as useless and

A model of the Walter Davidson Prefabricated Farm Units Project (1932). The unified farm building was an integral part of the small acreage farm for Broadacre City (1934). Photograph courtesy of the State Historical Society of Wisconsin.

meaningless as, for instance, the hauling of coal. One third of our yearly railroad tonnage is the coal haul. There is now no good reason why coal should not be burned at the mines and the resultant heat and light distributed from the place of origin. Nor is there good reason to separate agriculture and manufacturing from residence districts or from each other, provided we take the curse off these operations, as is done in Broadacre City. In Broadacre City every man is nearer every other man when he wants to be than he is in the present city. And the scaffolding still destroying our landscape—poles and wires, signboards, railroad and lumber yards, etc., etc., do not exist in Broadacres.

Especially is the curse taken off farm and factory. The farm becomes a most desirable and lovable place in which to live, the most lovely to see. Animals are housed in fireproof sanitary quarters. The farmer is no longer an isolated human unit in the nonsocial hinterland. The curse has been taken off industry, as well. The curse has been taken off poverty of all kinds—except spiritual poverty—because there is the highest standard of quality in everything available for use and there is left no inferior way of using anything. Differences now are only a matter of extent or of character. There is, however, a double curse on disorder.

Grouping may have *true* individuality, however. Both have been a blessing by three principal freedoms: free ground, free education, and a free medium of exchange for all labor or commodities. This means entire freedom from speculation. There can be no speculation in any three of these essentials to the commonwealth essentially by way of which the commonwealth lives. Broadacre City is still a *true* capitalist system but one wherein private ownership is based upon personal use and public service—genuine *capitalism.* Capitalism made *organic,* since it is broadly based upon the ground and the individual upon the ground. After meeting the needs of all, then, according to the contribution of each, so may each receive. And any man's contribution, whatever the character or extent it may assume, must here be integral with the life of the citizen, with the circumstances by and for which he lives, and concerning which he cannot lose the freedom of personal choice if he will work. If he will not work, he becomes a charge upon the state and treated accordingly.

This, of course, is not the capitalism we have now, any more than it is communism. Let us call it *Organic Capitalism,* because a citizen of Broadacre City is an actual capitalist, not merely a potential one. He is no longer a mere gambler, although there is still romance with which he may gamble. The fact is he owns himself first of all—the first condition of an *organic* capitalist—and he may then choose and own if he pleases all that makes his life and the lives of those he loves worthwhile. He may own the fruit of his own labor or, adding his unit of effort to a whole effort, become entirely sympathetic and cooperative. He gives up to government only those matters into which no individuality can possibly enter, where there can be no question of sacrificing that in his *nature* which is himself. And that is the promise of *true* democracy.

Government would especially be concerned with such things a public utilities. Government would be more an affair of business administration than meddling in politics. For instance, there is no longer need for one man to in some way regulate the money getting of the other four. Competitive concerns are not needed to employ the citizenry. For instance, in Broadacre City, gasoline is at the curb, so is water, gas, electricity, and compressed air. Sewage is handled on a nationwide basis to be redistributed to the soil as fertilizer. Any society is much better off if these material things are thus organized as features of government in which every man has a direct business interest. Government would not then be as now—a matter of politicians. This is a much more economic and effective basis for the development of industries and arts that are human and desirable, as well as the growth of efficiencies that have real and happy human value. The citizen would have about one-tenth of government which he has now, and that government would be the business administration of popular necessities, together with impersonal social affairs of a great nation. He would take active interest in such government because it would be his own business.

The major problem of the means of distribution-mobility comes in here. We have to solve the vexing traffic problem. It is one of the most important problems. First, the speed involved in general automobile traffic requires much space. And in solving these various problems we have made architecture out of roads. We have turned the road the other way up. We have made it concave with no ditches, so that one may stay on it, instead of the usual convex road with ditches. The road also serves for good drainage with a single deep grating-covered gutter in the middle draining to a conduit below. Beside this central conduit are smaller ones which are the conduits for wires and service pipes—all easily reached by removing a section of the continuous iron grating at the center of the road. The grating takes the place of the white or yellow road line now on the highways.

The top-turn intersection which we have devised, as architecture good to see, reduces the possibility of accident to pedestrian or motor traffic to one-tenth of one percent. Left turns overhead in full sight are this one-tenth and chance of accident there is small. Stop-and-go lights are eliminated. The road itself is lighted from the sides by low flood lights contained in floral features two feet above the ground, thus becoming a bright well-lighted ribbon with no lights glaring in the eyes of the driver. Wherever you see a road surface in Broadacre City it is a luminous surface at night and a dull red toned surface in the daytime. Steel in tension is extensively used for the pass-overs and for all other construction where wide spans are desirable—and wide spans are now desirable everywhere.

An interesting thing to consider in studying this model of Broadacres is the way distribution is effected. It is a fact that there is little or no back-and-forth haul and but little wasted to and fro. At the same time the scaffolding of our present

Two models of designs for the single-family Prefabricated Residences Project (1932) for Broadacre City (1934). Photograph courtesy of the State Historical Society of Wisconsin.

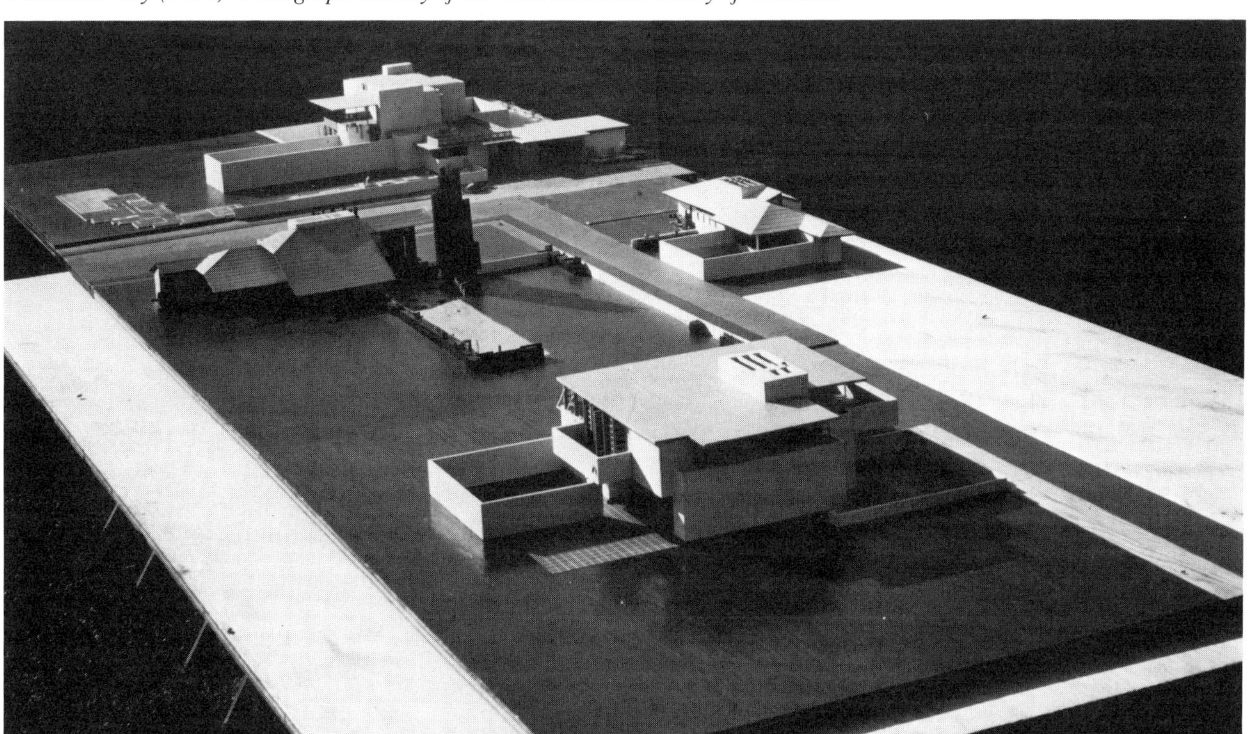

Models of various designs for the single-family Prefabricated Residences Project (1932) for Broadacre City (1934). Photograph courtesy of the State Historical Society of Wisconsin.

social set-up—especially telephone wires and poles, billboards, storage yards for coal and building materials, etc.—is all gone from this future city. To the ugly scaffolding of our present life the telephone and telegraph companies have contributed the worst features, and, no longer needed, they disappear in this city of the future.

It follows naturally from all this genuinely constructive way of life that in the administration of Broadacre City the county architect is important. He has a certain disciplinary as well as cultural relationship to the whole, and since he maintains the harmony of the whole his must be one of the best minds the city has, and it will inevitably become the best trained. He could hardly be very young nor could he be much educated by present standards. With the necessary apprentices, the county architect is located in a work place which is also an exhibition gallery placed by or near the county seat. He and his staff design the new buildings, develop and preserve the landscape of the county, and decide all questions affecting such matters. Nothing is left without continual provision for a better plan, keeping the way open to consistent growth. For this purpose careful studies and designs are prepared in advance for the better thing—that which has *truest* relation to the whole. The people themselves would be likely to express an interest in these things because these future citizens of Broadacres would all be learning the features of that fundamental relationship at the university while young and are growing up in it here. So the county architect would never lack for effective criticism. Wherever there is a nature feature he would be sure to take advantage of it, as we have done here, and develop it through his knowledge of the principles and the way of life of an *organic* architecture.

As to what is called landscape, here are the parks. Because Broadacre City is a different type of architectural expression, one much more abstract than usual, we now make a great rising tree wall for the park. The trees which make up the wall rise in height from the ground level inside, up and out toward the surrounding streets. The tree wall slopes upward from blossoming shrubs to higher blossoming trees, then to conifers, and finally to elms and on to the other majestic trees. Inside there is a more informal relationship. There are acres of flowerbeds, mosaics of color. At one end of these great spaces, thus sequestered, is a spacious out-of-doors music garden with enclosed spaces for dancing and refreshment.

The blocklike effects seen in this model would not be so apparent as "blocklike" in reality. But, here we have presented everything in the abstract; it is the architect's way. But in the ultimate Broadacres it is *true* that landscape becomes architecture just as architecture becomes landscape. But both are integral with the ground and are an orchestration of form according to *nature.* Right in the midst of the future city we have fields of flowers and grain. Right in the farming section are the buildings of industry, culture, recreation, and residence. Right in the midst of all is the marketplace, a perpetual fair. And anywhere in it all folk may live happily at work.

Most landscape architects would say: "But I love the natural scenery." Well, so do we. We augment natural "scenery." We develop for it by way of human *nature,* a collateral complementary scenery in the block of tree plantings in the ordered fields, even more beautiful than "nature." No, we outrage no scenery. We aim to make it complementary to whatever we do—or the other way round—adding the cleverest of human occupation as a feature in keeping with it. All the various features of life in Broadacres are appropriate to each other because the curse of ugliness and confusion has been removed from them all. Nothing can offend anything else, even if it would. There is nothing offensive to either the rich man or the farmer in the proximity of each to the other nor the proximity of industry. The spacing of all is ample for all purposes, and it is remarkable that it is all so simple and that it is, in the main, all so right here now. We need only the slight concerted political effort to remove the key logs from the jam.

Of course there will be religion. Protestants, Catholics, Darkies [sic], and the Synagogue will be

Early realization of the Broadacre City Project. This Usonian house on a flat site is the Goetsch-Winckler residence (1939) at Okemos, Michigan. It was to have been constructed as one of the seven residential structures of the aborted Usonia I Development Plan Project (1939) but was constructed later at another site. Photograph by the editor.

with us. Instead of each taking a little shovel full of coals and going off to start a little hell of his own discord, we have under construction—as always—the great cathedral, which is in fact a group of cathedrals. In the center there is a great concourse or meeting place where all groups gather together to worship by way of the elements—fire, music, water, and pageantry. In this way they might grow toward unity. But perhaps not. That depends more upon education as it would be in the future city where culture would largely take its place.

Speaking of education, notice that the children go in toward the inner spaces away from the highways and find their way from peaceful homes to peaceful schools along peaceful byways. Each schoolboy and schoolgirl has his garden at school. Each has to begin with a hoe in his hand. In each one-story school place there is a little outdoor classroom, a little cinema, a little museum. But museums are all traveling museums. In Broadacre City you will find most things decentralized, traveling continually, kept in continual circulation. All the personal, individual concerns of life are decentralized wherever possible to be applied at the desirable places as time and circumstance may give opportunity or vary the need. We begin at the root of society with culture of the children. Everything here seeks to begin again at the beginning, hoping to avoid the mistakes that have all but put our democracy to flight by now.

And the citizens must die here as elsewhere. Life is still a coming in and a going out. As man ap-

The realization of the Broadacre City Project. The Eric Pratt residence (1948) at Galesburg, Michigan, was constructed at the Frank Lloyd Wright-designed residential subdivision of twenty-two circular lots known as Galesburg Country Homes Acres. Photograph by the editor.

proaches death, he usually becomes sentimental. He likes to see where he is to lie. So the cemetery here is mainly another greater forest reservation adjoining the cathedral. When a man dies, the trees which cover the place in which he is to be buried are cut down. His plot may be then made into a flowerbed or become a marble pavement—the choice being his or what may be in his mind. And the crematory and columbarium is nearby as another choice. Thus ends the exploitation by the monument makers in common with most forms of exploitation. We have planned to end it.

Over here we have the commercial center—the market place—a perpetual fair where the citizen and his wife come to buy and sell and see and learn. There is no reason why this still necessary barter function shouldn't be beautiful, too. Flowers and vegetables picked fresh every hour are displayed here. Meats, game, and fish are supplied fresh from farms and pools. And beside this market every little community center has its exhibition gallery where the finer things made by workers of all kinds are displayed to be sold. This market, as you see, is a perpetual functioning county fair of a finer sort. There would be demonstrations all the time of better ways of keeping house, planning, preserving, conserving. And there will be cultural exhibitions, examples of fine art and the universal crafts for sale. The curse is taken off commerce by its mutuality and here again—beauty. And I have not yet touched upon the beauty parlors, wayside inns, sanatoriums, hotels, skyscrapers in the country, various apartments, the clubs, cinema houses, race courses, aerodromes [airports] and various public memorials.

The traffic problem being solved, Broadacre City is a delightfully safe place to live and to work in or go places near by or far away. Social intercourse is facilitated not impeded by the increased spacing and the freedom gained. Whatever you want to be or do, there is an appropriate place for either. But

The realization of the Broadacre City Project. The Ward McCartney residence and alterations (1949) in Kalamazoo, Michigan, at the Frank Lloyd Wright-designed residential subdivision known as Parkwyn Village. Photograph by the editor.

the greatest thing here is to be able to do them all in harmony with a great altogether. The way of life as planned here kills off the specialist, eventually. But there are little compounds, with clinics or studios in gardens for doctors, scientists, architects, and artists. Every professional man has his own little place of work and the people come to him. He does not waste his time and energy going to the city and back again as now.

So here, in this little model and in its collaterals, you have a definite cross section and new form for everything needed for a complete modern USONIAN civilization. A *true* culture. But the model you see here is only for this particular type of ground in these particular circumstances. Never would the same plan be imposed on land that is otherwise or when the circumstance changed. Instead, the resources of the land would be brought out and new forms wrought according to the circumstances.

PART NINE

The Architecture of a Free Democratic Government

An exterior view of the Thomas E. Keys residence (1950) at Rochester, Minnesota. The construction is concrete block. Photograph by the editor.

28 Government and Architecture

What can government do with an advanced idea? If it is still a controversial idea, and any good idea must be so, can government touch it without its eye on at least the next election? It cannot.

Introduction

This chapter presents Frank Lloyd Wright's speech to about 600 federal architects assembled in the ballroom of the Mayflower Hotel, Washington, D.C., on Tuesday, October 25, 1938. Many topical areas, including the architecture of historic Williamsburg, were addressed. Among his remarks was the following:

> *Studying . . . Williamsburg closely . . . one may see why and how, now, this nation was contrived by the monied man for the monied man by the money-minded. . . .*

Mr. Wright also talked at length about *organic architecture*, culture, education, and Broadacre City (see also Chapters 26 and 27). The session closed with a brief question-and-answer period in which he solicited the audience's reactions and voiced strong views about government building and buildings. An original typescript copy of the text of this speech is housed in the Speech and Article File-1938 of the Frank Lloyd Wright Papers of the Manuscript Division

---

Text of a speech reprinted with minor editing from Frank Lloyd Wright's "Speech to the AFA," *The Federal Architect*, Vol. IX, January 1939, pp. 20–23.

of the Library of Congress. In addition, an edited and somewhat revised version of this speech appeared in Frederick Gutheim (Editor), *Frank Lloyd Wright On Architecture: Selected Writings (1894–1940),* New York: Duell, Sloan, & Pearce, 1941, pp. 241–246.

At least twenty-eight government-related projects, not including those for public schools and university-related buildings, were designed by Mr. Wright between 1893 and 1958. Unfortunately their construction eluded him for almost his entire career because only four were built; among them the grandest are the Marin County Administration Building, the Hall of Justice, and the Post Office for Marin County, California, San Rafeal (1957—see Chapter 29).

Three other government-related designs (built) were the Banff National Park Pavilion (with Francis C. Sullivan, architect) at Alberta, Canada (1911), the Los Angeles Exhibition Pavilion for the display of Mr. Wright's travelling exhibition titled "Sixty Years of Living Architecture" at Los Angeles, California (1954), and the Dallas Theater Center at Dallas, Texas (1955). The twenty-four remaining unexecuted designs for government-related projects are the Municipal Boat House for the Madison Improvement Association for Madison, Wisconsin (1893), the competition for the City of Milwaukee Library and Museum for Milwaukee, Wisconsin (1893), Sherman Booth's Municipal Art Gallery for Chicago, (1907), Sherman Booth's Town Hall for Glencoe, Illinois (1909), the Post Office and Carnegie Library Project for Ottawa, Ontario (1913); the US Embassy for Tokyo (1914), the project for six playhouses for the Oak Park Playground Association at Oak Park, Illinois (1926), two designs for the Monona Terrace Madison Civic Center complex for Madison, Wisconsin (1938 and 1955), the US Government "Cloverleaf Quadruple" Housing Project for Pittsfield, Massachusetts (1941), two designs for the Point Park Community Center for Pittsburgh (1947 and 1948), a concrete "Butterfly" bridge over the Wisconsin River, Spring Green, Wisconsin (1947), twin suspension bridges at Point Park in Pittsburgh (1947), a concrete bridge for the San Francisco Bay Southern Crossing (1949), a bridge for Echo Park at Wisconsin Dells, Wisconsin (1951), a restaurant for Yosemite National Park, California (1953), the Barnsdall Park Municipal Gallery for Los Angeles (1954), the Marin County Amphitheatre for the Marin County Civic Center at San Rafael, California (1957), the Arizona State Capital "Oasis" Project for the State of Arizona at Phoenix (1957), the Baghdad Art Museum, the Plan for Greater Baghdad, the Post and Telegraph Building, the Opera House and Gardens, and the University Complex and Gardens for Baghdad, Iraq (1957), and post office and community center/auditorium projects for Spring Green, Wisconsin (1957 and 1958, respectively).

The Speech

WRIGHT: Ladies and gentlemen, I have often said that it is impossible for a man to be a good architect and a gentleman at the same time. But, there you are—out there—so let each man judge for himself of this introduction I have just received and the remarks I am about to make.

I think the first thing we should, perhaps, do here tonight is to get this noisy Williamsburg matter—anyhow, in our own minds—on straight. Now, I did *not* say "Williamsburg is all wrong." I did say that it was—Eastern newspaper editorials to the contrary—"quite all right"; but I don't think I meant, when I said that it was quite all right, what Rockefeller meant when he restored Williamsburg. It is an admirable restoration—authentic replica of the setting of our early historic settler's life. As a museum piece it is invaluable to us because it is placed where we can see it and see through it. We may read—as I read there—something of what really was the matter with our forefathers when they got here—the men who came here, rebels against oppression later to become revolutionists, to find a new and better land. They came and lived within shooting distance of the Indians and brought that culture with them which we now see in detail at Williamsburg. We see that it was all just what they had there, "back home." Of course, "back home" is what all Englishmen in foreign lands wish for. If you watch Englishmen conduct their lives as their lives run around the whole world you will find them doing just *what* was done and just as near as possible *as* it was done back home, whether they are doing it in India, Africa, Australia, or at the North Pole. Whatever they did at home, that same thing they do so far as they can do it—south, north, east, or west in the new land in which they find themselves.

Concerning Williamsburg . . . they there ran *true* to form. We must say that the restoration *is* a fine museum piece and as such valuable to Americans if they would only let it be a museum piece and not an *illusion,* studying it for what significance it has where our life is concerned, not attempting to live in it, still. As an object lesson to the nation in architecture, it *is* valuable. Studying the exhibit at Williamsburg closely—from the inside—one may see why and how, now, this nation was contrived by the monied man for the monied man by the money-minded; see why property was the criterion by means of which this union was to survive, if it could survive at all. You can read in this search for the elegant solution that the culture which the colonists had on them, or with them, when they arrived was French culture unified by a century or two of English taste. England had little elegance of her own, so turned to that of the French, imitated French culture, and, inevitably, brought the imitation to these shores. That is plain *truth* concerning the culture of our colonists. Now, why not, indeed, have a fine restoration of that culture where we can look it in the face for what it is today and see what the culture was that lay in behind the culture of a mixed nation such as this one of ours? That early culture, as you will see, had little of reality in it but did have a certain reticence, a fine cleanliness when in poverty and a finer simplicity in general than is generally practiced now. But, when, later, modern devotees of English colonial culture became rich and could spend money like drunken sailors, it is easy to see how and why we got Queen Anne, Medieval Gothic, General Grant Gothic, etc., etc.—"the 57 varieties"—and easy to see why we have all these blind-as-a-bat government buildings to work in; why, and how, we got the kind of grandomania the government always so generously provides for us, for official purposes, especially, and for its popular heroes, regardless.

Facing reality as it soon did, how in actuality could that colonial culture prove itself equal to the strain soon to be put upon it? You may see the consequences all around you here in Washington. Now, with deeper thought, ignoring colonial *culture,* you'll find something in the Colonial life of our forefathers that was clean, something sweet and straightforward, something out of the *nature* of the *true* liberal. The ideals of our forefathers were fine and high. And you will see that among them were great men—endowed with greatness and generosity, *true* aristocrats. That older nation from which they came knew that they were worth having but didn't know how to keep them.

But unfortunately, for the ideals of freedom and democracy, old feudal hangovers from England came along with them. The colonials brought in

A detailed view of the brick masonry exterior of the Arthur C. Mathews residence (1950) at Atherton, California. Photograph by the editor.

the feudal land system, the feudal idea of money, the feudal notion of property rights in everything on earth *as a speculative commodity.* Among these high-minded men was one Tom Paine who did know something of a technical basis for the practice of individual human rights. But not until long after the colonial rebels had set up the constitution for this democracy was anything at all written into it concerned with the *nature* of human rights. Therefore—tonight—standing here, an architect, I want to speak of the culture of *organic architecture* as opposed to this culture, we call it "colonial," brought to the great experiment here by our forefathers. It would be silly for me to say "modern architecture" in speaking to you because modern architecture means merely the architecture of today, or architecture à la mode. But, when you say *organic architecture* you immediately run up a flag to the masthead. You use a term that really compels thought. Now, of course, the architecture we had by way of the colonials nobody has been compelled to think much about. It has not demanded nor has it received any thought at all. Even they had ceased to think about it. Sometimes I think it has gone as far as it has gone only to give a break to the inferior desecrator and allow educated men to stop thinking, never allowing the nation to begin to make something of itself by way of its own life. *Organic architecture* is something that must come out from the ground by way of the life of the people—not out of the universities. It comes out of the circumstances of the time, the place, and the man. Universities do not know it, yet. They do, however, begin to suspect. *Organic* architecture rejects art as a mere aesthetic and clings to the creative evolution of principle.

So, today, *organic* architecture knows that during all these years we have suffered severely from a dreadful hangover—an illusory dream of culture—to such an extent that light and life have gone out of architecture, gone out of the building itself and the work that makes the building—perhaps for no better reason than because of the superficialities that came over to us in early days as culture, borrowed as they were even then by way of our colonial forefathers. I am not one so silly as to suppose that a man of Thomas Jefferson's caliber, were he living today, would wear knee breeches, buckles on his shoes, powdered hair, lace at throat and wrists, and the other elegancies indulged in by gentlemen of his day. He was in advance of the thought of his time. He was leader of his kind in his day. He held in high esteem the generous, fine ideal called then, as now, democracy—an ideal that is about as far from realization now, as then, probably. Why has that ideal flourished so little here among us? Why have we so little of it that even England, from whom we received it as a reaction, now has more of it than we? Do we really know why? Can our universities tell us—do you imagine? Ask them!

Because of this deadly cultural lag—for that is what all this is and it is precisely what we suffer from—we have allowed ourselves to learn nothing of architecture. So—we, at this late day, are now where we have to begin at the beginning because the boys whom we sent to be cultured as architects were never allowed to begin at the beginning. As though some man who wanted to learn to fly had gone to a high precipice to jump off so they went to the top of a tall building to jump off. Well—we have had to begin where they fell. Now *organic* architecture has come to you out of your own country by way of the circumstances in which our national flag was planted; something natural and genuine out of our own ground has come to be in spite of current education and foolish sentimentality. It is the new reality—and it is a demand for the finer integrity than business yet knows. You may treat it lightly; you may scoff; you may play horse with it if you wish—but it is the beginning, the rise of a centerline of *true* culture for America.

I am talking of *organic* architecture for America. But America—I should say—now goes quite completely around the world; probably the America to which I refer can be found more abroad than found at home. This *organic* way is the *spiritual* way of doing things, a spirited way of being and doing that is already around the world. Sad to admit, however, that if *organic* architecture is to come home and now live here at home we must import what we exported. In this matter of architecture we have been turning to Europe for our own export because, it seems, the kind of eclecticism which has flourished so rankly among us can only get a genuine architecture that way. I am not reconciled to that. And yet I know it to be *true*. And I know that our learning is such that it can only arrive at the benefits which come from any *true* philosophy of building or being when some hallmark from abroad is upon it; Oxford once but Paris now preferred. Any country other than our own country might do for us to imitate in this matter of culture. Nothing our own, nothing *true* to ourselves coming from the tall grass out on our great Midwest prairies, could get much credence in our very best circles. It had to go abroad for recognition. So, our own creative effort in architecture has languished here in America as every great idea has languished or died as the price of too much learning where there should be *vision*. This peculiar trait of our kind of learning brings to mind Lieber Meister's [Louis H. Sullivan] definition of a highbrow: "a man educated far beyond his capacity." I think that we as a nation have now been educated far beyond our capacity; educated out of thinking for ourselves; educated away from the things that mean life to the American people. Of course, we have unemployment and misery because we have no ideas by way of which to utilize our sciences and mechanical inventions; no ideas by way of which we might use these newer riches—glass and steel, no honest ideas by way of which these things could come into the possession of the life of the American people. No. Our people today, being so badly overeducated still lack, most of all, what we properly call "culture." The same lack of culture—the cultural lag—is here that exists in Russia today, which does not flatter us. Russia—a great nation—ninety-one percent illiterate [and] mostly serfs who had far less than nothing, is now free. Eating during their lifetime, out of the hand of a superior class—seeing what culture the upper classes had—their tall ceilings, glittering glass chandeliers, sensual paintings, statues, with fountains playing on wide terraces: utter magnificence—now what? Can you talk to these freed serfs of simplicity? Can you talk to them of the things of the *spirit* and mind? You cannot. They want that which they did not have and were subject to when they were slaves—only now they want all of it twice as tall, want twice as many glittering chandeliers, more sensuality, more and bigger statues, more *magnificence,* in short. And today, in what we call culture, how much better are we where this cultural lag is concerned? May *we* look down on *them* do you think? Not while Williamsburg is [the] criterion.

Unfortunately nothing in education today genuinely suffices as a solution for this deadly wasteful lag because nothing is being done from the inside out. What have we done with our cultural lag? We have had our way or will have it if the education of the corporate, by the corporate, for incorporation doesn't loosen up a little; and it still stands: we've got it to show for itself in the grandomania of our public buildings, in private palaces in these modern equivalents of barons, princes, and dukes, completely *commercialized.* And this deadly lag has not served life well in our case. We are bankrupt, culturally, by way of these hangovers from feudal times, impotent by a silly idealism, made ridicu-

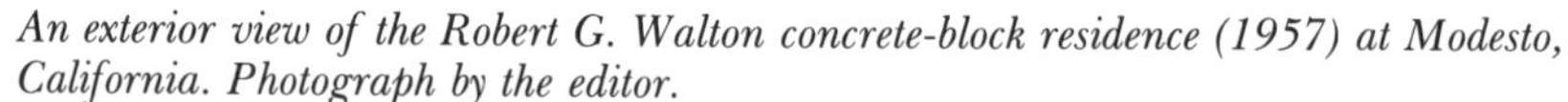
An exterior view of the Robert G. Walton concrete-block residence (1957) at Modesto, California. Photograph by the editor.

lous by a mawkish sentimentality that will keep on keeping men from demanding their own. The cultural influences in our country are like the floo-floo [sic] bird. I am referring to the peculiar and especial bird who always flew backward. To keep the wind out of its eyes? No. Just because it didn't give a darn where it was *going* but just *had* to see where it had *been.*

Now, in the floo-floo bird you have the *true* symbol of our government architecture too, and in consequence how discredited American culture stands in the present time! All the world knows it to be funny except America. What prevented us and still prevents us from knowing it? Armchair education, let's say. Now, all this has parallels in history. The Romans were just as incognizant as we of the things of the *spirit.* They, too, had no culture of their own. England had none of her own and we, having none, got what we have as substitute second, third, or fourth hand from them all. Roman culture, for instance, was Greek. The Romans did have, however, great engineers—you have all heard of the arch—but what did the Romans do with their greatest invention—the arch? You know well enough that for centuries they wasted it by pasting a travesty of Greek trabeation over it to conceal the *truth* of structure, until finally, some vulgar Roman, more uncultured than the rest, one day got up and said: "Hell! Take it all away! What's the matter with the arch? It's a genuine, beautiful and noble thing"—and finally they got it, got the common arch as indigenous architecture. We, the modern Romans, probably, are going to get architecture something like that the same way. We are going to have a *true* architecture of glass—steel—and the forms that gratify our new sense of space. We are going to have it. No colonial Eden is able—long—to say us nay. Culture, given time, will catch up and assert itself in spite of reaction—even if asserting itself as reaction itself. This thing which we call America, as I have said, goes around the world today. It is chiefly *spirit* as yet, but that *spirit* is reality. Not by way of government can we find encouragement of any help. No, we can have nothing by way of official government until the thing is at least ten years in the past. What can government do with an advanced idea? If it is still a controversial idea, and any good idea must be so, can government touch it without its eye on at least the next election? It cannot. I know of nothing more silly than to expect government to solve our advanced problems for us. If we have no ideas, how can government have any? That is a sensible question to ask, and the answer is that government as a majority affair can never have any. So, I see the tragedy of entrusting to government billions to spend on billions. Why should government ever be entrusted to build buildings? Inevitably buildings are for tomorrow. That is the last thing government should be expected or allowed to do because in entrusting building to government, we must go ten or one-hundred years backward instead of ten years ahead into the future. Tragic! But to talk against it is just so much water over the dam. The driver may not know where to go but he is in the driver's seat. So what?

Perhaps you feel, as I feel in the circumstances, a burning indignation in my soul when I see the desecration everywhere with us in the name of culture and realize it as all our own fault. You know something of the degradation of the cultural fabric of your nation when you see our billions now being spent to give us human slums taken from the region of the body and poverty fixed as an institution in the realm of the American soul. That is what most of this so-called "housing" means to me and what it will come to mean to America in [the] future. I stand here and challenge our America to reflect that any honest, willing, *busy* workman of today with his family can own no home of his own at all unless by grace and beneficence of *government.* That should make it time to sit up and raise hell with what made it that way. At least, so I think and so you would think, if you thought about it at all.

And I will tell you now that when any man in our nation has the courage to stand up and challenge the accustomed and is therefore accused of being a *sensationalist* do not trust that accusation. In the accusation there speaks, usually, the self-styled *conservative* in our country—than which I know of nothing more wearisome as obstruction to growth. By the term *conservative* as in popular use we've come to use it we mean—really, some stand-patter or a lid-sitter, some man who having got his, doesn't want and won't have a change. But, *truly* speaking, a *conservative* is a radical by *nature* and character. He can be nothing else. The word *radical* means of the root and the word *conservative* means keeping life in the thing conserved—keeping it *growing* in other words . . . And how can you do that unless you know and understand that thing at the beginning—at the root, that is. How can you consider yourselves *conservative* when you do not know that root or when you consider that root to be money—and, having made money, are determined by hook or crook to hang on to it? No . . . they so-minded have got it all—all wrong. They now remind me of the man who got the measure of a door by holding his hands just so wide apart. He ran down the street keeping his hands as he had them saying, "Get out de way, ev'ybody, I'se got de measure of a do'!"

Well—yes, the would-be conservative *has* got the measure of a door—and everybody must get out [of] the way as best he can, but he hasn't the actual measure of *the* door. I suppose it is unbecoming, at least ungracious, to talk in this way about the people out of whose hands we must all eat as things are with us. I suppose standing here I am biting the hand that feeds *me*. But perhaps less so than any other architect in America. Nevertheless, directly or indirectly, we are all eating out of the hand of the man higher up, as he is eating out of the hand above him until finally *government* takes a hand. And we call it a system. Well, God knows it is no system. It is an adventitious hangover from feudal times—let's face it. If we had allowed ourselves to learn anything of culture or if we had a genuine American culture on the way, we would now insist upon a more *organic* structure for our society.

I am not talking to you like this out of any books at all. I am speaking here as an architect who has

An exterior view of the Seth Petersen residence (1958) at Lake Delton, Wisconsin. This small, one-room cottage is constructed of native stone and wood. Photograph by the editor.

The Nakoma Warrior Sculpture (1924) by Frank Lloyd Wright was conceived for the Nakoma Country Club and Winnebago Camping Ground Indian Memorial Project (1924) at Madison, Wisconsin. It was constructed in the late 1970s for the Johnson Wax Administration Building in Racine. Photograph by the editor.

The Nakomis Woman Sculpture (1924) by Frank Lloyd Wright was intended for the Nakoma Country Club and Winnebago Camping Ground Indian Memorial Project (1924) at Madison, Wisconsin. It was constructed in the late 1970s for the Johnson Wax Administration Building at Racine. Photograph by the editor.

built more than 200 buildings for his own people, every one of the buildings an honest experiment in behalf of the man it was built for—always building, professedly and openly, as an experiment. To what end? That I might become famous as an architect? That I might make a reputation for myself which I might follow up with profit? No! Not that—I persisted with will and patience because there is something compelling in this country and it is the people of the country. They are right-minded and sincere—at bottom, patient, long-suffering, generous, and wonderful. I love my people as I love architecture. You put those two loves together and what will you get? You will get a way of building born that is an honest way of building and a more genuine life by way of the building. You will see those things we call buildings blossoming into new forms, free patterns for new life, and a wider life for all.

Every decent design for any building should be a design for better living—a better design for a richer, fairer way of life instead of being a shallow hangover from feudal times to please grandmother.

Perhaps this is as good a place to stop as any. I've said very little of what I meant to say. But I do want to say to you that there was—once upon a time—a great modern who was less neglected in his time than he would be were he living among us now—Victor Hugo. Victor Hugo had a prophetic mind. He wrote in the great chapter on architecture, which is not in most editions of *Notre Dame,* included in some under the title "The Book Will Kill the Edifice," to the effect that late in the nineteenth century and early in the twentieth century architecture would come alive again into the world after having languished and all but died for 500 years. I think he based the prophesy on the fact that the nineteenth century would have given us the new means, new ways he foresaw as *the machine,* and that by that time—the twentieth century—life would be impassioned again, intolerant of the back drag of old unsuitable forms. Now, bearing him out—in the wake of the printing press—came mobilization, the motorcar, electrifications. The little village designed for horse and buggy or footwork, now gives over to a new scale at least one-hundred times that norm. Multiply the normal speed of movement today by God knows what, multiply—say steel and glass, the automobile, the radio, electrical communication—and what might we not have? And yet today the country is littered with the scaffolding of poles and wires, stumpage, dumpage [sic], and ghastly derelicts of all kinds. We might move freely and speak to each other a thousand miles away by a little thing fixed in our coat lapel, provided patents had not been bought up and suppressed.

I wanted to put cool [fluorescent] light in my latest building. [I] offered the Johnson Wax building for a further experiment to an experiment already used successfully but I found I could not have it. General Electric had bought the patent and was not prepared to give it to the public for two years—or until the way to commercialize the idea could be economically squared. That same thing in more important ways has been going on by utility companies' making speculative commodities out of ideas by means of which society lives, moves, and has its being—and that way still is the only way our society has of getting these ideas at all. In fact, life itself is now a speculative commodity unless one has $2500 a year or more. Then how can you still think of this as *a free country?* Now, what do you, as architects, think of all this?

The only justification I have for being here at all to talk is that I have earnestly tried to do something about it myself. The Broadacre City models were one of the things. And for that I asked for my country three things—three things I needed for Broadacre City—in order that it might go.

First: Free land to those who could use it. No absentee ownership of land. The land to be held by the *improvements,* not the improvements held by some other holder of the land.

Second: A free medium of exchange. No monster we call money to go on working while we sleep—no more of this thing called money as an accretion, working endlessly for any man, good or bad, who gets a little of it, regardless of his contribution to society. No—because here again is another speculative commodity so artificially set up that it can be thrown behind a vault door and still work for itself. That is wrong. That is a monstrosity.

Third: Let us have done with this making of speculative commodities out of common human needs, this patenting and selling of human ideas—the basis of life itself—by way of which society lives, loves, and has its being. These three things we should ask, we—architects—I am talking as an architect still, and for my country and the people of this country—in order that we may live our own lives in *deed* as well as in *theory.* As it now stands—architects—I ask you to observe—this country of ours does not own its own ground, unless the banks and insurance companies that do own it are the country. A nation that does not own its own ground has gone far toward extinction as a civilization. We are going there too fast now. If that is not food for thought for any architect—if that does not start him trying to work something out, I do not know what could.

All this may sound like socialism, communism, or what not. I am no student of socialism, but I *am* a student of *organic;* and in searching for it in the bases of our civilization today I could not find it. I have read Henry George, Kropotkin, Gesell Prondhon, Marx, Mazzini, Whitman, Thoreau, Veblen, and many other advocates of freedom, and most of the things that applied in those great minds in the direction of freedom as conditions exist for us today point to a great breakdown. Before the long depression we, as architects, did not think much of this—but this is no depression. It is certainly a breakdown. One that cannot be fixed by tinkering. Any architect speaking with understanding, making things stand up by way of the *nature* of materials and science of structure, his eyes open and on *entity,* must know in head and bones that this is so. Therefore these three freedoms—*free land, free money, free ideas*—we must have or there is no great life to come for this idea we love and are proud to call democracy.

Questions and Answers

QUESTIONER: Who should design government buildings—private architects or government employees?

WRIGHT: Certainly no government employees because no employee is free to do creative work. And I am not so sure about private architects as they stand at present. I think if we could forget about *official* designing, allowing buildings to be built simply, naturally, by builders—their hands in the mud of the bricks of which the buildings are made, a lot would come out of the ground a little more simply for the honest purposes of life—forgetting entirely architecture as we have now come to know it from the books. I think something good might then happen. I think we could somehow get many traditions off our necks in order that the great traditions might live and we would learn to see that in *truth* the cultural lag persists and obstructs our path by way of too many little traditions with no great sense at all of *tradition.* Then I think what we call great building might live again among us. But what hope when building has been turned over lock, stock, and barrel to college boys who are now in training to the books?

QUESTIONER: If private capital will only build for profit and government will not build except on the old

An exterior view of the Johnson Wax Administration Building (1936–lower building*) and the Johnson Wax Research and Development Tower (1944*–center tower*) at Racine, Wisconsin. Photograph by the editor.*

An interior view of the lobby of the Johnson Wax Administration Building at Racine. Note the use of incandescent lighting. Photograph by the editor.

lines, how shall we hope for change in building conditions?

WRIGHT: That I leave up to you as it is now squarely up to all of us.

QUESTIONER: You have made obvious criticism of conditions of today—have you anything constructive to offer?

WRIGHT: I do not think what I have said has reached this gentleman behind the flag of December 7, 1887, hanging over the balcony over his head. So I ask you of what use for me to come here and speak to him? Perhaps he has not been listening. I have said constructive things but there must be a lot of destructive work, much satire before anything can be done in America today that is really constructive. I have planted *organic* buildings all around the world—over 200 of them, I said—themselves in the *nature* of the thing. If they mean nothing, then what can I *say* that would mean anything constructive?

QUESTIONER: In domestic architecture, what do you say are the trends for small families?

WRIGHT: Building small homes for the small families of little or no means is a very definite trend in the life of our country now. And—means or no means—I see that everybody is eager for space. The sense of space has become an American characteristic. Perhaps the new ideal of freedom we call democracy had something to do with it. We will no longer be pigeonholed by way of classic colonialisms or by anything else, I think. My prescription for a modern house? One—a good site. Pick that one at the most difficult spot—pick a site no one wants—one that has features making for character; trees, individuality, a fault of some kind in the Realtor mind. That means getting out of the city. Then—standing on that site—look about you so that you see what has charm. What is the reason you want to build there? Find out. Then build your house so that you may still look from where you stood upon all that charmed you and lose nothing of what you saw before the house was built. See that architectural association accentuates character. Now, if you want a diagram—just come in sometime!

QUESTIONER: What do you think of the Jefferson Memorial?

WRIGHT: Representative [Tom] Amlie asking the question and he knows damn well what I think of the memorial but thanks to him for the "come on." That belated monstrosity is obviously across the grain of indigenous American feeling for architecture. It is the greatest insult yet and pure extravagance as such.

QUESTIONER: The highest culture has always been achieved by nations which are almost on the decline or at least have passed through the many stages of civilization. We are in that era now. Do you think we are justified in expecting the architects to do away with the culture lag?

WRIGHT: You can wait for the lag to take itself off if you want to. I am not going to wait!

Frank Lloyd Wright working with his drawings, circa mid-1950s. Photograph by Carmie A. Thompson, courtesy of The Capital Times, *Madison, Wisconsin.*

29 Building for Local Government: The Marin County Civic Center

The carelessness with which our people get their buildings built [and] who they will let plan them is almost as though anybody that could poke a fire could plan a building. It should take the greatest experience that can be had to so plan. The best is none too good! And when people choose an architect they ought to prayerfully go at it and if necessary go on their hands and knees as far as they could go to get the best there is. . . .

Introduction

In late April of 1957 Frank Lloyd Wright was invited to the University of California, Berkeley, to give a number of lectures and seminars to architecture students as a guest Bernard Maybeck Lecturer.[1] It was during this trip to Berkeley that his

---

The text of Frank Lloyd Wright's public talk before the Marin County Board of Supervisors, Marin County, California, is reproduced with minor editing from the public record of published minutes of the Marin County Board of Supervisors public meeting on July 31, 1957.

[1] For the complete text of these lectures see Patrick J. Meehan (Editor) *The Master Architect: Conversations with Frank Lloyd Wright*, New York: John Wiley and Sons, 1984, pp. 185–228. These lectures took place on April 24 and 27, 1957.

creative genius was focused on the design of a new government complex for Marin County, California:

> *A meeting was arranged with him privately at the Grant Avenue offices of the Frank Lloyd Wright Foundation in San Francisco on April 26, 1957 . . . four [Marin County] supervisors . . . along with the entire Civic Center Committee met with Frank Lloyd Wright and his associate, Aaron Green, that day and heard his lecture in Berkeley that night, and the Marinites came away convinced apostles of Louis Sullivan's "Spiritual Child." [Mr.] Wright is reported to have said, "So Marin County wants an architect!" . . . Wright's suggestion that the building should reflect the personality of the county was the magic that settled the issue. Marin County had an architect.*[2]

On June 27 the Marin County Board of Supervisors voted four to one to open negotiations with Mr. Wright for his architectural design services. He arrived in San Francisco on July 31 and was disappointed when a welcoming committee met him with an automobile for his eighteen-mile trip north to San Rafael that Wednesday night. He was reported to have commented "I had rather hoped for a helicopter."[3] Mr. Wright was scheduled to appear at the San Rafael High School. Regarding his first meeting with the citizenry of Marin County, the following has been reported:

> *Everybody who was anybody attended. . . . "He talked for one and a half hours. He insulted everybody and they ate it up. . . ." After his usual explanation of organic architecture, Wright launched into a hefty attack on Realtors as the arch enemies of architecture. Many present that night remember the charisma of the man and the hero worship that developed from his first visit to Marin. The old Wright devotees and the new converts lined up solidly . . . in . . . determined drive for a Wright-designed building.*
>
> *But the detractors and dissidents were equally obdurate. A contract with Wright had been approved by the [Marin County] Board [of Supervisors] and was to be signed the next day [Thursday, August 1, 1957]. Having overheard a conversation . . . concerning the possibility of the contract being mislaid . . . [the Chairman] brought his copy to the San Rafael meeting with him which was signed by the four Board members present and by Mr. Wright in the hallway of the San Rafael High School on their way into the meeting.*
>
> *Mr. Wright remained in Marin [County] that night to be present at the formal Board meeting the next day in order to answer any questions concerning the contract.*[4]

---

[2] From Evelyn Morris Radford, *The Genius and the County Building: How Frank Lloyd Wright Came to Marin County, California, and Glorified San Rafael,* unpublished dissertation submitted to the Graduate Division of the University of Hawaii in partial fulfillment of the requirements for the degree of Doctor of Philosophy in American Studies, August 1972, pp. 128–130.

[3] "Young at Heart," *The Capital Times* (Madison, Wisconsin), Vol. 80, No. 26, August 1, 1957, p. 2.

[4] Evelyn Morris Radford. *The Genius and the County Building,* pp. 130–131.

On the following Friday, August 2, in a brief but disquieting period at a meeting with the Marin County Board of Supervisors, Mr. Wright was accused by an irate citizen of being a Communist:

> *He [Mr. Wright] walked out of a meeting . . . while the charges were being read. . . .*
>
> *"I am what I am", he told the supervisors. "If you don't like it, you can lump it. To hell with it all."*
>
> *He waved his cane angrily as he paused in his exit and upped with a tag line:*
>
> *"This is an absolute and utter insult and I will not be subject to it". . . .*
>
> *Two hours after his stormy exit from the courthouse, Wright had cooled sufficiently to sign the official contracts retaining him for the civic center project.*
>
> *But first, he lunched at the Meadow Club in Fairfax with several county officials and played the piano for their entertainment. . . .*
>
> *Wright . . . privately, defied anyone to prove he is or ever has been a Communist sympathizer.*
>
> *"I challenge any one to prove one act or one association of a character that could be called subversive," said Wright. "If the kind of belief I have is subversive, then I am the greatest subversive in America."*[5]

Later that same day Mr. Wright and members of the Marin County Board wandered through knee-high grass over the 130-acre proposed civic center building site:

> *The spry old man explored the terrain with the eagerness of a child at a picnic.*
>
> *He ducked between the strands of barbed wire fence and climbed over another one, jumped across several ditches and fought his way through knee high grass and thistles.*
>
> *Finally, he rendered his appraisal.*
>
> *"Splendid," he said. "It's as beautiful as California can have."*
>
> *Two 15-year old Santa Venetia girls . . . asked Wright to pose for snapshots. He agreed amiably.*
>
> *"Are you going to knock down all these hills?" one girl inquired.*
>
> *"Not a single hill," said the master architect, now beaming with enthusiasm.*
>
> *Some one asked if he planned to make further site inspections before getting to work on the plans. Wright evidently considered that something of an insult too.*
>
> *"I don't have to drink a tub of dye to know what color it is," he replied.*[6]

---

[5] Francis B. O'Gara. "Red Charge Stirs Wright to a Boil," *The San Francisco Examiner* (San Francisco, California), August 3, 1957, p. 3, columns 1 and 2.

[6] *Ibid.*

Frank Lloyd Wright points to a sectional drawing of the Marin County Administration Building, as a listener looks on at Marin County, California, on March 25, 1958. Photograph by Ken Yimm, courtesy of the San Francisco Archives of the San Francisco Public Library.

As discussed earlier in the introduction to Chapter 28, Mr. Wright designed at least twenty-eight government-related projects, among which the Marin County Civic Center Administration Building, Hall of Justice, and Post Office at San Rafael were the grandest. Before his death in April 1959 he also designed the (unbuilt) Marin County Amphitheatre (1957). Construction of the Marin County Civic Center Administration Building began in 1960 and was completed in 1962. Ground was broken for Marin County Hall of Justice in 1967 and the building was occupied in 1969. The complex was located on a tract of wooded land in the hills of Marin County.

This chapter presents the complete text of Mr. Wright's July 31, 1957, talk at the San Rafael High School, as recorded in the Marin County public record of minutes from that public meeting. In addition to the residents who were in attendance on this historic occasion, members of the Marin County Board of Supervisors were Walter Castro, Sr. (Chairman), Mrs. Vera Schultz, James Marshall, and William Gnoss. Other Marin County public officials were Mrs. Mary Summers (Planning Director), Leon de Lisle (County Auditor), Marvin Brigham (Director of Public Works), and Alan Bruce (Deputy County Administrator). Architect Henry Schubart, Jr., opened the meeting and introduced Mr. Wright to the citizens of Marin County. A short question-and-answer period followed his talk.

The Talk

HENRY SCHUBART, JR.: I would like to take a very few minutes to try to set the stage for tonight's meeting for you, if I may. If you [will] put yourselves in the position of being a member of the Board of Supervisors of Marin County, I think you will appreciate what a tremendously difficult job they have had to do and what enormous responsibility lies on their shoulders in making decisions for building and for plans that not only we will enjoy but our children and our children's children. I think that we all owe, if I can speak for myself and perhaps for most of you, a great debt of gratitude [to them] for having had the courage not to make small plans. We have a great tendency these days to do the expedient thing, to do the easy thing, and to select ways and means that will perhaps please everybody, and, as a result, in the process we often get mediocrity. I think [it was] for this reason that the Board has seen fit to make a bold decision to bring to Marin County one of the really great architects of all times. [It] is something that, in spite of [the] differences or fears we may have, certainly we must realize that they have made a very difficult and a very firm decision.

All of us have a tendency to think of buildings and civic centers in terms of money [and] in terms of time. We want to build it cheaply, we want to build it quickly, and I think it is most important that we realize that this civic center is going to be the focus of our political and cultural life in this county for many, many years to come. I think for any man—and I speak here very personally as an architect—for any man to approach a project of this magnitude without fear and without trembling and to be able to bring a very personal and a very creative thing to the work he is doing it isn't just business. It isn't just a plan for money but it is something which will create a whole aura for our life in the county; and I think for such a project we need a very special man and I think perhaps this had something to do with the Board's decision. I think we need an innovative [man] and I think we need a great creative man and who is very fearless and who has always been. We also need an older man, because to plan a structure or group of structures of this magnitude requires great wisdom and great foresight and the architect we have with us tonight is a man who was able thirty, forty, fifty years ago to build and plan buildings which are satisfactory and beautiful and contemporary for our own life today. In introducing such a man I would also, especially for those of you who are not architects, try to convey to you the stature of this man. I don't want to embarrass Mr. Wright, but I feel personally that if I were to introduce a musician to you of the stature of a Bach or a scientist of the stature of a Pasteur or a Newton there would be no misunderstanding as to the man's stature. We don't have today as great an understanding of the art of architecture as we do have of some other fields of endeavor but I want you to know that throughout the world Mr. Wright is considered one of the greatest architects of all times. In introducing Mr. Wright to you, I would like to ask him to speak to you informally as he always does. He is always very much at ease and I would like him to talk to you, if he will, about what a civic center is, about what he thinks a civic center is, and what kind of life we may have here in Marin County. I think this is probably one of the most important and most honored moments as far as I am concerned. I would like to introduce Mr. Wright to you.

WRIGHT: [Mr. Wright puts his arm around Mr. Schubart] Gentlemen! Gentlemen, little Hank has grown up and grown up, how nicely! [Editor's Note: Mr. Schubart was an apprentice of Mr. Wright's Taliesin Fellowship from July 1933 to August 1934.]

Well, here you all are. Here I am. You wouldn't have [had] to go so far for an architect if you had waited until winter. I would then have been nearer to you in Arizona. This whole country of ours I had to cross today to get here three hours late. Well, here we all

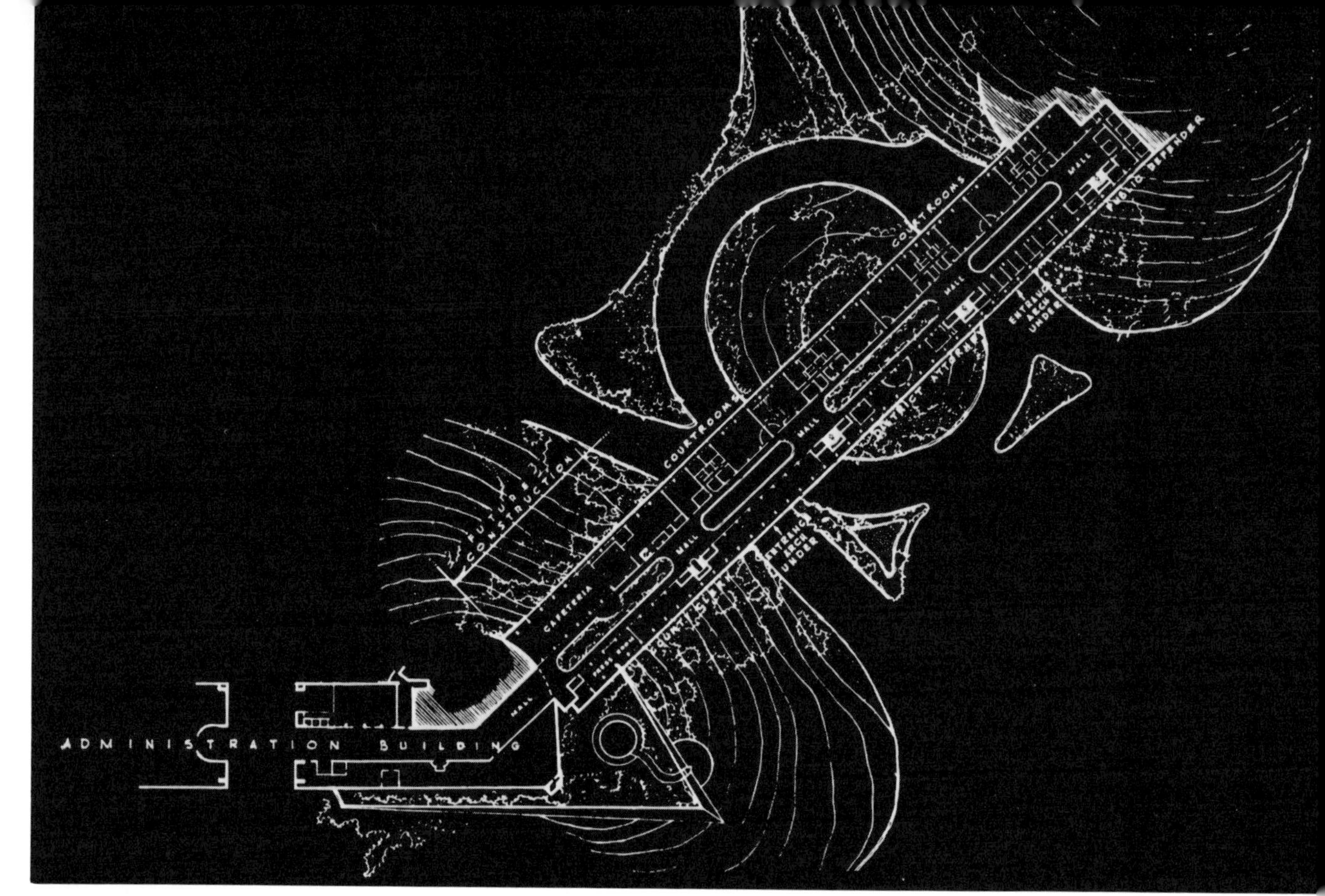

Partial site plan of the Marin County Administration Building (left) and Hall of Justice (right), Marin County, California (1957). Note from the location of the topographic contour lines how the Hall of Justice spans between two significant hills. The site-plan drawing was reproduced from the November 1962 issue of Architectural Forum. *Drawing used by permission of Billboard Publications, Inc., 1515 Broadway, New York, New York 10036.*

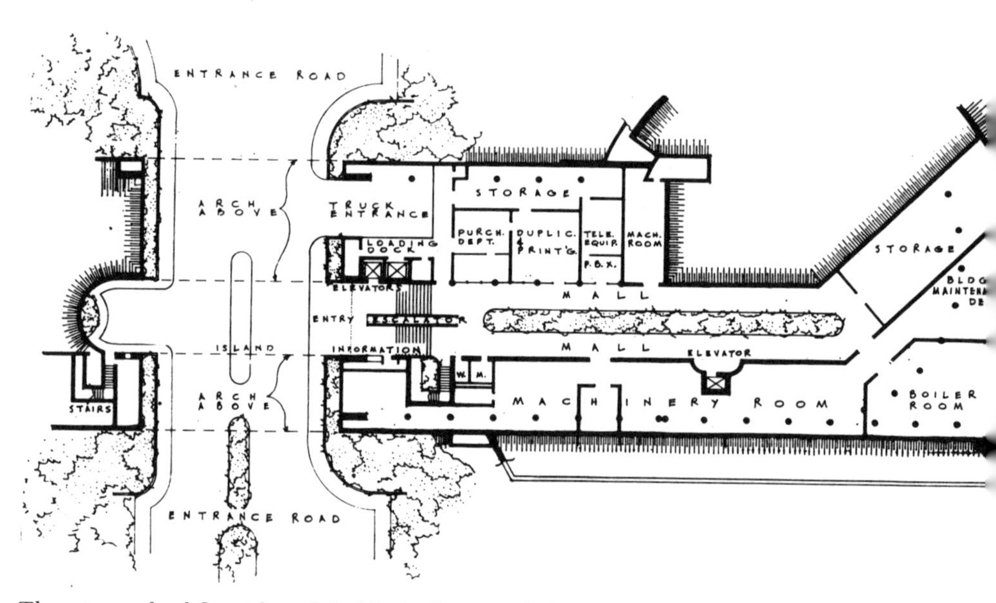

The entrance-level floor plan of the Marin County Administration Building (1957). This level generally houses the machinery and boiler rooms, the building maintenance department, storage space, and truck-loading dock facilities. The floor-plan drawing was reproduced from the November 1962 issue of Architectural Forum. *Drawing used by permission of Billboard Publications, Inc., 1515 Broadway, New York, New York 10036.*

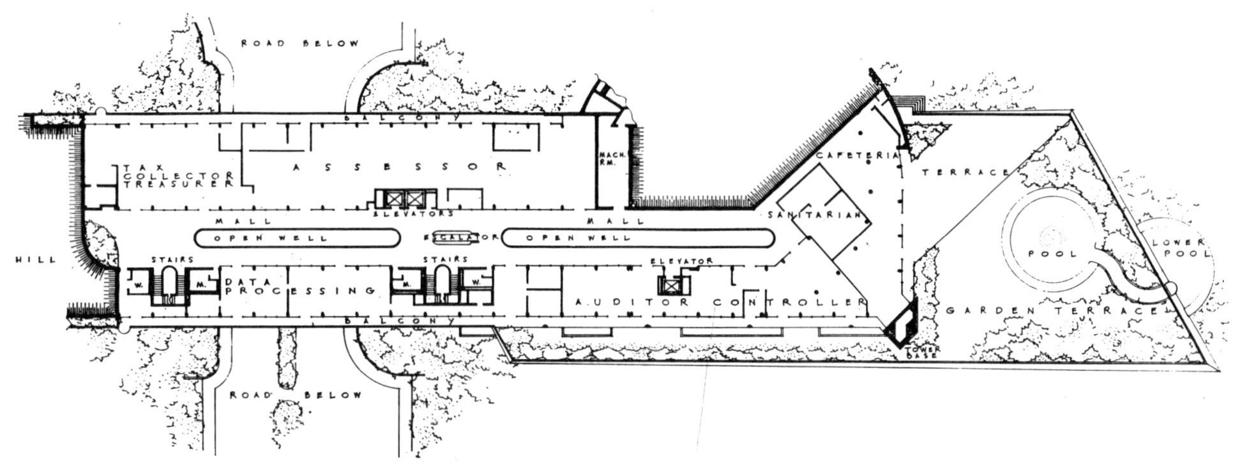

The first-level floor plan of the Marin County Administration Building (1957). This level accommodates the offices of the tax collector, treasurer, and assessor, data processing facilities, the offices of the auditor/controller, and a cafeteria. These rooms are accessible from the linear centrally located, mall-type corridor. The garden terrace and pool are reached from the cafeteria. The floor-plan drawing was reproduced from the November 1962 issue of Architectural Forum. *Drawing used by permission of Billboard Publications, Inc., 1515 Broadway, New York, New York 10036.*

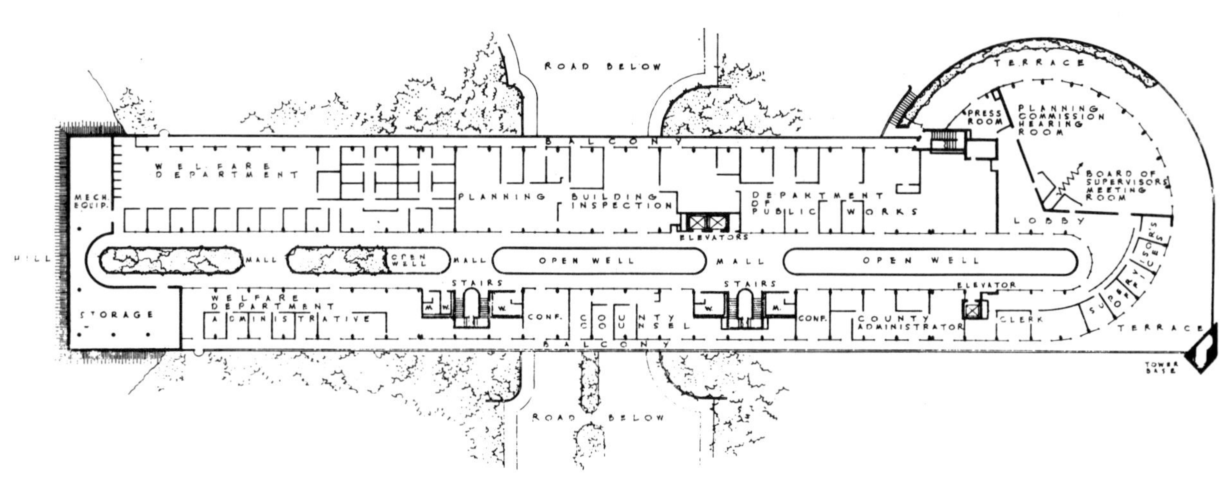

The second-level floor plan of the Marin County Administration Building (1957). This level houses the offices of the welfare department, planning and building inspection department, the department of public works, the county counsel, county administrator, county clerk, supervisors, and public hearing rooms of the Board of Supervisors and Planning Commission. All are accessible from the linear central open, mall-type corridor. Outside are terraces and balconies. The floor-plan drawing was reproduced from the November 1962 issue of Architectural Forum. *Drawing used by permission of Billboard Publications, Inc., 1515 Broadway, New York, New York 10036.*

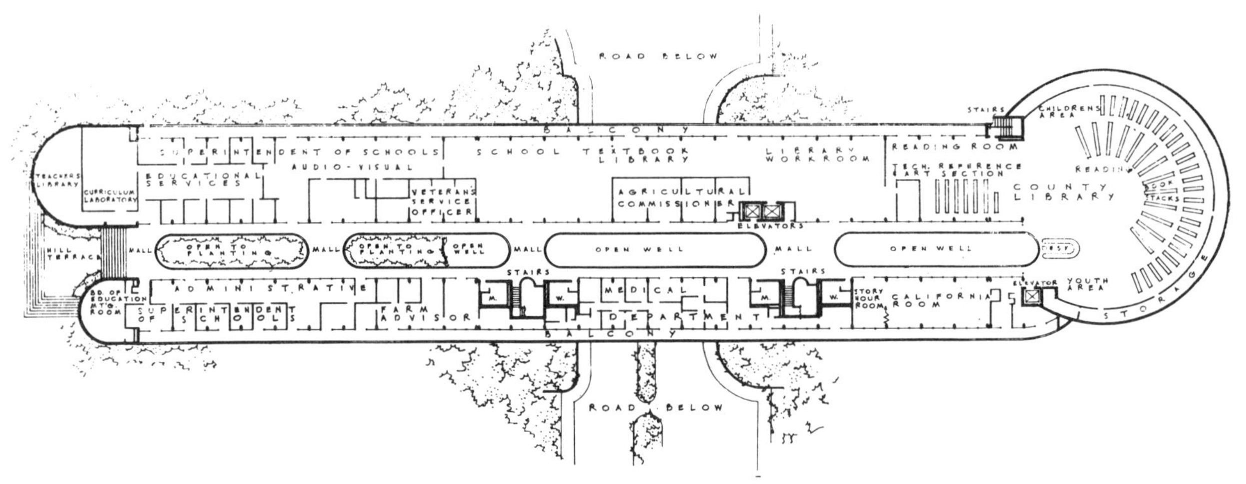

The third-level floor plan of the Marin County Administration Building (1957). The floor accommodates the offices of the superintendent of schools, public library, farm advisor, medical department, agricultural commissioner, veteran's service officer, and other administrative offices. As on levels one and two, all offices are accessible from the central corridor. Outside two elongated balconies afford an excellent view of the countryside. The floor-plan drawing was reproduced from the November 1962 issue of Architectural Forum. *Drawing used by permission of Billboard Publications, Inc., 1515 Broadway, New York, New York 10036.*

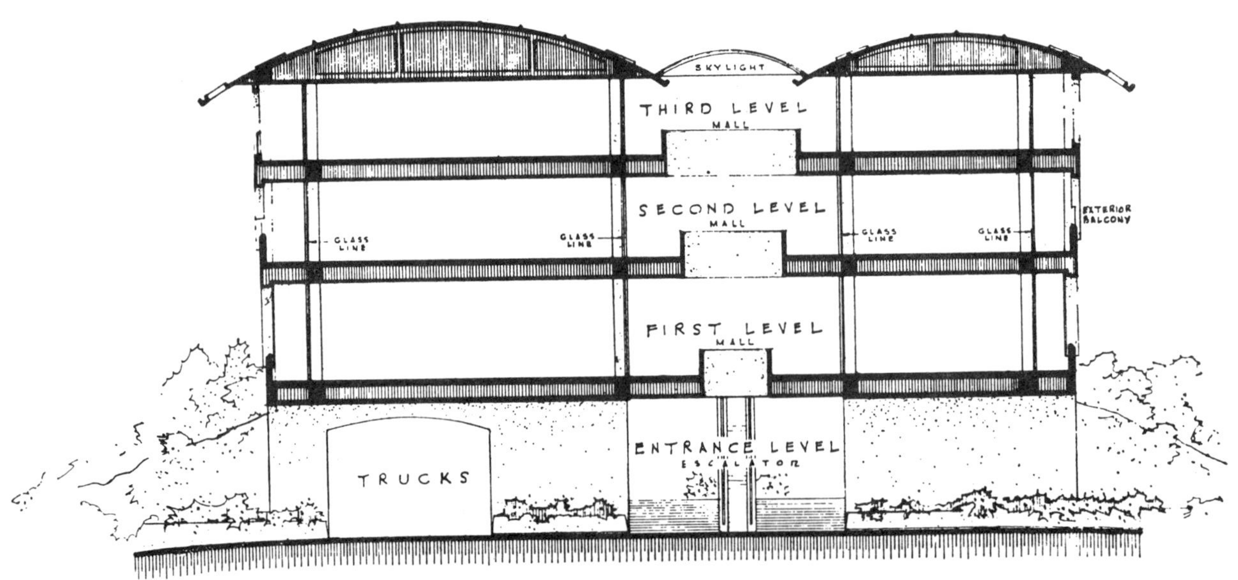

The four levels of the Marin County Administration Building (1957), located at the center of the structure, looking from the entrance level which passes beneath the upper floors. Building section drawing reproduced from the November 1962 issue of Architectural Forum. *Drawing used by permission of Billboard Publications, Inc., 1515 Broadway, New York, New York 10036.*

The Marin County Administration Building (1957) under construction in May of 1961. Photograph courtesy of The Capital Times, *Madison, Wisconsin.*

are. I feel as though I had come here on a mission to save Marin County! Because, as you know, of course you must know because most of you have been to school, that you learn nothing about architecture really worth knowing in school. And, as a consequence, architecture is the blind spot today in our culture as a nation. This is *true.* Look at our colleges, the buildings you went to, your children now go to school in; see the buildings still being built. These have little or no sense of architecture. Architecture [is] the cornerstone of any culture of our own.

We will never have a culture of our own until we have an architecture of our own. Now an architecture of our own doesn't mean something that is ours by way of our own taste. It is something that we have knowledge concerning. We will have it only when we know what constitutes a good building and when we know that the good building is not one that hurts the landscape but is one that makes the landscape more beautiful than it was before that building was built.

Now, in Marin County you have one of the most beautiful landscapes I have seen. I haven't seen Marin County before and I am proud to be here since I am here to help make the buildings of this county characteristic of the beauty of the county.

Now we are going to learn, as we're learning a little I think all through the nation, that there is only one thing after all has been said and done that really is the "payoff" and that is *beauty.* If we don't succeed in developing beauty at home, this civilization is just another one of those that hasn't mattered much and goes to destruction with nobody's sorrow. The atom bomb might as well drop if by building for Marin County we can't show intelligence, sympathy, beauty, [and] understanding. I think most of our American towns would be beautiful if they had proper know-how; if only they knew how to do the things that all would love if their architects were as competent *spiritually* as they are technically. *True* education should have done that for them. Well, at least by now, this should have been done because we are already

The roof trusses are placed and roof construction has begun in this view of the Marin County Administration Building (1957), June 1961. Photograph courtesy of The Capital Times, *Madison, Wisconsin.*

165 years old [and it's] high time now that Marin County [and] all the other counties realized this.

I don't think you can expect much from big cities now because they are doomed by excess. You see, it is *true* [that] our modern advantages are made, by them, totally disadvantageous so far as our big cities are concerned. Everyone of them is bankrupt—not solvent—if over 100,000 population. And a great rush is on just now by its owners to cash in before the crash comes. The cities are building broad freeways not for the people to get out but to get in, whereas they are only going to be used for the citizens to get out. I think getting out is inevitable and has started. I think that in 1921 to 1932 I was modeling this escape from the city to the country. And if the country was like Marin County I don't think it would be difficult at all to persuade most of the citizens that live in the city now to come to Marin County.

What we now want to do, so I think and I may be wrong, is to get a real *poetic* expression of modern life here. *Poetic* is a dangerous word to use in this society at the present time because we have so far missed the *poetic principle.* Therein lies everything that endures, that comes from the human *spirit* to us in civilization. Now can we get that *spirit* into what we do to represent Marin County in these buildings that Marin County builds in the scheme that Marin County will adopt for its citizenry and its official life? If we do this, we'll have done something not only for Marin County but for this whole country. There is nothing yet built officially in

A view of the Marin County Administration Building (1957) from the west during the final phases of construction, circa late 1961 or early 1962. Note the scaffolding on the spire at the left. Photograph courtesy of The Capital Times, *Madison, Wisconsin.*

The great dome with projecting prowlike wall and 217-foot pylon on the Marin County Administration Building (1957). Photograph by the editor.

The Marin County Administration Building (1957) spans the valley between two significant hills with rhythmic circular forms and arches. Photograph by the editor.

The pattern on the light blue roof of the Marin County Administration Building (1957). This view shows the two office wings on the building's third level. The filigreed half-domes are almost flush with the hillside. Housed beneath the dome (left) *is the teacher's library and beneath the dome* (right) *is the Board of Education meeting room. Both domes open out onto a hill terrace. Photograph by the editor.*

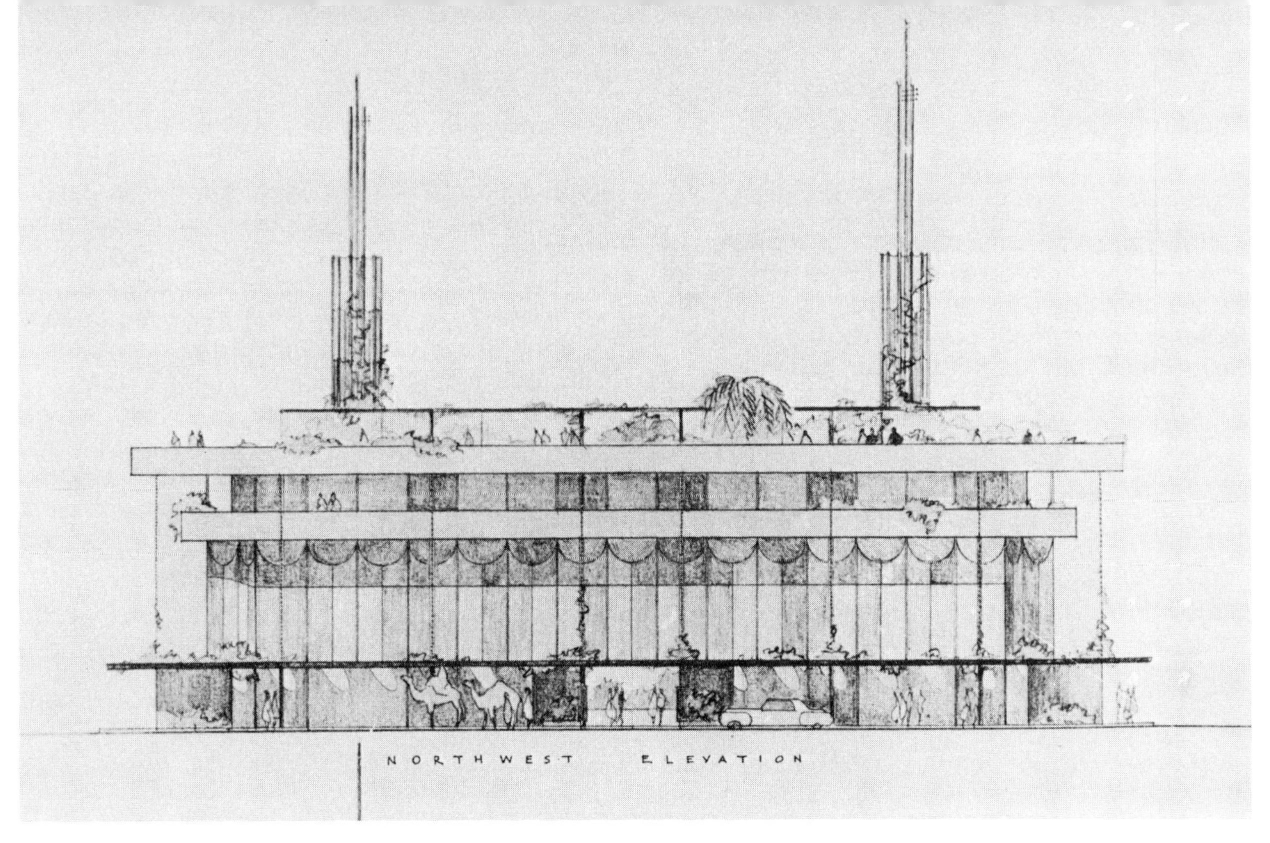

A drawing of an elevation of the Baghdad Post and Telegraph Building Project (1957), Baghdad, Iraq. Wright: "The basis of the construction is the hollow steel tube filled with concrete . . . the whole structure provides translucent, well-lighted interior space under adequate shelter in the hot climate of Baghdad." Drawing reproduced from the May 1958 issue of Architectural Forum. *Drawing used by permission of The Frank Lloyd Wright Foundation.*

this whole country that can be pointed to as adequately measuring up to these possibilities of our present life and time that hasn't been tainted and is soon to be destroyed by this universal traffic problem.

Now, at present, I happen to be doing a cultural center for the place where civilization was invented—that is Iraq. Before Iraq was destroyed it was a beautiful circular city built by Harun al Rashid but the Mongols came from the north and practically destroyed it. Now what is left of the city has struck oil and they have immense sums of money. They can bring back the city of Harun al Rashid today. They are not likely to do it because a lot of western architects are in there already building skyscrapers all over the place and they are going to meet the destruction that is barging in on all big western cities. So it seems to me vital over there to try and make them see how foolish it is to join that western procession.

I think it would be foolish, too, for Marin County to join that procession or one they will find calling itself "civic center" all over the country. Well, what is a civic center? In Marin County it would be something commensurate with the beauty of the county—wouldn't it? It would be something in harmony with the spirit of the people of the county [and] not necessarily displeasing the chief citizens of the county—who probably live in ugly buildings themselves—but something far ahead of Marin

County at the present time; probably more commensurate with the ideas of the young people here.

I am an architect who believes not implicitly but conservatively in the fresh mind of the young. I am for the teenagers. I think the teenager is often reprehensible as he is now seen but is so, largely, because the old people are stupid. If they were not, I think we might proceed in the direction of a beautiful architecture for a beautiful life with much more pleasure and a great deal more unhindered results. So here among you we have a great opportunity—I regard it as such.

I am trying now to bring to Iraq the glory and beauty of that old Sumerian civilization which really left to the Greeks very little to do in the fine arts. There they are now in need of evidently everything they once had and I am proud to be able to help them get some of it back again. But Marin County is no similar case. Marin County has nearly everything that Iraq hasn't got—except oil! The county has beauty, whereas the only beauty that Iraq has left is the Tigris and the Euphrates—very muddy and the whole place is flat as a pancake. If the Iraqi could only see Marin County! I think they would all come over here and settle. Now having such beauty as a gift, loving it, I don't know that you have inherited a love for it, but have you? How did you all get it? But here it is and you are here and it is all yours to make or break. Now what is to be done with you in that connection and how?

First of all, we've got to agree upon some way to take care of this confounding, insensible, immobile

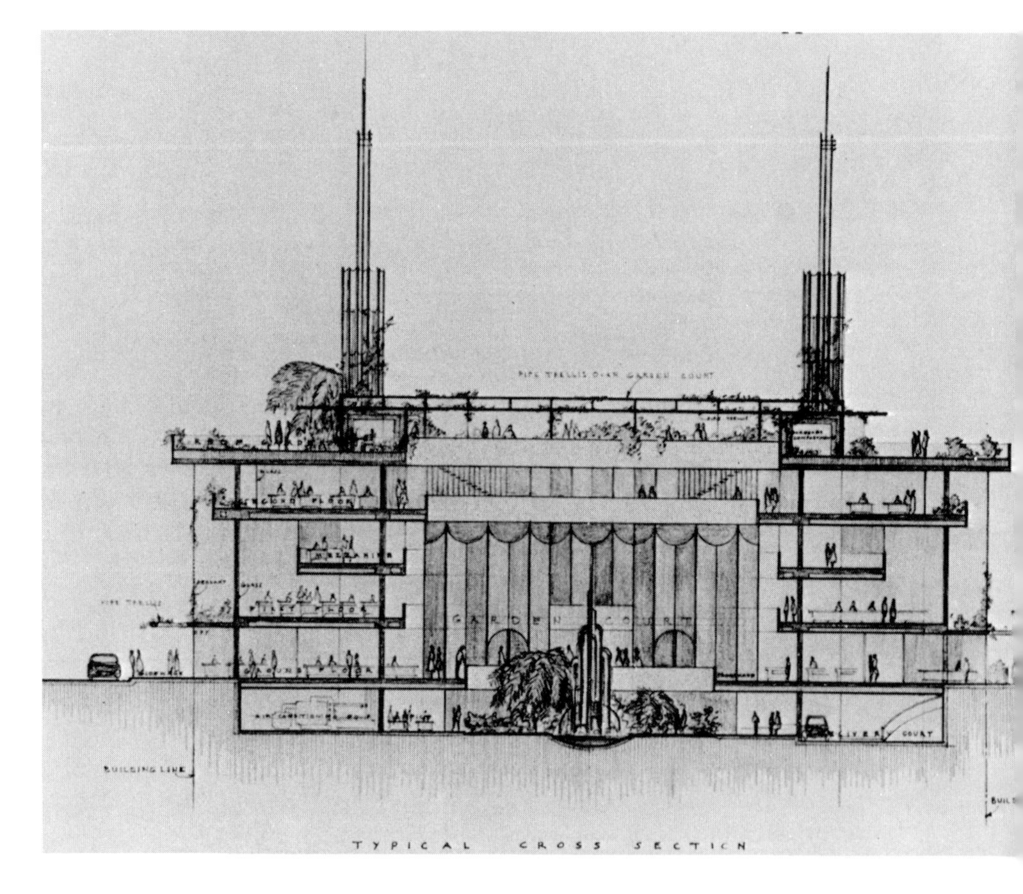

A drawing of a cross section of the Baghdad Post and Telegraph Building Project (1957), Baghdad, Iraq. Wright: ". . . glass walls sheltered under cantilever floor slabs–set in mastic free of structure itself–an arbor of steel rods suspended from overhead is arranged as an outer pattern to carry suitable greenery." Drawing from the May 1958 issue of Architectural Forum. *Drawing used by permission of The Frank Lloyd Wright Foundation.*

automobile. I think nothing is more degrading to the *spirit* of good design than the motorcar of today. I would refuse one as a gift. They tell me it was all done for "madam" but I don't believe that. They had to please her, of course, but that doesn't account for all this swank and style for a ferryboat instead of an automobile. She—madam—may have wanted to look long and stylish and as though designed to fight all the other cars behind her in the streets, but. . . . Well, anyway, we have to dispose, first of all, of this traffic problem in any planning for a civic center for Marin County.

You can't dispose of it on any basis that we know anything about at the present time. No, you see, a man seated in his car requires today about twenty times [more space], at least, [than] anything he did in the foot-and-walker age or the horse-and-buggy era. Now, multiply him by twenty times and then consider the area movement to and fro which he has had to have in order not to kill his neighbor and the space his neighbor must have not to kill him and you will see that nowhere today is there any adequate consideration being given to the spacing in the architect's planning that is due to the absolute necessity the motorcar forces upon us even as the car exists now. And what you see running along the roads almost anywhere around Wisconsin—and I am sure it is the same here as in Milwaukee—you see new ones coming in by fives. They don't come in by threes anymore. They put five on one truck. And consider now that they are going to multiply three to five times in the next three years. So in area what that means is the doom of the big city—the city doomed by *the machine!* Citizens are going to give up their cars or they are going to give up the city. They will give up the city because the city doesn't mean much to them now when they can get everything they had in the old-time cities and stay right at home.

The feudal city was built as a cultural necessity not a gregarious animal resource. There was then no way of humane culture otherwise. But not so now! Everything is in your own hands now. You can be an individual at home or abroad; you can be yourselves. But to be so what you need is space—broad spacing on the ground. This old habit of a little lot and a little house cheek by jowl with other little houses, each with neighboring elbows in its ribs, treading on each other's toes, all the time crowding. Why? Because crowding is so easily exploited! *Freedom* isn't!

I see here in Marin County this *new space* opportunity and before you a great chance for free open spacing—groundroom. Let us start in with this general idea of a free ground plan, taking into account not only conditions as they are at present but looking at least ten years ahead. I believe that nobody has [a] right to build anything that he hasn't planned for ten years ahead. I have often told my clients when they come in to talk about things at the present time that that is the way they should begin to plan how they should now be involved. Marin County should begin to plan this civic center for at least twenty years ahead because Marin County buildings should last about 300 years.

The carelessness with which our people get their buildings built, who they will let plan them, is almost as though anybody that could poke a fire could plan a building. It should take the greatest experience that can be had to so plan. The best is none too good! And when people choose an architect, they ought to go at it prayerfully and if necessary go on their hands and knees as far as they could go to get the best there is because in the realm of such planning none is good enough because, as people, we are over technized [sic] and deficient in the *spirit* of architecture. Architecture is the blind spot of our nation. We have not grown the right kind of architects yet because their education is not on the side of proper growth. It is still cherishing the blind spot in our civilization. Hence the lust for ugliness of which [Henry] Mencken speaks. But now here comes a crucial opportunity to open the eyes not of Marin County alone but of the country to what officials gathering together might themselves do to broaden and beautify human lives, [to] make living fascinating, [to] bring to the life of the *spirit* that they can afford.

Wright: ". . . we have to dispose, first of all, of this traffic problem in any planning for a civic center for Marin County." This well landscaped parking area serves the Marin County Civic Center (1957). Photograph by the editor.

So I do think that is exactly what we should aim to do in planning the scheme of your Marin County Civic Center. Your civic center should not have the usual kind of ominous ring. The sound of "civic center" now is a little bit like the center of business, you know, that looks as though everything was jammed to a concussion; as though everybody was going to get hit or be standing in everybody else's way. But let's avoid that kind of too much *centering.* Let us not—meaning expedient—be too *practical.* Let's be sensible and let's be understanding and have appreciation, sensitivity too, for it. You [will] really see the beauty of Marin County. You are really going to see the beauty of the buildings we're going to propose to build for you in the county. They are going to be built by and for the county landscape and to be built by and for *you*—no less!

Well, *organic architecture* is new to you in that interior sense but it is only architecture humane; the architecture that is out of *nature,* for human *nature.* And that means great *nature, nature* with a capital "N. "I guess I use the word *nature,* as I always have, in rather a confusing way because I always put a capital "N" on the word, and why? Because we write the word God with a capital "G" don't we? Now *Nature* is all the body of God we are ever going to see! As you study it, instead of looking *at* it, look *into Nature.* The reason is the *why* of this or that and by way of such interior *Nature* study, increase your knowledge of what constitutes *truth.* Do this concerning anything and you will soon find that it's Nature is the *beauty* of it.

I'm not going to give you too long a lecture on the philosophy of architecture here now. I am here, just as one of the family, now that I have signed the contract with you, to try to do this thing I have been talking about. *You* are here now, but, where are *we*? Well, *you* are entitled to take me apart and find out what it is that *I* mean. If *you* don't yet understand *me,* I am happy to answer any questions even from the gallery—even *especially* from

The four distinct levels of the Marin County Administration Building (1957) can be viewed from the roadway that crosses through the entrance level beneath the upper levels of the building. Photograph by the editor.

the gallery and I suppose the best ones usually come from the gallery, but I don't know. So who wants to know what I am able to tell them about what? Son Hank [Schubart] has given me a very nice introduction here tonight—please don't let it scare you!

Now, after all, it's not so much to be [the] greatest architect in the world because there aren't great ones left. I never felt particularly flattered by such accusation because I wish there were more architects who understood the *Nature* of *organic architecture*. It's new—not very old yet but the *principles* are as old as Lao-tse, at least. Jesus was the original advocate when He said, "the Kingdom of God is within you"; from *there* could have come this idea of building from the inside out. That is what *organic architecture* is—building the way *Nature* builds. How does *Nature* build? Build you, for instance? How does she build a tree? How does she do this thing that is so marvelously deep but vague and beautiful, so expressive? *She* always builds from inside outward. Now, somehow or other, architecture has got the other way around. Some of this in my own name, too! Yes, the other way around. Architects build an outside steel frame structure and fill in the frame with glass. The rest of the building comes from outside in. So the old box frame is still nineteenth-century architecture. Whereas, now in mid-twentieth century it is the interior way of construction that stabilizes all and the walls are merely integuments—thin, light, and hang from the interior structure. In other words, *organic* means a very natural simple process.

The old steel frame matches what we see in Mexico City just now. All of the so-called International Style structures have not only crashed the glass panels [but] the steel frames have exploded it—sent it flying. The steel frames themselves are twisted and wrecked. Conclusive enough evidence that when building, if you want to meet earthquakes, you cannot start from the outside and go inward but must start from the inside and go

The half-dome over the third-level, Board of Education meeting room opens out onto a hillside terrace in the office wing of the Marin County Administration Building (1957). Photograph by the editor.

outward. Well, here at least you will have in Marin County what you'll safely call earthquakeproof buildings. I don't know that it is very important here, but [it's] a good thing to have.

Is there anybody who really has an idea about what particular character this group of buildings for you should have? Because [it has] to be something altogether, a unit. You can't just build one building here and another building there and another one over there without reference to a great coherent scheme for the whole—a scheme, in itself like anything *organic* in *Nature, coordinate.* That scheme *coordinate* is what you expect from me. I hope. I know, in conceiving this, it would be greatly helpful to me to know if any of you have some particular feeling about what buildings or any particular building. I think my audience [is] not very articulate tonight!

CARMEL BOOTH: Mr. Wright, I am Carmel Booth of San Anselmo. I do want to say that I am most happy that the County of Marin, particularly our Board of Supervisors, has seen fit to hire the services of one of the outstanding gentlemen of our age. We know that you will give us everything we want. I don't think we can tell you anything. We are so stupid you will have to tell us, Mr. Wright.

WRIGHT: My dear lady, you shouldn't break down, weep, and confess in front of all these county people of yours, but even if what you say were not *true* I should much like to hear you say what you say, what you have just said.

GENTLEMAN FROM THE AUDIENCE: Mr. Wright, I feel that within the next twenty years Marin County could very well have a population in excess of a million and a quarter people. . . .

WRIGHT: I agree.

GENTLEMAN FROM THE AUDIENCE: . . . In San Francisco we have an area of twenty-six square miles . . .

WRIGHT: Yes.

GENTLEMAN FROM THE AUDIENCE: . . . with 800,000 people, here we have 525 square miles and the most beautiful county in all California . . .

WRIGHT: Right!

GENTLEMAN FROM THE AUDIENCE: . . . and I do claim that it is going to be recognized as the "jewel county" of the State of California.

WRIGHT: And, therefore, be wrecked if you don't watch out!

GENTLEMAN FROM THE AUDIENCE: . . . and you certainly should bear in mind that we want your kind of a building and I am sure you will follow it out. The shortage of time element is constantly getting shorter. We now cross the United States in three hours. We'll soon be able to cross the United States and the Pacific Ocean in less than three hours. The population is moving West . . .

WRIGHT: It is going to be hard to keep up with all that. I'm booked as Admiral on the American Fleet for the first passage clear across the country within two years on a jet flight taking two hours and twenty minutes. Yes, sir . . . and it is not only time that flies!

GENTLEMAN FROM THE AUDIENCE: Mr. Wright, I would like to ask what have you to suggest so we can start at the present time to prevent further injurement from a cancerous growth of building developments that is completely spoiling our beautiful Marin County and that would spoil any of the things that you are standing for? How can we stop this thing?

WRIGHT: Well, there is the atom bomb! And there is, of course, the virtue of what we call American freedom. We are not very well up on freedom in our country at the present time. We have taken license to a very great extent in the name of freedom and our towns which could be so beautiful and our village life could also be beautiful. But licentious—there are ugly poles and wires, roadside signs and buildings right on the sidewalks—no attention whatever paid to spacious ground plan because . . . why? Crowding! No space! No room! Who is responsible? Don't tell me that you people yourselves aren't responsible because really you are. Why are these poles and wires here with us now? Don't you all take them for granted? Who is complaining about them? I never hear anybody making a fuss about this mortgage on our native landscape but they do have a mortgage and have foreclosed it on our American landscape. That is most tragic. It is so in every region; not yet so bad here as it is elsewhere.

But there is one bad thing we cannot seem to get rid of yet. Why? They are not needed now. And why can't we get rid of the fifty-foot lot or even the

Pattern in the ornament, detail, and structure (foreground) *of the Marin County Civic Center (1957), against the hilly natural surroundings* (background). *View from the second-level outdoor terrace that encircles the joint Planning Commission hearing room/Board of Supervisors meeting room. Photograph by the editor.*

Pattern in the roof, windows, and ornament of the Marin County Administration Building (1957). The third-level "portholes" provide sun control and a walkway for a secondary means of pedestrian circulation between the various county departments. Photograph by the editor.

A narrow third-level balcony with "portholes" (right)*, which runs the full length of the Administration Building, is a secondary means of connecting the numerous county departments. Window-walls line the exterior of the balcony and interior mall. No office is totally without natural light. Photograph by the editor.*

The first-level outdoor pool is set in the landscaped garden terrace on top of the prowlike wall adjacent to the great dome of the Marin County Administration Building (1957). Photograph by the editor.

View of the great dome of the Marin County Administration Building (1957) from the first-level garden terrace pool. Photograph by the editor.

one-hundred-foot lot? Have we got to begin by abolishing the Realtor? Because as I understand him—I have hated him ever since the inception of my architectural career—he is the man who watches to see which way the crowd is going to go; is already moving and he'll run out there ahead, buy all the ground, and cut it up into little pieces, and sell a little piece at a time. The little pieces look smaller and smaller and smaller as the cars grow bigger. Well, we fall. Now the discouraging feature in all these situations, to me as an architect, is that you are yourselves so supine. You don't do anything about it! You don't even say anything! A woman got up the other day—[in an] audience in Madison [Wisconsin] where I was speaking—speaking of a terrible housing project [on] one side of town, suburban to Madison. I had never seen anything so benighted—so utterly regardless of the human interest. Well, the woman got up and said: "But Mr. Wright, what else can we do? We haven't anything else to buy." And I said, "My fair lady, do you know why you don't have anything else to buy? Have you ever asked for it out loud? Did you ever stand up for something better? Ever refuse to buy these damnable impoverishments? No. You bought one. You are paying for it now. You will buy another. And why? Why didn't you get a tent instead? Go out and live in it until you could get something decent you could approve. You'd soon get it." That's *true,* ladies and gentlemen, just so long as you will take this imposition without complaining. What shall I call it? There is a name for it but it isn't fit for this assembly. You will get it just so long as you let poles and wires murder your landscape and spoil the buildings you build.

You'll have them so long as the cars come to you the way they're now so badly overdone—you'll get them. Who buys these cars now? We know hardly any of them are bought but just rented. But even so, who should want to even rent one? You must know that if you didn't rent them they would change.

I am old enough now in the practice of architecture to know that the main, the basic fault of all the trouble lies in the eye of *vox populi* itself. Remember the July orator who said: "My friends, the eye of the *vox populi* is upon us?" Yes, the *populi,* the people, you, you Marin County people. Well at least you have now spoken up, lined up for something better. I say Marin County is going to get it but what a struggle It was for you. Wasn't it? Now why not line up to get better homes, line up to get more ground and better ground? More ground isn't worth what Realtors set for it just because of your own crowding. They make it cost you more by compressing you, the population, into a popular small package. Do you squawk? No sir, you mumble and mutter, but why don't you get up and act? Now what is *true* of you is *true* of nearly every abuse in our daily lives today. You people can change it! Have you tried to change it? If you really know what you want, then do your best to insist upon it. Throw the fellows out of office that officiously stand in your way and elect no more unconscientious objectors. They have become a political sect!

So what of politics today? You all know it is the triumph of conformity to mediocrity or vice versa. You know that mediocrity—say the common man—was started on this way by our dearest, most devastating president Franklin D. Roosevelt in his fireside chats. There the common-man misnomer was told how great he was, and he became so conscious of himself that at the present time I would say that the uncommon man is unconstitutional and I wouldn't be surprised if pretty soon he will have to sue for a pardon. Now who is this common man? There is really no such man. Try and find one. When I think of the common man, I think of him as a character, perhaps, now high up in politics or driving a truck. He may be a rich man. He's one of the merchants of our success. He can be on the farm, be anywhere; that is my common man. My common man is mediocre because he is the man who believes only in what he can see and he can see only what he can put his hand on. Now there lies our political trouble. There is our mediocre man. He is all right, he is, maybe, the basis of things but without the uncommon man he has no vision—though he may not know it—without him, he is sunk. At the present time he seems to be get-

Ornamental lighting accents the vehicular passageway that passes through the building at ground level at the Marin County Civic Center (1957), Marin County, California. Photograph by the editor.

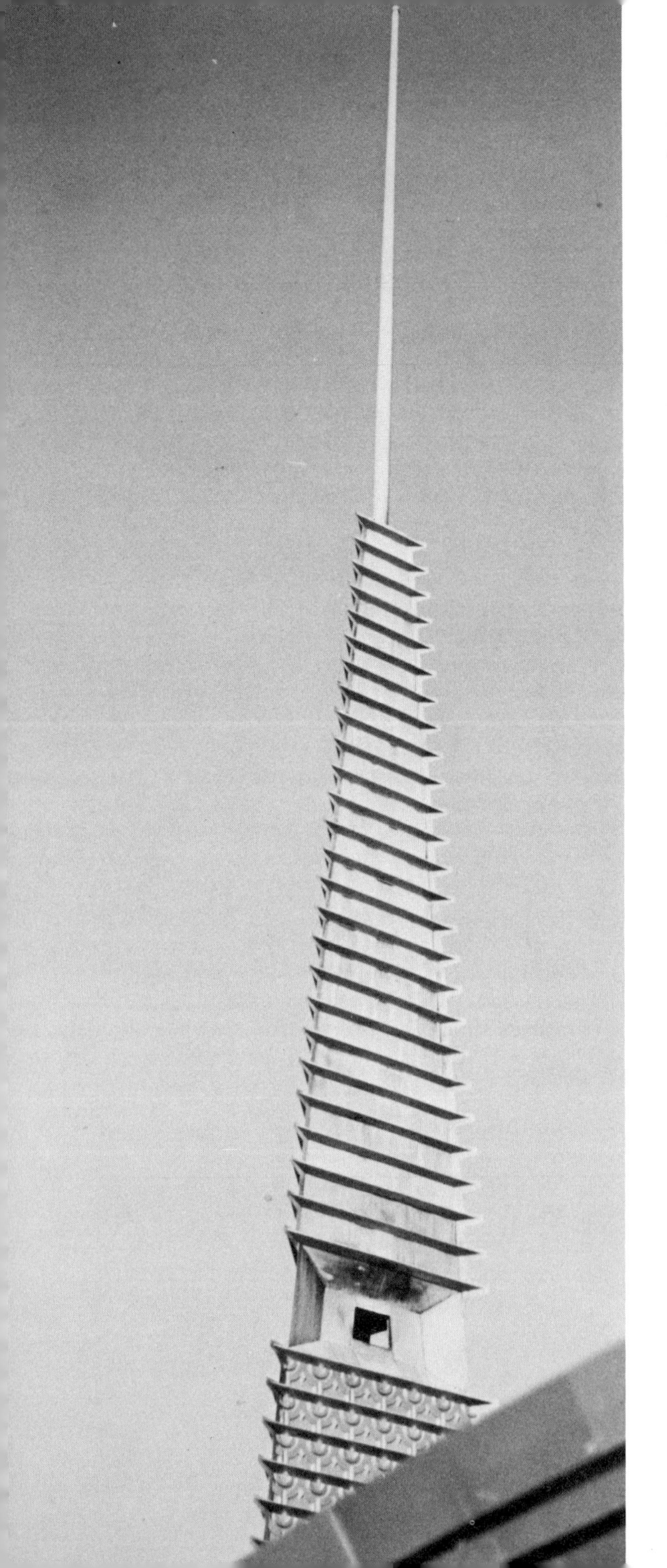

ting jealous of the uncommon man. He says: "Well, what's the punk got we ain't got? He just got the breaks—that's all." Now that is no *true* American sentiment. He is the end of democracy—the end of rule by the bravest and the best. But he votes and so is catered to by the politician until mediocrity, a block to progress, has risen into high places. Look at this McCarthy thing in Wisconsin. You have it just as bad way out here in your state. So I dare say. The mediocre are all coming up but not from the grass roots. No root [do] they come from. It is only the mud—the scum of things. Well, I don't know. So I will get back to where I belong. I am not a politician. I have always distrusted politics and not justly, as I dare say, has this distrust been only a fault of mine because politics must enter into everything; you've been through all this to get me to build these buildings. I guess so.

But what we are talking about now is something even closer to you. Until you see yourselves as individuals, what else does freedom in this country mean? What does our national freedom mean unless it means the sovereignty of the individual? For the individual who signs his sovereignty away under any circumstances I have no respect. Nor have you—really. We all have certain inalienable rights and as individuals they belong especially to us as Americans. But the most important privilege of all is opportunity to live beautifully in a way you like because it is suitable to you. The pursuit of happiness is not enough now—that will do for awhile but happiness consists in what I have just described. I can't bear to see us all sitting around here in our country in ugliness. My God, look at our national ugliness not only out here but look [at] any town in America! Look at these poles, look at the wires, look at the trucks on our highways—and look! Well, there are so many other things discordant. What are we all going to do? The railroads have died or are dying because the freight cars [that]

The great 217-foot pylon at the Marin County Civic Center (1957) is an ornamental concealment of the building's boiler stacks. Photograph by the editor.

have come off the rails now run on our streets. I've lost two members of my own family and a young Italian who came over to get me to do a building for him on the Grand Canal in Venice. He was killed near Pittsburgh by a truck and I know of five others. Why? Because nobody is saying anything. Have you ever heard anybody publicly complain? I haven't. Why don't you? Well, why don't we all? I don't know what is the matter with us. Perhaps too much to eat? Perhaps our mattresses are too soft? Perhaps we do live in too great comfort and all we're asking for is three squares a day and some kind of schooling for Min and Timmy and some fun. We let it go at that, but is it enough to amount to the pursuit of happiness?

LADY FROM THE AUDIENCE: I have been away on vacation. May I inquire what these buildings are that are to be built?

WRIGHT: Well, that is yet to be determined. Dear lady, the number of buildings and what buildings are to be included are probably those buildings that make your life better worth living and make the job of engineering the county, caring for the sick and disabled of the county, and interests of the individuals of the county fresh, convenient, and beautiful entertainment. Now [that's] what those buildings [are] like.

LADY FROM THE AUDIENCE: Is there a recreation center as well as the government buildings?

WRIGHT: Of course there will be a recreation center! Good buildings themselves are all recreation centers, too. Well, we shall see.

GENTLEMAN FROM THE AUDIENCE: Mr. Wright, I would like to ask you about the sovereign rights of the individual and I would like to bring up one point. When you design these buildings, do you intend to furnish them with your own furniture and your own fabrics or is that going to be put out to open bids for other peoples' ideas?

WRIGHT: Well, my buildings are always open to anything I can find which is better. If I can't find

The circular system of signs at the Marin County Civic Center (1957) reflects the circular design elements used throughout the facility. Photograph by the editor.

anything good enough, I'll do it myself. But if I am able to find something good enough I will be happy to use it.

GENTLEMAN FROM THE AUDIENCE: The Supervisors have selected you as the architect for the Civic Center. I believe they have selected the site prior to getting your services. [Let's] say that you do not agree that

An interior view of the Marin County Administration Building (1957) illustrates the central open corridor on the second level. All governmental offices are functionally as well as visually accessible to this corridor. Photograph by the editor.

An interior view of the corridor on the second level of the Marin County Administration Building (1957). Note the translucent skylight above the mall which allows for the penetration of natural light. Photograph by the editor.

the site is the logical spot for this development; what will be the outcome?

WRIGHT: The logical spot for this development, my dear sir, will be the most beautiful one that you have!

GENTLEMAN FROM THE AUDIENCE: This has already been selected.

WRIGHT: I think, from what I hear, that *beautiful* is the word, but I haven't seen your site yet. I am to see it on Friday [August 2, 1957]. It is near water, as it should be, and what the environment is I don't know. But I am sure it is beautiful. All so tell me. What do you think?

GENTLEMAN FROM THE AUDIENCE: Well, if it isn't up to expectations, would you suggest shifting the site?

WRIGHT: If it isn't, we would move [it] if I could have a hand in it. Marin County certainly shouldn't roost upon a spot unworthy of its character, unworthy of its beauty.

GENTLEMAN FROM THE AUDIENCE: Mr. Wright, how many millions of dollars will this cost?

WRIGHT: Who knows? That is always a more or less, ruinous question.

GENTLEMAN FROM THE AUDIENCE: I just made a comment. I thought that you might just bring some of those people from East India or the Near East with all the oil wells. Are you going to get them?

WRIGHT: This young man is afraid Marin County, because of no oil, is going to be sunk! Is Marin County afraid that it's going to be pushed over its head? It need have no such fear.

GENTLEMAN FROM THE AUDIENCE: Mr. Wright, really, sincerely, with this spiraling cost of our economy, there must be some specific goal. In other words, is it going to cost two million, or one million, five million, fifty million? How will you be able to handle the spiraling cost of our economy?

WRIGHT: My dear boy, we shall have to cut our cloth—I mean our suit according to our cloth, and

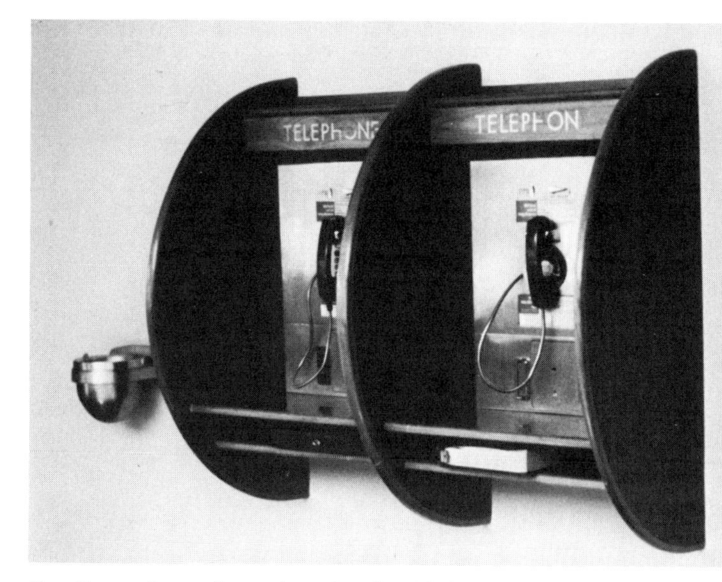

Questioner: ". . . do you intend to furnish the building with your own furniture . . . ?" Wright: ". . . my buildings are always open to anything I can find that is better. If I can't find anything good enough, I'll do it myself." Circular telephone booths at the Marin County Civic Center (1957), Marin County, California. Photograph by the editor.

what Marin County feels that it can afford is the perimeter of our endeavor; this and all together with what building intelligence we do have. No good architect sells buildings. He doesn't sell projects. He sells his services to help people get what they want in the best possible way. Now that is what I am going to do for Marin County. I'm going to find out what Marin County wants and, itself, feels it can afford. Then, within that I am going to try and give Marin County all that the economic laws allow. All we can get, but how much, specifically, who knows? We'll see. Those things are all as per trial, per cut, fit, and try. No man is enough of a scalawag—even if he is an architect—to tell any man that his house is going to cost him just so much money. Especially if it is an unusual house that has never been seen by man before. Also, if the man for whom he builds doesn't himself specifically know what he wants. I have never had much trouble in that respect, although houses often cost

The circular interior sign system used in the Marin County Civic Center (1957) reflects the circular elements adapted by Frank Lloyd Wright throughout the facility. These elements can also be seen in the design of the ashtray (center), *the bulletin board* (left), *and the indirect lighting luminaires that illuminate the interior wall surface* (upper right). *Photograph by the editor.*

a lot more than the people wanted to pay for them but they have usually been responsible for that themselves. They want a lot more than they can afford at the time, and when they see how easy it is to get it now for their future they will have their architect get it for them now. None of them I know have turned and blamed me. Now maybe Marin County will. I don't know.

GENTLEMAN FROM THE AUDIENCE: I would like to answer that question a little more specifically. A space study which has been made was before the County Board of Supervisors, who set aside, as a rough preliminary estimate, a total sum for the construction of the Civic Center of approximately five and a half million dollars. This was the original budget for a long-term program.

WRIGHT: That does not include the site . . .

GENTLEMAN FROM THE AUDIENCE: I believe that does not include the site.

WRIGHT: . . . because we shall want lots of site!

GENTLEMAN FROM THE AUDIENCE: I believe that I might ask a question that some of you might ask if it crossed your mind. We all know that Mr. Wright is not going to build a building with stark columns. On the other hand, I think perhaps we all might be concerned with what his feelings are about monumentality, about the scale of a group of public buildings, about whether they will be on pedestals or whether they will be a place for people to wander in and out with their children. What kind of buildings?

WRIGHT: Now you must know the answer to that? But why don't I just tell you that one of the manifestations of *organic* architecture is simplicity because it is of the quality of life itself. It is for your own life and will look that way. The buildings will feel to you that way. Could you see the letters written to me—someday we will publish many of them—you would get from them the feeling that the environment we made for them has changed life for the better for all those people [and] how the children

Aerial view of the Marin County Post Office (1957), Marin County, California. This is the only post office constructed from a Frank Lloyd Wright design. Photograph by the editor.

A ground-level view of the Marin County Post Office (1957). As in the Marin County Civic Center, circular patterns formed the basis for the overall design. Photograph by the editor.

seem to have taken an interest in these good things they never even thought of before. So it is. An *organic* building is a tremendously important basis of our future culture. You can't have a culture without this kind of building. You can't live life beautifully without living in a beautiful environment, and *organic* building is basic to environment. We can't live up to the top of our *spiritual* stature without such beautiful environment. Why do you all love Marin County? It is beautiful. Why are you here? Because here it is beautiful. Why are you going to have the Civic Center the way you want it? You fought to have it [as a] superior environment. Why? Because you love beauty. And the understanding of it finally is that it is the ultimate payoff, so-called, and is so, no matter how much you may value other things. Beauty is the moving cause of nearly every issue worth the civilization we have. And don't you know that a civilization without culture—such as ours—is like a man without a soul? Our civilization is only a civilization and fit to die, and die soon, unless it achieves for itself a culture—a soul—of its own! Culture consists of the expression by the human *spirit* of the love of beauty. Well, this sounds too much like a sermon.

SCHUBART: Now that you have met Mr. Wright I would like you to meet a man who is going to do a lot of hard work, that is Mr. Aaron Green, who is Mr. Wright's representative in San Francisco and will be working with us on the Civic Center. Mr. Aaron Green. I would also like to ask Mr. Walter Castro, Chairman of the Board of Supervisors, to make a short announcement to you.

WALTER CASTRO: Mr. Wright, ladies and gentlemen, on behalf of [the] Marin County Board of Supervisors I want to thank you all for the fine attendance tonight to meet Mr. Wright.

Frank Lloyd Wright and Robert Richman, Director of the Institute of Contemporary Art at the door of the White House in Washington, D.C., on May 26, 1949, on a visit to President Harry S. Truman. Photograph by Harris and Ewing, courtesy of the Library of Congress.

30 A National Cultural Center

. . . I believe that government has no affair with culture. I think it should stay out of culture unless it can enable it. Any enabling act on the part of government toward the growth of a culture would be a welcome act on the part of government but any interference with it should be resented.

Introduction

On Wednesday, September 24, 1958, Frank Lloyd Wright, accompanied by Mrs. Wright, left Taliesin, near Spring Green, Wisconsin, to embark on a ten-day trip to view progress at the Guggenheim Museum, under construction in New York City, to speak at a dinner on Thursday, October 2nd, given by the Bethesda-Chevy Chase Chamber of Commerce at Chevy Chase, to speak at the Institute of Contemporary Art in Washington on Friday, October 3rd, and to lecture at the University of Virginia, Charlottesville, on Saturday, October 4th. This chapter presents Mr. Wright's complete talk on October 3 on the subject of the proposed National Cultural Center.

On his arrival at the airport in Washington on October 2nd it was reported

The text of this heretofore unpublished talk with Frank Lloyd Wright is reproduced in its entirety from the National Educational Television Film Service *Platform* series and the motion picture film titled *A National Cultural Center* by permission of WNET/Thirteen television of New York.

that Mr. Wright had "voiced his contempt for the architecture in the nation's capital. 'I am going to stay away from the Capitol,' he said, 'I have seen it.' Wright refused to be hurried by the welcoming committee and insisted on shaking hands and talking with his baggageman."[1]

A short time later Mrs. Wright reflected:

> *We arrived in the Washington Airport to the welcome of sunshine, reporters, photographers and Robert Richman, the founder of the Institute of Contemporary Art. He and his wife worked for the development of culture in Washington for 12 years.*
>
> *"This town cared for nothing but politics a few years back," Mrs. Richman said, "and now people are beginning to be interested in art, poetry, literature, music, dance and the theater. We gradually gained wide membership [in the Institute of Contemporary Art]—beginning with a mere hundred, there are now 2000 members. This enables us to bring to Washington great men—leaders in their chosen field."*[2]

Mrs. Wright further described the circumstances relating to Mr. Wright's October 3rd talk to the Institute of Contemporary Art at George Washington University regarding the proposed National Cultural Center:

> *Through the unceasing efforts of Robert Richman, the founder of the Institute of Contemporary Art, the United States government gave 10 acres of land on the Potomac River, evaluated at 1 1/2 million dollars for the building of the National Cultural Center, part of which will be the Institute of Contemporary Art. The approximate cost of this building will be about 27 million dollars.*
>
> *Mr. Richman asked Mr. Wright to speak on the subject of this proposed building. When we arrived at George Washington University an overflow audience had already gathered in the new auditorium. . . .*
>
> *During the discussion Mr. Wright and Robert Richman were televised on the platform by the Ford Foundation. The questions submitted were from prominent people involved, including engineers and architects.*
>
> *Mr. Richman introduced Mr. Wright as the one man whose opinion regarding the project would be most valuable.*[3]

Later that month Mr. Wright also participated in a two-part, hour-long television program for the WTTW-Chicago Channel 11 series called *Heritage*, which featured an in-depth interview in which he discussed his philosophy of *organic architecture.*[4]

---

[1] "Gets Ovation At Chevy Chase: Wright Lashes at Suburban 'Blight' and Universities," *The Capital Times* (Madison, Wisconsin), Vol. 82, No. 97, October 3, 1958, pp. 1, 4.

[2] Olgivanna Lloyd Wright, "Our House," *The Capital Times* (Madison, Wisconsin), Vol. 82, No. 103, October 10, 1958, p. 3.

[3] Olgivanna Lloyd Wright, "Our House," *The Capital Times* (Madison, Wisconsin), Vol. 82, No. 105, October 13, 1958, p. 3.

[4] For a discussion of this program and its complete text see Patrick J. Meehan (Editor), *The Master Architect: Conversations with Frank Lloyd Wright*, New York: John Wiley and Sons, pp. 75–104.

An interior view of the John F. Kennedy Center for the Performing Arts (1962), Washington, D.C. Edward Durell Stone, Architect. Photograph by the editor.

Mr. Wright's talk before the Institute was released as a motion picture in 1960 (a year after his death) by the National Educational Television (NET) Film Service. This motion picture, titled *A National Cultural Center,* included a filmed introduction to Mr. Wright's talk of October 3rd before the Institute of Contemporary Art by John Noble Richards, then president of the American Institute of Architects (AIA). This chapter also presents the complete transcript of Mr. Richards' introductory statement. The proposed National Cultural Center was subsequently designed by architect Edward Durell Stone and later constructed and renamed the John F. Kennedy Center for the Performing Arts.

In Mr. Wright's presentation before the Institute he talked a great deal on the design of theaters, opera houses, and symphony orchestra halls—an area of study in which he had considerable knowledge and experience from his past architectural projects. During his lengthy architectural career he designed at least thirty-four facilities for the performing arts, of which twelve were constructed.

The built projects of this type are the Midway Gardens Orchestra Shell and Stage at Chicago, Illinois (1913), the Imperial Hotel Theater in Tokyo, (1915); the Arizona Biltmore Hotel Auditorium at Phoenix (1927); the Hillside Home School Theater/Playhouse at the Taliesin Fellowship Complex, Spring Green, Wisconsin (1933), the Annie Merner Pfeiffer Chapel (used sometimes as a recital hall and for musical performances) at Florida Southern College, Lakeland (1938), the Ordway Industrial Arts Building Circle Theater also at Florida Southern College (1942 and 1950), the Taliesin West Cabaret Theater at Scottsdale, Arizona (1949), the Hillside Home School Theater/Playhouse Reconstruction, Spring Green, Wisconsin (1952), the Dallas Theater Center (sometimes known as the

Kalita Humphreys Theatre), Dallas, Texas (1955), the Solomon R. Guggenheim Museum Auditorium in New York City (1956), and the Grady Gammage Memorial Auditorium for Arizona State University at Tempe (1959).

Twenty-two unbuilt project designs were made including designs for a motion picture theater at Los Angeles(?) (1897–1900), the Aline Barnsdall Residence and Theater Project, also at Los Angeles (1917–1920), a movie theater project in Tokyo (1918), a cinema and shops in collaboration with Mr. Wright's son John Lloyd Wright at Michigan City, Indiana (1932), the "New Theater" Project for Broadacre City (1932), two designs for the Madison Civic Center/Monona Terrace Project at Madison, Wisconsin (1938 and 1955), the Crystal Heights Hotel, Theater, and Shops Project in Washington, D.C. (1940), the Arch Obler Residence (with small motion picture theater) at Malibu, California (1941–1956), the Music Building Complex with Symphony Hall and Stage Project at Florida Southern College, Lakeland (1944 and 1958), two designs for the Point Park Community Center Project at Pittsburgh (1947 and 1948), the Huntington Hartford Theatre Square Project in collaboration with Lloyd Wright in Hollywood, California (1949), the Huntington Hartford Vine Street Theatre Project (also in collaboration with Lloyd Wright) in Hollywood (1951), the Huntington Hartford Fine Arts Galleries, Outdoor Theater and Sculpture Gardens Project (again in collaboration with Lloyd Wright) in Hollywood (1953), the Marin County Amphitheatre Project for the Marin County Civic Center at San Rafael, California (1957), the Baghdad Opera House and Gardens Project at Baghdad, Iraq (1957), the Spring Green Auditorium Project at Spring Green, Wisconsin (1958), and two designs for the Michael Todd Universal Theater Project in Los Angeles (1958).

AIA Introductory Statement

ANNOUNCER: Appearing on *Platform* today is Frank Lloyd Wright who will speak of his convictions on a National Cultural Center.

JOHN NOBLE RICHARDS: I am John Noble Richards, an architect and president of the American Institute of Architects (AIA). On April 8, 1959, our profession and the world lost one of the *truly* great thinkers and creative designers of our age. Our organization honored itself in 1949 by adding to his many citations our highest award for architectural achievement—the Gold Medal of the American Institute of Architects [see Chapter 16]. Frank Lloyd Wright was and may remain controversial in the best and most stimulating sense. His ideas and his buildings are a challenge flung into the face of our time to arouse us and move us forward. You will witness some of his characteristic provocative candor in this interview, one of his last public appearances. The subject of this interview is the proposed new cultural center for Washington, D.C. We need this center, a proper setting for the presentation of music, opera, and other performing arts not only for the capital city itself but as a symbol of our national concern for culture and the arts. Frank Lloyd Wright also felt this need. He came to Washington to speak on the center, although in frail health he visited the site—a piece of land on the Potomac now [1960] partly occupied by an old brewery. The government will donate the land if enough money can be raised for the buildings. Mr. Wright studied the street plans drawn up by the Capital Parks and Planning Commission. In his own words he preferred "honest arrogance to hypocritical humility." He left little doubt as to who he thought should be the architect. In fact, he offered his services free. He once also said: "My best building is my next one"—it was not to be.

We, of the AIA, feel that the architect of this important project should be selected in a national competition. I so testified before Congress. I am sure Frank Lloyd Wright's thoughts will stimulate whoever may be chosen as they do all who love architecture. Here he speaks before a large audience in the Lisner Auditorium [of George Washington University] in answer to questions raised by various citizens and put to him by Robert Richman, Director of the Institute of Contemporary Art.

The Talk

ROBERT RICHMAN: Dr. David Findlay who is Chairman of the Fine Arts Committee asked this question and Commissioner [Robert] McLaughlin—both district commissioners—has asked a corollary question. I thought I'd read them together, Mr. Wright, and have your opinion on that. The first is: "Do you think there is a satisfactory architectural solution in which all of the functions of the cultural center, as I mentioned, can take place under a single building and under one roof? For example, do you envision a large central stage in the middle of a structure that would be adaptable for symphony concerts, operas, ballets, or plays in an auditorium seating, say, 3000, whereupon another section of that stage might be used for a string quartet recital being played simultaneously before 800 in a small chamber theater?" President McLaughlin of the Commissioners has asked: "Do you feel that it's

An interior view of seating and stage from beneath the balcony at the Hillside Home School Theater (1933), near Spring Green, Wisconsin. All furnishings, including the stage curtain, were designed by Frank Lloyd Wright. Photograph courtesy of The Capital Times, *Madison, Wisconsin.*

An interior view of seating and balcony at the Hillside Home School Theater (1933). All interior furnishings were designed by Frank Lloyd Wright. Photograph courtesy of The Capital Times, *Madison, Wisconsin.*

architecturally possible to incorporate in the National Cultural Center project a hall large enough to accommodate conventions of large national societies or organizations, in a sense taking the stage out and using the whole thing?" Well sir, those are two questions to start with.

WRIGHT: Well, ladies and gentlemen, this is a whole lot to render for one admission but . . .

AUDIENCE: (loud laughter)

WRIGHT: . . . let's go on with it. Of course it is! Of course, the single building for a multipurpose building is the modern thing. In Marin County we have substituted one building for thirteen [see Chapter 29] and I think possibly a cultural center would be more effective and certainly more a piece of architecture as one than as a dozen or more subsidiary things. The more we can concentrate, the more we can simplify, the more we can eliminate the unnecessary—that is what I would call *modern.*

Now modern architecture, of course, has a great many misapplications. Anything built today is modern, isn't it? But I'm a representative of that thought in architecture which is *organic* and, of course, the *organic* thing in relation to a civic center for Washington would be as nearly one grand whole as possible.

Now I suppose there will be other questions coming along, but fundamentally the traffic

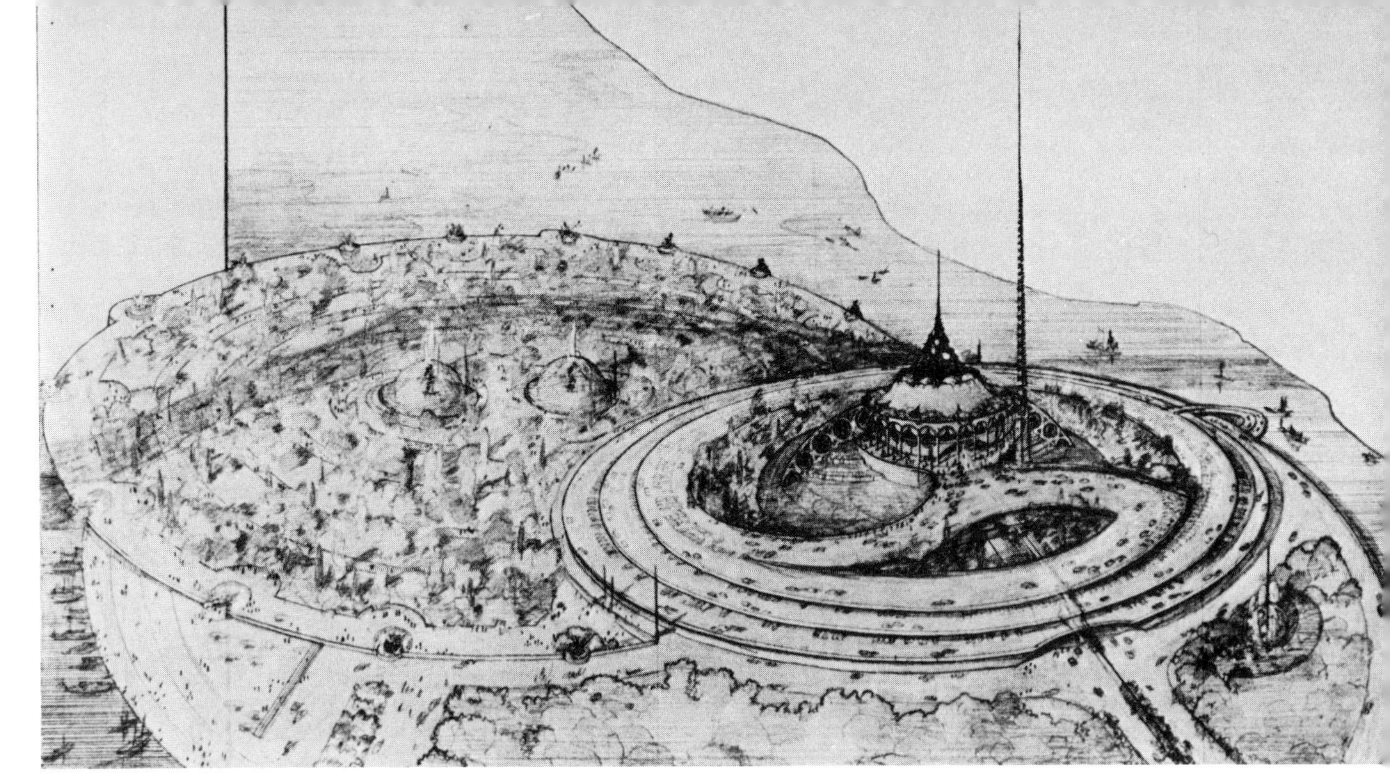

Frank Lloyd Wright's aerial perspective rendering of the Baghdad Opera House and Gardens Project (1957), Baghdad, Iraq, shows the water gardens surrounded by a motorcar ziggurat. The Baghdad Opera House at the center of the ramp is crowned with an ornamental spire. Drawing from the May 1958 issue of Architectural Forum. *Drawing used by permission of Billboard Publications, Inc., 1515 Broadway, New York, New York 10036.*

problem is the problem the architect must meet and solve first. Now in Baghdad there are already 30,000 motorcars. So in solving the Baghdad Cultural Center problem I began with the motorcar first.

Now there's not much use in building a beautiful building and swamping it with a sea of motorcars. Unless the motorcar problem is first of all solved—approached and saved—I see no reason [to] build beautiful, expensive, monumental buildings. So, I think now the building level begins above the parking level and the entire area of this lot, as I've seen it with Robert Richman this afternoon, would seem to be already practically turned over to the car, already possessed by the automobile. The automobile runs the river front. The automobile comes in across and destroys the beautiful little island and altogether the trampling of the herd has practically made of this site a parking lot!

AUDIENCE: (some hesitant laughter)

WRIGHT: So what! Go on with your questions!

AUDIENCE: (laughter)

RICHMAN: That representative, Frank Thompson [sic] of New Jersey, who sponsored the bill in the House [of Representatives], asks a question: "What do you believe are the advantages of the waterfront site, aesthetically, for the National Cultural Center and should that be incorporated into the plan?" As it

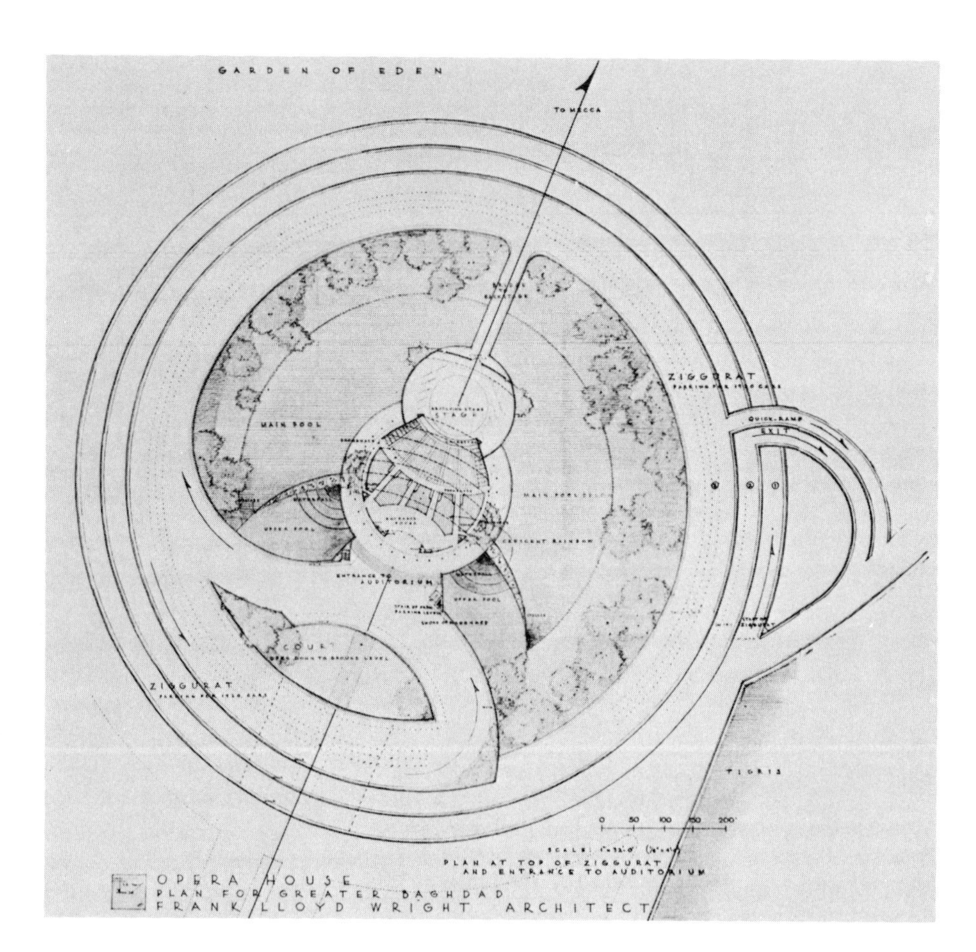

Floor plan and partial site plan of the Baghdad Opera House and Gardens Projects (1957). Drawing from the May 1958 issue of Architectural Forum. *Drawing used by permission of The Frank Lloyd Wright Foundation.*

stands now, you remember, the parkway bounds it on the . . .

WRIGHT: Well, this plan would take the building over to the parkway to the waterfront, which, of course, should be done, because if the building were cut off from the waterfront by a driveway with motor cars on it it would be robbed of the greatest asset the site could give as it now stands. The building should extend to the water and, in some instances perhaps, over the water. Why not! But the concept of a noble building as a complete whole is not very simple and it's not easy. It might really degenerate into one of these . . . just one of those things, you know?

AUDIENCE: (laughter)

RICHMAN: I think that the question that Mr. Nordlinger [sic], Chairman of the Washington Ballet Company, asks—he asks three very good questions which will come later—but this [question] having to do with the large overall plan which would be, say, lifted above the entire site and go to the waterfront, says: "Realizing the financial problem is one of our most important considerations, what type of building . . ."

WRIGHT: Why!

RICHMAN: ". . . could be recommended to give us the utmost facilities for the smallest expenditure and could you sort of do it in part? That is . . ."

WRIGHT: Well, here it is again!

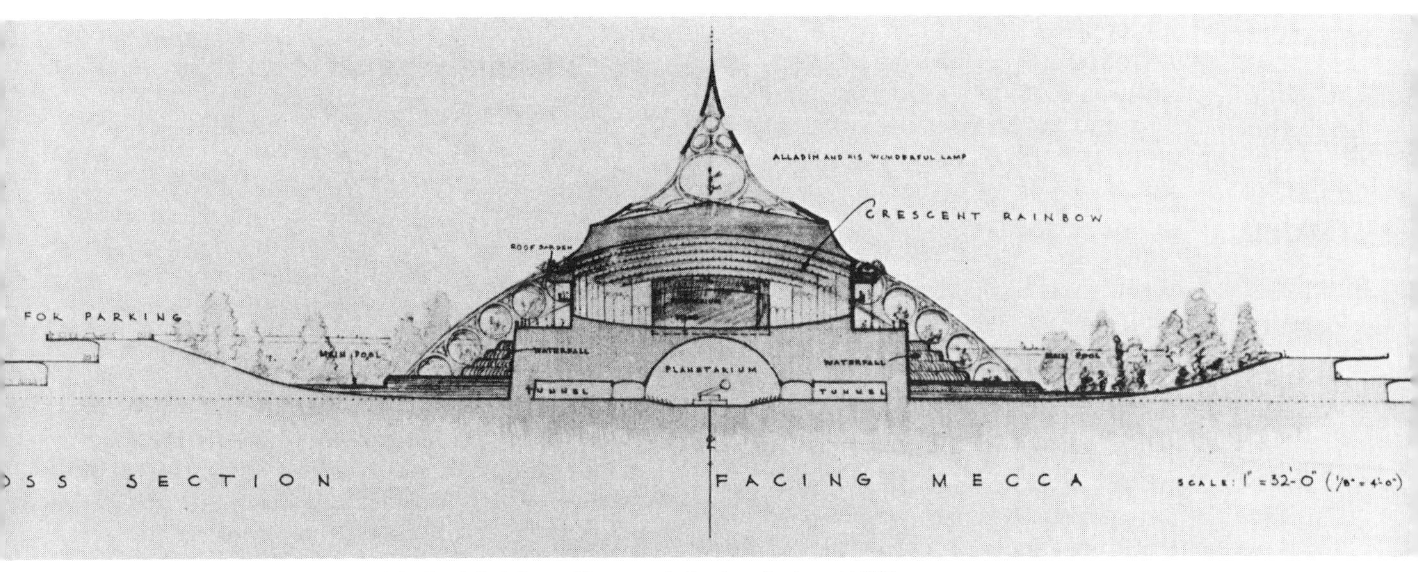

A building cross-section drawing of the Baghdad Opera House and Gardens Projects (1957). Drawing from the May 1958 issue of Architectural Forum. *Drawing used by permission of The Frank Lloyd Wright Foundation.*

RICHMAN: ". . . add some each time?"

WRIGHT: Is this political?

AUDIENCE: (laughter)

WRIGHT: I see no reason if you're going to Washington, the capital of the nation that's going to champion culture at this late date—160 years old . . .

AUDIENCE: (loud laughter and applause)

WRIGHT: . . . it had not ought to be a question of some thrifty businessman's idea of money!

AUDIENCE: (laughter)

WRIGHT: Well now, I don't know the gentleman that proposes the economical basis and I have no intention of slighting him! Because, of course, we know that money talks and I think it doesn't cease talking where culture is concerned but it's got to!

RICHMAN: Well, in this particular case the bill calls for the funds to be raised from private sources and it sets up the . . . Board of Trustees. Representative Thompson [sic] says this:

> *Should President Eisenhower, who has all the appointments to make under the National Cultural Center Act, appoint people like Andrew Mellon who donated the Mellon Gallery and John D. Rockefeller who is head of the Lincoln Square [Lincoln Center] Project in New York City?*

WRIGHT: There you have it!

RICHMAN: The National Cultural Center . . .

AUDIENCE: (laughter)

RICHMAN: . . . clearly does not add up to a federal subsidized center. You see, politically they've taken that stance.

WRIGHT: It adds up to the trend of a nation, however! Toward being a great big corporation—the biggest corporation on earth! And I don't know how you're going to raise a culture in Washington—the center of the political drift and trend—to the basis where you can consider it a platform from which culture would emanate to the world under the Declaration of Independence, according to the sovereignty of the individual. Do you think you could?

RICHMAN: Well, I'm going to ask you my one . . .

WRIGHT: I'm going to ask *you* a question!

RICHMAN AND AUDIENCE: (loud laughter)

RICHMAN: I would like to answer that by asking this back: If this is conceived of in something like the Lincoln Square Center fund raising, which has raised 35 million dollars of their 75 million dollars and all from private sources, how would you square that with your remark to me the day before yesterday that you felt that the government, as a client in a building like this, is a rather dangerous client to deal with?

WRIGHT: Well, I believe that government has no affair with culture. I think it should stay out of culture unless it can enable it. Any enabling act on the part of government toward the growth of a culture would be a welcome act on the part of government but any interference with it should be resented. I don't believe government is capable or ever will be capable now that the day of the aristocrat is over and we have a new type of aristocrat—one from within, outward. I think that the funds should come largely by aids of government and the will of the people who are *truly* interested in the continuation of the civilization of the United States.

RICHMAN: To move now to the general problems of the design of the building and the engineering

The Lincoln Center for the Performing Arts. Shown are the Metropolitan Opera House (center)*, designed by Wallace K. Harrison, architect, the New York State Theater* (left)*, designed by Philip Johnson, architect, and the Avery Fisher [Orchestra Hall] Hall* (right)*, designed by Max Abramovitz, architect. Photograph courtesy of the New York Convention and Visitors Bureau.*

problems involved, we have some rather specific questions there and thought we might touch the engineering first. Dr. Paul Calloway [sic], the Conductor of the Washington Opera Society and the National Cathedral Choirs, has said that we have the following needs:

> *The stage [to be] large enough for all opera and ballet, modern lighting and scene shifting mechanisms which are not built on the models of New York but look to the future, a pit large enough for an orchestra of 100 pieces, a large organ chamber located on or above the stage so that the organ can either be a solo instrument or a part of the orchestra . . .*

WRIGHT: . . .and equipment for stereophonic sound and all the modern ways of reproducing thought, ideas, music, [and] everything else—that's all detail; that's all automatic and goes taken really for granted.

RICHMAN: All right now, in order to—for example, to get something to compare this with and I know that you met this problem in the Dallas Cultural Center [Dallas Theater Center].

Herman Kraowitz [sic] has told Mr. Patrick Hayes [sic], Washington's leading impresario, of the new dimensions for the Lincoln Center. They have asked for 115 feet from the stage to the grid for the new opera house, another fifteen feet clearance to the roof top, the architect at his own option may add twenty-five feet for a maximum height from the street to the top of the building of 140 feet.

WRIGHT: Umm!

RICHMAN: Well, this all seems to be envisioning the vertical use of scenery. How did you meet that problem in the Dallas Cultural Center?

WRIGHT: It's all old stuff!!! I threw it all out to start with twenty-seven years ago!

AUDIENCE: (laughter)

WRIGHT: I came to [the] conclusion that the proscenium was a thing of the past and that to force the performance through a hole in the wall to the audience in one room and the performance in another room was all that was the matter with drama, with stage, with the theater. And, if that were brought about . . . if it were brought about that the audience and the performance were sympathetically related to each other as one and the stage equipped so that transformations of scenery could be effected in an instant [so] that the drama would have new life and that's the Dallas Theater. And I think that if Washington ever built a theater along the old lines it would just serve it right! That's all!

AUDIENCE: (loud laughter)

RICHMAN: What you propose might be fine for, let's say, Greek drama. [It would] be excellent for contemporary drama. What about Mozart opera which itself was conceived behind the proscenium?

WRIGHT: Well now, an opera house is not a theater!

RICHMAN: Well I meant to point out, sir, that we very much want an opera house and I was giving the opera house dimensions of the new Metropolitan [Opera House in New York].

WRIGHT: Well the opera, of course, is pretty well standardized and all the operas have been scenarioed [sic] and those scenes are stored away in stock and an opera house would have to be so devised as to use stock stuff. So the opera house is not in the same plane or in the same case as the theater. A theater would be totally different. The opera house would be more or less standardized and more or less the old, old ritual.

RICHMAN: So that would take the tall [proscenium] . . .

WRIGHT: You'd have that for the scenery now in existence—you'd have to have the tall proscenium but no not as tall as usual because you must remember that the theater was—the height of the theater—the height of the proscenium was determined by the gallery. Now, no theater could make a living without the gallery and up in the gallery

RAMP
DR. RM.
GREEN RM.
DR. RM.
TERRACE
SIDE STAGE
REVOLVING STAGE
SIDE STAGE
FOYER
EL.
STOR.
BALCONY ABOVE
0 10 25 FEET
AUDITORIUM LEVEL

Site plan and floor plan of the auditorium level of the Dallas Theater Center [The Kalita Humphreys Theater] (1955), Dallas, Texas. The building is situated on a rocky one and one-half-acre site on Turtle Creek. Fundamental to the auditorium level plan is the stage "in the round" on which the performers and staging appear to be more like sculpture than like stage painting. A thirty-two-foot revolving stage is used to change scenes and to indicate the passage of time. Drawing from the March 1960 issue of Architectural Forum. *Drawing used by permission of Billboard Publications, Inc., 1515 Broadway, New York, New York 10036.*

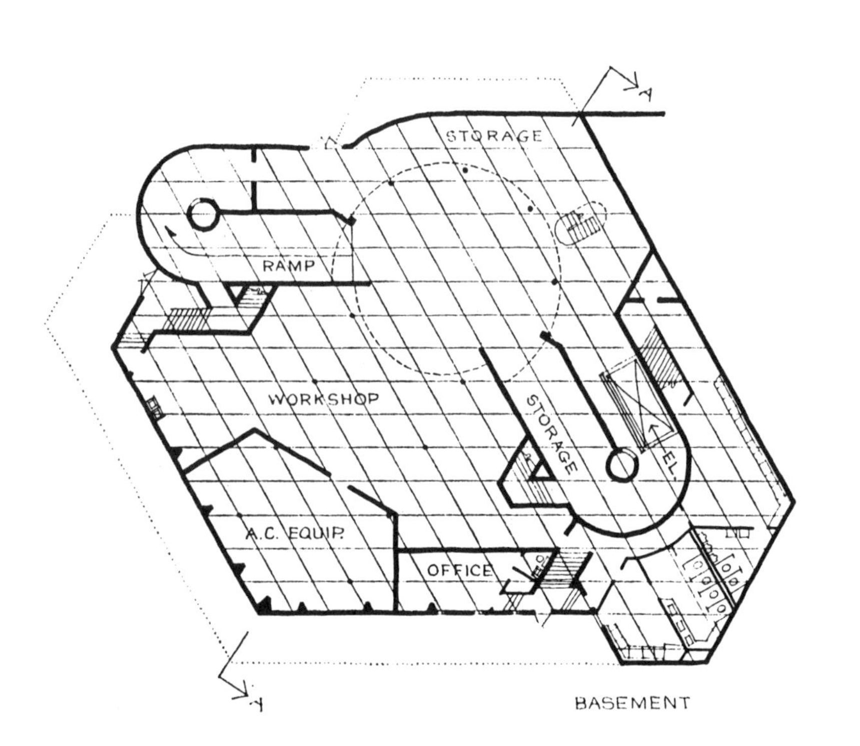

The basement plan of the Dallas Theater Center (1955). Drawing from the March 1960 issue of Architectural Forum. *Drawing used by permission of Billboard Publications, Inc., 1515 Broadway, New York, New York 10036.*

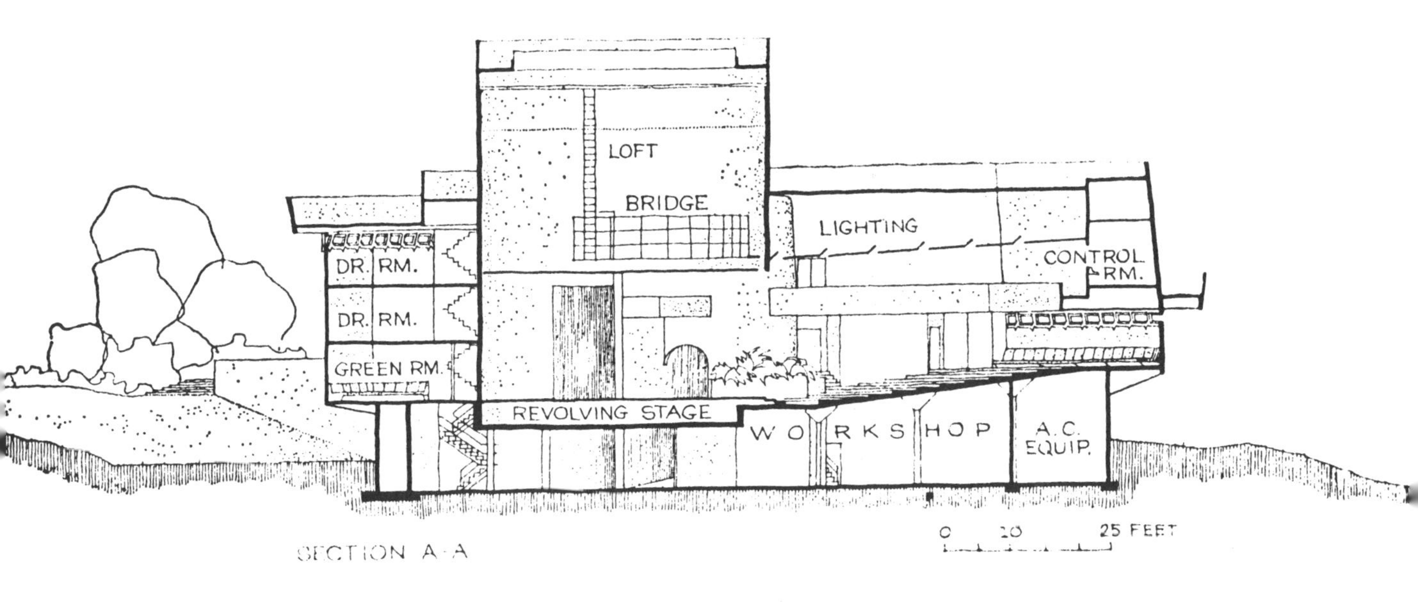

A building section drawing of the Dallas Theater Center (1955). Drawing from the March 1960 issue of Architectural Forum. *Drawing used by permission of Billboard Publications, Inc., 1515 Broadway, New York, New York 10036.*

A daytime exterior view of the 31,188 square-foot Dallas Theater Center (1955), looking toward the building from the approach. Photograph by the editor.

A nocturnal exterior view of the Dallas Theater Center (1955), looking from the drive toward the building. Photograph by the editor.

were the ten-centers and thirty-centers and so on and they were very high up. Now to get a view of the stage the proscenium had to be lifted high. Now a high proscenium is a very bad thing acoustically—nothing could be worse. But it had to be high and the scenery had to be tall and so the old theater and the old theatrical condition made a tall proscenium and a high overhead because when you pull the scenery up it had to be as high as the proscenium above the proscenium in order to get rid of the scenery!

AUDIENCE: (slight laughter)

WRIGHT: Well, there's the origin of the present standardized opera house and theater. The gallery, the upper regions that have to be accommodated on the stage. Now once you eliminate from the audience or the idea of the audience the element of the gallery there's no need for the tallness of the stage. There's no need for the great overhead and the tremendously expansive arrangements for scenery that were occasioned by the tall house.

The Dallas Theater is not going to be tall. The proscenium of the Dallas Theater is sixteen feet high as against, perhaps, sixty or forty or thirty, and there is no overhead except enough for a man to walk around above and shift the scenes such as they are. But the scenery changes. Now scenery becomes sculptural; it's in the open; it's as you are sitting in the audience. It's on the stage complete in itself and the stage revolves and is divided in the center so that the stage turns about and the new scene is right there. So the transportation of scenery—one scene from another—takes about counting ten and you don't have to wait. There are no waits between the scenes.

Well, you have to have in Washington, no doubt, accommodation for all the old standardized operas and you would have to have a standardized opera house but not for the theater meant to be modern—[its] got to be advanced. I see no hope for modernizing opera, do you?

RICHMAN: No sir.

WRIGHT: All right.

RICHMAN: Because, even now, opera is cast into—like new design of automobiles based on four

The main entrance to the Dallas Theater Center (1955). The terrace which overhangs the entrance, has been enclosed since this photograph was taken. Photograph courtesy of The Capital Times, *Madison, Wisconsin.*

wheels—new opera is based on that tradition certainly . . .

WRIGHT: Yah.

RICHMAN: . . . of the proscenium and the scene. That would mean, perhaps, then that we would need three different kinds of stages or auditoria [sic], as I see it now. The theater and symphony concert hall would have to double. An opera house for the opera, classical and modern, ballet, and modern dance and then the small chamber auditorium for poetry reading and chamber music and small chamber theater.

WRIGHT: Or why not the ideal thing for each?

RICHMAN: Under one roof?

WRIGHT: It's limitless, isn't it? Of course under one roof.

RICHMAN: Under one roof. Then that . . .

WRIGHT: All this under one roof and what a roof!!!

RICHMAN AND AUDIENCE: (loud laughter)

WRIGHT: And don't neglect the interior courts also, letting sunlight in behind on the court. An edifice of that description would be, of course, one of the grand things of earth and probably beyond anything ever yet built! Why not?!

RICHMAN: Is acoustical engineering so advanced now that it's possible to have these large halls without sound reproduction?

WRIGHT: Well, somebody asked me that long ago in New York what the difference was between an engineer and an architect and I said it was simple. The difference was that an engineer was a rudimentary undeveloped architect.

AUDIENCE: (loud laughter)

Frank Lloyd Wright presenting his architectural concepts, circa late 1950s. Photographs by C. A. Thompson courtesy of The Capital Times, *Madison, Wisconsin.*

Frank Lloyd Wright presenting his architectural concepts, circa late 1950s. Photographs by C. A. Thompson courtesy of The Capital Times, *Madison, Wisconsin.*

Interior view of the foyer of the Dallas Theater Center [The Kalita Humphreys Theater] (1955), Dallas, Texas, shows two specially detailed doors that open to the lobby, which has a low ceiling of only eight feet. Photograph by the editor.

An interior view of the library of the Dallas Theater Center (1955). Photograph by the editor.

The gently sloping seating of the Dallas Theater Center (1955). The 444-seat house banks back in three angled tiers to a main promenade at the back of the hall. A narrow balcony above, which has one row of seats, doubles as a lighting area. Photograph by the editor.

The stage and seating of the Dallas Theater Center (1955). Unfortunately, after the theater was constructed the revolving stage was covered over. Above the stage is a drumshaped stagehouse–forty feet high and forty feet in diameter. Photograph by the editor.

A view of the construction of the Grady Gammage Memorial Auditorium at Arizona State University (1959), in Tempe. The foreground of the photograph shows the structural and decorative elements of the elevated walkway. Photograph courtesy of Arizona State University, Tempe, Arizona.

An exterior view of the Grady Gammage Memorial Auditorium at Arizona State University (1959). Photograph courtesy of Arizona State University, Tempe, Arizona.

An interior view of the stairway and ramp of the Grady Gammage Memorial Auditorium at Arizona State University (1959). Photograph courtesy of Arizona State University, Tempe, Arizona.

An interior view of the seating area of the Grady Gammage Memorial Auditorium at Arizona State University (1959). The rows of seats slope gently to the stage area [not shown]. Photograph courtesy of Arizona State University, Tempe, Arizona.

The stage of the Grady Gammage Memorial Auditorium at Arizona State University (1959). The screen at the back of the stage forms a circular ornamental backdrop. Photograph courtesy of Arizona State University, Tempe, Arizona.

WRIGHT: And you know, the engineers themselves liked the definition! (slight laughter)

RICHMAN: So you're answering this question by hedging. You propose an acoustical architect to take care of the problem.

WRIGHT: Well, acoustics is not where we've arrived at the point where it is an exact science.

RICHMAN: I see.

WRIGHT: You have to have had some experience in building buildings for sound in order to arrive at a good result. Dankmar Adler, who built the Chicago Auditorium, was called a great sound engineer. He himself knew by experience what he knew and he never had reduced it to a science and it never yet has been done, although they profess to have done so. He never built a bad house acoustically and Carnegie Hall in New York is one; the Auditorium in Chicago was the great demonstration of his power and prowess because even today it is the best room for opera in the world.

RICHMAN: Well that seems to, as most of us knew, dictate the answer to the next question. But for various reasons this does present a considerable problem. For one thing, the Fine Arts Commission has to pass on the plans. For another thing, the National Capital Planning . . .

WRIGHT: Now, now, there would be the problem!!!

AUDIENCE: (loud laughter)

WRIGHT: That would be difficult—I know! Because in a fine arts commission I don't believe there would be a member who didn't know *all* about *everything* connected with the problem!!!

AUDIENCE: (laughter)

RICHMAN: And it's awfully hard to convince all people who are equally well educated about those specific details, certainly.

WRIGHT: Architecture, being the blind spot of the nation—nobody who has been educated, at least, knows what constitutes the virtue of a building. Now how are you going to get judgment? You'll get damnation not judgment!!!

AUDIENCE: (laughter)

RICHMAN: Well, as the Director of the National Capital Planning, Mr. Findlay, asks: "Does this not present a unique opportunity for such a building of unusual characteristics geared to the cultural needs of the people far into the next century?" and I'd like to combine that with a question by Representative Thompson: "Doesn't this mean that the building or buildings can be purely functional and not serve as decorative monuments related to the monuments

A detailed view of the stage of the Grady Gammage Memorial Auditorium at Arizona State University (1959). The leaves (or walls) of the stage shell may be extended or retracted as needed. Photograph courtesy of Arizona State University, Tempe, Arizona.

This backstage view from wall to wall of the Grady Gammage Memorial Auditorium for Arizona State University (1959), Tempe, Arizona, shows the leaves of the stage shell in a retracted position. Photograph courtesy of Arizona State University, Tempe, Arizona.

This backstage view of the Grady Gammage Memorial Auditorium at Arizona State University (1959), shows the leaves of the stage shell extended half-way and the lighting system dropped for maintenance. Photograph courtesy of Arizona State University, Tempe, Arizona.

An exterior view of the Auditorium Building at the northwest corner of Michigan Avenue and Congress Street (1886—1890), Chicago, Adler and Sullivan, Architects. Photograph courtesy of the Illinois Department of Conservation.

and government buildings now existing in Washington?"

WRIGHT: I don't blame the senators for being suspicious.

AUDIENCE: (laughter)

WRIGHT: I think that it would probably inevitably result in a fantastic phantasmagoria of this, that, and the other. But, if it were really *organic* in character and designed as a whole by the study of *nature* and according to its *nature* by someone who had studied *nature* to learn about architecture, it could have no such disastrous result! The study of *nature* has saved—is going to save—architecture; it would save politics; it has saved nearly everything human *nature* has committed itself to and it would save this project. Is that (slight laughter) a satisfactory answer?

AUDIENCE: (slight laughter)

RICHMAN: Very decidedly. I should think that just a specific question might nail that down. Is it architecturally possible to relate this building, for example, to the architecture of the Lincoln Memorial which will be . . . ?

WRIGHT: It is not! The Lincoln Memorial is related to the toga and the civilization that wore it!!!

AUDIENCE: (slight laughter)

WRIGHT: And I think it would be absurd to try and maintain the weakness and follies of the old lack of

An interior view of the theater in the Auditorium Building (1886—1890) in Chicago, Adler and Sullivan, architects. Photograph courtesy of the Illinois Department of Conservation.

Wright: "The Lincoln Memorial is related to the toga and the civilization that wore it! . . . the Lincoln Memorial is not *an indication of culture. It's an indication of the lack of it." The Lincoln Memorial, designed by Henry Bacon, was completed in Washington, D.C., in 1917. Photograph by the editor.*

culture! Now, the Lincoln Memorial is *not* an indication of culture. It's an indication of the lack of it. The old Capitol is not an indication of culture, although I'm in favor of preserving these old mistakes—these old evidences of the *old* life in order that the *new* life may shine the brighter . . .

AUDIENCE: (laughter)

RICHMAN: Yes sir.

WRIGHT: . . . and so forth. You know the story!

AUDIENCE: (loud laughter and applause)

WRIGHT: The question is, I imagine, if a man has made a mistake once, should he keep on making it?

AUDIENCE: (slight laughter)

RICHMAN: That's *true.* I'm sure that you envisioned just in the two times—three times—that you've seen the site—I'm sure you have seen some sort of vision of what that large multiple-unit building under one roof would be. Do you . . .

WRIGHT: Could be!

RICHMAN: Do you want to project that vision? Should I ask that question after I've asked whether you think that the selection of an architect, for example, or architects for it . . .

WRIGHT: Now that's a very touchy question. You want to know . . .

RICHMAN AND AUDIENCE: (loud laughter)

WRIGHT: . . . You want to know if I'd contribute an idea of what I'm talking about on paper! And I would! Because my one real aim is not only to get better architects for America but to leave behind me some better architecture! And I believe I might suggest something that would amount to that and would never be paid for it in this world—I would have to *give* it!!!

RICHMAN: Do I under . . .

AUDIENCE: (very loud applause)

WRIGHT: Democracy has yet to demonstrate it *can* serve the beauty of life and serve the culture of the nation by backing something genuinely noble, *true,* and beautiful! And it hasn't done it yet!!! [Mr. Wright rises from the table at which he was seated and walks toward the exit, waving and smiling at the audience as he leaves the stage.]

AUDIENCE: (very loud applause)

Epilogue

. . . *life is only worth living if you can make it more beautiful than it was when you found it. That is* true. . . .

. . . *It is what a man does that he has.*

Bibliography

"Architect Models New Type of City," *New York Times*, March 27, 1935, p. 16.

"Art and the Machine," *Chicago Daily Tribune*, March 4, 1901, p. 6.

Art Institute of Chicago. *Catalogue of the Seventh Annual Exhibition of the Chicago Architectural Sketch Club.* Chicago: Art Institute of Chicago, May 1894.

"Arts in Industry Glorified in Show," *New York Times*, April 16, 1935, section 1, p. 23.

"At Parade of Homes: Wright House Draws Big Crowds at Show," *The Capital Times* (Madison, Wis.), June 22, 1959.

Barney, Maginel Wright. *The Valley of the God-Almighty Joneses.* New York: Appleton-Century, 1965.

"Cincinnati Convention Charts Course for '32," *National Real Estate Journal*, July 1932, p. 17.

Daughters of the American Revolution (Ill.). *The New Industrialism.* Part III. Chicago: National League of Industrial Art, 1902.

Davis, Patricia Talbot. *Together They Built a Mountain.* Lititz, Pa.: Sutter House, 1974.

"Fighting the Box," *The New Yorker*, July 5, 1952, pp. 16–17.

Fishman, Robert. *Urban Utopias in the Twentieth Century: Ebenezer Howard, Frank Lloyd Wright, and Le Corbusier.* Cambridge, Mass.: MIT Press, 1977.

"FLLW Designed This Big 'One Space' Prefab," *House and Home*, August 1959, pp. 176–77.

"FLLW's Dallas Theater," *Architectural Forum*, March 1960, pp. 130–35.

"Florida Southern College Revisited for Glimpses of the Administration Group in Wright's Organic Campus," *Architectural Forum*, September 1952, p. 125.

"Frank Lloyd Wright Designs for Baghdad," *Architectural Forum*, May 1958, pp. 89–101 and cover.

"Frank Lloyd Wright Lecture," *Michigan Society of Architects Monthly Bulletin*, May 1954, p. 17.

"Frank Lloyd Wright On Hospital Design: A Modern Hospital Interview With the World-Famous Architect," *Modern Hospital*, September 1948, pp. 51–54.

"Gets Ovation At Chevy Chase: Wright Lashes at Suburban 'Blight' and Universities," *The Capital Times* (Madison, Wis.), October 3, 1958, p. 1.

"The Good Building Is One That Makes the Landscape More Beautiful Than It Was Before," *Architectural Forum*, November 1962, pp. 122–29.

Green, Aaron G. *An Architecture for Democracy: The Marin County Civic Center.* San Francisco: Grendon Publishing, 1990.

Gutheim, Frederick, ed. *Frank Lloyd Wright On Architecture: Selected Writings, 1894–1940.* New York: Duell, Sloan, and Pearce, 1941.

Hanks, David A. "Frank Lloyd Wright's 'The Art and Craft of the Machine,'" *The Frank Lloyd Wright Newsletter* 2, no. 3, second quarter 1979, pp. 6–9.

———. *The Decorative Designs of Frank Lloyd Wright.* New York: E. P. Dutton, 1979.

Hanna, Paul R., and Jean S. Hanna. *Frank Lloyd Wright's Hanna House: The Clients' Report.* New York and Cambridge: Architectural History Foundation and MIT Press, 1981.

"Here Is Prefabrication's Biggest News for 1957," *House and Home*, December 1956, pp. 117–21 and cover.

Hitchcock, Henry-Russell. *In the Nature of Materials: 1887–1941, the Buildings of Frank Lloyd Wright.* New York: Duell, Sloan and Pearce, 1942.

"Hospitals Taken To Task—Frank Lloyd Wright Declares Most Are Monstrosities," *New York Times*, April 28, 1953, p. 30.

Jordan, Robert Furneaux. "A Great Architect's Visit to Britain: Robert Furneaux Jordan on Frank Lloyd Wright," *The Listener* (London), September 28, 1950, pp. A15–A16.

———. "Lloyd Wright in Britain: Mr. R. Furneaux Jordan's Radio Talk," *Builder: An Illustrated Weekly Magazine for the Architect* (England), November 24, 1950, p. 540.

Kaufmann, Edgar J., Jr., and Ben Raeburn, eds. *Frank Lloyd Wright: Writings and Buildings.* New York: Horizon Press, 1960.

McArthur, Shirley DuFresne. *Frank Lloyd Wright American System-Built Homes in Milwaukee.* Milwaukee, Wis.: Northpoint Historical Society, 1985.

Meehan, Patrick J., ed. *Frank Lloyd Wright Remembered.* Washington, D.C.: Preservation Press, 1991.

———. *The Master Architect: Conversations with Frank Lloyd Wright.* New York: John Wiley & Sons, 1984.

"Mid-'50s Frank Lloyd Wright Prefab House To Be Relocated," *Architecture: The AIA Journal*, March 1985, p. 32.

National Educational Television Film Service. *Platform: A National Cultural Center* (film). New York: WNET/Thirteen, 1958

O'Gara, Francis B. "Red Charge Stirs Wright to a Boil," *San Francisco Examiner*, August 3, 1957, p. 3.

Orr, Douglas William. "Citation with the Gold Medal to Frank Lloyd Wright," *AIA Journal*, April 1949, p. 163.

Porter, Franklin, and Mary Porter, eds. *Heritage: The Lloyd Jones Family.* Spring Green, Wis.: Unity Chapel, 1986.

"Presentation of the Frank P. Brown Medal," *Journal of The Franklin Institute*, September 1954, pp. 217–18.

Radford, Evelyn Morris. *The Genius and the County Building: How Frank Lloyd Wright Came to Marin County, California and Glorified San Rafael.* Unpublished dissertation submitted to the Graduate Division of the University of Hawaii in partial fulfillment of the requirements for the degree of Doctor of Philosophy in American Studies, August 1972.

Raymond, Antonin. *An Autobiography.* Rutland, Vt.: Charles E. Tuttle Company, 1973.

"Ready for Parade of Homes Here: New Wright Prefab Home To Be Marketed in Spring," *The Capital Times* (Madison, Wis.), February 9, 1959.

Richards Company. *The American System-Built Houses, Designed by Frank Lloyd Wright.* Milwaukee, Wis.: Richards Company, 1916.

Robinson, Sidney K. *Life Imitates Architecture: Taliesin and Alden Dow's Studio.* Ann Arbor, Mich.: Architectural Research Laboratory, University of Michigan, 1980.

Robinson, Sidney K. *The Architecture of Alden B. Dow.* Detroit: Wayne State University Press, 1983.

"Second Annual Convention of the Architectural League of America," *The American Architect and Building News*, June 16, 1900, p. 87.

"Second Annual Convention of the Architectural League of America, held at Chicago, June 7–9," *The Brickbuilder*, June 1900, pp. 112–15.

Sergeant, John. *Frank Lloyd Wright's Usonian Houses: The Case for Organic Architecture.* New York: Whitney Library of Design, 1976.

Spencer, Brian A. *The Prairie School Tradition.* New York: Whitney Library of Design, 1979.

Sorensen, Sterling. "Receipt of Architects' Award Is Highlight in Wright's Stormy Career," *The Capital Times* (Madison, Wis.), March 10, 1949, p. 5.

Sprague, Paul E. "The Marshall Erdman Prefabricated Buildings." In *Frank Lloyd Wright and Madison: Eight Decades of Artistic and Social Interaction*, edited by Paul E. Sprague. Madison, Wis.: Elvehjem Museum of Art, University of Wisconsin-Madison, 1990.

Storrer, William Allin. *The Architecture of Frank Lloyd Wright: A Complete Catalogue*, 2nd ed. Cambridge, Mass.: MIT Press, 1979.

Tafel, Edgar. *Apprentice to Genius: Years with Frank Lloyd Wright.* New York: McGraw-Hill, 1979.

Twombly, Robert C. *Frank Lloyd Wright: An Interpretive Biography.* New York: Harper & Row, 1973.

———. *Frank Lloyd Wright: His Life and His Architecture.* New York: John Wiley & Sons, 1979.

Wright, Frank Lloyd. "AA 125 Echoes from the Past: Frank Lloyd Wright—The Annual Distribution of Prizes—1950," *Architectural Association Quarterly*, January/March 1973, pp. 46–47.

———. "AA: Frank Lloyd Wright," *The Architect's Journal* (England), July 27, 1950, pp. 86–87.

———. "Acceptance," *Proceedings of the American Academy of Arts and Letters and the National Institute of Arts and Letters*, second series, no. 4, 1954, pp. 16–17.

———. "Acceptance Speech of Frank Lloyd Wright Upon Receiving the Gold Medal for 1948," *AIA Journal*, May 1949 pp. 199–207.

———. "Address at the Meeting of the Student Chapter Members, the American Institute of Architects." In *Architecture in America: A Battle of Styles*, edited by William A. Coles and Henry Hope Reed, Jr. New York: Appleton-Century-Crofts, 1961.

———. *An Address by Frank Lloyd Wright: In Connection With Founders Week.* Lakeland, Fla.: Florida Southern College, 1950.

———. "An Adventure in the Human Spirit," *Motive*, November 1950, pp. 30–31.

———. "American Architecture," *Journal of The Franklin Institute*, September 1954, pp. 219–24.

———. "The American System of House Building," *The Western Architect*, September 1916, pp. 121–23.

———. "America's Foremost Architect Speaks On Prefabrication and the Role of Creative Man in the Machine Age: 'Quality and Quantity Must Be Partners, Science and Art Must Live Together'—Frank Lloyd Wright," *House and Home*, April 1958, pp. 120–22.

———. "Annual Prize-Giving: Presentations by Mr. Frank Lloyd Wright," *The Architectural Association Journal* (London), August/September 1950, pp. 32–37.

———. "The Architect," *The Brickbuilder*, June 1900, pp. 124–28.
———. "The Art and Craft of the Machine." In *Catalogue of the Fourteenth Annual Exhibition of the Chicago Architectural Club. Chicago: Architectural Club*, Art Institute of Chicago, 1901.
———. *The Arts and Industry in a Controlled Economy.* Chicago: Henry George School of Social Science, October 1951.
———. "At Taliesin," *The Capital Times* (Madison, Wis.), February 26, 1937, p. 9.
———. *Ausgeführte Bauten und Entwürfe von Frank Lloyd Wright.* Berlin: Ernst Wasmuth, 1910.
———. *An Autobiography.* New York: Horizon Press, 1977.
———. "Building a Democracy," *A Taliesin Square-Paper*, no. 10, October 29, 1946, pp. 1–4.
———. "Building A Democracy," *Albright Art Gallery, Gallery Notes* (Buffalo Fine Arts Gallery, Buffalo, N.Y.), June 1947, pp. 14–18.
———. "By Frank Lloyd Wright." *Michigan Society of Architects Monthly Bulletin*, June 1954, p. 9.
———. "Dinner to Mr. and Mrs. Frank Lloyd Wright," *The Architectural Association Journal* (London), August/September 1950, pp. 44–46.
———. "Education and Art in Behalf of Life," *Arts in Society*, June 1958, pp. 5–10.
———. "Ethics of Ornament," *The Prairie School Review* 4, no. 1, first quarter 1967, pp. 16–17.
———. "Frank Lloyd Wright," *Architectural Forum*, January 1948.
———. "Frank Lloyd Wright Addresses the Students of the Architectural Association," *Architectural Design*, August 1950, p. 219.
———. *Frank Lloyd Wright: Ausgeführte Bauten.* Berlin: Verlegt bei Ernst Wasmuth A.G., 1911.
———. *Frank Lloyd Wright On Architecture: Selected Writings (1894-1940).* Chicago: Duell, Sloan, and Pearce, 1941.
———. "Frank Lloyd Wright On the Right To Be One's Self," *Marg* (Bombay, India), January 1947, p. 20.
———. "Frank Lloyd Wright Speaks On Hardware," *Weekly Bulletin, Michigan Society of Architects*, August 16, 1949, pp. 1–3.
———. "Frank Lloyd Wright Townhall Lecture, Ford Auditorium, Detroit, October 21, 1957," *Michigan Society of Architects Monthly Bulletin*, December 1957, p. 23.
———. "The House of the Future," *National Real Estate Journal*, July 1932, pp. 25–26.
———. "The House of the Future," *National Real Estate and Building Journal*, October 1957, p. 43.
———. "I Don't Like Hardware," *Hardware Consultant and Contractor*, May 1949, p. 22.
———. "Let Us Go Now and Mimic No More: An Address by Frank Lloyd Wright at Princeton University," *The Capital Times* (Madison, Wis.), August 17, 1947, p. 1.
———. *The Living City.* New York: Horizon Press, 1958.
———. "Mimic No More," *A Taliesin Square-Paper: A Nonpolitical Voice from Our Democratic Minority*, no. 11, March 6, 1947.
———. "Mr. Frank Lloyd Wright at the AA," *The Architectural Association Journal* (London), May 1939, pp. 268–69.
———. "Mr. Wright Talks On Broadacre City To Ludwig Mies van der Rohe," *Taliesin I*, no. 1, October 1940, pp. 10–18.
———. *The Natural House.* New York: Horizon Press, 1954.
———. "A New Freedom for Living in America," *Taliesin I*, no. 1, October 1940, pp. 35–37.
———. "On Organic Architecture," *Michigan Society of Architects Weekly Bulletin*, April 10, 1945, pp. 8–9.
———. *An Organic Architecture: The Architecture of Democracy.* London: Lund Humphries and Co., 1939, 1941, 1970.
———. "On Ornamentation: Frank Lloyd Wright Pleads for New Culture Before Nineteenth Century Club—Other Events," *Oak Leaves* (Oak Park, Ill.), January 16, 1909, p. 20.
———. "Planning Man's Physical Environment," *Berkeley—A Journal of Modern Culture*, no. 1, 1947, p. 5.
———. "Progress in Architectural Education," *Line Magazine* 2, no. 1, 1953, unpaginated (6 pages).
———. "Quality, Not Quantity, Seen as Big Need by Mr. Wright," *The Southern* (Florida Southern College), November 23, 1951, p. 2.
———. "The Right To Be One's Self," *Husk* (Mount Vernon, Iowa), December 1946, pp. 37–40.
———. Speech, *Proceedings of the Southern Conference on Hospital Planning, Hotel Buena Vista, Biloxi, Mississippi.* Montgomery, Ala., February 22, 1950, pp. 105–14.
———. "The Speech of Acceptance," *A Taliesin Square-Paper: A Nonpolitical Voice from Our Democratic Minority*, no. 13, 1949(?), pp. 2–7.
———. "Speech to the AFA," *The Federal Architect*, January 1939, pp. 20–23.
———. "This Is American Architecture," *Design*, January/February 1958, p. 112.
———. "Wright Calls for Organic Architecture to Match Growth of Democracy," *The Capital Times* (Madison, Wis.), November 10, 1946, p. 11.
———. "Wright is Right," *Newsweek*, May 11, 1953, pp. 97–98.
Wright, Olgivanna. "Our House," *The Capital Times* (Madison, Wis.), October 10, 1958, p. 3.
———. "Our House," *The Capital Times* (Madison, Wis.), October 13, 1958, p. 3.
———. *Our House.* New York: Horizon Press, 1959.
"Wright 'Unveils' Prefab Houses," *Chicago Sun-Times*, January 22, 1958, p. 3.
"Young at Heart," *The Capital Times* (Madison, Wis.), August 1, 1957, p. 2.

Index

Page numbers in **boldface type** refer to illustrations.